Global Environmental Politics

Global Environmental Politics is the perfect introduction to this increasingly significant area. This fully revised and updated new edition combines an accessible introduction to the most important environmental theories and concepts with a series of detailed case studies of the most pressing environmental problems.

Features and benefits of the book:

- Explains the most important concepts and theories in environmental politics;
- Introduces environmental politics within the context of political science and international relations theories;
- Demonstrates how the concepts and theories apply in a wide variety of real world contexts;
- New case study chapters on the role of technology, the role of China, endangered species, biodiversity and the politics of conservation, the politics of food, and forests;
- Each chapter is written by an established international authority in the field;
- Fully up to date with the latest topics such as climate change negotiations, transnational governance, new indicators for sustainable development goals and much more;
- More in-text support, such as end of chapter web links and discussion questions.

This exciting textbook is essential reading for all students of environmental politics and will be of key interest to students of international relations and political economy.

Gabriela Kütting is a Professor of Global Politics at Rutgers University, USA.

Kyle Herman is a Researcher at the Division of Global Affairs, Rutgers University, USA.

Global Environmental Politics

Concepts, Theories and Case Studies

Second Edition

EDITED BY GABRIELA KÜTTING AND KYLE HERMAN

Routledge
Taylor & Francis Group

LONDON AND NEW YORK

Second edition published 2018
by Routledge
2 Park Square, Milton Park, Abingdon, Oxon OX14 4RN

and by Routledge
711 Third Avenue, New York, NY 10017

Routledge is an imprint of the Taylor & Francis Group, an informa business

First edition published by Routledge 2011

British Library Cataloguing in Publication Data
A catalogue record for this book is available from the British Library

Library of Congress Cataloging in Publication Data
Names: Kütting, Gabriela, 1967- editor.
Title: Global environmental politics: concepts, theories and case studies/ edited by Gabriela Kütting and Kyle Herman.
Description: Second edition. | New York: Routledge, 2018. | "First edition published by Routledge 2011"–T.p. verso. | Includes bibliographical references and index.
Identifiers: LCCN 2017060144 | ISBN 9781138895287 (hardback) | ISBN 9781138895355 (paperback) | ISBN 9781315179537 (ebook)
Subjects: LCSH: Environmental policy–International cooperation.
Classification: LCC GE170.G5557 2018 | DDC 363.7/0526–dc23
LC record available at https://lccn.loc.gov/2017060144

ISBN: 978-1-138-89528-7 (hbk)
ISBN: 978-1-138-89535-5 (pbk)
ISBN: 978-1-315-17953-7 (ebk)

Typeset in Avenir and Dante
by Sunrise Setting Ltd., Brixham, UK

Contents

Figures

Tables

Contributors

Frederike Boll is a policy advisor for business and human rights at the Friedrich-Ebert-Foundation in Germany. Her research interests include the power of transnational corporations, decent work worldwide and questions of global environmental governance.

Timothy Ehresman is adjunct faculty in the political science department at Belmont University in Nashville, Tennessee. His primary teaching focus is classes on global environmental politics and political theory of the environment.

Lucy Ford is senior lecturer at Oxford Brookes University. Her current research focuses on the psychoanalytic and ecopsychological dimensions of the global ecological crisis.

Doris Fuchs is Professor of International Relations and Sustainable Development and Speaker of the Center for Interdisciplinary Sustainability Research at the University of Muenster. Her research focuses on sustainable consumption, power (especially corporate power) and agrifood, climate, finance and energy policy.

Wendy Godek is an Associate Researcher at the International Center for Tropical Agriculture (CIAT) in Managua, Nicaragua. Her research focuses on the theory and practice of building more sustainable, socially-just food and agriculture systems, and she has written articles on food sovereignty policies and practice in Latin America.

Paul G. Harris is the Chair Professor of Global and Environmental Studies at the Education University of Hong Kong. He is author/editor of many books on global environmental politics, policy and ethics. See: www.paulgharris.net

Kyle Herman is a researcher and entrepreneur. He has worked for a Danish NGO for six years negotiating UNFCCC global climate policy and European Union renewable energy directives. He recently obtained his PhD from Rutgers University, Division of Global Affairs. He founded a cleantech data analytics start-up in 2016 that employs machine-learning and AI to cull millions of data points in order to better equip policymakers and investors for the cleantech energy evolution.

Thomas Hickmann is a Post-Doctoral Researcher and Lecturer at the Faculty of Economics and Social Sciences, University of Potsdam in Germany. His research mainly deals with global environmental and development politics with a particular focus on the role and function of sub-national and non-state actors in global sustainability policy-making.

Hannah Hughes is a Lecturer in International Relations in the School of Law and Politics at Cardiff University. She is interested in the relationship between knowledge and power in climate change and global environmental politics more broadly.

David Humphreys is Professor of Environmental Policy at the Open University. He has written and edited several books and articles on deforestation and forest policy. In 2008 he received the International Studies Association's Harold and Margaret Sprout Award.

Gabriela Kütting is Professor of Global Politics at Rutgers University, Newark. Her research focuses on critical global environmental politics, environmental justice, and global political ecology.

Markus Lederer is Professor of International Relations at the Institute of Political Science, Technical University of Darmstadt in Germany. His research focuses on global climate politics, the role of the state in green transformations in the global South, and the interlinkages of development and climate politics.

Judith Shapiro is Director of the Natural Resources and Sustainable Development Dual MA program at American University's School of International Service. Her books on China include *Mao's War against Nature* (Cambridge) and *China's Environmental Challenges* (Polity). Her website is www.judithshapiro.com.

Dimitris Stevis is Professor of International Politics in the Department of Political Science at Colorado State University. His current research focuses on labour environmentalism and just green transitions.

Maria Julia Trombetta is assistant professor of International Relations and International Security at the School of International Studies, Nottingham University, Ningbo Campus, China. Her research focuses on securitization, environmental conflict and energy security.

Alice B. M. Vadrot is political scientist and Erwin Schrödinger Fellow of the Austrian Research Fund (FWF). Currently, she is visiting research fellow at the Centre for Science and Policy (CSaP) of the University of Cambridge and Senior Post Doc at the Department of Political Science at the University of Vienna. Her research interests include the interrelations between science, policy and politics, international biodiversity politics and global environmental governance. In 2014, she published the book *The Politics of Knowledge and Global Biodiversity* (Routledge).

John Vogler is Professorial Research Fellow in International Relations at Keele University, UK. He has researched and published on the International Relations of the environment over many years. His most recent book is *Climate Change and World Politics* (2016), published by Palgrave.

Introduction

Gabriela Kütting and Kyle Herman

The world has changed since the first edition of this book was published in 2010. The way global environmental politics is conceptualized has become more diverse. At the same time, the environmental challenges the world is facing have not changed very much, yet we are definitely at the beginning of an energy revolution. While the political discourse has not changed dramatically, changes have happened in the global political economy and at levels below, above, and parallel to the state that are quietly challenging the way we think about global environmental politics.

The second edition of this textbook tries to reflect these changes and put them into perspective and make sense of them. The original framework in the first part of the book has not changed because we believe that these concepts are still the best tools for analyzing and understanding the global arena in which environmental politics is enacted. Part two has seen fundamental revisions in that new challenges have arisen that deserve our detailed scrutiny. To that effect, chapters on technology, on energy, and on China as a political actor have been added. Rather than studying a selection of institutions or policies, chapters in part two reflect the diversity of issue areas that arise in global environmental politics, and not all of them are driven by institutions or global policy frameworks.

This textbook is also unique in that it tries to reflect the field of global environmental politics, which is not dominated by one single approach. We feel that students should learn and understand the diversity of approaches that exist, and the best way to do this is to be exposed to differing accounts rather than a single narrative that presents the field as one homogeneous field, which it very clearly is not.

The book kicks off with an introductory chapter on theoretical perspectives which explains the various approaches to studying global environmental politics, placing it within the discipline of international relations. Initially, it was a relatively marginal concern, but the demands of the 'real world' forced the environment on to the academic agenda. Inevitably, existing theories and approaches were deployed in the study of the novel problems of transboundary pollution and global environmental change, but environmental specialists were soon making their own distinct contributions. In order to make sense of this, it is useful to consider the purpose of theory and its underlying assumptions. For example, the many theories discussed will all have a different starting point and a main focus which will lead them to prioritize different issues, values, and constructs as the most important ones and will also lead them to different conclusions. This brings us to the basic questions of the role and significance of various actors, most notably the state, but also prompts us to define the exact problem that we should seek to address. Are we primarily interested in actors such as the state or civil society, and do we believe that change for the better will be initiated and pushed through by them? Are we more skeptical and want to focus on consumptive or equity issues? Do we believe that the environment is a security issue and the best way forward is to treat it as such? John Vogler addresses these questions in a theoretical context and they will be followed up and discussed in more detail in subsequent chapters.

Lucy Ford explains and discusses transnational actors in global environmental politics. Transnational actors engage in international activities across national boundaries but do not do so on behalf of a state or international organization. In fact, there are many non-state actors who contest this concentrated global power in the hands of political and economic elites. Non-state actors championing a particular issue such as the environment are challenging nation-states and, by extension, inter-state organizations – claiming they are failing to solve global issues. Their aim is to redefine the issues, agendas, and problems by pointing out where these institutions are failing, promoting the reform of these institutions, working with these organizations sometimes bypassing the nation-state, and sometimes even calling for these organizations to be downgraded. When defining transnational actors, then, we are referring to all those non-state actors such as TNCs, NGOs, or social movements that operate *across* the globe and form part of global politics. They are neither states nor international organizations, but they act alongside them, sometimes collaborating with and sometimes challenging them, and at other times ignoring them altogether. Many of the issues highlighted by NGOs have to do with North–South issues, a theme that is picked up in the next chapter.

In their chapter on global political economy and development issues, Markus Lederer and Thomas Hickmann focus on the linkages between the economy, the environment, and development. They analyze the relationship between the economy and the environment in a global context, particularly relating to distributional issues. They discuss different theoretical and conceptual approaches to the interplay between economic globalization and environmental issues. Particularly, they address two major themes: they debate whether the terms 'sustainability' and 'development' can be reconciled. They also discuss who the relevant actors in the global political economy are.

Hannah Hughes, in her chapter on environmental security, sees environmental improvement not in economic tools but in the way the environment is perceived as a security issue and the policy consequences arising thereof. Environmental security is a contested concept. Generally, proponents of linking environment and security point to the roots of resource scarcity and environmental degradation in promoting intra-state and inter-state violent conflict and wars. The traditional definition of security, restricted to the polemics of state sovereignty, military affairs between states, and the threat of inter-state war as a function of threats to territorial integrity, should be expanded to include other issues, such as the environment. These analysts have also regarded the linkage itself as important in elevating environmental issues to the forefront of national security affairs, creating the political urgency to resolve environmental problems. Yet, critics of the linkage between the concepts of environment and security generally dismiss the relationship on several grounds. First and foremost, these analysts (regarded as traditionalist thinkers) believe that expanding the definition of security, as it is traditionally regarded, waters the concept down to something too vague to be analyzed rigorously. Others criticize the link claiming that the environment is antithetical to everything society often regards as security and, for that reason, connecting the two concepts will prevent us from thinking critically about dealing with environmental problems. Specifically, the chapter contends that, if the concept is generally couched in the discourses of war, conflict, sovereignty, and traditional power dynamics, then associating the environment with security is problematic.

Chapter 5 (Doris Fuchs and Frederike Boll) introduces a still young concept to global environmental politics. Sustainable consumption has become a pivotal topic in global environmental politics in recent years. Trends in resource depletion and environmental degradation caused by consumption levels and patterns, particularly in industrialized countries, combined with sharp rises in consumer demand in high growth countries, such as China and India, highlight one of the most fundamental problems facing human kind today as well as its causes. Consumption deals with the household level and how consumer and citizen actions influence political and economic governance. Thus, it is part of global political economy approaches but a subfield in its own right. The chapter describes the rise in importance of the study of consumption as well as identifying the actors of global sustainable consumption governance.

The last chapter in part one (Timothy Ehresman and Dimitris Stevis) brings environmental and ecological justice to the forefront of political concepts to consider in global environmental politics. The topic of environmental and ecological justice has come to occupy a unique and useful place in the field. Some of the earliest attempts to parse issues of justice as to the international environment arose in works by legal scholars attending to international environmental law. However, the field of international relations has itself come to embrace environmental justice issues as central to wider discourses on international justice and fairness, and as integral to studies of global environmental politics. Scholars in the field of international relations have, for some time, raised concerns regarding the fairness and moral urgency of problems in global environmental politics. And, as scholarly work on global environmental issues, initiatives, and institutions has advanced over time, the concept of justice has become central to broader environmental policy debates. Motivated by the growing significance of justice and equity for global environmental politics, this chapter offers a historical and analytical overview of international environmental justice, covering concepts as well as the application of justice issues.

The second section of this chapter offers case and policy studies, which apply the concepts discussed in the first section of the book. The case studies kick off with the most prominent and pressing issue of all – climate change. It reflects all dimensions of global environmental politics, ranging from classical regime analysis to critical approaches, from state-centric analysis to transnational networks, addressing conflict and cooperation in the field of political economy, environmental justice, and dilemmas over consumption. In this chapter, the historical trajectory of institutional action on climate change is retraced from the Climate Change Convention to the Kyoto Protocol and its various Conferences of the Parties (COP) meetings. The problem is then addressed in a wider framework, placing the dilemmas of equity, North–South divisions, civil society activism, economic constraints, and scientific consensus in perspective. The students will understand the full complexity of this multi-layered challenge to global cooperation and the challenges global society faces in the 21st century.

Judith Shapiro addresses the challenges of China taking on the role of a new super-power. Both domestically, with its insatiable appetite for resources and energy, and globally, with its newfound role at international conferences, China faces manifold environmental challenges which are discussed and contextualized in detail in this chapter.

Likewise, Kyle Herman confronts one of the most formidable challenges of the 21st century, namely the role of technology in global environmental politics. He engages the reader in a discussion premised not so much on the potential destructive forces of fossil fuels, but rather what new technologies are emerging, and at a rapid rate, to mitigate against global carbon emissions. The analysis takes a global political economy approach to drive home the point that climate policies are, in fact, already proving valuable to innovation, development, and diffusion of renewable energy and other clean technologies.

Julia Trombetta takes on the third major challenge, namely the role of energy policy. Access to energy services is a fundamental aspect of contemporary life. We rely on energy for transport, production, communication. Energy empowers. Access to energy sources is a strategic priority for many nation states, and the provision of energy services is essential for the economy and for development. Yet, even if energy is fundamental to fulfil human potential, 1.2 billion people have no access to electricity (IEA 2016). At the same time, without a radical transformation of existing energy systems, ensuring existing consumption, allowing for growth, and broadening access to energy services will have catastrophic consequences for the environment. Contemporary energy systems are unsustainable. Using the changing conceptualization of energy security as an analytical tool, and drawing on insights from the global governance literature, this chapter will analyze the transformation of energy politics, the emergence of forms of global energy governance, and the main actors involved in it.

Alice Vadrot addresses another vital issue, namely that of biodiversity and species protection. The term biodiversity, though used widely and liberally by researchers and practitioners, refers to a complex and under-researched environmental policy area. Deforestation, habitat destruction, wildlife conservation, over-fishing, species extinction, and the introduction of genetically modified organisms have all necessitated the adoption of a biodiversity regime at the United Nations level in the form of the Biodiversity Convention of 1992 and subsequent Biosafety Protocol of 2000. In order to develop a better understanding of the underlying dynamics at the intersection between science, politics, and policy, this chapter examines the historical, conceptual, and institutional conditions of the emergence of 'biodiversity' as global environmental concern and a policy issue. Subsequently, the regulatory framework, which has been established to tackle what is increasingly conceived to be the 'sixth mass extinction' will be described and emerging power struggles between the Global North and the Global South discussed.

The importance of enhancing the sustainability of food systems (Wendy Godek) is an issue that continues to be on the top of global agendas. This is attributed to the deepening of multiple environmental, social, and economic challenges that have compromised the ability of food systems to ensure food security, or when 'all people, at all times, have physical, social and economic access to sufficient, safe and nutritious food that meets their dietary needs and food preferences for an active and healthy life for all' (FAO 1996). While hunger has declined over the last decade, global food insecurity continues to be a significant problem, with an estimated 795 million hungry people worldwide (FAO 2015), or about 11% of the world population, most of whom live in poverty in the Global South. This chapter analyzes the concepts of food security and food sovereignty and how they relate to environmental and development concerns.

Forests are a political economy issue which, apart from playing such an important ecological role, have been at the forefront of innovative institutional efforts to develop more inclusive policy tools. As the subject matter of deforestation is such an obviously fraught example of the point where economic needs and wants clash with scientific advice, it is an ideal study of exactly where the problems are located in this ambiguous relationship. It brings to the fore all the issues that are pertinent in global environmental politics and globalization in general in the early 21st century: questions of governance, the role of transnational actors, the meaning of sustainable development, North–South relations, problems of development and poverty, the connection between poverty and environmental degradation, and the relationship between Western science and indigenous knowledge, to name but a few. This complex relationship is explained and analyzed here.

In sum, the second part of this book offers a broad view of the issues and challenges environmental politics and policies will face in the 21st century. These case studies bring together a range of different views, but together are hinged on one underlying perspective: global environmental politics and policies are changing drastically, and this is due to economic, political, and environmental changes occurring in parallel. With this, the next several decades are ripe for any number of technological, political, and economic changes related to the environment.

References

FAO (1996) Rome Declaration on World Food Security and the World Food Summit Plan of Action. World Food Summit, Rome, Italy, 13–17 November [Online]. Available at: www.fao.org/docrep/003/w3613e/w3613e00.htm

FAO (2015) *The State of Food Insecurity in the World*. Rome: Food and Agriculture Organizations of the United Nations.

IEA (2016) *World Energy Outlook 2016*. Paris: IEA. The 2016 energy access database. Available at: www.worldenergyoutlook.org/media/weowebsite/2015/WEO2016Electricity.xlsx (last accessed 2/10/2017).

Part I

Concepts and theories

International relations theory and the environment

1

John Vogler

This first chapter aims to situate the study of environmental questions within the broader context of international relations (IR) theory. It then seeks to provide a brief review of the main theoretical strands in IR thinking about the environment, including the institutionalist study of international cooperation and regime formation; the emergence of ideas on global environmental governance and the radical critique to which they have been subjected. The chapter concludes with a consideration of what may be regarded as the foundational security concerns of IR as a discipline and the ways in which the relationship between security and environmental degradation have been portrayed.

Classical IR theory

The study of IR as a distinct discipline was essentially a product of the Great War of 1914–18, the experience of which prompted urgent questions about how the old European inter-state system might be reformed in order to provide a new basis for security. European history had been punctuated by armed conflict, but it was the unprecedented scale of industrialised warfare that made any repetition appear unthinkable. International public law and functional international cooperation over such matters as the organisation of railways, telegraphs and postal services was already well established by the end of the nineteenth century, but it was the question of security and the avoidance of war that dominated all others. How was peace and order to be achieved in what was usually assumed to be an anarchical system of conflict-prone nation states? The then dominant school of liberal internationalists (sometimes also described, usually by their opponents, as idealists) proposed the strengthening of international law and the building of new international institutions for cooperation. If not providing for world government, this would at least serve to provide some insurance against a repetition of 1914 through the institutionalisation of a collective approach to security in the newly formed League of Nations. The conditions for this experiment may not have been right, or the idea itself may have been fatally flawed (Claude 1962), but disillusionment with the failure of the League and the onset of another world war gave rise to the ascendancy of a rival school of 'realist' thought, owing much to European traditions of *realpolitik* in a process famously described by Carr ([1939]1946) on the very eve of the Second World War. Realism, a label adopted to highlight the supposed inadequacy of the ideas of pre-war 'idealist' thinkers, became the dominant approach in the 1950s and arguably, with writers such as Kissinger (1970), Waltz (1979) and Mearsheimer (2001), along with a host of similarly inclined practitioners and commentators, remains so until this day. Realism shared with its 'idealist' protagonists a view of a world system constituted by sovereign states. Where it differed was in its stress on the primacy of national interests, power politics and the ultimate significance of armed force. If there was to be any security, it would be achieved through deterrence and power balancing, rather than through international cooperation and the pursuit of illusory common interests.

For much of the period since 1945, it was possible to write an IR textbook without specific mention of the environment. Nowadays, if not impossible, it would be unlikely![1] In more traditional writing, natural resources were the object of competition and conflict between states or constituents of national power (Morgenthau 1948). The natural environment provided the, often overlooked, context of international politics. It did not constitute a subject in its own right and, significantly, was regarded as a constant, rather than a site of dangerous or destabilising change. As Stevis (2006) notes, in his study of the trajectory of academic work on the international politics of the environment, most of the relevant research before the 1970s was conducted by economists, geographers and others from outside the IR discipline, even if their focus was fixed upon the geopolitics of resource scarcity.[2] There were also some, largely technical and legal, studies of resource conflicts and transboundary legal problems, but it was not until environmental issues became firmly implanted on the actual agenda of international politics, around the time of the 1972 United Nations Conference on the Human Environment at Stockholm, that the growing problems of transboundary, and then global, degradation attracted substantial theoretical interest amongst IR scholars.

As the discipline of IR developed, these established approaches have been subject to waves of criticism: from positivists demanding scientific evidence for theories; from Marxist-inspired critical scholarship and, more recently, by constructivists and post-modern theorists, challenging some of the core assumptions of the established discipline. Since the late 1960s, the study of IR has, thus, fractured in many ways, but it is probably true that, if they share little else, the majority of scholars have a core concern with security and peace, even if they now define them in rather different ways. A major criticism (Smith 1993) levelled at the work of those who came to specialise in the IR of the environment is that they continue to reside at the periphery of this theoretical ferment, failing to fully engage with the twists and 'turns' of theoretical debate in the discipline. There may be some truth in this for, as we shall see below, there has been a dominant concern with promoting inter-national environmental cooperation inspired by a largely liberal institutionalist approach. However, as we shall also see, there have been alternative voices. Deriving from very differ-ent assumptions and traditions, often denying the relevance of a state-centric world view, they have called for radical action. With respect to these challenges, Cox (1981) made an influential distinction between 'problem solving' and critical theory. 'Problem solvers' work within the prevailing assumptions of the international system, trying to find ways in which inter-state cooperation can be advanced, scientific findings better integrated into policy and regimes made more effective in their implementation. As we shall see, this description covers the bulk of the work that has been done on the international politics of the environ-ment. By contrast, 'critical theorists' are not interested in solving what are regarded as intermediate and technical problems. They are more concerned with probing the under-lying assumptions of prevailing practice, which may include the relations between the state and capital or the way in which accepted discourses implicitly privilege some groups and disadvantage others. Writers on international environmental politics also share with their counterparts, elsewhere in the discipline, a tendency to react to trends in world politics, a parallelism with events and an inevitable concern with normative issues. This often, but not always, extends to a common problematic – the question of how global governance is to be achieved and, increasingly, to questions of environmental security.

The study of inter-state cooperation and regimes

At the beginning of serious consideration of the international dimension of environmental problems, there was a prevailing academic focus upon international cooperation as a means to their solution. As a well-known text of the early 1990s put it, the problematic was:

> Can a fragmented and often highly conflictual political system made up of over 170 sovereign states and numerous other actors achieve the high (and historically unprece-dented) levels of co-operation and policy co-ordination needed to manage envi-ronmental problems on a global scale?
>
> (Hurrell and Kingsbury 1992:1)

It is noteworthy that the necessity for international cooperation in the 'management' of the global environment and the primacy of state governments in this enterprise were usually taken for granted. Equally, this view rested upon the assumption of international anarchy and the need to provide some functional equivalent to a world government if transboundary and global problems were to be addressed. A 'liberal institutionalist' approach came to dominate the field.

Those who studied the fast-developing network of multilateral environmental agree-ments (MEAs), such as the Montreal Protocol of 1987, were intellectually indebted to work that had been developed in the field of international political economy since the 1970s.[3] This was readily adaptable to the emerging study of international environmental coopera-tion. The approach utilised the concept of a regime, often attributed to a seminal article by

Ruggie (1975) and developed and defined by Krasner (1983) and his collaborators, as a means of describing and analysing international institutions. It is important to realise that the term institution is here used in a sociological sense – as a pattern of human roles and rules – rather than in the more established international usage that would term an organisation, such as the World Bank, an institution. The regime concept was first deployed to understand how 'cooperation under anarchy' could occur in international economic relations, a specific case in point being provided by the travails of the world economy in the 1970s, when it appeared that an apparent loss of US hegemony, manifested by the ending of the gold standard in 1971, would lead to the permanent unravelling of the international monetary order. The argument was advanced that such regimes could survive 'after hegemony' (Keohane 1984) because there were very good self-interested reasons for nations to cooperate. Such cooperation, understood in regime terms, did not only rest upon the existence of international legal rules and formal organisations (which, since the 1920s, had been assiduously studied by IR specialists) but also upon sets of more intangible principles and norms, which were the key characteristics of a regime – constituting, in effect, an international level institution. The central task was to analyse such sets of '. . . principles, norms, rules and decision-making procedures around which actors' expectations converge in a given area of international relations' (Krasner 1983:3) and then to comprehend the circumstances under which regimes were created and subject to change.

This regime-centred 'liberal institutionalist' approach provided a readily available means to comprehend the very rapid development of MEAs during the 1980s and 1990s when well over a hundred such agreements were negotiated at both regional and global levels. Managing the global environment posed many similar problems to those encountered in stabilising the global economy. However, there were some significant differences. While self-interested behaviour provides the dynamic for the operation of global markets, from an environmental perspective it can lead to a 'tragedy' of the global commons. The global commons are areas and resources that do not fall under the sovereign jurisdiction of any state: the high seas, Antarctica, outer space and the atmosphere. If users pursue their own short-term interests, and access to the commons is unrestricted and resources are finite, then the probable result, according to Hardin (1968), would be ecological collapse and general ruin. There are many sobering examples of such behaviour: the fate of whale and fish stocks and the reckless pollution of the atmosphere and oceans. Extensive work on local commons has demonstrated that the problem can be solved, either through privatisation (Hardin's solution) or by some form of collective agreement amongst users (Ostrom 1990). At the global level, 'privatisation' has limited application (for example, in the extension of Exclusive Economic Zones at sea) and there is, of course, no central government to control and regulate access to the commons. It is here that regimes may provide the necessary institutional equivalent to the kind of commons governance that is exercised in a voluntary way at the local level (Vogler 2000).

It is also the case that, although the origins of regime thinking may lie elsewhere, its elaboration and development have been heavily influenced by the work of those concerned with international environmental cooperation (Young 1997, Underdal 1992). There have also been attempts to build cumulative data on the characteristics of environmental regimes (Young and Zürn 2006, Pettenger 2014). Environmental regime creation was investigated in terms of established models for the resolution of collective action problems relying, in particular, on game theoretical and micro-economic analysis. The use of such formal models to analyse strategic behaviour and to account for cooperation has a long history in IR (Schelling, 1960). The game of 'prisoners' dilemma' has been particularly significant in that it highlights the difficulties of cooperation, from which both parties might benefit, under conditions of suspicion and imperfect information. If played on a 'one off' basis, the rational strategy is to avoid cooperation, but as Axelrod (1990) has demonstrated, if the game is iterated, then parties will benefit from developing patterns of cooperation. It may be argued, by analogy, that regimes can provide a stable institutionalised setting within which governments can learn the benefits of cooperation. This important insight, encapsulated in Young's (1994) notion of 'institutional bargaining' and marking a sharp difference from realist theorising, is the understanding that institutions matter in themselves and serve to modify the behaviour of the governments that participate in them. Alongside attempts to explain the formation of regimes, significant effort was also directed to an understanding of regime effectiveness in solving transboundary and global environmental problems (Victor et al. 1998, Andresen 2015). Less attention has been directed at how regimes alter over their life-cycle as institutions, but there has been significant recent work on how various environmental and other regimes affect each other in what has become known as 'institutional interplay' (Young 2002) and how several may combine in a 'regime complex' (Keohane and Victor 2010).

The critique of regime analysis

At the genesis of regime thinking, Strange (1983) made the critical point that there really was no such thing as a distinct theory of regimes, rather a re-use and re-direction of existing approaches in IR theory. The realist account of international cooperation, termed 'hegemonic stability theory', posited that it could only be sustained by the authority and dominance of a hegemonic power. This was hardly an attractive proposition for students of environmental politics, confronted with US abdication of its previous leading environmental role from the 1980s onwards (Falkner 2005), although it may retain some validity in discussions of whether the climate change regime can progress without US engagement and leadership. Instead, as we have seen, liberal institutionalism became the mainstream approach within which most of the work on international environmental cooperation has been conducted. Institutions or environmental regimes were seen as significant determinants of government behaviour and sources of learning, leading to potential absolute gains for all concerned and, most significantly, to the joint management of a shared vulnerability to environmental change.

Yet it is also true that there have been more recent theoretical departures that would not fit with Strange's assertion. Again, none are necessarily specific to the study of international environmental cooperation. Realists and liberals share a rational actor model which tends towards fixed assumptions on the motivation of states. Indeed, the difference between the two schools of thought can perhaps be narrowed down to a dispute over whether gains are seen to be relative or absolute. In the realist world view, there is always a struggle for power, only achievable at the expense of others, while for those of a more liberal inclination, states pursue their interests, which can often be realised through cooperation that serves to increase joint benefits. Game theorists characterise these two positions in terms of 'zero sum' conflict games or 'positive sum' cooperative gains. Other scholars have challenged the often unspoken assumptions that constrain this classic debate. They point out that interests are not 'given' and cannot be assumed as the basis of rational policy strategies. Instead, they are subject to those shifting perceptions of reality held by political actors. This is often described as a 'cognitivist' position because the crucial variable is seen to be knowledge. Thus, regime change and development are not solely explicable in terms of the calculus of power and interests within an institutional setting. Here, attention has been directed towards the important interface between scientists and policy-makers where, for example in an influential account by Haas (1990), knowledge based, transnational *epistemic communities* determined the way in which the Mediterranean anti-pollution regime was constructed. In another important study, Litfin (1994) considered the discourses suffusing the complex relationships between scientific advice and policy-making that conditioned the negotiation of the 1987 Montreal Protocol on the restoration of the stratospheric ozone layer.

These 'cognitivist' approaches reflect a broader trend in IR theorising that rejects strict positivistic social science explanation in favour of understanding based upon the analysis of discourse and meaning (Ruggie 1998). 'Post-structuralist' scholarship, frequently based upon the influential ideas of French theorist Michel Foucault, denies that the physical world has any inherent meaning and emphasises the power relations embedded in dominant forms of socialisation and discourse. It has its adherents amongst those who study 'governmentality' and environmental issues (Epstein 2008, Death 2010, Stripple and Bulkeley 2014). A related application is to be found under the heading of 'constructivism'. Wendt (1992) famously made the point that international anarchy was not an objective condition but 'what states make of it'. This constructivist view appeared to challenge rational choice accounts of state behaviour, although Wendt (1999) and other writers have attempted to argue that it can be married to existing types of explanation in IR.[4] Constructivism has great potential for the study of international environmental cooperation because it is centrally concerned with the evolution of norms of behaviour, the identity of actors such as the European Union (EU) and questions of compliance (Bernstein 2001, Vogler 2003, Stevenson 2012). Potentially, it can surmount a key theoretical contradiction in regime analysis which, simply stated, is that while regimes are made up of a sets of norms, principles and rules which are essentially social constructs, regime analysts have applied the positivistic methods of social science to them. In more formal terms, there is a clash between the ontological status of regimes and the epistemology of those who study them. On the other hand, a wholesale adoption of a constructivist or 'post-positivist' approach would have to grapple with the point that environmental regimes are predicated upon what Searle (1995) has called the 'brute' physical facts of nature, such as deforestation or climate change, that exist independently of our observations. We may construct and interpret them in many ways, but the most authoritative and useful, in terms of bringing about the physical changes upon which human survival depends, must remain the method of positivistic natural science. Perhaps a distinctive feature of the study of international environmental politics is that it raises such fundamental questions in starker terms than in other areas of IR.

Global governance

As discussed by Hickmann and Lederer in Chapter 3, globalization can mean many things, but in essence it represents a move away from a world divided into distinctly separate national economies and societies, presided over by sovereign state authorities, towards economic and perhaps even social systems that transcend national boundaries and, by some accounts, operate on a global basis. One of the clearest examples is provided by the evident integration of what were national and regional financial markets into what now appears to be one single, tightly interconnected, world system. Something similar has occurred with production processes that are now seen to be globally distributed, although such globalisation remains patchy, with some sectors, such as agriculture, still subject to extensive national control and protection. Although such processes of globalisation were accelerated by the ending of the Cold War, they have been evident over a long period, and IR scholars responded to such trends by considering the threat that they posed to the prevailing 'Westphalian' order of nation states. Burton (1972), for example, proposed a 'world society' model of a complex overlapping 'cobweb' of human systems that was radically different from the orthodox international political conception of state-to-state interaction. Transnational processes were analysed linking the international and the local as well as the emergence of a whole variety of supposedly 'new actors' (Keohane and Nye 1972, 1977, Mansbach et al. 1976, Rosenau 1980). Such a pluralist view of international politics included international organisations, the European Union and, most prominently, transnational business corporations and Non-Governmental Organisations (NGOs). If these new types of actor did not supplant the state, they might certainly rival it and provide alternative and appropriate forms of 'global governance' over phenomena that seemed to have outrun the capabilities of states. There was, too, an element of wishful thinking. This harked back to an idealist 'world government' tradition whereby nation states would be replaced by a less war-prone and more rational form of political organisation. Much of the discussion of NGOs and the possible emergence of a 'global civil society' has this normative dimension, described by Lucy Ford in the following chapter of this book.

Environmental degradation is often transnational in character and intimately associated with the processes of economic globalisation, although the relationship between growth, increases in trade and adverse environmental impacts remains a matter of academic dispute. Nonetheless, students of international environmental politics had good reason to pursue some of the trends in IR outlined above. Dissatisfaction with the environmental performance of governments and inter-state institutions was typified by the disappointments of the 'Rio process', where so many of the promises made at the 1992 Earth Summit failed to be realised and progress with the newly established climate and biodiversity regimes proved to be agonisingly slow. In particular, NGOs, many of which had achieved great prominence through their environmental actions, seemed to provide not only a significant focus for empirical study (Princen and Finger 1994, Newell 2000) but also a virtuous alternative to the self-interested machinations of state governments. There was also the empirical observation that non-state actors, whether regional entities such as the EU, transnationally organised NGOs or the private business sector, were playing an increasing part in environmental politics. Thus, for example, NGOs had a significant role in transmitting local protest at environmental destruction to the international level (Wapner 1996, Willetts 2008).

Although government spokespersons increasingly acknowledge 'multi-stakeholder' involvement, it is often the case that when they speak of 'global governance' they frequently mean no more than a rearrangement of existing international agencies. The long debate over whether the United Nations Environment Programme (UNEP) should be promoted from the status of a UN Programme to that of an independent specialised agency, and whether there should be an over-arching world environmental organisation, provides a case in point. This is far from what is understood by the term in academic discourse (Lederer 2015). The whole point of using the term 'governance', rather than the more orthodox 'government', is to capture the idea that, in an increasingly globalised system, many of the control functions traditionally the preserve of nation states have been transferred elsewhere (Paterson et al. 2003). Thus, global governance theorising breaks with the state-centric focus of the regime analysts and puts NGOs or private actors at the centre of its analysis (Pattberg 2007). As demonstrated by the development of privately based rules on forest products, they can provide governance for sustainability where states have failed to engage in effective international cooperation (see Humphreys, Chapter 13). The prolonged failure of formal international cooperation under the United Nations Framework Convention on Climate Change (UNFCCC) to produce an effective climate change regime, from the Kyoto Protocol of 1997 through to the outline of future action under the 2015 Paris Agreement, stimulated a mass of both theoretical and empirical work on the transnational and private alternatives (Abbott 2012, Andonova et al. 2009, Bulkeley et al. 2014). Transnationally linked cities, subnational initiatives and business schemes for carbon reporting and reduction were all part of the policy mix. The involvement of so many different entities at different scales led to an inevitable institutional fragmentation (Biermann et al. 2009), raising the question not so much of whether global governance or international action provided the more effective response to climate change, but how they might usefully fit together.

Radical ecopolitics

Realism and liberalism never entirely monopolised the study of international relations. There were always other more radical approaches in the sense that they refused to accept the prevailing order of nation states and market-based economies that provided the axioms upon which the dominant approaches in the field were founded. In the early twentieth century, radical approaches to IR often had a basis in Marxist historical materialism and the understanding that the state had an essentially class nature; Lenin referred to it as the 'executive committee of the bourgeoisie'. It followed that international conflicts arose from the contradictions within the world capitalist system. Thus, Lenin (1916 & 1965) explained the First World War as a conflict arising not from inter-state anarchy and the breakdown of the balance of power system, but from clashing imperialisms driven by the imperatives of capitalist accumulation and, in particular, a declining rate of return on investments. Other theorists in the Marxist tradition provided explanations similarly based upon the various crises of capitalism, notably under-consumption, to which states were bound to respond, often by engaging in aggressive behaviour. Marxist approaches to international relations have been further developed in the study of Global Political Economy. Here, the focus has been on the underlying dynamics of capitalist accumulation in the world system and the patterns of dominance and dependency that arise – notably in North–South relations. Such dependency is not simply based upon disparities in the ownership and control of material wealth, but also operates in the realm of ideas. Thus, Marxists who have developed the ideas of the Italian theorist Antonio Gramsci on hegemony have been able to make some connection with those, like the constructivists, who prioritise the role of discourse and 'ideational' factors.

The environmental problematic was not a central concern of twentieth century Marxist scholars of IR. Advocating class-based revolution as the necessary basis for a new and fairer international order, they would have been hard put to establish that socialist societies were also environmentally virtuous societies. While there was ample evidence that the growth trajectory of the capitalist world gave rise to massive resource exploitation and ecological damage, this was rivalled by the malign environmental consequences of the policies pursued by the Soviet Union and other avowedly socialist states. Nonetheless, as environmental issues have risen to prominence, Marxist scholars have found that their fundamental critique of capitalist accumulation does provide a powerful means of analysing the interconnected crisis of the world economy and environment (Newell and Paterson 2010). Various frameworks, including a neo-Gramscian one, can be deployed to understand how firms come to dominate an issue area such as forestry, biodiversity and biosafety (Levy and Newell 2005; Vadrot, Chapter 11). In this, market-based globalisation is the driver of degradation and states (acting as the agents of capital) are regarded as part of the problem rather than, as in mainstream work, the solution (Vogler 2005). It follows that the global ecological crisis cannot be regarded as a 'collective action problem' between states and that international regimes are 'epiphenomenal' in the sense that they merely give the impression that something is being achieved without affecting the underlying operations of global capitalism.

This rejection of the significance of the state and the whole enterprise of inter-state cooperation in the solution of environmental problems represents a fundamental attack upon mainstream international relations theorising. Nor is such a critical approach exclusive to those who fully subscribe to Marxist ideas and historical materialism. There are many other types of radical scholarship that also insist that the roots of the problem cannot be addressed through the encouragement and development of international environmental cooperation. The feminist critique of existing IR theory seeks to expose the gender bias inherent both in the state system and even those NGOs and other actors associated with global environmental governance. This fundamental critique both relocates the sources of the problem and challenges mainstream approaches to environmental management (Bretherton 1998). Other writers (Laferrière and Stoett 1999, Saurin 1996) have been inspired by ideas derived from radical green political thought. With these approaches, the study of global environmental politics has moved a long way from the mainstream preoccupation with inter-state institutions. Kütting (2004), for example, delves into production and supply chains in the global economy that give rise to complex interactions at local and global levels, linking environment with development and thus providing the drivers of both economic growth and degradation. Possibly, this may help us to understand that the politics of the global environment have always depended not only upon the earnest attempts of developed country reformers to institute regimes for conservation, but critically upon the urgent demands of the global South for development and redistribution.

The return to security

The achievement of security in a disorderly and anarchic system has historically been regarded as the overriding concern of IR theory, as outlined by Hughes in Chapter 4. While the IR theory of the environment built upon the tradition of the study of international cooperation, it did not initially engage with questions of war and peace. These were implicitly understood to be separate from the concerns of students of environmental politics, except perhaps when it came to the environmental consequences of the nuclear arms race and the possibility, much debated in the 1980s, of a 'nuclear winter' following an 'exchange' between the United States and the Soviet Union. In retrospect, it may seem strange that such a central concept as security was not subject to critical interrogation in the IR literature during most of the Cold War period. This may well have been because the threat of a collision between two nuclear armed superpowers was such an evident possibility that fear of the consequences of their involvement tended to prevent, or limit the extent of, other violent conflicts, at least in Europe. Security continued to be defined as the security of the state and to be assessed in terms of its ability to ward off armed incursions across its frontiers.

In the 1980s, this neglect of the theorisation of security began to change. Buzan (1983) made important distinctions between the referent objects of security. Whereas the orthodox referent object was the state, one could now also speak of 'societal security' or even 'environmental security'. In some officially sponsored accounts, a focus on the security of the state and its borders was replaced with a new concept of 'human security' (UNDP 1994). This multi-dimensional idea comprised a range of threats against which human beings should be secured. They included hunger, poor health, physical violence and the destruction of the physical environment. In the academic world, 'critical security studies' burgeoned and connections were made between security and emancipation (Booth 1991). The so-called 'Copenhagen School' adopted a constructivist inspired approach in which what mattered was the attribution of the security label to an issue by means of a 'speech act' (Buzan et al. 1998). 'Securitising' an issue involved raising its political profile and, in the wake of the ending of the Cold War, there were numerous examples of such activities relating to the environment. For activists, portraying environmental problems in terms of their link to national security had the advantage of raising their political salience and, accordingly, the amount of public expenditure likely to be dedicated to them. 'Security' threats are usually judged by publics to have sufficient gravity and urgency to give them priority over other calls upon governmental expenditure. At the same time, military establishments were under (what turned out to be) the mistaken impression that the ending of the Cold War would yield a 'peace dividend' under which major cuts in military expenditure would be sought. Environmental conservation was argued to provide a new and alternative role for the military, and organisations like NATO (the North Atlantic Treaty Organization) began to discover a whole range of alternative threats to security, including environmental degradation. As Deudney (1990) pointed out at the time, there remained a profound antipathy between the methods and mindset of military establishments and those of the environmental movement; thus, those who engaged with the securitisation and militarisation of the environment did so at their peril.

At this point, it is important to make a crucial distinction. Scholarly work on environmental security falls into two broad categories. On the one hand, there is the question of how environmental change and degradation relate to violent conflict and the integrity of the state and its territory – the orthodox concerns of strategic studies and IR. As with the activity by military establishments referred to above, this merely extends existing ideas of security by adding a range of new triggers for violent conflict and corresponding analysis and action by the armed forces. The other category has more radical implications because, by incorporating the environment problematic, it seeks to redefine the very meaning of security. It is essentially part of the critical and human security movements discussed above. Thus, the referent object of security ceases to be the state but becomes the survival of the biosphere. It is in this sense that reference is made, for example, to climate security. While the first category fits in well with established realist thinking and the concerns of policy-making elites, merely adding a new area of state security concern, the latter is firmly embedded in critical approaches to IR and connects with the radical ecopolitics discussed above.

The ending of the Cold War and the rising international profile of global scale environmental issues, as evidenced by the signing of the climate change and desertification conventions at Rio in 1992, helped to focus policy and academic attention on their potential to provoke conflict. In the longer term, this may be regarded as a concern, dating back to the gloomy predictions of Thomas Malthus in the nineteenth century, with the problems of over-population resource scarcity and social collapse. It was, also, very much a developed world perspective in that, faced with these challenges, 'state failure' in the South might lead to a variety of undesirable consequences in the North, including terrorist attacks, migration pressure and the interruption of supplies of raw materials. Accordingly, substantial and well-funded academic effort was directed from the 1990s towards an empirical investigation of the connections between environmental degradation and armed conflict. Such research was generally framed within the orthodox concerns of realist IR. 'Environmental security' was defined in terms of managing threats to the integrity of the state and its territory and the preservation of international stability in the face, for example, of the ill-understood consequences of climate change and desertification in Africa.

Extensive work in this area was undertaken by Homer-Dixon (1991, 1999) and his collaborators. They developed and attempted to test three hypotheses on environmental change, scarcity and conflict. War and insurrection could arise from struggles over diminishing resources brought about by environmental degradation in ways that would be instantly recognised by realist students of international conflict. Alternatively, the loss of livelihood occasioned by ecological collapse could force large scale population movements and armed confrontation over territory. Finally, internal insurrection and the collapse of the fragile institutions found in the developing world might also be triggered, leading to the transnational spread of conflict and intervention. Causal chains were complex and uncertain but it did become clear that many current conflicts had their origins in a morass of poverty, under-development, ethnic hatred and ecological collapse. However, the findings of the research were that there was no clear and direct relationship between environmental change and conflict (Barnett 2001, Gleditsch 1998). In another important study by Baechler (1999), environmental change was seen as just one component of a syndrome of 'maldevelopment' in which the developed North and its practices were deeply implicated.

The uncertainties thrown up by these empirical studies did not prevent policy-makers from commissioning work that attempted to provide practical guidance to political and military elites on the management and, indeed, prosecution of environmentally induced conflicts. In the late 1990s, for instance, NATO produced a study (Lietzmann and Vest 1999) that attempted to identify a set of syndromes and early warning indicators that would alert decision-makers to potential conflicts. Also, as the scientific evidence for climate change became more and more convincing in the first years of the twenty first century, military analysts began to prepare scenarios for national security policy in the context of a radically altered world (Schwartz and Randall 2003). Environmental change was conceptualised as a 'threat multiplier', but still in a fairly orthodox way. Events in the Arctic as the ice receded, and national claims to territory and control of the North West Passage, provide a graphic illustration (European Council 2008).

Of much greater theoretical significance was the re-evaluation of the key concept of security that was proceeding elsewhere in the discipline. In fact, as Swatuk (2006: 216) observes, 'almost as soon as the "environment" appeared on the policy map of state security apparatuses, dissenting and critical voices could be heard questioning the appropriateness of linking environmental issues to (national) security practices'. By detaching the concept from the referent object of the state and its territory, space was opened up to consider whether environmental issues should not just be an extension of security, but part of a wholesale reconfiguration in which it was possible to think about environmental questions as security issues in their own right (Lautensach and Lautensach 2014). Such thinking takes a holistic view of natural and human systems and is fully aware that pre-existing security debates, even when they take the environment into account, are constructed in such a way as to privilege the interests of the powerful and the 'developed'. The dire systemic consequences of climate change may be regarded as so devastating that they replace inter-state war as the principal problematic facing the international system.

This analysis is not confined to radical scholars. Elements of it have entered mainstream discourse. For example, after the attacks on the World Trade Center in 2001, security issues tended to be narrowly defined in US and European policy-making circles as involving 'terrorism, failed states and weapons of mass destruction'. However, this was soon challenged by assertions that, in fact, in terms of the potential for destruction and loss of human life, climate change represented a greater threat than terrorism (King 2004). Followers of the Copenhagen School would recognise a securitisation move here, with interested parties attempting to divert resources away from the 'war on terror' to the mitigation of, and adaptation to, the effects of climate change. Much of this may simply have been rhetoric, but it was surely of some significance that climate security was placed on the agenda of the UN Security Council in April 2007 and again in 2011. Were this to become widely accepted, it would denote not so much a 'return to security' issues but a thoroughgoing redefinition of what it means to be secure – with the most profound implications for the study of IR. As Corry and Stevenson (2017) argue, this may imply that 'the environment' is no longer simply an issue taken up or neglected by various IR approaches, but is becoming 'constitutive of IR as an academic field'.

Conclusion

This chapter has described the ways in which the study of international environmental politics has evolved within the discipline of IR. Initially, it was a relatively marginal concern, but 'real world' developments forced the environment on to the academic agenda. Inevitably, existing theories and approaches were deployed in the study of the novel problems of transboundary pollution and global environmental change, but environmental specialists were soon making their own distinct contributions in regime analysis, in the study of non-state actors and in the redefinition of the central concept of security.

In order to make sense of this, and to think through the ways in which the various theoretical approaches converge or contrast, it may be useful to ask four, often highly inter-related, questions that are relevant to any form of IR theorising. They are:

- What is the purpose of theory?
- What are the underlying theoretical assumptions, both ontological (those things that are believed to exist) and epistemological (how we may know about them).
- What is the role and significance of the state?
- What is the problem that we should seek to address?

Theories may simply be regarded as attempts to make explanatory generalisations about phenomena, following the example of the natural sciences (positivism). Such theorising often has a political agenda, other than enquiry for its own sake. Scientific investigation is directed to the solution of problems. This would provide a fairly accurate description of much of the work in international environmental politics that addresses the circumstances under which regimes may be built and developed. As we have seen, many other approaches in the field have a distinctly different critical approach which may be subversive rather than 'problem solving'. Radical ecopolitics has this characteristic, but it is always worth remembering that such distinctions have a long pedigree. Thus, after the First World War, some theorists were concerned with reform and institution building while others, on the political left, sought the establishment of world peace through the overthrow of the prevailing economic and social order.

It is also necessary to tease out the assumptions that guide theoretical work. Mainstream regime analysis, and indeed the bulk of realist and liberal theorising, is predicated on a model of human action: that people, or indeed states, are assumed to make rational choices amongst alternative courses of action in terms of a set of relatively fixed interests or preferences. As we have seen, a critical distinction between realist and liberal thinkers is whether the negotiation of these preferences leads to essentially conflictual or cooperative outcomes. Liberal institutionalism is founded upon the latter view. Quite different are those who adopt a constructivist approach. In their view, preferences are never fixed but always subject to change and this, rather than the distribution of power or the conjunction of interests, provides the key to obtaining international cooperation on environmental issues. A critical question is whether discourse or constructivist analysis can be combined with rational choice accounts or whether they have fundamentally different epistemologies. There are some interesting questions for environmental scholarship here because of the significance of natural science for policy-making alongside the socially constructed nature of the norms of behaviour that are the essential characteristic of regimes.

IR in general, and the definition of security in particular, has prioritised the state. While regime theorists continue to focus upon inter-state cooperation, much of the most innovative work in environmental politics has challenged its supremacy. In particular, the study of global environmental governance has focussed upon the advocacy and regulatory activities of non-state entities. There is a sense that the state, far from being regarded as part of the solution to global environmental degradation, is itself a major part of the problem. Analysts adopting the standpoint of radical ecopolitics would have no dispute with this characterisation of the state. Although the tendency amongst environmental activists and green theorists has been to distrust the state and to seek alternative forms of governance, there is now a growing realisation that, in any time frame that is relevant to the solution of pressing environmental problems, the state cannot be excluded. Critical questions, not least for the future of inter-state environmental regimes, are whether it is possible to 'green' the state (Eckersley 2004) and whether inter-state environmental cooperation can be an ecologically relevant activity (Vogler 2005, 2016).

A theme of this chapter has been that, whereas theories of IR and the growth of the discipline were predicated upon the problem of war and insecurity, in a conception that excluded environmental issues, the latter have become an integral part of a contemporary redefinition of security. The ending of the Cold War, the advance of globalisation and a growing understanding of the magnitude of the threat to human existence posed by global environmental change have led to a perceptible shift in the definition of security and hence the problem that policy-makers and IR theorists feel called to address. Environmental change is recognised as a significant driver of contemporary conflicts which in themselves are very different from the large scale inter-state warfare that provided the impetus for early realist and liberal internationalist writing. But, more than this, the stability of the climate and the survival of ecosystems have, in some ways, replaced the integrity of the state as that which is to be secured in a world system that is far removed from that confronting international theorists in the first half of the twentieth century.

Notes

1 Despite the magnitude of the problem of climate change and the increasing salience of environmental and resource issues at high level international meetings such as the G7 or G20, it is evident that such issues still have a relatively marginal status in the textbooks.

2 A major exception was provided by the work of Sprout and Sprout (1971). Currently, the concept of 'geopolitics' is often used merely as a synonym for world or international power politics. Here, it is used in its classical sense of the physical determinants of foreign policy and inter-state conflict.

3 A rather similar process may be observed in the way in which the very substantial work on monitoring and verification, which had arisen in response to the need for arms control during the Cold War, was adapted to meet the requirement to ensure the implementation of international agreements.

4 For an accessible treatment of this issue and refutation of Wendt's argument that rational choice and constructivist approaches can be combined in IR, see Smith and Owens (2008).

Bibliography

Abbott, K. W. (2012) The Transnational Regime Complex for Climate Change. *Environment and Planning C: Government and Policy*, 30(4), 571–590.

Andonova, L. B., Betsill, M. M. & Bulkeley, H. (2009) Transnational Climate Governance. *Global Environmental Politics*, 9(2), 52–73.

Andresen, S. (2015) Regime Effectiveness, in Bäckstrand, K. and Lövbrand, E. (eds) *Research Handbook on Climate Governance*. Cheltenham: Elgar. pp. 425–434.

Axelrod, R. (1990) *The Evolution of Co-operation*. London: Penguin.

Baechler, G. (1999) *Violence Through Environmental Discrimination: Causes, Rwanda Arena and Conflict Model*. Dordrecht: Kluwer.

Barnett, J. (2001) *The Meaning of Environmental Security: Ecological Politics and Policy in the New Security Era*. London: Zed Books.

Bernstein, S. (2001) *The Compromise of Liberal Environmentalism*. New York: Columbia University Press.

Biermann, F., Pattberg P., van Asselt, H. & Zelli, F. (2009) The Fragmentation of Global Governance Architectures: A Framework for Analysis. *Global Environmental Politics*, 9(4), 14–40.

Booth, K. (1991) Security and Emancipation. *Review of International Studies*, 17(4), 313–326.

Bretherton, C. (1998) Global Environmental Politics: Putting Gender on the Agenda. *Review of International Studies*, 24(1), 85–100.

Bulkeley, H. et al. (2014) *Transnational Climate Change Governance*. Cambridge: Cambridge University Press.

Burton, J. W. (1972) *World Society*. Cambridge: Cambridge University Press.

Buzan, B. (1983) *People States and Fear: The National Security Problem in International Relations*. Brighton: Wheatsheaf.

Buzan, B., Waever, O & de Wilde J. (1998) *Security: A New Framework for Analysis*. Boulder: Lynne Rienner.

Carr, E. H. ([1939]1946) *The Twenty Years' Crisis 1919–1939. An Introduction to the Study of International Relations*. London: Macmillan.

Claude, I. L. (1962) *Power and International Relations*. New York: Random House.

Corry, O. & Stevenson, H. (eds). (2017) *International Relations and the Earth: Traditions and Trends in Global Environmental Politics*. London: Routledge.

Cox, R. (1981) Social Forces, States and World Orders: Beyond International Relations Theory. *Millennium Journal of International Studies*, 10(2), 126–155.

Death, C. (2010) *Governing Sustainable Development: Partnerships, Protests and Power at the World Summit*. London: Routledge.

Deudney, D. (1990) The Case Against Linking Environmental Degradation and National Security. *Millennium*, 19(3), 461–476.

Dunne, T., Kirkl, M. & Smith, S. (2016) *International Relations Theories: Discipline and Diversity.* 4th edition. Oxford: Oxford University Press.

Eckersley, R. (2004) *The Green State: Rethinking Democracy and Sovereignty.* Cambridge, MA: MIT Press.

Epstein, C. (2008) *The Power of Words in International Relations: Birth of an Anti-Whaling Discourse.* Cambridge, MA: MIT Press.

European Council. (2008) *Climate Change and International Security: Paper from the High Representative and the European Commission to the European Council.* S113/08, Brussels: Council of the European Union.

Falkner, R. (2005) American Hegemony and the Global Environment. *International Studies Review*, 7(4), 585–589.

Gleditsch, N. P. (1998) Armed Conflict and the Environment: A Critique of the Literature. *Journal of Peace Research*, 35(3), 381–400.

Haas, P. M. (1990) Obtaining Environmental Protection Through Epistemic Consensus. *Millennium Journal of International Studies*, 19(3), 347–363.

Hardin, G. (1968) The Tragedy of the Commons. *Science*, 162(3859), 1243–1248.

Homer-Dixon, T. (1991) On the Threshold: Environmental Changes as Causes of Acute Conflict. *International Security*, 16(2), 76–116.

Homer-Dixon, T. (1999) *The Environment, Scarcity and Violence.* Princeton: Princeton University Press.

Humphreys, D. (1996) Hegemonic Ideology and the International Tropical Timber Organisation, in Vogler, J. & Imber, M. (eds), *The Environment and International Relations.* London: Routledge. pp. 197–215.

Humphreys, D. (2006) *Logjam: Deforestation and the Crisis of Global Governance.* London: Earthscan.

Hurrell, A. & Kingsbury, B. (eds). (1992) *The International Politics of the Environment: Actors, Interests and Institutions.* Oxford: Clarendon Press.

Keck, M. E & Sikkink, K. (1998) *Activists Beyond Borders: Advocacy Networks in International Politics.* Ithaca: Cornell University Press.

Keohane, R. (1984) *After Hegemony: Cooperation and Discord in the World Political Economy.* New Jersey: Princeton University Press.

Keohane, R. & Nye, J. S. (eds). (1972) *Transnational Relations and World Politics.* Cambridge, MA: Harvard University Press.

Keohane, R. & Nye, J. S. (1977) *Power and Interdependence: World Politics in Transition.* Boston: Little Brown.

Keohane, R.O. & Victor, D.G (2010) *The Regime Complex for Climate Change,Discussion Paper 10–33.* Harvard: Belfer Center for Science and International Affairs, Harvard Kennedy School of Government.

King, D. A. (2004) Climate Change Science: Adapt, Mitigate or Ignore? *Science*, 9, January, 303(5655), 176–177.

Kissinger, H. (1970) *The White House Years.* Boston: Little Brown, Ch.III.

Krasner, S. D. (ed). (1983) *International Regimes.* Ithaca: Cornell University Press.

Kütting, G. (2000) *Environment, Society and International Relations.* London: Routledge.

Kütting, G. (2004) *Globalization and Environment: Greening Global Political Economy.* Albany: SUNY Press.

Laferrière E. & Stoett, P. J. (1999) *International Relations Theory and Ecological Thought: Towards a Synthesis.* London: Routledge.

Lautensach, S. W. and Lautensach, A. K. (2014) Environmental Security, International National and Human, in Harris, P. G. (ed) *Routledge Handbook of Global Environmental Politics*. London: Routledge. pp. 246–258.

Lederer (2015) Global Governance, in Bäckstrand, K. and Lövbrand, E. (eds) *Research Handbook on Climate Governance*. Cheltenham: Elgar. pp. 3–13.

Lenin, V. I. (1916 & 1965) *Imperialism The Highest Stage of Capitalism: A Popular Outline*. Peking: Foreign Languages Press.

Levy, D. & Newell, P. J. (eds). (2005) *The Business of Global Environmental Governance*. Cambridge, MA: MIT Press.

Lietzmann, K. M. & Vest, G. (eds). (1999) *Environment and Security in an International Context*. Brussels: NATO Committee on the Challenges of Modern Society; no.232.

Litfin, K. (1994) *Ozone Discourses: Science and Politics in Global Environmental Co-operation*. New York: Columbia University Press.

Mansbach, R., Ferguson, Y. & Lampert, D. (1976) *The Web of World Politics*. Englewood Cliffs, NJ: Prentice-Hall.

Mearsheimer, J. (2001) *The Tragedy of Great Power Politics*. New York: W. W. Norton.

Morgenthau, H. J. (1948) *Politics Among nations: The Struggle for Power and Peace*. New York: A. A. Knopf.

Newell, P. (2000) *Climate for Change: Non-State Actors and the Global Politics of the Greenhouse*. Cambridge: Cambridge University Press.

Newell, P. and Paterson, M. (2010) *Climate Capitalism: Global Warming and the Transformation of the Global Economy*. Cambridge: Cambridge University Press.

O'Neill, K. (2017) *The Environment and International Relations*. 2nd edition. Cambridge: Cambridge University Press.

Ostrom, O. (1990) *Governing the Commons: The Evolution of Institutions for Collective Action*. Cambridge: Cambridge University Press.

Paterson, M. (2001) *Understanding Global Environmental Politics: Domination, Accumulation, Resistance*. Houndmills: Palgrave.

Paterson, M., Humphreys, D. & Pettiford, L. (2003) Conceptualizing Global Environmental Governance: From Interstate Regimes to Counter-hegemonic Struggles. *Global Environmental Politics*, 3(2), 1–10.

Pattberg, P. H. (2007) *Private Institutions and Global Governance: The New Politics of Environmental Sustainability*. Cheltenham: Edward Elgar.

Pettenger, M. E. (2014) International Environmental Regimes: Formation, Effectiveness and Trends, in Harris, P. G. *Routledge Handbook of Global Environmental Politics*. London: Routledge. pp. 111–123.

Princen, T. & Finger M. (eds) (1994) *Environmental NGOs in World Politics*. London: Routledge.

Rapoport, A. (1974) *Fights Games and Debates*. Ann Arbor: University of Michigan Press.

Rosenau, J. N. (1980) *The Study of Global Interdependence: Essays on The Transnationalisation of World Affairs*. London: Frances Pinter.

Ruggie, J. G. (1975) International Responses to Technology: Concepts and Trends. *International Organization*, 29(3), 557–583.

Ruggie, J. G. (1998) *Constructing the World Polity: Essays on International Institutionalization*. London: Routledge.

Saurin, J. (1996) International Relations, Social Ecology and the Globalisation of Environmental Change, in Vogler, J. & Imber, M. (eds), *The Environment and International Relations*. London: Routledge. pp. 77–98.

Schelling, T. (1960) *The Strategy of Conflict*. New York: Oxford University Press.

Schwartz P. & Randall, D. (2003) *An Abrupt Climate Change Scenario and its Implications for National Security*. Jet Propulsion Laboratory Pasadena California, www.dtic.mil.dtic/tr/fulltext/u2/a469325.pdf

Searle, J. R. (1995) *The Construction of Social Reality*. Harmondsworth: Penguin.

Smith, S. (1993) The Environment on the Periphery of International Relations: An Explanation. *Environmental Politics*, 2(4), 28–45.

Smith, S. & Owens, P. (2008) Alternative Approaches to International Theory, in Baylis, J., Smith, S. & Owens, P. (eds), *The Globalization of World Politics: An Introduction to International Relations*. 4th edition. Oxford: Oxford University Press. pp. 174–191.

Sprout, H. & Sprout, M. (1971) *Towards a Politics of the Planet Earth*. New York: van Nostrand Rheinhold.

Stevenson, H. (2012) *Institutionalizing Unsustainability: The Paradox of Global Climate Change Governance*. Berkeley: University of California Press.

Stevis, D. (2006) The Trajectory of the Study of International Environmental Politics', in Betsill, M. M., Hochstetler, K. & Stevis D. (eds) *Palgrave Advances in International Environmental Politics*. Houndsmills: Palgrave Macmillan. pp. 13–54.

Strange, S. (1983) *Cave! Hic Dragones: A Critique of Regime Analysis*, in Krasner, S. D. (ed) *International Regimes*. Ithaca: Cornell University Press, pp. 337–354.

Stripple, J. & Bulkeley, H. (eds). (2014) *Governing the Climate: New Approaches to Rationality, Power and Politics*. Cambridge: Cambridge University Press.

Swatuk, L. A. (2006) Environmental Security, in Betsill, M. M., Hochstetler, K. & Stevis D. (eds) *Palgrave Advances in International Environmental Politics*. Houndsmills: Palgrave Macmillan. pp. 203–236.

United Nations Development Programme (UNDP) (1994) *Human Development Report 1994*. Oxford: Oxford University Press.

Underdal, A. (1992) The Study of International Regimes. *Journal of Peace Research*, 32(1), 227–240.

Victor, D., Raustiala, K. & Skolnikoff, E. (eds). (1998) *The Implementation and Effectiveness of Environmental Commitments*. Cambridge, MA: MIT Press.

Vogler, J. (1996) The Environment in International Relations: Legacies and Contentions, in Vogler, J. & Imber, M. (eds), *The Environment and International Relations*. London: Routledge. pp. 1–21.

Vogler, J. (2000) *The Global Commons: Environmental and Technological Governance*. Chichester: John Wiley.

Vogler, J. (2003) Taking Institutions Seriously: How Regime Analysis can be Relevant to Multilevel Environmental Governance. *Global Environmental Politics*, 3(2), 25–39.

Vogler, J. (2005) In Defense of International Environmental Cooperation, in Barry, J. & Eckersley R. (eds), *The State and the Global Ecological Crisis*. Cambridge, MA: MIT Press: 229–254.

Vogler, J. (2016) *Climate Change in World Politics*. Houndsmills: Palgrave.

Waltz, K. (1979) *Theory of International Politics*. Reading, MA: Addison-Wesley.

Wapner, P. (1996) *Environmental Activism and World Civic Politics*. Albany: State University of New York Press.

Wendt, A. (1992) Anarchy is What States Make of it: The Social Construction of Power Politics. *International Organization*, 46(2), 391–425.

Wendt, A. (1999) *A Social Theory of International Politics*. Cambridge: Cambridge University Press.

Willetts, P. (2008) Transnational Actors and International Organizations in Global Politics', in Baylis, J., Smith, S. & Owens, P. (eds), *The Globalization of World Politics: An Introduction to International Relations*. 4th edition. Oxford: Oxford University Press. pp. 331–347.

Young, O. R. (1989) *International Cooperation: Building Regimes for Natural Resources and the Environment.* Ithaca: Cornell University Press.

Young, O. R. (1994) *International Governance: Protecting the Environment in a Stateless Society.* Ithaca: Cornell University Press.

Young, O. R. (ed). (1997) *Global Governance: Drawing Insights from the Environmental Experience.* Cambridge, MA: MIT Press.

Young, O. R. (2002) *The Institutional Dimensions of Environmental Change: Fit, Interplay and Scale.* Cambridge, MA: MIT Press.

Young, O. R. & Zürn, M. (2006) The International Regimes Database: Designing and Using a Sophisticated Tool for Institutional Analysis. *Global Environmental Politics*, 6(3), 121–141.

Transnational actors in global environmental politics[1]

2

Lucy Ford

Introduction

After a month long campaign by indigenous and environmental activists to prevent an access pipeline from being drilled under the Missouri River in North Dakota, the Army Corp of Engineers refused the permit on 4 December 2016, handing initial victory to the protesters (Wong 2016). Commenting on this success, Shannon Jackson, Executive Director of Our Revolution, a movement to reclaim democracy in the United States, stated:

> Today's decision clearly demonstrates the power of the political revolution. When people come together from all walks of life – veterans, Native Americans, environmentalists, farmers, young and old – to protect the health of our planet and generations to come, there is nothing we cannot accomplish. This victory sends a clear signal to those at the top: we are united and not giving up. We will continue to stand together and expect the decisions made by our government to benefit all of us, not just the rich and corporations.
>
> (Our Revolution 2016)

Not two months later, on 24 January 2017, US president Donald Trump overturned the verdict of the experts and ignored the voices of the water protectors by signing the executive order to approve the pipeline, demonstrating support for the fossil fuel industry (Eilperin and Dennis 2017). At this time, Trump also hinted at his intention to withdraw from the Paris Climate Agreement.

Across the ocean in Europe, water and earth protectors are resisting the first fracking site in Lancashire, UK, after successful local government opposition to Cuadrilla's application to drill for shale gas was overruled by the UK central government (Ambrose 2017) (Figure 2.1).

Environmental politics, whether national or international, it would seem then, still lies in the hands of the state, much in line with traditional, state-centric realist international relations (IR) theory. And yet, clearly, other actors have influenced these processes, from the water protectors attempting to halt projects to the gas and oil companies successfully lobbying governments to go ahead.

Liberal and critical approaches to IR want to highlight that beyond the realm of inter-state politics there is an array of actors, such as transnational social movements, non-governmental organizations (NGOs) or transnational corporations (TNCs), sometimes collectively referred to as non-state actors, transnational actors or civil society actors, that have a bearing on politics and political outcomes. Questions about 'who acts and how' are fundamentally about what constitutes 'the political' in global environmental politics.

This chapter is concerned with transnational actors in global environmental politics. The first section of the chapter starts by locating transnational actors in IR, defining more clearly some of the key concepts and how these have evolved over time, and how they relate to developments within the discipline of IR. It further provides some conceptual tools for analyzing the role of transnational actors in global environmental politics, including contested theoretical approaches and challenges to explaining their significance. In particular, it analyzes the sphere of global civil society, where transnational actors are said to be located. The second section then focuses on a variety of transnational actors, including transnational environmental movements, NGOs and transnational corporate actors. It asks what motivates them and how they act and engage in global environmental politics.

Figure 2.1 'Women's Call for Calm' 15 minute silence at the site entrance at the Preston New Road Cuadrilla fracking site, Lancashire, 12 July 2017. Photo courtesy of Peter Yankowski.

Locating transnational actors in international relations

The discipline of IR is notorious for its confusing variety of concepts that are sometimes used interchangeably and sometimes mean different things. So, for example, while International Relations in its origin was concerned with analyzing the international relations between nation-states as well as their interactions with international organizations such as the UN (United Nations) or NATO (North Atlantic Treaty Organization), more recent scholars now often understand International Relations to be about social, economic, cultural or political interactions across the globe. They might want to talk about transnational politics, world politics, global politics or indeed global political economy. Similarly, the term non-state actor can be confusing. Although strictly it appears to be referring to any actor that is not a state or government, the boundaries between what constitutes state and non-state are not always clear. For example, the UN might be seen as a non-state actor in that it stands alone as an institution. However, it is clearly an international – indeed intergovernmental – organization and a channel through which states (and other actors) operate. The UN claims moral authority over world politics. It is, as it were, the closest body to a world government. Some would argue that international organizations, such as the UN, the World Bank, the IMF or the WTO, embody a quasi world state that holds a lot of power to direct world affairs (see, for example, Shaw 2000).

However, there are many non-state actors who contest this concentrated global power. Non-state actors championing a particular issue, such as the environment, are challenging nation-states and, by extension, inter-state organizations – claiming they are failing to solve global issues. Their aim is to contest the agenda, to point out where these institutions are failing, to promote reform of these institutions, to work with these organizations, sometimes bypassing the nation-state, and sometimes even calling for these organizations to be abolished, as seen, for example, in the 'WTO - Shrink or Sink' campaign, organized and signed by a transnational, heterogeneous collection of networks, associations and NGOs, self-defined as transnational civil society (see, for example, TWN, no date). When defining transnational actors, then, we are referring to all those non-state actors, such as TNCs, NGOs or social movements, that operate *across* the globe and form part of global politics. They are neither states nor international organizations, but they act alongside them, sometimes collaborating with and sometimes challenging them, and at other times ignoring them altogether.

The evolution of some of the key concepts to do with understanding transnational actors can usefully be related to the historical development of the discipline of IR in general and global environmental politics in particular. Within IR, the study of transnational actors came to the fore during the 1970s with the theoretical developments of pluralism and complex interdependence (Keohane and Nye 1977). Out of this developed the study of international regime theory, which focuses on the importance of institutions and shared norms amongst actors (see Vogler, Chapter 1). The emphasis in this body of literature is on the effectiveness of international institutions that deal with transboundary issues and the institutional settings and arrangements as well as power structures that enable or constrain international cooperation. In the field of the environment, this literature looks particularly at international environmental regimes, or Multilateral

Environmental Agreements (MEAs) as they are most often referred to. While much of regime theory stands accused of state-centrism, there is within this school of thought acknowledgement of the role of non-state actors, known as epistemic communities. They are transnational networks of knowledge-based experts from the world of science, NGOs or business that contribute expertise to the policy-making process in particular issue areas, such as the environment, trade or security, which fosters institutional and wider institutional learning (for example Vogler 2003).

From international regimes to global governance

The analytical framework of international regimes has tended to be replaced by that of global governance. The concept of governance has become prominent in IR since the end of the Cold War. No longer was the world seen as divided into a simple bi-polar system maintaining international order. A lot of the literature has focused on how processes of globalization are generating a more complex, multi-level world political system which implicitly challenges the old Westphalian assumptions about the nation-state. Questions about how to govern the new world order have become prominent, not least in relation to transboundary issues, such as environmental degradation. Governance as a concept is distinguished from government. A government is backed by formal authority; by police powers to ensure implementation of policies. Governance, on the other hand, is more encompassing than government, including institutions as well as non-governmental mechanisms. Held and McGrew (2003: 8) describe governance as

> [T]he structures and processes of governing beyond the state where there exists no supreme or singular political authority . . . it constitutes a broad analytical approach to addressing the central questions of political life under conditions of globalization, namely: who rules, in whose interests, by what mechanisms and for what purposes?

It is thus a vision of a global institutional architecture that is multilayered, pluralistic and structurally complex, with national governments still acting as strategic sites for enmeshing global governance. The shift from regimes to governance is also visible in global environmental politics, and much of the literature now talks about global environmental governance as the sphere of global environmental politics (Lipschutz and Mayer 1996; Paterson et al. 2003). A move away from state-centric analysis has also occurred, with the focus on analyzing transnational environmental movements and NGOs as well as TNCs as actors in global environmental politics (see, for example, Princen and Finger 1994; Lipschutz and Mayer 1996; Wapner 1996; 1997; Keck and Sikkink 1998). More recently, the co-creation of global environmental governance between state and non-state actors has been described as 'hybrid multilateralism' (Bäckstrand et al. 2017).

There are a variety of theoretical approaches to global governance. The universalizing liberal language of global governance, as seen, for example, in the Report of the UN Commission for Global Governance (UNCGG), *Our Global Neighbourhood*, claims we are entering a new era of democratization, economic transformation, multilateralism and collective responsibility (UNCGG 1995: 1). While international governance was once played out in intergovernmental relationships, *Our Global Neighbourhood* claims this new global era is marked by the involvement of NGOs, citizens' movements, TNCs, and the global market alongside states and intergovernmental organizations (UNCGG 1995: 3). In the liberal academic literature, too, this inclusion of transnational actors in the policy-making process is what is perceived to be new about global governance (Young 1997).

Increasing transnational activism is attributed to the perceived powerlessness of the state in a globalizing world, particularly when it comes to so-called global issues, such as environmental degradation. Alongside the forces of globalization, pressure from grass-roots movements is seen as a challenge to the power and authority of states (UNCGG 1995: 10–11). The response, according to the report, is for the states-system – organized around a reinvigorated UN – to welcome these challenges in the form of a widened global governance. Non-governmental actors, according to the report, have brought about a 'global associational revolution' (1995: 253) consisting of 'a multitude of institutions, voluntary associations, and networks . . . [which] channel the interests and energies of many communities outside government, from business and the professions to individuals' (UNCGG 1995: 32).

Alongside NGOs, global business is considered to be an 'even more clearly identifiable sector with a role in global governance' (UNCGG 1995: 255). Business is seen as being 'in the forefront of "futures" research, mapping out long-range global scenarios and assessing their implications for corporate responsibility', following the lead of the Business Council on Sustainable Development (BCSD), which is 'illustrative of this new role' (Ibid). In this liberal, pluralist account, this wide range of non-governmental actors is seen as standing alongside states. Moreover, it is seen as enabling the democratization of global governance.

Critics of the liberal discourse caution that there is a danger of overemphasizing the diffusion, or even loss, of state power. The importance and centrality of state sovereignty do not disappear. The key institutions remain inter-governmental ones. Despite claims that environmental issues, because of their global nature, challenge the sovereign, interstate system, and despite claims to be creating some global civil space, the political framework of the liberal global political economy has not fundamentally altered. While states may appear to have lost autonomy, juridically their claim to sovereignty is not undermined (Paterson 1997: 175). Critical voices in the global governance debate draw connections to Foucauldian and neo-Gramscian discourse. Here, global governance does not mark the retreat of the state, but rather the ultimate form of government rationality or, as Foucault termed it, 'governmentality', the 'unspoken rationality of neoliberal globalization' (Douglas 2000: 116). Neo-Gramscians similarly liken global governance to a strategy of global capitalist hegemony, a process of institutionalization that stabilizes and perpetuates world order (Cox 1981: 136; Ford 2003: 122). In these views, global environmental governance is not so much about managing global environmental problems as about perpetuating dominant capitalist structures and practices. Yet again, other writers, recognising the complexity and diversity of global environmental governance, highlight the role of networks amongst a range of actors, deploying Social Network Analysis (SNA) to identify the complex structures of networks and how they might enable information flow, coordination and cooperation (Paterson 2016).

The space of global civil society

Within the literature on global governance, transnational actors are often said to be located within the sphere of global civil society. The concept of civil society itself is an old and complex one that has seen shifts over time in its boundaries with state and market, also varying theoretically from liberal to critical positions. However, as some authors have pointed out, there are problems with constructing bounded spheres due to the often trans-national dimension of social relations (Shaw 1994). The extrapolation of civil society to global civil society is open to different interpretations. Predominantly, it is claimed that changing circumstances under conditions of globalization have affected non-state actors and the way they organize, as well as who and what they target. The sphere in which they are said to be operating has also become globalized. If national social movements were located in civil society, now transnational and global social movement activism is growing in a sphere of global civil society (see, for example, Shaw 1994; Lipschutz and Mayer 1996).

The term global civil society is now widely used amongst social movements, NGOs, business as well as government representatives and the institutions of global governance. It is actively shaping a political sphere and creating new transnational political identities and subjects (Drainville 2004). Some writers see global civil society as consisting of 'self-conscious constructions of networks of knowledge and action, by decentred local actors, that cross the reified boundaries of space as though they were not there' with the aim 'to reconstruct, re-imagine, or re-map world politics' (Lipschutz 1992: 390). In his view, global civil society is a *parallel sphere* that seeks to bypass the state-system and construct 'new political spaces' (1992: 393).

This leads to questions about what the sphere of global civil society adds to our analysis of transnational actors. Different theoretical viewpoints have different takes on the meaning and importance of global governance and global civil society.

The dominant liberal view, as depicted in documents such as *Our Global Neighbourhood*, envisages a pluralistic, relatively harmonious, emancipatory political sphere (see also Lipschutz and Mayer 1996; Wapner 1997; Kaldor 2003). Liberals refer to it as that 'domain that exists above the individual and below the state but also across state boundaries, where people voluntarily organize themselves to pursue various aims' (Wapner 1997: 66). In this view, global governance is constituted by the addition of global civil society to international society, made up of both NGOs and business actors. It is portrayed as a space of 'civility' and not a potential site for conflicting interests.

On the other hand, traditional IR theorists are sceptical about the importance of global governance or global civil society (for example Grieco and Ikenberry 2003). They see any institutional mechanisms above the state level as inevitably subject to distortion and abuse by the most powerful nation-states who will further their interests through these institu-tions or ignore and bypass them.

Critical voices agree partially with some of the realist analysis about the abuse of such institutional mechanisms by powerful states, but they locate the whole scenario within global capitalism, seeing powerful states as seeking to expand their control over global capitalism, not just for the sake of political power in and of itself. Neo-Gramscians, for example, emphasize the role of ideology as well as institutions in maintaining capitalist hegemony. Here, the sphere of global civil society is in danger of contributing to the enclosure of the global public sphere, by creating an elite space that legitimizes global governance. However, the neo-Gramscian view also sees global civil society as a site for potential contest to hegemony, and thus a site of struggle and resistance. They see global civil society as the terrain where progressive forces are challenging the increasing power of capital and seeking to create transnational links and new political spaces for mobilizing on global problems such as social injustice and environmental degradation (for example Gill 2003).

In line with the perceived transformative potential of global civil society, sections of social movements – in particular established NGOs – consciously define themselves as members of global civil society, invoking the language of democratization and participation. They see the sphere of global civil society as a political space for engaging with the institutions of global governance in an attempt to make up for the democratic deficit that these non-transparent and unaccountable institutions create. Civil society actors clearly are active and important participants in a less state-centric global environmental governance, though claims that they democratise, or even lend greater legitimacy, require careful scrutiny (Bernauer and Betzold 2012; Stevenson and Dryzek 2014), and further investigation into the impact of transnational actors shows varying degrees of success (Betsill and Corell 2008; McCormick 2011; Newell 2000; Park 2013).

On the other hand, less institutionalized grassroots movements with radical agendas are suspicious of a politics of engagement, which they view as a form of co-optation (Ford 2003). In the neo-Gramscian view, the establishment of an enlarged liberal sphere of global civil society where people can participate in the management of the environment is consistent with the notion that civil society is a mechanism of hegemony. In this view, civil society's involvement and perceived contribution to policy making are a concession to the people in return for their acquiescence in preserving the dominant social, political and economic capitalist model. Further, they see such discourses of global civil society as strategies for absorbing and neutralizing potentially counter-hegemonic ideas (Cox 1993: 55). However, they also stress that civil society is the space for change; the space where hegemony is challenged. It is where the struggle over environmental policy is played out. Global civil society thus is not only a sphere of action, but it has *agency*, as do the actors operating from the sphere, be they transnational environmental movements, TNCs or transnational business networks.

We saw that there are different interpretations of the phenomenon of global civil society and its democratizing potential. While one can argue that there has, indeed, been an increase in activity of transnational actors in the sphere of global civil society and, therefore, increased *participation* of these actors in global governance, that does not necessarily translate into democracy; although some argue it could potentially enhance democracy within global governance (for example Held and McGrew 2003; Stevenson and Dryzek 2014). Reports such as *Our Global Neighbourhood* may be slightly exaggerating the claims of democratization because participation does not necessarily equal representation. Here, NGOs are situated in the same sphere as business actors, competing for participation in global institutions. Previously, the UN's Agenda 21 had, for the first time ever, called upon the global population to participate in the saving of the planet (UN 1992). However, the locus of authority remains entrenched in the inter-state system, with a growing recognition of the role of business as by far the dominant section of this so-called global civil society. Critical scholars view environmental issues as being depoliticized through the orthodox discourse of global environmental governance building within the liberal global political economy (e.g. Paterson 2000). That is to say that environmental problems are separated out from economic and political issues, seen as discrete issues that are capable of being fixed through institutions, market-based mechanisms or changed behaviour, yet without challenging the parameters of the current system.

At heart, the study of the role of transnational actors in global environmental politics is about power relations. As we saw above, global environmental governance is the arena of global environmental politics. It is here that the global management of transboundary environmental issues is fought out. Global civil society is now most readily identified as the space in which transnational actors operate. It is portrayed as a democratizing force for global governance in the dominant liberal literature. However, critical scholars want to deconstruct this space and make the power relations explicit. Ultimately, we might want to ask in what way does an analysis of transnational actors in global environmental politics challenge conventional approaches to understanding political outcomes in global environmental politics. For this, we now turn to an illustration of a variety of transnational actors.

Transnational actors in global environmental politics

The previous section of the chapter has illustrated the context and space of transnational activism. Traditionally, the role of transnational actors in the policy-making process, like in the discipline of IR more generally, has not been at the centre of analysis. Although regime theory, in its analysis of environmental regimes and multilateral environmental agreements, acknowledges epistemic communities as contributors to global environmental politics, the emphasis has been on the role of scientists and technical experts contributing expertise to the understanding of environmental issues (Vogler 2003). This has been particularly important where controversy or uncertainty has been an issue, for example over the phenomenon of climate change. The presence of epistemic communities, however, has not radically unsettled the state-centricity of regime analysis. While it has introduced actors other than states, these have been limited to elite experts. These types of elite actors must not be confused with the broader transnational environmental movement and might better be described as part of broader advocacy networks (Keck and Sikkink 1998).

This section will focus on transnational environmental movements, NGOs and transnational business / TNCs as actors in global environmental politics. It will use the concept of NGOs generally, although they are sometimes also referred to as International NGOs (INGOs) or Transnational NGOs (TNGOs). Although this book's focus is on global environmental politics, and the focus of this chapter is on the transnational actors in global environmental politics, this is not to say that environmental issues can be seen in isolation. Indeed, focusing on single issues can be counterproductive because it may fail to challenge the fragmented, disciplinary technical-rational discourse that is a key contributor to environmental degradation and current global environmental governance. If environmental issues are separated out of their social, political and economic context, the root causes are rendered invisible, leading to techno-fix solutions that may exacerbate the problem (Ford 2003). Indeed, concerns amongst transnational actors are rarely limited to discrete environmental problems. The analysis of global environmental change and issues of sustainability is mostly couched in a much broader framework, looking at the relationship between environment and human economic, social, cultural and political development. The growing discourse around environmental and ecological justice exemplifies this (Gillard et al. 2017).

Transnational environmental movements and NGOs

Particularly since the 1960s, global environmental movements have proliferated with the awareness and politicization of environmental degradation and its relationship to the wider organization of modern societies in their economic, political and cultural aspects. Increased awareness around the connection between globalization and environmental degradation has led movements to take their struggle out of a purely national context. The 1992 UN Conference on Environment and Development (UNCED) is usually quoted as the watershed for transnational actor involvement in global environmental politics, where close to 1,500 NGOs organized a parallel conference and many more movements and NGOs rallied from across the globe. Ten years later, over 6,000 officially registered NGOs gathered in Johannesburg for the 2002 International Summit on Sustainable Development, alongside countless 'unofficial' groups and movements. A myriad of movements and organizations across the world, from business to NGOs, campaigned on climate change around the various Conferences of the Parties (COPs) running up to the Paris Climate Conference in 2015.

It is hard to find a consensus among social movement theorists as to how a social movement might be defined. Scholars have challenged the social movement literature that has tended to see social movements as bounded by nation-states, or geographically limited to regions or cultures, particularly the North (see, for example, Walker 1994; Stammers and Eschle 2005). Broadly, social movements, including environmental movements, are heterogeneous groups that share collective identity, solidarity and common purpose (e.g. Diani 2000). They vary in size, issues and tactics and the environmental movement itself spans various shades of green. Despite the diversity of identities and experiences, these movements do identify commonalities in the experience of late capitalist modernity and connections are sometimes forged across space and place.

Transnational movements, then, are movements that are building transnational cooperation around common goals and purposes (Smith et al. 1997: 59–60). Sydney Tarrow defines them as: '. . . socially mobilised groups with constituents in at least two states, engaged in sustained contentious interactions with power-holders in at least one state other than their own, or against an international institution, or a multinational economic actor' (2001: 11).

Thus, transnational environmental movements are movements that are creating transnational links and acting transnationally because they perceive the root causes of environmental degradation to be tied up with the forces of globalization, such as the increasing globalization of capital and, with it, the globalization of governance structures. That said, there are many movements that campaign solely on national, regional or local issues. But, increasingly, there is an awareness of the relationship between the local and the global.

Indeed, 'think global act local' became a prominent slogan within the green movement, linking global awareness with the importance of connectedness to place and rooted action, as seen, for example, in the Transition Movement (for example Griffiths 2009).

While many movements campaign on specific issues, it is important to note that the boundaries between issues are not necessarily always rigid. Transnational movements campaigning on human rights abuses, gender inequality or labour issues often share similar concerns and goals to environmental movements, in that their individual causes may all in some ways stem from the nature of the current global economic and political system. Indeed, many environmental movements would not want to separate the environment and human development. They argue that sustainability and social justice go hand in hand.

The terminology for describing transnational movements has varied enormously: for example, INGOs, International Social Movement Organizations (ISMOs), international pressure groups or interest groups, or transnational advocacy groups or networks (e.g. Keck and Sikkink 1998; Stammers and Eschle 2005). Within the field of the environment more specifically, they have been described as environmental transnational coalitions (Princen 1995). More broadly, they have been identified as world civic politics (Wapner 1996), global citizen action (Edwards and Gaventa 2001) or people's movements (Shiva 2005). Many movements have identified globalized capitalist structures and distant, unaccountable governance structures as part of the problems they care about and have identified themselves as anti-globalization movements, anti-capitalist movements, pro-democracy movements, and global justice movements or, more boldly, the 'movement of movements' (Mertes 2004).

There is a danger of conflating organizations with movements (Stammers and Eschle 2005). The environmental movement broadly conceived contains a wide variety of groupings. While some NGOs could be seen to be located on a spectrum within the environmental movement, it is not the case that all NGOs are *part of* the movement as such. Some large, established NGOs, such as IUCN (International Union for the Conservation of Nature) or the WWF (World-Wide Fund for Nature), have a high degree of cross-fertilization with established institutions of governance. These large, bureaucratic, professional environmental NGOs are far removed from the grassroots of the environmental movement, though they may share common concerns.

Others, such as pressure groups like Friends of the Earth or Greenpeace, are financially independent of governmental institutions and sometimes take an anti-state position as well as lobbying at the state and inter-state level. As such, they have a two-pronged approach. On the one hand, they have been involved, along with organizations such as IUCN and WWF, in setting and monitoring the implementation of institutional responses, in the context of international environmental regime formation and maintenance and within the United Nations as well as within national governments or at the EU level. On the other, they are working in solidarity with grassroots environmental movements, sometimes taking direct action (Young 1999; Ford 2003).

Grassroots movements are largely marginalized from institutional processes, often by choice. They might not fit neatly into a 'transnational' category because they may be campaigning on a particular local issue and may lack resources to network transnationally. However, they clearly identify transnational structures as the root cause of environmental destruction. Movements such as Via Campesina, Climate Camp or Earth First! are challenging the top-down governance process through direct action. They are highly critical of the institutional channels available and their responses to environmental problems. They are also critical of institutionalized environmental NGOs that they see as co-opted by the dominant powers of global governance. These grassroots activist movements perceive themselves to be engaged in an emancipatory struggle for freedom from dominating discourses to pursue alternative, equitable and sustainable ways of living, working for a redistribution of power and carving out political space. Their strategy is not necessarily to influence the agenda of the global governance process but rather to take direct action to increase awareness about issues and to directly challenge and confront the state and economic powers that be. Although they may be active in specific places and localities, they are forging transnational links through networks such as the Peoples' Global Action or the World Social Forum (Williams and Ford 1999; Ford 2003; Mertes 2004). The movement of movements could be seen as the transnational heart of a large variety of groups and movements across the globe. Within this movement, diverse groups from across the globe are campaigning for the preservation of economic, political, cultural and ecological diversity, which they perceive to be under threat from a globalizing monoculture (see Shiva 1993; Gill 2003).

The intention here is not to measure which movements have been most successful in, for example, lobbying the institutions of global governance or attempting to shut them down. Rather, the emphasis is on the political and cultural process of activism and the impediments which may be preventing successful outcomes, and on the portrayal of these movements as agents of change. Indeed, instrumentally, these movements may be relatively powerless compared to large business lobby groups. However, there is a powerful, cultural element to the movements for social change, which through global action and the global media, are spreading new discourses and challenging existing ones.

Importantly, movements do not just arise as a means to an end but are actively engaged in processes of socio-cultural change, bringing forth alternative ways of knowing and doing. Progressive movements are thus not just challenging the organization of the global political economy but actively showing what an alternative could look like. This cultural aspect of social movements is something that has been largely ignored in social movement theory that focuses on the reasons for mobilization of collective behaviour. Melucci (1996) has warned that social movements must not be reduced purely to a political dimension for this would deny the communicative role they play (p. 2). His project is concerned with analyzing the actors' *construction* of their own action (1996: 16), the actual processes of cultural change. Yet, such an approach must not lose sight of the context, which remains the global political economy. Social movements need to be reflexive about their position within this hegemony as well as the dangers of co-optation. As seen above, they need to be able to contextualize their agency within the global matrix.

TNCs and business advocacy groups

Like transnational environmental movements and NGOs, TNCs have mushroomed in the last three decades, and they constitute important players in the modern, hyper-globalized capitalist world economy, responsible for large amounts of investment and trade. A TNC is a corporation that is active in more than two countries – that is, it may have a host state, but it operates subsidiaries in various other locations and involves the movement of capital, resources and people across national boundaries. Examples might include oil corporations such as Shell or BP, or food giants such as Unilever or Nestle. Apart from TNCs, though, there are also related business advocacy groups who act in the interests of transnational business, such as the International Chamber of Commerce (ICC), the World Business Council for Sustainable Development (WBCSD) or the European Chemical Industry Council (CEFIC), to name a few examples.

TNCs and business advocacy networks are clearly important transnational actors in global environmental politics because of the close link between the global economic system and global environmental degradation. Unlike transnational movements and NGOs, they are pursuing instrumental goals rather than acting on principled beliefs (Keck and Sikkink 1998; Clapp 2005b). They are motivated by profit, which leads to the growth imperative and resulting increased demand on resources that can contribute directly to environmental degradation, given that many TNCs are operating in environmentally sensitive sectors, such as natural resource extraction. While some TNCs invest in and produce environmentally benign goods and services, generally trade and investment patterns within the capitalist global economy tend to exacerbate, rather than mitigate, environmental degradation due to the growth imperative. The distantiated processes of global capitalism, including the activities of TNCs, contribute both directly and indirectly to processes of environmental degradation. This leads to a tension between global environmental governance as pursued through MEAs and the freedom to do business. TNCs and transnational business advocacy networks acting on their behalf are eager to minimize regulation that is designed to limit environmental (and social) degradation. Fundamentally, then, there is a conflict of interest between their aims and those of global environmental policy. Like NGOs, they are involved in lobbying within the global environmental policy-making process, though they are often pursuing very different outcomes from those of NGOs. While NGOs and social movements may be seeking to challenge the very culture of capitalist relations that *systematically produce* environmental degradation and social injustice, TNCs are attempting to influence the agenda to prevent measures that could be harmful to business. There is no denying the power of TNCs, as some TNCs have greater assets than nation-states. However, not all commentators see TNCs as necessarily an obstacle to sustainable development. Some argue that these assets can be used to positively contribute to sustainable development, such as through the transfer of innovative and clean technology and the investment in infrastructure and job creation (Murphy and Bendell 1997, Herman, Chapter 9). In this way, the world has seen a greening of some businesses.

The greening of business or greenwash?

Apart from official lobbying in opposition to global environmental policy, business has also been very busy recreating itself as a vanguard of sustainable development (Schmidheiny 1992; ICC 1991). The institutionalization of this concept is not limited to governments and international organizations. In addition to UN documents and government policies, the concept of sustainable development has entered the corporate world. However, business is not blind to the environmental movement's criticisms and, in the concept of sustainable development, has found a way to discursively integrate environmental problems without substantially changing its social and material productive practices. The link between economic growth and environmental degradation remains solid, despite the corporate sector's promotion of sustainable development (ICC 1991).

During the 1992 UNCED conference, business was brought on board and the WBCSD (formerly the BCSD) was born. This lobby group managed to ensure that, during official negotiations, the role of business in environmental degradation was played down. Agenda 21, signed at UNCED as a comprehensive blueprint for global action on sustainable development (UN 1992), only mentions corporations in order to emphasize their role in sustainable development but eschews any mention of the need for business to be regulated. More fundamentally, at the same time as UNCED was being held, UN reforms were underway that dismantled the United Nations Centre on Transnational Corporations (UNCTC) (Clapp 2005a: 25). Attempts by the UNCTC to include corporate accountability measures within Agenda 21 had been rejected by industrialized countries during preparatory meetings. The controversy over the lack of provisions in Agenda 21 regarding corporations was further enhanced by the fact that corporations such as ICI (Imperial Chemical Industries) and ARCO (Atlantic Richfield Company), major environmental polluters with a track record of funding anti-environmental lobby groups, were found to be contributing to the funding of UNCED itself (Doran 1993; Chatterjee and Finger 1994).

Critical voices would argue that business is using the discourse of sustainable development as a way of subverting environmental concerns through greenwash (Beder 1997). As far back as 1984, UNEP (the United Nations Environment Programme) and ICC organized the World Industry Conference on Environmental Management (WICEM), which three years prior to the Brundtland Report's promotion of sustainable development, was discussing the possibility of achieving economic growth and sound environmental management. The position was a distinctly corporatist one. At WICEM, it was recommended that industry should become more strongly involved in formulating environmental policy in general, as well as in formulating national environmental regulatory frameworks (Trisoglio and ten Kate 1991). By 1991, in the run up to UNCED, WICEM II was clearly carving out the niche for industry in defining and spearheading their particular model of sustainable development.

As part of this quest, WICEM II further called on business and industry to foster harmonious relations with local communities in order to gain their confidence and to become better integrated into the community and wider society. The result of WICEM II was *The Business Charter for Sustainable Development: Principles for Environmental Management*, adopted in 1990 and first published in 1991. This states, for example,

> economic growth provides the conditions in which protection of the environment can best be achieved, and environmental protection . . . is necessary to achieve growth that is sustainable . . . In turn, versatile, dynamic, responsive and profitable businesses are required as the *driving force* for sustainable *economic* development and for

providing managerial, technical and financial resources to contribute to the resolution of environmental challenges. Market economies, characterised by entrepreneurial initiatives, are essential to achieve this . . . making market forces work in this way to protect and improve the quality of the environment – with the help of standards such as ISO 14000, and judicious use of economic instruments in a harmonious regulatory framework – is an ongoing challenge that the world faces in entering the 21st century.

(ICC 1991, emphasis in original)

It is clear from this passage that business, in line with conventional economic orthodoxy, perceives environmental degradation to be something *outside of* economic processes. The environment is something that is separate from, and that impinges on and challenges, economic and corporate structures and processes. Business and growth cannot be questioned in themselves, the task is to 'manage' the challenges within the given framework. Business is clearly bidding for its narrow view of sustainable development to be implemented and for business to take on a major role in the implementation. While, on the one hand, aiming to become more closely integrated with community and society, business is actually lobbying for autonomy and self-regulation or, at most, market-based instruments such as carbon-trading.

The privatization of global environmental governance

Another key dynamic in the provision of global public goods has been that of public authority versus private power. Global governance has sometimes involved a shift away from public authority to private agencies, as seen, for example, in the public–private partnerships such as Global Compact, which includes over 4,700 corporate participants as well as stakeholders from over 130 countries. At heart, it advocates responsible corporate citizenship to the challenges of globalization in the areas of human rights, labour, environment and anti-corruption, contributing to a more sustainable and inclusive global economy (UNGC no date).

Likewise, business advocacy groups, such as WBCSD, and institutions, such as the International Organization for Standardization (ISO), promote voluntary codes of conduct that, as well as safeguarding the autonomy of business, also implicate business in environmental management. The growth in voluntary codes of conduct is blurring the boundary between public and private and leading to what has been called 'mixed regimes', involving states and private authorities in the 'creation and maintenance of international principles, norms, rules and decision-making procedures' (Clapp 1998: 295).

There has been a tension between the general liberalization and deregulation trend in the globalized political economy on the one hand and the growing need for environmental regulation on the other, which has led to a search for 'new and private forms of (environmental) regulation, such as (environmental) standards . . . as a way out of this *tension* between deregulation and re-regulation' (Finger and Tamiotti 1999: 9). On the one hand, there has been a move from traditional 'command and control' style policy to an increased privatization of environmental politics involving the private sector and non-state actors (see also Clapp 1998). On the other, there is an argument that a fundamental reorganization of international society is taking place, as seen in the growth of global governance (Finger and Tamiotti 1999).

A privatization of environmental governance is taking place, as seen in the growing influence of private actors on decision making, which in some cases, is outweighing the influence of states. Evidence suggests that more and more private actors are initiating regimes which are later recognized by states and incorporated into their regulatory structures, one example being the ISO 14000 series, which specifies environmental management standards (Clapp 1998). In line with the mainstream belief that global environmental problems demand global solutions, the notion of global standards would seem an essential basis upon which to build harmonized global solutions. However, also in line with the mainstream, it ignores the unequal power structures within the global political economy. The membership of ISO, true to its hybrid nature, consists of a mixture of governments, mixed public–private actors and private industry associations. The government members are predominantly made up of developed countries, while the private members' majority come from within the OECD (Organisation for Economic Co-operation and Development). Given that the decision-making process is heavily dominated by private interests, the voice of developing countries in the establishment of these global standards is marginalized (Clapp 1998: 296–301).

The idea of establishing environmental standards within the remit of ISO was a response to Agenda 21's recommendation for the role of industry in sustainable development (Clapp 1998: 302). The setting up of environmental *management* standards involved a change of direction from the ISO's traditional remit of *technical* standards (Finger and Tamiotti 1999: 12).

The shift towards global standards must further be seen in the context of trade liberalization and the WTO (World Trade Organization). The WTO's Agreement on Technical Barriers to Trade (TBT) encourages the use of international standards rather than national ones, which are seen as *technical* barriers to trade (Finger and Tamiotti 1999: 13; Clapp 1998: 305). In effect, the ISO environmental management standards, which were recognized by the GATT (General Agreement on Tariffs and Trade), create a lowest common denominator and act as a mechanism for avoiding trade barriers. More importantly, they demonstrate the role of privately agreed voluntary standards in the re-regulation and public management of international trade.

With the latest global crisis in neoliberal capitalism and a seeming return to neo-Keynsian style intervention, some green voices are proposing a 'Green New Deal' as a solution to the interlinked crises of capital, energy and climate. This would involve business and government as well as labour and environmental movements in bringing about a shift to green energy and green collar jobs financed by re-regulating finance and taxation (GNDG 2008).

From the above, we can see that transnational environmental movements and TNCs and their advocates and lobbyists are all clearly visible actors in global environmental politics. The question of the power of these diverse actors in global civil society is a complex one. For one, we have seen that this sphere includes a large variety of different types of actors – NGOs, transnational advocacy groups, TNCs, social movements. The liberal pluralist descriptions of this sphere do not analyze power relations within civil society. It seems questionable that business actors and NGOs are working on an equal footing. Business actors clearly have more 'tacit power' over state actors due to their close connection to economic growth creation (Newell 2000: 159). Further, amongst NGOs themselves, there are differentiations that cannot be ignored. NGOs, like social movements, are not a homogeneous, or necessarily a progressive, force and are not immune to power relations of class, race or gender or between North and South and are further differentiated on the basis of ideologies and strategies. Critical voices, on the other hand, embrace the diversity and complexity of the sphere, seeing it as a site of struggle for hegemony as well as counter-hegemony.

Conclusions

This chapter has provided an overview of transnational actors and their agency in global environmental politics. Over the last two decades, we have seen a growing literature on the role of transnational actors in world politics. Few IR scholars would argue that they are completely irrelevant. Most would agree that transnational actors need to be part of the analysis in understanding the framework and processes of global politics. Transnational actors are, of course, a broad church, encompassing anything from transnational social movements to global business. They do not all operate on the same footing, nor do they employ the same tactics to achieve their goals. Different theoretical perspectives provide different analyses of how and why transnational actors matter to global environmental politics. Solving global environmental problems is clearly a political as well as an economic, cultural and social struggle. States are not the only actors in this arena, and it is clear that transnational actors are an important part of the picture.

Note

1 I would like to thank Peter Doran, Jenneth Parker, Stephen Hurt and Neil Stammers for feedback on the first edition of this chapter.

Recommended reading

Betsill, M. M. (2011) Transnational actors in international environmental politics, in Betsill, M. M., Hochstetler, K. & Stevis, D. (eds), *Palgrave Advances in International Environmental Politics*, 2nd edition. Basingstoke: Palgrave Macmillan.

Betsill, M. M. & Corell, E. (2008) *NGO Diplomacy: The Influence of NGOs in International Environmental Negotiations*. Cambridge, MA: MIT Press.

Park, S. (2013) Transnational Environmental Activism, in Falkner, R. (ed), *The Handbook of Global Climate and Environmental Policy*. Chichester: Wiley & Sons, 268–285.

References

Ambrose, J. (2017) Cuadrilla's Fracking Plans Cleared by High Court. *The Telegraph*, 12 April. Available at: www.telegraph.co.uk/business/2017/04/12/cuadrillas-lancashire-fracking-plans-cleared-high-court (last accessed 19/07/2017).

Bäckstrand, K., et al. (2017) Non-State Actors in Global Climate Governance: From Copenhagen to Paris and Beyond. *Environmental Politics*, 26(4), 561–579.

Beder, S. (1997) *Global Spin: The Corporate Assault on Environmentalism*. Totnes: Green Books.

Bernauer, T. & Betzold, C. (2012) Civil Society in Global Environmental Governance. *The Journal of Environment and Development*, 21(1), 62–66.

Betsill, M. M. & Corell, E. (2008) *NGO Diplomacy: The Influence of NGOs in International Environmental Negotiations*. Cambridge, MA: MIT Press.

Chatterjee, P. & Finger, M. (1994) *The Earth Brokers*. London: Routledge.

Clapp, J. (1998) The Privatisation of Global Environmental Governance: ISO 14000 and the Developing World. *Global Governance*, 4(3), 295–316.

Clapp, J. (2005a) Global Environmental Governance for Corporate Responsibility and Accountability. *Global Environmental Politics*, 5(3), 23–34.

Clapp, J. (2005b) Transnational Corporations and Global Environmental Governance, in Dauvergne, P. (ed.), *Handbook of Global Environmental Politics*. Cheltenham: Edward Elgar.

Cox, R. W. (1981) Social Forces, States and World Orders. *Millennium*, 10(2), 126–151.

Cox, R. (1993) Gramsci, Hegemony and International Relations: An Essay in Method, in Gill, S. (ed.), *Gramsci, Historical Materialism and International Relations*. Cambridge: CUP.

Diani, M. (2000) The Concept of Social Movement, in Nash, K. (ed.), *Readings in Contemporary Political Sociology*. Oxford: Basil Blackwell.

Douglas, I. (2000) Globalization and the Retreat of the State, in Gills, B. K. (ed.), *Globalization and The Politics of Resistance*. Basingstoke: Macmillan.

Doran, P. (1993) The Earth Summit (UNCED): Ecology as Spectacle. *Paradigms: The Kent Journal of International Relations*, 7(1), 55–65.

Drainville, A. (2004) *Contesting Globalization: Space and Place in the World Economy*. London: Routledge.

Edwards, M. & Gaventa, J. (eds) (2001) *Global Citizen Action: Lessons and Challenges*, London: Earthscan.

Eilperin, J. & Dennis, B. (2017, February 7) 'Trump Administration to approve final permit for Dakota Access Pipeline' *Washington Post*, Available at: www.washingtonpost.com/news/energy-environment/wp/2017/02/07/trump-administration-to-approve-final-permit-for-dakota-access-pipeline/?utm_term=.b54d53055ae3 (last accessed 25/08/17).

Finger, M. & Tamiotti, L. (1999) New Global Regulatory Mechanisms and the Environment: The Emerging Linkage between the WTO and the ISO. *IDS Bulletin*, 30(3), 8–15.

Ford, L. H. (2003) Challenging Global Environmental Governance: Social Movement Agency and Global Civil Society. *Global Environmental Politics*, 3(2), 120–134.

Gill, S. (2003) *Power and Resistance in the New World Order*. Basingstoke: Palgrave Macmillan.

Gillard, R., Ford, L. & Kütting, G. (2017) Justice Discourses and The Global Environment: Diverse Perspectives on an Uneven Landscape, in O. Corry & H. Stevenson (eds), *Traditions and Trends in Global Environmental Politics: International Relations and the Earth*. London: Earthscan.

GNDG (Green New Deal Group). (2008) *A Green New Deal: Joined Up Policies to Solve the Triple Crunch of the Credit Crisis, Climate Change and High Oil Prices*. London: New Economics Foundation.

Grieco, J. M. & Ikenberry, G. J. (2003) *State Power and World Markets*. New York and London: Norton.

Griffiths, J. (2009) The Transition Initiative: Changing the Scale of Change. *Orion Magazine*, July/August. Online. Available at: www.orionmagazine.org/index.php/articles/article/4792 (last accessed 29/06/2009).

Held, D. & McGrew, T. (eds). (2003) *The Global Transformations Reader*. Cambridge: Polity.

ICC (International Chamber of Commerce) (1991) *The Business Charter for Sustainable Development: Principles for Environmental Management*. Paris: ICC, leaflet.

Kaldor, M. (2003) *Global Civil Society*. Cambridge: Polity.

Keck, M. E. & Sikkink, K. (1998) *Activists Beyond Borders: Advocacy Networks in International Politics*, Ithaka/London: Cornell University Press.

Keohane, R. & Nye, J. (1977) *Power and Interdependence*. Boston: Little, Brown and Company (Inc.).

Lipschutz, R. D. (1992) Reconstructing World Politics: The Emergence of Global Civil Society, *Millennium*, 21(3), 389–420.

Lipschutz, R. D. & Mayer, J. (1996) *Global Civil Society and Global Environmental Governance*, Albany: SUNY.

McCormick, J. (2011) The Role of Environmental NGOs in International Regimes, in Axelrod, R. et al. (eds), *The Global Environment: Institutions, Law and Policy*. Washington, DC: CQ Press, 92–109.

Melucci, A. (1996) *Challenging Codes: Collective Action in the Information Age*. Cambridge: CUP.

Mertes, T. (ed.) (2004) *A Movement of Movements: Is Another World Really Possible?* London: Verso.

Murphy, D. F. & Bendell, J. (1997) *In the Company of Partners: Business, Environmental Groups and Sustainable Development Post-Rio*. Bristol: Policy.

Newell, P. (2000) *Climate for Change: Non-State Actors and the Global Politics of the Greenhouse*. Cambridge: CUP.

Our Revolution. (2016) Statement on Army Corp's Decision to Block Dakota Access Pipeline Route. Available at: https://ourrevolution.com/press/our-revolution-army-corps-decision-block-dakota-access-pipeline-route/ (last accessed 19/07/2017).

Park, S. (2013) Transnational Environmental Activism, in Falkner, R. (ed.), *The Handbook of Global Climate and Environmental Policy*. Chichester: Wiley & Sons, 268–285.

Paterson, M. (1997) Institutions of global environmental change: sovereignty, *Global Environmental Change*, 7(2), 175–177.

Paterson, M. (2000) *Understanding Global Environmental Politics*. Basingstoke: Palgrave Macmillan.

Paterson, M. (2016) Networks and Coordination in Global Climate Governance, in Stavins, R. N. & Stowe, R. C. (eds), *The Paris Agreement and Beyond: International Climate Change Policy Post-2020*. Cambridge, MA: Harvard Kennedy School Project on Climate Agreements, 83–86.

Paterson, M., Humphreys, D. & Pettiford, L. (2003) Conceptualising Global Environmental Governance: From Interstate Regimes to Counter-Hegemonic Struggles. *Global Environmental Politics*, 3(2), 1–10.

Princen, T. & Finger, M. (1994) *Environmental NGOs in World Politics*. London: Routledge.

Princen, T. (1995) Ivory, conservation and environmental transnational coalitions, in Risse-Kappen, T. (ed) *Bringing Transnational Relations back in: Non-state actors, domestic structures and international institutions*, Cambridge: CUP, 227–256.

Schmidheiny, S. (1992) *Changing Course*. Cambridge, MA: MIT Press.

Shaw, M. (1994) Civil Society and Global Politics: Beyond a Social Movements Approach. *Millennium*, 23(3), 647–667.

Shaw, M. (2000) *Theory of the Global State: Globality as Unfinished Revolution*. Cambridge: CUP.

Shiva, V. (1993) *Monocultures of the Mind*. London: Zed Books.

Shiva, V. (2005) From Doha to Hong Kong via Cancun. Online. Available at: https://zcomm.org/znetarticle/from-doha-to-hong-kong-via-cancun-by-vandana2-shiva/ last accessed 20/01/2009).

Smith, J., Pagnucco, R. & Chatfield, C. (1997) Social Movements and World Politics: A Theoretical Framework, in Smith, J., Chatfield, C. & Pagnucco, R. (eds), *Transnational Social Movements and Global Politics*. Syracuse: Syracuse University Press.

Stammers, N. & Eschle, C. (2005) 'Social Movements and Global Activism', in de Jong, W., Shaw, M. & Stammers, N. (eds), *Global Activism Global Media*. London: Pluto.

Stevenson, H. & Dryzek, J. S. (2014) *Democratising Global Climate Governance*. Cambridge and New York: CUP.

Tarrow, S. (2001) Transnational politics: contention and institutions in International Politics, *Annual Review of Political Science*, 4(1), 1–20.

Trisoglio, A. & ten Kate, K. (1991) *From WICEM to WICEM II: A Report to Assess Progress in the Implementation of the WICEM Recommendations*. Geneva: UNEP.

TWN (Third World Network) (no date) WTO—Shrink or Sink. Online. Available at: www.twn.my/title/shrink.htm (last accessed 12/12/2008).

UN (1992) *Agenda 21*. UNCED, Geneva: UN.

UNCGG (UN Commission on Global Governance) (1995) *Our Global Neighbourhood*. Oxford: OUP.

UNGC (UN Global Compact) (no date) Online. Available at: www.unglobalcompact.org/AboutTheGC/index.html (last accessed 15/01/2009).

Vogler, J. (2003) Taking Institutions Seriously: How Regime Analysis can be Relevant to Multilevel Environmental Governance. *Global Environmental Politics*, 3(2), 25–39.

Walker, R. B. J. (1994) Social Movements/World Politics. *Millennium*, 23(3), 669–700.

Wapner, P. (1996) *Environmental Activism and World Civic Politics*. Albany: SUNY.

Wapner, P. (1997) Governance in global civil society, in Young, O. (ed.) *Global Governance: Drawing Insight from the Environmental Experience*, Cambridge, MA: MIT Press, 65–84.

Williams, M. & Ford, L. (1999) The World Trade Organisation, Social Movements and Global Environmental Management, in Rootes, C. (ed.), *Environmental Movements Local, National, Global*. London: Frank Cass.

Wong, J. C. (2016) Dakota Access Pipeline: US Denies Key Permit, A Win for Standing Rock Protesters. *The Guardian*, 5 December. Available at: www.theguardian.com/us-news/2016/dec/04/dakota-access-pipeline-permit-denied-standing-rock (last accessed 19/07/2017).

Young, O. R. (ed.) (1997) *Global Governance: Drawing Insights from the Environmental Experience*. Cambridge, MA: MIT Press.

Young, Z. (1999) NGOs and the Global Environmental Facility: Friendly Foes, in Rootes, C. (ed.), *Environmental Movements Local, National, Global*. London: Frank Cass.

Global political economy and development

3

Thomas Hickmann and
Markus Lederer

Introduction

Over the past few decades, we have witnessed a tremendous increase of cross-border economic relations. The expansion of economic globalization has led to an unprecedented integration of the global economy and produced a broad range of economic and social benefits. Proponents of economic globalization highlight that the increasing flows of transboundary trade, investment, and finance have reduced poverty, fostered technological advancement in both developing and industrialized countries, and supported regional integration (Bhagwati and Panagariya 2014). However, it is clear that neither all national economies nor all parts of the society benefit equally from this economic development (Lindert and Williamson 2007; Piketty 2014). While certain countries continue to show robust economic growth rates, other countries suffer from intensified competition, the fluctuation of investments, and financial speculation. Moreover, critics claim that certain societal groups are entirely excluded from the monetary wealth produced by a liberalized global economy (Dasgupta 2004; Ostry et al. 2014).

Beyond these distributional problems – where one could argue that, when considering absolute numbers, growth still moves more people out of poverty – it becomes increasingly obvious that economic globalization has huge impacts on the natural environment. Several studies underscore that intensified global economic relations have caused or accelerated dramatic changes in the Earth System, defined as the sum of our planet's interacting physical, chemical, biological, and human processes. This is most prevalent in the issue-areas of climate change, biodiversity loss, and land degradation (Rockström et al. 2009; Steffen et al. 2015b). In this context, the term *Anthropocene* has received widespread attention (Pattberg and Zelli 2016). Although still controversial among different scholar groups, it denotes a new geological epoch in planetary history, in which humans become the main drivers of environmental change (Crutzen 2002). Human-induced climate change, species extinction, ocean acidification, plastic seas, desertification, the overexploitation of natural resources, and other problems prompted by economic globalization restrain and endanger the habitability of the planet. Governments at all levels are now at a critical juncture to set sustainable development paths for the 21st century and beyond. The overarching question, therefore, is how we can reconcile the global political economy with environmental conservation and the existing planetary boundaries to sustain the natural basis of life on earth for us, as well as for future generations.

After this introduction, the chapter proceeds as follows. In the next section, we discuss different theoretical and conceptual approaches to the interplay between economic globalization and environmental issues. Thereafter, we refer to two major themes: *(i) Is sustainable development possible?* Under this heading, we reflect on whether the terms "sustainability" and "development" can be reconciled and *(ii) Who are the relevant actors in the global political economy?* In this context, we portray the broad array of actors and the related actor constellations that have emerged in this field. Finally, we draw some conclusions, highlight relevant open questions, and point to avenues for further research.

Theoretical and conceptual perspectives

There are various debates surrounding the question of how economic growth and environmental stewardship can be reconciled. In this section, we introduce four different approaches that have tackled this issue: Environmental Economics, International Political Economy and Development Studies, Global Environmental Governance and Earth System Governance, as well as Political Ecology. In particular, we introduce these perspectives and highlight their main contributions to the literature in their historical context.

Environmental economics

The academic discipline of Economics has always dealt with the question of how humans appropriate natural capital. Historically, the focus of this field of study has not been on how to protect nature, but on how to exploit natural resources most effectively. Those resources were perceived as either completely inexhaustible (e.g. air) or, at least, as highly abundant and self-replenishing. Access to these goods might be denied – but enough of the asset is available for free (e.g. water, wood, or fertile land). However, in the late 1960s, a group of scholars started to contend that the rate of exhaustion of natural capital is outgrowing the rate of natural replenishment and that we thus face "limits to growth" (Meadows et al. 1972). At about the same time, a debate on negative externalities was initiated, stating that markets by themselves often do not lead to optimal social outcomes. A typical example of such a negative externality is the pollution of rivers that is caused by a certain company upriver, while residents downriver have to live with the consequence of highly polluted water.

Over the last 20 years, highly interesting discussions have moved center stage of how to deal with such issues. On the one hand, the neo-classical answer within the field of Economics has been that either an increase of efficiency, and thus less waste and pollution, or of market-based instruments, such as taxes and trading systems, would work best to decrease environmental degradation (Solow 1991). From such a perspective, more globalization decreases pollution and should be promoted as better technologies and more efficient markets will help overcome market failures. The main tool of most mainstream approaches to estimate whether specific policies might be worth establishing are cost–benefit analyses (Dietz 2015). Currently, many studies in behavioral economics use a similar approach focusing on how "nudging" could substantially reduce environmental destruction (Campbell-Arvai and Arvai 2015). On the other hand, a number of critical voices claim that more efficiency does not solve the problem of ever scarcer natural resources. Authors like Hermann Daly argue that the underlying growth fetishism of neo-classical perspectives is outright utopian. Only non-growth, or in the words of Daly a "steady-state economy", is a realistic possibility (Daly 2007). Daly and many of his followers can thus be seen as the intellectual founding fathers of what is today known as the *degrowth model* (see below).

International political economy and development studies

Likewise, the academic traditions of Political Science and International Relations did, for a long time, not focus on environmental protection (Lederer 2017). If at all, nature was perceived as something that had to be dominated for human well-being or at least taken into account when human interaction from trade to war to state-building had to be explained. This is nicely displayed in the sub-discipline of International Political Economy. In the early 1970s, authors like Robert Gilpin studied the relationship between "States and Markets" (Gilpin 1987), but Gilpin did not seriously engage in the *problematique* that both the economy and politics are dependent on a specific form of natural exploration. In a similar vein, critical scholars from the same field, like Susan Strange (Strange 1996) or Robert Cox (Cox 1981), for all their merits when it comes to understanding power structures within global affairs, mostly neglected the ecological repercussions of the global political economy.

This changed only in the 1990s when a younger generation of scholars became aware of the political economy of sustainable development (e.g. Clapp and Dauvergne 2005). Different from Environmental Economics, many of these approaches went beyond material analyses and focused on the ideational basis of power and hegemony. Inspired by Critical Theory and Gramscian approaches, authors like Peter Newell (Newell 2012) or Chukwumerije Okereke (Okereke 2008) criticize the ideological domination of (neo-)liberal thinking. They argue that many of the propagated mainstream solutions to ecological problems were not tackling the fundamental power structures of a transnational elite causing ecological mayhem. These critical approaches also emphasized the role played by non-state actors in the global political economy, particularly that of transnational companies. They show that business actors often very subtly influenced environmental policies through different material and non-material channels (Fuchs and Lederer 2007). This line of critical environmental scholarship is today well established and brings together elaborated theoretical perspectives with classical themes of the global political economy (Death 2013).

A similar development can be observed in the field of development studies. Again, the environment in all classical approaches – be it Modernization, Dependence, or Liberal Theory – was only conceptualized as a means for a higher end that traditionally was equated with growth (Hönke and Lederer 2013). For a long time, the slogan that "the environment cannot be improved in conditions of poverty" prevailed, uttered first by India's former Prime Minister Indira Gandhi at the first global environmental conference in 1972. The underlying idea that the global North has to take full (financial) responsibility for global environmental problems is, however, no longer prevalent, neither in academic nor in contemporary policy discourses. On the one hand, the upper and middle classes of the global South, particularly in China, are now also heavily contributing to environmental problems, including climate change (Kahn and Zheng 2016). The notion of "common but differentiated responsibilities", which is one of the main principles of all global environmental treaties, should, therefore, not too easily be perceived as an antagonism of "North vs. South". On the other hand, the good news is that many of the most innovative notions of low-carbon development are now being developed in cities and countries of the global South (Urban 2014).

Global environmental governance and earth system governance

The long period of academic neglect of the interplay between economic globalization and environmental issues has given rise to the approaches of Global Environmental Governance and Earth System Governance. These evolving fields of study have their roots in the broader analytical perspective of Global Governance, which goes back to the early 1990s (Rosenau and Czempiel 1992). Scholars in this tradition study the politics of cross-border environmental problems from the notion that agency and authority have diffused to include numerous public and private actors that are commonly involved in (global) environmental policy-making (Hickmann 2017). In contrast to classical accounts, which locate agency and authority exclusively with national governments, these newer approaches point to the great diversity of problem-solving and decision-making capacities that sub- and non-state actors have developed in recent years (Dellas et al. 2011).

Furthermore, adherents of these governance approaches analyze the interplay between the different actors and point to the increasing institutional complexity in global environmental politics. Scholars have developed various concepts to describe this development, such as "fragmentation" (Biermann et al. 2009), "multi-level governance" (Bulkeley and Newell 2010), or "polycentrism" (Ostrom 2010). Instead of focusing on individual environmental regimes, scholars now explore the overarching governance architecture and the links between the different actors and governmental levels dealing with different issue-areas of environmental policy-making (Biermann et al. 2010). In addition, authors concerned with global environmental governance pay attention to normative issues related to the proliferation of actors and growth of institutional complexity like democratic legitimacy, accountability, and environmental justice (Bäckstrand et al. 2010; Schlosberg 2013). While these scholars have provided important insights into contemporary environmental politics, they have largely neglected the economic dimension of global environmental politics.

Political ecology

Another approach that is concentrated on studying the drivers and solutions of trans-boundary environmental challenges is the field of Political Ecology. Adherents of the Political Ecology approach adopt a critical perspective on the existing power relations and constellations in the global political economy (Clapp and Fuchs 2009; Fuchs et al. 2016). In general, they focus their studies on the interactions between humans and nature and set out to observe the "shifting dialectic between (. . .) social groups and their physical environment" (Blaikie and Brookfield 1987: 17). By presuming a dialectic relationship between human societies and their environment, nature is no longer a passive entity trans-formed by human behavior. In contrast, it is perceived as a factor that actively influences systems of human behavior as well as the interactions within human societies. Political Ecology is hence understood as "combining the concerns of ecology and political econ-omy that together represent an ever-changing dynamic tension between ecological and human change, and between diverse groups within society at scales from the local individ-ual to the Earth as a whole" (Peterson 2000: 325).

When the Political Ecology approach gained salience in the 1980s, it spread out into different academic sub-fields and complemented other theoretical strands, such as liberal-ism or feminism. Parallel to the levels of analysis in social sciences, political ecology inves-tigates interactions on local, regional, national, or global levels (Walker 2005). Phenomena that are relevant to Political Ecology simultaneously influence, and are a product of, both societal and environmental functions on multiple levels (Adger et al. 2001). Thus, the Political Ecology approach starts from the assertion that it is worth studying the various complex processes at work at different levels, but at the same time, offers insights which approaches focused on either side of the human/environment dynamic may not.

Major themes

After having discussed some of the most important existing theoretical and conceptual approaches to the interplay between economic globalization and environmental issues, the following section takes up two major themes that are crucial to gain a thorough overview and understanding of key concepts, relevant actors and institutions, as well as the social and political dynamics in the interplay of the global political economy, development, and environmental issues.

Is sustainable development possible?

A first major theme deals with the question of whether sustainable development is possible and the terms sustainability and development can be reconciled. The concept of sustainable development was put onto the agenda by the so-called *Brundtland Report*, which defines the term as development that "meets the needs of the present generation without compromising the ability of future generations to meet their own needs" (World Commission on Environment and Development 1987: 43). This definition has come under severe criticism due to its vagueness. According to Kates et al., the concept "allows programs of environment or development; places from local to global; and institutions of government, civil society, business, and industry to each project their interests, hopes, and aspirations onto the banner of sustainable development" (Kates et al. 2005: 10).

The *Johannesburg Declaration* adopted at the 2002 *World Summit on Sustainable Development* made an attempt to introduce a more precise definition and identified three pillars of sustainable development. On this occasion, the participating nation-states enshrined a "collective responsibility to advance and strengthen the interdependent and mutually reinforcing pillars of sustainable development – *economic development, social development*, and *environmental protection* – at local, national, regional, and global levels" (World Summit on Sustainable Development 2002: 1, emphasis added). Several actors, perhaps most prominently the European Union, build upon these three pillars of sustainable development and seek to translate/integrate the three dimensions into their policy-making systems (European Union 2009). However: The issue of how the three pillars (*economic development, social development*, and *environmental protection*) are defined in concrete cases needs to be addressed over and over again at different governmental levels. In this section, we discuss a number of concepts related to the above-mentioned question.

Limits to growth

The first two decades after the Second World War were marked by unprecedented growth, increasing prosperity in industrial nations, and expanding middle classes. The economic future looked bright for the Western side of the Cold War and economic progress at this time has rightly been labeled the "Great Acceleration" (Steffen et al. 2015a). Gross domestic products were rising and unlimited growth seemed possible. Nevertheless, economic growth was heavily fueled by the industrialized exploitation of natural resources. A warning occurred in the early 1970s with the outbreak of the first oil crisis, which epitomized the increasing dependency on the availability of resources in many industrialized countries (Buttel et al. 1990).

At about the same time, a transdisciplinary conglomerate of scientists, now known as the *Club of Rome*, published the book *Limits to Growth*. The group of scholars compiled a list of 66 critical problems, which contained poverty, war, pollution, crime, resource depletion, and economic instability. When the scholars tried to find common causes, or at least a common denominator, they identified exponential economic growth as a possible solution (Meadows 2007). In the book *Limits to Growth*, they point to a lack of consideration for resource availability in predominant models of exponential economic growth. Both production and consumption strain the planets' ecosystems in a way that is destined to come to an end once resources run dry. The authors composed a world model in which they simulated different economic growth rates. None of the 66 critical problems was solved by any possible configuration of growth. In fact, some problems, especially that of resource depletion, even got worse at roughly the same speed growth rates were rising (Meadows et al. 1972). Accordingly, the Club of Rome came to the conclusion that economic growth is not only limited but can be perceived as the underlying cause of several problems the world was facing in the early 1970s and until today.

Kuznets-Curve

The Kuznets-Curve shows a different picture. It supposes increasing strains on natural resources and ecosystems until a certain level of growth, prosperity, and average income is reached. Yet, after societies have achieved a certain threshold and development stage, further economic growth decreases environmental pressure (Stern et al. 1996). According to proponents of the Kuznets-Curve, reasons for this development are a shift to clean production chains, rearranging consumer priorities, and a turn to more sustainable policies. The idea of a natural move towards sustainability, once a certain level of growth has been achieved, is underlined by the development paths of a certain group of industrialized countries, such as Northern European countries. Germany and the Scandinavian countries, for example, have successfully recovered large forest areas that were heavily depleted and they cleaned up many heavily polluted rivers and lakes. The Kuznets-Curve thus can work for particular ecosystems and within specific countries. The question is, however, whether the Kuznets-Curve also works for the largest environmental problem, climate change.

In an empirical study, Cole, Rayner, and Bates highlighted the correlation between income levels and the decline of different kinds of emissions in several OECD (Organisation for Economic Co-operation and Development) countries (Cole et al. 1997). Their finding pointed to certain thresholds for the emission levels of certain pollutants in developed, growth-oriented societies. However, Cole et al. also accounted for carbon dioxide emissions, the pollutant mainly responsible for the greenhouse effect. This indicator did not reach a turning point at any stage during the study (Antal and Van Den Bergh 2016), and in those cases where emissions at least grew slower, like in the United Kingdom or Germany, the question arises whether these countries have not simply outsourced some of their most emission-intensive industries to China and other emerging economies.

Apparently, the same applies to other environmental indicators, such as waste, energy use by transport, and traffic volumes. While the Kuznets-Curve may hold true for certain pollutants and environmental indicators for some countries, it does not pass the test on other relevant environmental issues and on a global level. The projected thresholds of growth may be attained, but the turn towards sustainable development does not come automatically. It, therefore, needs a framework of policies, regulations, and public awareness for a turn towards sustainable consumption and production, while maintaining growth levels (Panayotou 1997; Andreoni and Levision 2001).

Weak and strong sustainability

Sustainability has become a universally used term for future-oriented models of economic and societal processes. Yet, as indicated above, it can be interpreted in concurring ways. Two broad categories can be distinguished. On the one hand, the idea of "weak sustainability" is based on the assumption of equity between natural and reproducible capital (Hediger 1999; Pelenc and Ballet 2015). In other words, the extraction of resources and the production of commodities by other material means produce the same kind of capital. This assumption correlates with two solutions to environmental problems: First, damages that stem from the exploitation of nature can be compensated for with the profit it generates. Second, future technological innovations will be able to solve emerging ecological challenges. From this point of view, sustainability means securing the well-being of future generations by any means, decoupled from the integrity of ecosystems.

On the other hand, the term "strong sustainability" implies that natural capital has a unique worth, which is not interchangeable with human-made commodities. Ecosystems are an essential part to human well-being; hence, they cannot be destroyed irreparably in the name of economic growth. This assumption leads to an understanding of sustainability that competes with contemporary growth-maximizing economic policies. Whereas economic growth remains an essential factor to development, strong sustainable development would need to cut growth levels in order to maintain critical ecosystems and avoid irreversible effects of human activity on the natural environment. Both terms understand natural resources as a certain kind of capital that can, and should, be commodified for accelerating economic growth. However, they differ on the maximum level of resource extraction and the effect certain levels have on both human societies and ecological systems. Another difference, moreover, is the importance they ascribe to the integrity of nature in the interplay between human well-being and ecosystems.

Green growth vs. degrowth

Against the backdrop of ongoing economic globalization and existing development challenges, there is a controversial debate on the right way forward. In fact, there are numerous strategies and proposals on how to alter and reform the global economy to mitigate negative effects on the natural environment. Two existing approaches stand out and contrast sharply with each other. First, some experts propose a *leapfrogging/green growth/green economy* to bridge increased energy needs in developing countries with innovative green technologies.

The World Bank defines green growth as "making growth processes resource-efficient, cleaner and more resilient without necessarily slowing them" (World Bank 2011: 2). This can be interpreted as a manual for both "leapfrogging" developing countries and industrialized countries pivoting to sustainable industries. Developing countries could directly use energy and resource efficient, clean technologies, instead of building their economy on pollution- and resource-heavy industries. The green growth model still depends on the extraction of natural resources, but at a much slower rate, with non-renewable resources being a sort of backbone for an economy mainly based on renewable energy. Accordingly, the status quo in most industrial countries requires a slightly different approach to green growth. In these countries, it is essential to balance out the need for short-term growth with investments in sustainability (Smulders et al. 2014).

As a result, the pressure on ecosystems decreases and productivity will increase in the long-term, offsetting short-term losses. In contrast to the Kuznets-Curve, advocates of green growth are aware of the need for policies and regulation to foster a sustainable economic development and often call for a strong involvement of the state (UNEP 2011). The notion of green growth has now become the hegemonic discourse in most international organizations. For example, both the OECD and the World Bank call for the phasing out of fossil fuel subsidies, governmental regulation to enhance energy efficiency, and more widespread information on sustainability (Antal and Van Den Bergh 2016). Although the specific policy solutions of political actors vary, green growth, as an overall concept, therefore stands for the integration of environmental and economic objectives. Most prominently, the concept has been advocated by a group of senior scholars and elder statesman, including Nicholas Stern from the London School of Economics and Felipe Calderón, former president of Mexico. They lead the *New Climate Economy Project*, which issues influential reports conveying the message that better growth and better climate protection do not contradict each other (The New Climate Economy 2017).

Other experts take a more skeptical view and propose a degrowth approach, claiming that "Prosperity Without Growth" is not only possible but also necessary in order to effectively deal with the existing global environmental challenges (Jackson 2009; Klein 2014). Advocates of this approach understand economic growth as a fundamental obstacle to sustainability and ecologically sound societies. This is based on the observation that capitalist modes of production, consumption, and the sheer amount of commodified goods increase constantly – and with them also pollution, the exploitation of ecosystems, and greenhouse gas emissions (Alexander 2012: 356). Accordingly, Demaria et al. characterize degrowth as "an attempt to re-politicize the debate on the much needed socio-ecological transformation, affirming dissidence with the current world representations and searching for alternative ones" (Demaria et al. 2013: 192). The alternative that most advocates of the degrowth model put forward is a down-scaled global economy that is focused on local production to serve people's actual needs (Martinez-Alier et al. 2010).

Rather unsurprisingly in a hyper-globalized and growth-oriented world economy, the degrowth approach has so far not received widespread recognition among influential decision-makers, but is pushed by certain environmental groups and civil society organizations. This approach is much more radical than most mainstream ideas of weak sustainability (see above) as it challenges the underlying growth paradigm for our economic well-being. In addition, it criticizes many current practices of environmental protection, such as recycling, offsetting, and car-sharing, which all might do a little good but rather help privileged layers of society to maintain their lifestyles (Dauvergne 2016: speaks of "Environmentalism of the Rich").

Neo-extractivism and Buen Vivir

The development model advocated by the main actors in the global system has, over the last decades, been a neoliberal one. Whether this model has been successful is subject to contentious political and academic debates. However, some countries, especially in Latin America, have started to decouple their development from neoliberal policies (Burchardt and Dietz 2014: 470). Bolivia and Ecuador, for instance, have remodeled their economies on a state-controlled basis. Consequently, the extraction of their rich resources runs through state-owned institutions (Cori and Monni 2015). Raw materials represent an important share of the exports of many of these countries and are hence an essential factor in the development and funding of social welfare systems, infrastructure, and public services. This dynamic produces a certain power structure within societies that is relevant to both environmental and sociological analysis, often leading to new forms of rent-seeking and the danger of the resource curse (Cori and Monni 2015). Those who have power over nature (by extracting resources) are those who have power over society (courtesy of the selling of resources and spending those funds). As the extraction of natural resources is the main or sole basis of power for ruling classes (North and Grinspun 2016), a shift away from this model of economic growth seems unlikely. Additionally, the dependency of development on raw material exports could lead to a severe backdrop of economic growth in a global economy that has shifted away from the use of natural resources for economic production, and is likely to shape the global political economy of the 21st century (Collier 2010).

Another alternative perspective on development relates to the concept of Buen Vivir (Acosta 2017). The origins of this concept go back to the *cosmovisions* of Andean peoples that advocate a legal standing for the natural environment (Walsh 2010). Such a rights approach to nature diverges from the mainstream modes of production and consumption in the global political economy. The philosophy behind the concept of Buen Vivir has inspired several social movements in Latin America and has lately even been expressed at political and institutional levels, including the international climate negotiations (Fabricant 2013). In 2008, Ecuador became the first country in the world to install the rights of nature, as well as a couple of related provisions, in its national constitution. In particular, the preamble of Ecuador's new constitution envisions a new form of citizenship that embraces diversity and harmony with the natural environment in order to live well (Becker 2011). Moreover, the constitution acknowledges the inalienable rights of ecosystems and requires the government to penalize violations of these rights.

Who are the relevant actors?

A second major theme focuses on who rules – thus, on the agents of environmental governance and development. Whereas most environmental scholarship was, at its very beginning, just as state-centric as all other sub-disciplines of Political Science, the current scholarship is highly aware of the multi-actor constellations that dominate environmental politics. Hence, many of the most important debates on how either regimes or international organizations, as well as business and non-business non-state actors, influenced politics were first explored in the field of economic, environmental, and development politics.

A good example of the role of various actors in the interplay between different policy spheres is the debate about global governance that, from its very beginning, had an analytical as well as a normative dimension (Dingwerth and Pattberg 2006). Particularly, researchers and non-governmental organizations working on the role of international financial institutions, as well as on the World Bank, criticized the negative impact these institutions have on the natural environment (Rock 1996). The International Monetary Fund or the World Trade Organization were perceived as much more powerful than the more weakly organized United Nations Environment Programme or the United Nations Development Programme. In fact, when comparing their financial means, the access these organizations have to the highest policy-making level, or their influence on hegemonic discourses, the World Bank, and other international financial institutions, clearly stand out.

Nevertheless, scholarship on the role of bureaucracies (Barnett and Finnemore 2005) or secretariats in environmental and developmental organizations (Biermann and Siebenhüner 2009), on synergies and conflicts between international institutions (Oberthür and Gehring 2006), the analysis of the advantages and disadvantages of fragmentation within the institutional setting of these organizations (Zelli and van Asselt 2013), or the debate on the emergence of regime complexes, e.g. in the field of climate politics (Keohane and Victor 2011), have all shown that these actors are often highly influential beyond their legal mandate. This can most prominently be observed in global climate politics, where the secretariat of the United Nations Framework Convention on Climate Change is currently loosening its straitjacket by gradually expanding its original spectrum of activity and original mandate in a creative way (Hickmann et al. forthcoming).

Finally, two developments underscore the ambivalence of the role and function of international organizations. First, the attempt to replace the United Nations Environment Programme with an International Environmental Organization (that might create a level-playing-field in the global arena between the policy domains of environment and economy) failed at the Rio+20 conference in 2012 due to the strong opposition of the United States and a couple of other countries (Bauer 2015). Second, a countervailing trend is that, at least rhetorically, all international organizations now have a very strong focus on sustainable development. Particularly, the World Bank is attempting to go beyond *green-washing* and has, for example, become very active in financing renewable energy projects in rural areas of the least developed countries. Still, their financing for conventional energy systems outweighs their financing for renewable energies.

The relevant agents in the global political economy also include non-state actors of various kinds. Whereas research in the 1990s fixated on whether either non-profit non-governmental organizations or for-profit business actors would, by themselves, become so important that they acquire "private authority" (Cutler et al. 1999), scholarship in the 2000s stressed the interaction effects of various non-state and state actors. Particular emphasis has, for example, been placed on the role multi-stakeholder partnerships have in the follow-up of the World Summit on Sustainable Development at Johannesburg in 2002, where the idea of partnerships was strongly advocated (Pattberg 2007). This hype has, however, slowed down as research showed that the effectiveness of these partnerships is not, *per se*, higher than state-led programs. Moreover, some of the most important elements that are necessary to increase the outcome and eventual impact of partnerships are a sustainable financial commitment and good management – aspects well known from classical development programs (Beisheim et al. 2014).

On a positive note, two trends are worth mentioning: First, non-governmental organizations in these policy fields no longer just act simply as watchdogs or agenda-setters. They have also become service and knowledge providers and are often implementing many of the most progressive programs in this field. This has been well researched for the field of global climate politics, where non-state actors became particularly active after the failure of national governments to adopt a new international climate treaty at the United Nations climate summit in Copenhagen in 2009. Non-state actors have thus initiated various climate governance experiments (Hoffmann 2011) or have acted in an entrepreneurial spirit and set rules by themselves, e.g. private standards for the carbon market (Green 2014). Second, similarly to the international organizations mentioned above, non-state actors and multi-stakeholder partnerships claim to have a sustainable development focus and thus at least try to mainstream action to address environmental problems.

The final actor that should not be forgotten is the nation-state. Most literature in the 1990s and in the 2000s either neglected the role of the nation-state as a potentially positive actor, and perceived it as a "dysfunctional form of political organization" (Falkner 2013: 252), or when dealing with the state as an agent, took it as a unitary actor or "black box" (Purdon 2015). Only more recently has the literature on green transformations started to consider the state as an actor more serious advancing the role of a "green state" (Meadowcroft 2005; Eckersley 2006). A particular focus has been put on the role bureaucracies play in also bringing about transformational change in environmental politics (Lederer et al. forthcoming). This literature builds on the insight that the administrative structures of modern nation-states can be extremely powerful institutions that can be used for "good" as well as "bad" policies (a more recent elaboration can be found in Fukuyama (2014); for the classical treatment of the power of bureaucracies, see Weber (1920/2013).

This focus on state capacities takes up insights of the literature on governance and development, arguing that the question of "Why nations fail" (Acemoglu and Robinson 2012) or why peace-keeping operations are successful (Paris 2004) cannot be answered without an understanding of how institutions, or in the words of Douglas North "the rules of the game", (North 1991) are being set up. This literature stresses that, on the one hand, effectiveness and legitimacy of any governance intervention strongly depends on specific capacities to ensure that public administrations, non-governmental organizations, multi-stakeholder partnerships, et cetera can deliver what they have promised. For the case of state-building, Fukuyama makes the simple argument that "before governments can be constrained, they have to generate power to actually do things. States, in other words, have to be able to govern" (Fukuyama 2014: 52). However, Fukuyama is also pointing out that strong governments (or, in fact, all institutions) also have to be supplemented by checks and balances.

This neo-institutionalist debate is nicely mirrored in the question of how much environmental stewardship can be brought about through bottom-up processes that primarily rely on deliberation (Stevenson and Dryzek 2014) or through top-down "environmental authoritarianism" e.g. in China (Beeson 2010; Gilley 2012). This issue is similarly taken up in the debate on how much of a "developmental state" is necessary in order to bring about growth – a factor that has been decisive in East and South East Asian "growth miracles" (Evans 1995; Wade 2004). Finding a balance that combines bottom-up and top-down elements in a satisfying manner is most likely one of the most important challenges of environmental and developmental governance in the time to come.

Conclusions and outlook

We face great challenges in the 21st century. The natural environment is threatened by intensified economic globalization but, at the same time, we have tremendous development challenges in many parts of the world that, most likely, can only be solved through increased economic activity and transboundary exchange. China is the perfect example of this dilemma. In the past decade, the Chinese government has significantly reduced the country's poverty rates through an unleashing of economic freedoms – yet, at the expense of political freedom and at the cost of enormous environmental devastation.

This example underscores the fact that new development paths need to be explored, and apparently, the ultimate question of our times is whether, and how, we will manage to reconcile economic growth, development in its multidimensional aspects, and the planetary boundaries that we are in persistent danger of transgressing. No matter if this will result in a new form of green growth or whether we, as societies, seriously turn to concepts of degrowth, evidence for a "great transformation" on a global scale is needed and already underway (WBGU 2011). Such a transformation will be first and foremost a political task since such transformative changes do not come about only through technological innovations or the power of markets (Scoones et al. 2015).

In practical terms, it is of utmost importance to understand, on the one hand, the agents of change and resistance and, on the other hand, the structural opportunities and barriers of such transformations. Particularly when focusing on the chances of low-carbon development, we should not be naïve about the fact that certain societal groups and countries will lose out and will try to act as spoilers. While it is easy to blame countries like Saudi Arabia or the current United States administration under President Trump as climate or environmental villains, we should not forget that very poor people will also often resist changes towards green technologies as the proposed changes do not bring about any short-term advantages for them and their families. And, even more problematic, it is "our" lifestyle of the upper and middle classes in the North and in the South that has to change drastically. Thus, coalitions of the willing will have to be built, compensation will have to be paid, and fights about distribution will have to happen if we seriously aim to divert from our current path of unsustainability.

Academia and scientists can play a key role in this endeavor, be it because their technical expertise is necessary or because academics might generate new ideas or engage as activist scholars within the environmentalist movement (Wapner 2016). From a more scholarly perspective, we argue that the following three issues warrant further attention to better understand the interrelationship between economic globalization and environmental protection/degradation:

- First, we need a better understanding of the interplay between the various actors concerned with the global response to existing environmental challenges. In fact, a key issue with regard to the solution of problems like climate change, biodiversity loss, and desertification is how to build a synergetic division of labor across different governmental levels and societal actors. For instance, to limit global warming to 1.5° Celsius, coordinated efforts at all levels of government, and by all parts of the society, are required, each utilizing their comparative advantage.

- Second, the disciplines of political science and global environmental politics still focus too much on Northern issues, whereas not enough attention is dedicated to the needs and priorities of people living in the so-called global South. As an example, take the role of cities: It is of course wonderful that cities like Bristol, Copenhagen, Freiburg, or Toronto become greener, but the future of the globe depends much more on the further evolution of Beijing, Jakarta, Lagos, and Rio de Janeiro. We thus need to redirect some of our scholarly attention to critical developments in other parts of the world.
- Third, studies of global environmental politics need to become more political, and this includes more analysis of the global political economy of development. Too often, our assumption is still that environmental policies lead to win/win situations and we pay attention neither to the (economic) losers of specific policies nor to the distributional consequences that transformative changes bring about. With Brexit, the Trump presidency, and far-right parties on the rise in numerous European countries, we should also be much more aware in our scholarly work that those who perceive themselves as losing out from progressive policies are a force to reckon with.

Thus, studies of global environmental politics have to overcome the old dichotomy of critical vs. problem-solving approaches (Cox 1992), as environmental scholarship, almost by definition, has to be both. In other words, we should not engage in academic in-fighting, pushing our respective epistemological, methodological, or ontological "camps", as time is running out in order to sustain the natural basis of life on earth, for us as well as for future generations.

Recommended reading

Biermann, F. (2014) *Earth System Governance*. Cambridge: MIT Press.
Dauvergne, P. (2016) *Environmentalism of the Rich*. Cambridge: MIT Press.
Hamilton, C. (2017) *Defiant Earth. The End of Humans in the Anthropocene*. Cambridge: Polity Press.
Rosa, H.; Henning, C. (eds). (2017) *The Good Life Beyond Growth: New Perspectives*. London: Routledge.
Scoones, I.; Newell, P.; Leach, M. (eds). (2015) *The Politics of Green Transformations. Pathways to Sustainability*. Routledge: Abingdon.
Stern, N. (2015) *Why Are We Waiting? The Logic, Urgency, and Promise of Tackling Climate Change*. Cambridge: MIT Press.
Urban, F. (2014) *Low Carbon Transitions for Developing Countries*. Oxon: Routledge.

Websites

- *European Union* (http://ec.europa.eu/environment/green-growth/index_en.htm)
- *IPCC* (www.ipcc.ch)
- *The New Climate Economy* (http://newclimateeconomy.net/)
- *UNEP* (www.unep.org)
- *World Bank* (www.worldbank.org/en/topic/environment)

References

Acemoglu, Daron; Robinson, James A. (2012) *Why Nations Fail. The Origins of Power, Prosperity, and Poverty.* New York, NY: Crown Publisher.

Acosta, Alberto (2017) Buen Vivir, in Rosa, Hartmut; Hennig, Christoph (eds), *The Good Life Beyond Growth: New Perspectives.* London: Routledge.

Adger, W. Neil; Benjaminsen, Tor A.; Brown, Katrina; Svarstad, Hanne (2001) Advancing a Political Ecology of Global Environmental Discourses. *Development and Change*, 32(4), 681–715.

Alexander, Samuel (2012) Planned Economic Contraction: The Emerging Case for Degrowth. *Environmental Politics*, 21(3), 349–368.

Andreoni, James; Levision, Arik (2001) The Simple Analytics of the Environmental Kuznets Curve. *Journal of Public Economics*, 80(2), 269–286.

Antal, Miklós; Van Den Bergh, Jeroen C.J.M. (2016) Green Growth and Climate Change: Conceptual and Empirical Considerations. *Climate Policy*, 16(2), 165–177.

Bäckstrand, Karin; Khan, Jamil; Kronsell, Annica; Lövbrand, Eva (eds) (2010) *Environmental Politics and Deliberative Democracy: Examining the Promise of New Modes of Governance.* Cheltenham: Edward Elgar.

Barnett, Michael; Finnemore, Martha (2005) The power of liberal international organization, in Barnett, Michael; Duvall, Raymond (eds), *Power in Global Governance.* Cambridge: Cambridge University Press, 161–184.

Bauer, Steffen (2015) United Nations Environment Programme, in Morin, Jean-Frédéric; Orsini, Amandine (eds), *Essential Concepts of Global Environmental Governance.* London: Earthscan, 229–232.

Becker, Marc (2011) Correa, Indigenous Movements, and the Writing of a New Constitution in Ecuador. *Latin American Perspectives*, 38(1), 47–62.

Beeson, Mark (2010) The Coming of Environmental Authoritarianism. *Environmental Politics*, 19(2), 276–294.

Beisheim, Marianne; Liese, Andrea; Janetschek, Hannah; Sarre, Johanna (2014) Transnational Partnerships: Conditions for Successful Service Provision in Areas of Limited Statehood. *Governance*, 27(4), 655–673.

Bhagwati, Jagdish; Panagariya, Arvind (2014) *Why Growth Matters: How Economic Growth in India Reduced Poverty and the Lessons for Other Developing Countries.* New York, NY: Public Affairs.

Biermann, Frank; Pattberg, Philipp; van Asselt, Harro; Zelli, Fariborz (2009) The Fragmentation of Global Governance Architectures: A Framework for Analysis. *Global Environmental Politics*, 9(4), 14–40.

Biermann, Frank; Pattberg, Philipp; Zelli, Fariborz (2010) *Global Climate Governance Beyond 2012: Architecture, Agency and Adaptation.* Cambridge, UK: Cambridge University Press.

Biermann, Frank; Siebenhüner, Bernd (eds) (2009) *Managers of Global Change. The Influence of International Environmental Bureaucracies.* Cambridge, MA: MIT Press.

Blaikie, P. M.; Brookfield, H. (1987) *Land Degradation and Society.* New York, NY: Methuen.

Bulkeley, Harriet; Newell, Peter (2010) *Governing Climate Change.* London: Routledge.

Burchardt, Hans-Jürgen; Dietz, Karin (2014) (Neo-)Extractivism – A New Challenge for Development Theory from Latin America. *Third World Quarterly*, 35(3), 468–486.

Buttel, Frederick H.; Hawkins, Ann P.; Power, Alison G. (1990) From Limits to Growth to Global Change. Constraints and Contradictions in the Evolution of Environmental Science and Ideology. *Global Environmental Change*, 1(1), 57–66.

Campbell-Arvai, Victoria; Arvai, Joseph (2015) The Promise of Asymmetric Interventions for Addressing Risks to Environmental Systems. *Environment Systems and Decisions*, 35(4), 472–482.

Clapp, Jennifer; Dauvergne, Peter (2005) *Paths to a Green World. The Political Economy of the Global Environment*. Cambridge, MA: MIT Press.

Clapp, Jennifer; Fuchs, Doris A. (2009) *Corporate Power in Global Agrifood Governance*. Cambridge, MA: MIT Press.

Cole, Matthew A.; Rayner, Anthony J.; Bates, John M. (1997) The Environmental Kuznets Curve: An Empirical Analysis. *Environment and Development Economics*, 2(4), 401–416.

Collier, Paul (2010) *The Plundered Planet. Why We Must – and How We Can – Manage Nature for Global Prosperity*. Oxford: Oxford University Press.

Cori, Andrea; Monni, Salvatore (2015) Neo-Extractivism and the Resource Curse Hypothesis: Evidence from Ecuador. *Development*, 58(4), 594–607.

Cox, Robert W. (1981) Social Forces, States and World Order. Beyond International Relations Theory. *Millennium*, 10(2), 126–155.

Cox, Robert W. (1992) Multilateralism and World Order. *Review of International Studies*, 18(2), 161–180.

Crutzen, Paul J. (2002) Geology of Mankind. *Nature*, 415(6867), 23–23.

Cutler, Claire A.; Haufler, Virginia; Porter, Tony (eds) (1999) *Private Authority and International Affairs*. Albany, NY: State University of New York Press.

Daly, Herman E. (2007) *Ecological Economics and Sustainable Development: Selected Essays of Herman Daly*. Cheltenham: Edward Elgar.

Dasgupta, Samir (ed) (2004) *The Changing Face of Globalization*. New Delhi: Sage.

Dauvergne, Peter (2016) *Environmentalism of the Rich*. Cambridge, MA: MIT Press.

Death, Carl (ed.). (2013) *Critical Environmental Politics*. Abingdon: Routledge.

Dellas, Eleni; Pattberg, Philipp; Betsill, Michele (2011) Agency in Earth System Governance: Refining a Research Agenda. *International Environmental Agreements*, 11(1), 85–98.

Demaria, Federico; Schneider, Francois; Sekulova, Filka; Martinez-Alier, Joan (2013) What is Degrowth? From an Activist Slogan to a Social Movement. *Environmental Values*, 22(2), 191–215.

Dietz, Simon (2015) Cost-benefit analysis, in Pattberg, Philipp; Zelli, Fariborz (eds), *Encyclopedia of Global Environmental Governance and Politics*. Cheltenham: Edward Elgar, 81–87.

Dingwerth, Klaus; Pattberg, Philipp (2006) Global Governance as a Perspective on World Politics. *Global Governance*, 12(2), 185–203.

Eckersley, Robyn (2006) From the Liberal to the Green Democratic State: Upholding Autonomy and Sustainability. *International Journal of Innovation and Sustainable Development*, 1(4), 266–283.

European Union (2009) Strategy for Sustainable Development. Available at: http://eur-lex.europa.eu/legal-content/EN/TXT/?uri=LEGISSUM:l28117 (last accessed 12/09/2017).

Evans, Peter B. (1995) *Embedded Autonomy: State and Industrial Transformation*. Princeton, NJ: Princeton University Press.

Fabricant, Nicole (2013) Good Living for Whom? Bolivia's Climate Justice Movement and the Limitations of Indigenous Cosmovisions. *Latin American and Caribbean Ethnic Studies*, 8(2), 159–178.

Falkner, Robert (2013) The Nation-State, International Society, and the Global Environment, in Falkner, Robert (ed.), *The Handbook of Global Climate and Environment Policy*. Chichester: Wiley & Sons, 251–267.

Fuchs, Doris; Di Giulio, Antonietta; Glaab, Katharina; Lorek, Sylvia; Maniates, Michael; Princen, Thomas; Røpke, Inge (2016) Power: The Missing Element in Sustainable Consumption and Absolute Reductions Research and Action. *Journal of Cleaner Production*, 132, 298–307.

Fuchs, Doris; Lederer, Markus (2007) The Power of Business. *Business and Politics*, 9(3), 1–17.

Fukuyama, Francis (2014) *Political Order and Political Decay: From the Industrial Revolution to the Globalization of Democracy*. London: Profile Books.

Gilley, Bruce (2012) Authoritarian Environmentalism and China's Response to Climate Change. *Environmental Politics*, 21(2), 287–307.

Gilpin, Robert (1987) *The Political Economy of International Relations*. Princeton: Princeton University Press.

Green, Jessica F. (2014) *Rethinking Private Authority: Agents and Entrepreneurs in Global Environmental Governance*. Princeton: Princeton University Press.

Hediger, Werner (1999) Reconciling "Weak" and "Strong" Sustainability. *International Journal of Social Economics*, 26(7/8/9), 1127.

Hickmann, Thomas (2017) The Reconfiguration of Authority in Global Climate Governance. *International Studies Review*, 19(3), 430–451.

Hickmann, Thomas; Lederer, Markus; Pattberg, Philipp; Widerberg, Oscar (Forthcoming) The Evolution of International Environmental Bureaucracies: How the Climate Secretariat is Loosening Its Straitjacket, in Jörgens, Helge; Kolleck, Nina; Saerbeck, Barbara; Well, Mareike (eds), *Still Managers of Global Change? Reassessing the Role and Influence of International Environmental Bureaucracies*. Cambridge: MIT Press.

Hoffmann, Matthew (2011) *Climate Governance at the Crossroads: Experimenting with a Global Response after Kyoto*. Oxford: Oxford University Press.

Hönke, Jana; Lederer, Markus (2013) Development and International Relations, in Carlsnaes, Walter; Risse, Thomas; Simmons, Beth A. (eds), *Handbook of International Relations*. London: Sage, 775–800.

Jackson, Tim (2009) *Prosperity without Growth: Economics for a Finite Planet*. London: Earthscan.

Kahn, Matthew E.; Zheng, Siqi (2016) *Blue Skies over Beijing. Economic Growth and the Environment in China*. Princeton, MA: Princeton University Press.

Kates, Robert W.; Parris, Thomas M.; Leiserowitz, Anthony A. (2005) What is Sustainable Development? *Environment: Science and Policy for Sustainable Development*, 47(3), 8–21.

Keohane, Robert O.; Victor, David G. (2011) The Regime Complex for Climate Change. *Perspectives on Politics*, 9(1), 7–23.

Klein, Naomi (2014) *This Changes Everything. Capitalism vs. The Climate*. New York, NY: Simon & Schuster.

Lederer, Markus (2017) Umwelt und internationale Politik, in Masala, Carlo; Sauer, Frank (eds), *Handbuch Internationale Beziehungen*. Wiesbaden: VS Verlag für Sozialwissenschaften, 1095–1118.

Lederer, Markus; Wallbott, Linda; Urban, Frauke (Forthcoming) Green Transformations and State Bureaucracy, in Fouquet, Roger (ed), *Handbook on Green Growth*. Cheltenham: Edward Elgar.

Lindert, Peter H.; Williamson, Jeffrey G. (2007) Does Globalization Make the World More Unequal? in Bordo, Michael D.; Taylor, Alan M.; Williamson, Jeffrey G. (eds), *Globalization in Historical Perspective*. Chicago: University of Chicago Press, 227–276.

Martinez-Alier, Joan; Pascual, Unai; Vivien, Franck-Dominique; Zaccai, Edwin (2010) Sustainable De-Growth: Mapping the Context, Criticism and Future Prospects of an Emergent Paradigm. *Ecological Economics*, 69(9), 1741–1747.

Meadowcroft, James (2005) From Welfare State to Ecostate, in Barry, John; Eckersley, Robyn (eds), *The State and the Global Ecological Crisis*. Cambridge, MA: MIT Press, 3–24.

Meadows, Donella H. (2007) The History and Conclusions of the Limits to Growth. *System Dynamics Review*, 23(2–3), 191–197.

Meadows, Donella H.; Meadows, Dennis L.; Randers, Jorgen; Behrens III, William W. (1972) *The Limits to Growth*. New York, NY: Universe Books.

Newell, Peter (2012) *Globalization and the Environment. Capitalism, Ecology and Power*. Cambridge: Polity Press.

North, Douglass C. (1991) Institutions. *The Journal of Economic Perspectives*, 5(1), 97–112.

North, Liisa L.; Grinspun, Ricardo (2016) Neo-Extractivism and the New Latin American Developmentalism: The Missing Piece of Rural Transformation. *Third World Quarterly*, 37(8), 1483–1504.

Oberthür, Sebastian; Gehring, Thomas (eds) (2006) *Institutional Interaction in Global Environmental Governance: Synergy and Conflict among International and EU Policies*. Cambridge, MA: MIT Press.

Okereke, Chukwumerije (2008) Equity Norms in Global Environmental Governance. *Global Environmental Politics*, 9(1), 58–78.

Ostrom, Elinor (2010) Polycentric Systems for Coping with Collective Action and Global Environmental Change. *Global Environmental Change*, 20(4), 550–557.

Ostry, Jonathan David; Berg, Andrew; Tsangarides, Charalambos G. (2014) *Redistribution, Inequality, and Growth*. Washington, DC: International Monetary Fund.

Panayotou, Theodore (1997) Demystifiying the Environmental Kuznets Curve: Turning a Black Box Into a Policy Tool. *Environment and Development Economics*, 2(4), 465–484.

Paris, Ronald (2004) *At War's End. Building Peace After Civil Conflict*. Cambridge: Cambridge University Press.

Pattberg, Philipp (2007) *Private Institutions and Global Governance: The New Politics of Environmental Sustainability*. Cheltenham: Edward Elgar Publishing.

Pattberg, Philipp; Zelli, Fariborz (2016) *Environmental Politics and Governance in the Anthropocene: Institutions and Legitimacy in a Complex World*. London: Routledge.

Pelenc, Jerome; Ballet, Jerome (2015) Strong Sustainability, Critical Natural Capital and the Capability Approach. *Ecological Economics*, 112, 36–44.

Peterson, Garry (2000) Political Ecology and Ecological Resilience: An Integration of Human and Ecological Dynamics. *Ecological Economics*, 35(3), 323–336.

Piketty, Thomas (2014) *Capital in the Twenty First Century*. Cambridge: Harvard University Press.

Purdon, Mark (2015) Advancing Comparative Climate Change Politics: Theory and Method. *Global Environmental Politics*, 15(3), 1–26.

Rock, Michael T. (1996) Pollution Intensity of GDP and Trade Policy: Can the World Bank Be Wrong? *World Development*, 24(3), 471–479.

Rockström, Johan; Steffen, Will; Noone, Kevin; Persson, Asa; Chapin, F. Stuart; Lambin, Eric F.; Lenton, Timothy M.; Scheffer, Marten; Folke, Carl; Schellnhuber, Hans Joachim; Nykvist, Bjorn; de Wit, Cynthia A.; Hughes, Terry; van der Leeuw, Sander; Rodhe, Henning; Sorlin, Sverker; Snyder, Peter K.; Costanza, Robert; Svedin, Uno; Falkenmark, Malin; Karlberg, Louise; Corell, Robert W.; Fabry, Victoria J.; Hansen, James; Walker, Brian; Liverman, Diana; Richardson, Katherine; Crutzen, Paul; Foley, Jonathan A. (2009) A Safe Operating Space for Humanity. *Nature*, 461(7263), 472–475.

Rosenau, James N.; Czempiel, Ernst Otto (eds) (1992) *Governance Without Government: Order and Change in World Politics*. Cambridge, UK: Cambridge University Press.

Schlosberg, David (2013) Theorising Environmental Justice: The Expanding Sphere of a Discourse. *Environmental Politics*, 22(1), 37–55.

Scoones, I.; Newell, P.; Leach, M. (eds) (2015) *The Politics of Green Transformations. Pathways to Sustainability*. Abingdon: Routledge.

Smulders, Sjak; Toman, Michael; Withagen, Cees (2014) Growth Theory and 'Green Growth'. *Oxford Review of Economic Policy*, 30(3), 424–446.

Solow, R. M. (1991) Sustainability: An Economist's Perspective, in Dorfman, R.; Dorfman, N. (eds), *Economics of the Environment: Selected Readings*. New York, NY: W. W. Norton, 179–188.

Steffen, Will; Broadgate, Wendy; Deutsch, Lisa; Gaffney, Owen; Ludwig, Cornelia (2015a) The Trajectory of the Anthropocene: The Great Acceleration. *The Anthropocene Review*, 2(1), 81–98.

Steffen, Will; Richardson, Katherine; Rockström, Johan; Cornell, Sarah E.; Fetzer, Ingo; Bennett, Elena M.; Biggs, Reinette; Carpenter, Stephen R.; de Vries, Wim; de Wit, Cynthia A. (2015b)

Planetary Boundaries: Guiding Human Development on a Changing Planet. *Science*, 347(6223), 736–747.

Stern, David L.; Common, Michael S.; Barbier, Edward D. (1996) Economic Growth and Environmental Degradation: The Environmental Kuznets Curve and Sustainable Development. *World Development*, 24(7), 1151–1160.

Stevenson, Hayley; Dryzek, John S. (2014) *Democratizing Global Climate Governance.* Cambridge: Cambridge University Press.

Strange, Susan (1996) *The Retreat of the State: The Diffusion of Power in the World Economy.* Cambridge: Cambridge University Press.

The New Climate Economy (2017) The Sustainable Infrastructure Imperative. Available at: http://newclimateeconomy.report/ (last accessed 15/09/2017).

UNEP (2011) *Towards a Green Economy: Pathways to Sustainable Development and Poverty Eradication. A Synthesis for Policy Makers.* Nairobi: UNEP.

Urban, Frauke (2014) *Low Carbon Transitions for Developing Countries.* Oxon: Routledge.

Wade, Robert H. (2004) *Governing the Market: Economic Theory and the Role of Government in East Asian Industrialization.* Princeton, NJ: Princeton University Press.

Walker, Peter A. (2005) Political Ecology. Where is the Ecology? *Progress in Human Geography*, 29(1), 73–82.

Walsh, Catherine (2010) Development as Buen Vivir: Institutional Arrangements and (De)Colonial Entanglements. *Development*, 53(1), 15–21.

Wapner, Paul (2016) Living at the Margins, in Nicholson, Simon; Jinnah, Sikina (eds), *New Earth Politics. Essays from the Anthropocene.* Cambridge, MA: MIT Press.

WBGU (2011) *World in Transition. A Social Contract for Sustainability. Summary for Policy-Makers.* Berlin: German Advisory Council on Global Change (WBGU).

Weber, Max (1920/2013) *Wirtschaft und Gesellschaft. Gesamtausgabe. Soziologie.* Tübingen: Mohr Siebeck.

World Bank (2011) *State and Trends of the Carbon Market 2011.* Washington, DC: World Bank.

World Commission on Environment and Development (1987) *Our Common Future.* Oxford: Oxford University Press.

World Summit on Sustainable Development (2002) *Johannesburg Declaration,* Johannesburg, 4 September 2002.

Zelli, Fariborz; Asselt, Harro van (2013) Introduction: The Institutional Fragmentation of Global Environmental Governance: Causes, Consequences, and Responses. *Global Environmental Politics*, 13(3), 1–13.

Environmental security

4

Hannah Hughes

Security is a popular term in the study and everyday discussion of politics. Most commonly, it is used in relation to war, nuclear weapons and terrorist threats. Governments and media representations will commonly identify these kind of issues as threats to national security. More recently, however, environmental problems are also identified and described as security threats, particularly climate change and its potential for causing widespread disruption to food production, extreme weather events, climate refugees and even climate wars. Despite the regularity of its usage, we should not accept security as a benign term – as merely a word to describe the reality of different kinds of threats. The term security carries with it baggage, and as we will see, the use of security does things – it changes the actors and events it is used to describe. The aim of this chapter is to identify this "baggage" and build a pathway that enables us to explore how the environment and environmental degradation have become linked to security. Through this journey, we will observe how the environment has been constructed as a threat to national survival, human survival and even the survival of the planet itself. We will also learn why it is important to think about security as exactly that, a social construct, where different definitions of the problem serve different interests, actors and purposes. Thinking about security in this way will enable us to ask what environmental security offers us as students, scholars and practitioners in terms of collectively understanding and responding to environmental degradation.

Traditional security thinking

To understand why there is a need to look carefully at the term "environmental security" and its usage, we need to have a closer look at how security is used within the discipline of International Relations (IR) and the study of politics more broadly. This is important because it gives us an insight into the significance of the security concept and the kinds of associations that are made when it is used. Traditionally, the study of IR was most concerned with war and peace: what are the causes of war and how can we prevent it? This focused scholars' attention on the role and purpose of the state and inter-state relations.[1] One of the first things that a student of IR learns is that the ultimate function of the state is to guarantee the security of its people. State survival comes before all else, because there are no social goods to be shared between a political community without security to attain and protect them. As such, one of the most critical functions of government is to ensure the security of its people. Through this lens, security comes before all else. This makes security – understanding how it can be established and maintained – one of the most important topics of study within IR. Most commonly, security is conceived as national security, where the greatest threat to national survival is another state, and scholars focus their attention on "the threat, use, and control of military force" (Nye and Lynn-Jones, 1988 in Walt 1991).

However, during the 1980s, scholars began to question the adequacy of the state-centric, military approach to security studies and to identify other kinds of threats, such as environmental degradation and economic decline, as threats to national security. Contributions by Ullman (1983) on *Redefining Security* and Buzan's (1983) book *People, States and Fear* are particularly important. Although their work remained focused on the state as threatened by and guaranteeing security, they challenged the narrow, military focus of security studies and identified the need to acknowledge the security implications and effects of non-traditional threats (see Table 4.1). This challenge to notions of security is also traceable in the international policy arena. In 1988, for example, Soviet leader Mikhail Gorbachev

Table 4.1 Types of security and what they identify as a threat/threatened

Type of "security"	Referent object	Threat/key concerns
National Security	The state	Traditional threats: other states (war, military, nuclear weapons)
National Security (broadened agenda)	The state	Non-traditional threats: terrorism, pandemics (e.g. ebola), migration, climate change
Environmental Security	The state	Environmental degradation, overpopulation and resource scarcity as sources of conflict, migration, etc.
Human Security	Individual human beings/ human freedom and wellbeing	Environmental degradation as a threat to development and human rights
Ecological Security	Biosphere (ecological systems and processes)	Human activities
Climate Security	Depends on who speaks it: The state Human beings Climate stability Life as we know it	Impacts of climate change are uneven and threaten: global health, food security, sea-level, mass migration, etc.

suggested that environmental issues, like climate change, could pose a greater "threat from the sky" than missiles (quoted in Norman Myers 1993, 11). The 1980s, then, marked the beginning of a shift in security thinking, both in academic and policy circles, away from a narrow focus on war and military to include a broader set of potential security issues; a shift that accelerated at the end of the Cold War. As we shall see, this shift in thinking would challenge both what scholars and practitioners identified as threats and how they conceived of the notion of security.

The most important event in the unravelling of traditional approaches to security is the end of the Cold War. Until 1989, the world of security threats mapped on to traditional security thinking, and vice versa: state stockpiling and deployment of nuclear weapons was the gravest threat to international peace and security during this period. But scholars of security studies did not predict the end of the Cold War, and they were limited in their capacity to explain this dramatically transformed international security environment. Security actors and institutions also suddenly found themselves in a situation where the threat they had focused on for decades – the Soviet Union – and, in many cases, their reason for being, no longer existed. As a result, there was suddenly both a need and space for rethinking the meaning of security, and the environment would become a critical component of security's remaking.

The emergence of environmental security

Above, we identified some of the key influences that have shaped the study of security in international politics: the centrality of the state, war and the military. This is important because these same influences have impacted how the environment and security have been linked, and thus how we think about and study environmental security in Global Environmental Politics (GEP) today. In order to understand how the concept of environmental security has evolved over time, it is necessary to trace its emergence and popularization with the end of the Cold War, which is when threats from environmental degradation and the term "environmental security" began to appear more frequently in scholarly literature, on policy agendas and in media analyses. The aim of the following two sections of this chapter is to identify important figures in the popularization of environmental security, and to explore some of the criticism and implications of linking environmental degradation with security thinking.

The security threat posed by environmental degradation was first identified in the 1970s (Brown 1977; Falk 1971), and in 1987, the phrase "environmental security" entered into international debates through the Brundtland Report on *Our Common Future* (Trombetta 2008; World Commission on Environment and Development 1987). The early literature on environmental security identified the environment and environmental degradation as the next great threat to **national security**. A notable example of this is an article by Mathews (1989) on "Redefining Security", which was published in *Foreign Policy*. Matthews suggests that the 1990s will demand a redefinition of what constitutes national security, with the need to broaden the definition to include "resource, environmental and demographic issues" (Mathews 1989, 162). While Mathews identifies resource scarcity, particularly water, for its potential to lead to conflict, she identifies downward economic performance and political instability as the main sources of insecurity arising from environmental decline. In her words:

> Human suffering and turmoil make countries ripe for authoritarian government or external subversion. Environmental refugees spread the disruption across borders.
>
> (Mathews 1989, 168)

The threat posed to national security by environmental degradation was more widely popularized by an apocalyptic vision from Robert Kaplan in "The Coming Anarchy", which appeared in *The Atlantic Monthly*. Kaplan depicts a scene of Third World countries scarce in resources, overpopulated and riddled with malaria and HIV collapsing into chaos and threatening Western interests and world order. As Kaplan writes:

> It is time to understand the Environment for what it is: the national-security issue of the early twenty-first century. The political and strategic impact of surging populations, spreading disease, deforestation and soil erosion, water depletion, air pollution, and, possibly, rising sea levels in critical overcrowded regions like the Nile Delta and Bangladesh—developments that will prompt mass migrations and, in turn, incite group conflicts—will be the core foreign-policy challenge from which most others will ultimately emanate, arousing the public and uniting assorted interests left over from the Cold War.

Many environmental scholars were critical of the environmental threat as depicted by Mathews and Kaplan, particularly its focus on the global South, and these are reviewed in the following section. Despite its critics, however, environmental security had broad appeal and some effect on the audiences it was addressing. One of the main motivations behind linking the environment to security was to capture the attention of policymakers. Precisely because national security is one of the core functions of governments, identifying the next great threat as environmental degradation and tying this to economic decline and mass migration raised the stakes in environmental policymaking. Part of what authors aimed to achieve, then, was to bring greater attention to the state of global environmental decline and to increase the pressure on policymakers to deal with this as a more urgent policy issue.

At the same time, identifying the environment as a security issue also provided new threats and new purposes for the security organizations that needed to reorientate themselves with the end of the Cold War in 1989. There is evidence of this is in the first appearance of environmental security in the United States National Security Strategy (NSS) in 1991. Kaplan's article is said to have been influential in this regard, with the Under Secretary of State for Global Affairs, Timothy Wirth, apparently having a copy sent to every US embassy (Matthew 2002, 111). Then, in 1993, the Clinton administration created the position of Deputy Under Secretary for Environmental Security within the Department of Defense (DOD). This institutional attention to environmental security is also apparent within Europe, where in 1995, a NATO (North Atlantic Treaty Organization) Committee on the Challenges of Modern Society (CCMS) initiated a study of environmental security, the results of which are said to have influenced the incorporation of environmental considerations into development programmes (Trombetta 2008, 592). The European Union (EU) is thought to have used these concerns over the security implications of environmental degradation to develop security capabilities and competencies at the EU level, including "the creation of a European satellite system for the 'global monitoring for environment and security'" (Council of the European Union 2000 in Trombetta 2008, 592). While these shifts in the security landscape are judged as relatively superficial (Floyd 2007; Thomas 1997), they nevertheless highlight how academic thinking and security practices began to reconsider what constituted a global threat in the post-Cold War era and provide evidence of the environment's place on this changing security agenda.

Environmental conflict and its critics

As the early environmental security literature indicates, a range of threats were identified as arising from and contributing to environmental degradation, one of the most often cited being **overpopulation** (see Table 4.1). The major concern was that as human populations expand, so too does the demand on finite resources such as water, food and oil. The fear is that this **resource scarcity** has the potential to generate **resource wars** – as populations attempt to secure the resources they need to sustain themselves, develop and grow. From what we have learnt about traditional security thinking above, it is not surprising that ideas around resource wars and environmental conflict were readily grasped and popularized. The idea of resource wars linked environmental degradation to traditional ways of understanding security – the state, war and military – and thereby made environmental security amenable to institutional practices for understanding and responding to threats. In order to take a closer look at this, the following section examines how the environmental conflict thesis has been treated academically, received by policy communities and, in turn, the criticism it has generated (see Table 4.2).

During the 1990s, considerable effort went into establishing the empirical relationship between resource scarcity and conflict. The work of Thomas Homer-Dixon is the most influential in this regard, underpinning Kaplan's apocalyptic vision and informing the White House through briefs with Vice President Gore (Matthew 2002, 111). Homer-Dixon led a number of international research projects during the 1990s that aimed to establish the relationship between environmental stress in poor countries and violent conflict. After nearly a decade of study, the main conclusion of these research efforts was that environmental scarcity was an indirect, rather than direct, driver of conflict. [2] As Homer-Dixon concludes:

> Environmental scarcity . . . can contribute to civil violence, including insurgencies and ethnic clashes . . . the incidence of such violence will probably increase as scarcities of cropland, freshwater, and forests worsen in many parts of the developing world. Scarcity's role in such violence, however, is often obscure and indirect. It interacts with political, economic, and other factors to generate harsh social effects that in turn help to produce violence.
>
> (Homer-Dixon 1999, p. 177)

Table 4.2 Critics and criticism of linking environment and security

Criticism	Argument	Author
North/South divide	Overlooks the role of colonial histories, unequal development, and related structural injustices "South" portrayed as the source of instability threatening the "North" Overshadows the responsibility of the global North Shared challenge	Matthew, 2002 Simon Dalby, 1999, 2000
Inappropriate mind-set	Links environmental degradation to the national security mind-set Risks undermining the globalist sensibility of environmentalism Us/them and threat/defense mentality of national security thinking	Daniel Deudney 1990 Ole Waever 1995
Inappropriate institutional response	Military and war destructive of the environment	Matthias Finger 1994

The research underpinning these conclusions suggested that developing countries were particularly at risk from the effects of resource scarcity because of the decreased capacity for social and technical ingenuity.

Despite the difficulty in precisely positioning environmental scarcity in the causal chain of conflict, resource wars and, more recently, climate wars (Dyer 2011; Welzer 2017) remain a popular way of linking environment and security. While many of these are dramatic accounts for popular audiences (Dyer 2011; Welzer 2017), the linkage is also drawn between climate change and recent conflicts in United Nations (UN) reporting and academic literature. A report by the United Nations Environment Programme (UNEP), for example, identifies environmental issues and competition over resources as important "causative factors in the instigation and perpetuation of conflict in Sudan" (UNEP 2007, 8). And, in Syria, the effects of drought, likely deepened by climate change, are considered important contributory factors to the conflict (Kelley et al. 2015). Drawing attention to, and emphasizing, the relationship between environmental degradation and conflict enables actors to raise the stakes in global environmental policymaking. It also makes it easier to incorporate environmental degradation and its impacts into existing national security institutions, and it is this that has generated criticism amongst GEP scholars.

The criticism generated by the environmental conflict thesis was directed at both the empirical approach of Homer-Dixon's conflict thesis (Barnett 2000) and at how this research was taken up and deployed (Matthew 2002) (see Table 4.2 for a summary). Richard Matthew, for example, highlights the ahistorical nature of the arguments, which overlook the role of colonial histories, unequal development and related structural injustices, which provide critical context for any conclusions drawn about the global South and the presence or likelihood of conflict. Matthew also reminds us that "societies of all types have usually proven resilient and innovative in the face of environmental change" (Matthew 2002, 114). Other scholars have greater concerns about linking the environment to the national security mind-set.

Daniel Deudney highlights that the traditional focus of national security on violent interstate conflict has little in common with either environmental problems or solutions. He warns that trying to raise attention of environmental degradation by linking it to security may be counter-productive, as "the nationalist and militarist mind-set closely associated with "national security" threatens to undermine the globalist sensibility more often associated with environmental scholarship" (Deudney 1990, 474). Scholars are concerned by the "us" and "them" mentality prevalent in national security thinking, which they suggest could lead to an inappropriate construction of our environment "as a threat/defence problem" (Waever 1995, 65). Such thinking is evidenced in the framing of environmental security by Mathews and Kaplan, which in effect, leads to environmental resources being identified as national interests that need to be protected from other nations, usually with the underdeveloped global "South" portrayed as the source of instability threatening the "North" (Dalby 1999, 2000). As Simon Dalby highlights, this reduces the opportunity for the industrialized North to take greater responsibility for causing environmental problems and acknowledging the shared nature of the challenge. In fact, as Matthias Finger reminds us, the military and war are directly destructive of the environment; thus, the military model of framing and dealing with environmental change is more likely to impede effective environmental action than contribute to a greener world (Finger 1994).

Deepening environmental security

What we have observed so far is the emergence of the environment on a broadened security agenda. This means that, in a relatively short period of time, the environment had a place on some national security agendas alongside other non-conventional threats, such as global health, economic decline and poverty. However, while the security agenda had been broadened, security thinking had not necessarily been challenged. As illustrated by the environmental conflict thesis, constructions of environmental security remained tied to the state, national interest and military threat and response. But the unravelling of security did not stop there. Scholars also began to conceive of environmental degradation as a threat to individual human beings (Barnett 2001; Page 2002) and to the biosphere itself (Barnett 2001). This is identified as the deepening of the security concept, where objects other than the state are identified as threatened (Krause and Williams 1996).

It is possible to identify this shift in thinking in the work of individual scholars. For example, in 1989, Norman Myers first conceptualized environmental issues along traditional national security lines (Myers 1989). However, in his 1993 book *Ultimate Security*, his definition of security had deepened to the individual as referent object:

> security applies most at the level of the individual. It amounts to human well being: not only protection from harm and injury but access to other basic requisites that are the due of every person on earth.

> (Myers 1993, 31)

Conceptions of **human security** shift the focus of attention from the state and the military to protecting individual human freedom and wellbeing (see Table 4.1). The notion of human security opens security to a broader range of threats, including extreme natural and technological disasters (Adger et al. 2014, 758), and in doing so, enables scholars and international organizations to highlight the transnational characteristics of environmental threats and the interdependencies between "development, human rights and national security" (UN 2009). Thus, while state-centred approaches to environmental security, like the notion of resource wars, were taken up by national security organizations, human security, understood as "freedom from fear and freedom from want", emerged as an important concept within the UN system, particularly in the development agenda (United Nations Development Programme 1994; UN Millennium Declaration 2000).

The linkage between environment and security has also been explored in relation to human's negative impact on the biosphere (Barnett 2001). Conceptions of **ecological security** move from the threat that environmental change poses to the nation state or individual human beings to the threat humans pose to ecological systems and processes (see Table 4.1). The aim of these conceptions of security is to draw attention to the ecological systems that we depend on as human beings and, ultimately, to maintain "the ecological equilibrium in the long term" that sustains us (Barnett 2001, 109). In this definition of environmental security, then, it is the biosphere that is at threat and which needs to be secured. While non-human centred approaches to security have not had the same impact as the environmental conflict-thesis or human security approaches, they have been promoted by some international bodies, such as the UNEP (Ibid). This brings us to an important feature of environmental security debates – the different ways of identifying and defining the threat of environmental security, i.e. what/whom is threatened and what/whom is secured, have very different human, environmental and policy implications and outcomes. Thus, while the resource wars approach was readily apprehended by traditional security actors and institutions, human security approaches fitted more with the ethos and policy goals of UN organizations and bodies. As students of GEP, we need to be attentive to the various actors and interests that these different ways of defining and practicing environmental security represent and affect. Developing this attentiveness requires acquiring the analytical skills and theoretical tools for understanding and unpacking the social constructed nature of security, which is why we now turn to the so-called securitization framework.

Security as a social construct

It is the initial broadening of security to include non-military threats, then the further challenge to notions of security by identifying individual human beings and the planet as referent objects, that has led scholars to label security as an essentially "contested concept" (Buzan 1991). Threats exist: nuclear weapons exist and the climate is changing, and both threaten our survival. However, the contested nature of security highlights that how we understand and respond to these threats depends upon how they are constructed as shared social and political problems. In this sense, security is a malleable notion, which means that it can be constructed in different ways, by different actors and for different purposes. What we need to do, then, is to look beyond the different ways that the environment and security have been linked and turn to the actors and interests behind these linkages. In order to do this, I introduce the Copenhagen School and the securitization framework, an approach that has enabled scholars and students alike to illuminate the social constructed nature of security.

In the mid-1990s, one scholar began to criticize attempts to broaden and deepen security (Waever 1995). Ole Waever suggested that there were no such things as individual or international security because these concepts did not have a history like the traditional notion of national security. The aim was not to claim that we should only think about and use security in the sense of military threats and war, but to draw our attention to the idea that security – as it is known and used today – has been constructed as a concept through its historical usage. This means that there is no pre-given meaning to security that we can somehow uncover through our research and relate definitively to the environment and environmental change. Instead, we need to focus our attention on understanding the practices of security, through which the term security has become meaningful and has had effects. Looking at it from this perspective, Waever suggested that one of the most important security practices is the "speech act", the process by which actors identify a threat and attempt to claim the authority and extraordinary measures to manage it. Waever identified this speech-act as a process of **securitization**. Below, I outline the main tenets of this approach and use it to study one particular actor's usage of security in relation to climate change: the UK government. This enables us to both explore security as a socially constructed phenomenon and also to explore how particular constructions of environmental security serve different actors, interests and purposes.

Identifying security as a speech act underlies the development of the securitization framework (Buzan et al. 1998). This framework combined Buzan's (1991) broadened agenda for security studies with Waever's (1995) speech-act approach. The central insight in the securitization framework is that the meaning of security "lies in its usage" (Buzan et al. 1998, 24), which enables us to explore how security is socially constructed through language. The Copenhagen School identifies successful securitization – when both the threat and means to deal with it are accepted by the relevant audience – as a three step process:

1 **Existential threat:** actors declare an issue to be an existential threat to a designated referent object (the state, human beings, the biosphere).
2 **Emergency measures:** if the declaration of a security threat is accepted by the relevant audience(s), then the right to enact absolute priority and emergency actions are legitimized.
3 **Effects**: the effects on interunit relations by breaking free of the normal rules of politics (Buzan et al. 1998, 26).

Actors may declare an issue an existential threat (a securitizing move), but it is only when this threat and means to deal with it are accepted that the securitization is successful. The outcome of successful securitization (and thus a motive in securitizing moves) is "absolute priority", enabling "emergency actions" to tackle the issue, and "justifying actions outside the normal bounds of political procedure" (Buzan et al. 1998, 24). In theory, then, any actor may identify an issue an existential threat and make a securitizing move. However,

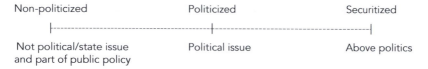

Figure 4.1 The spectrum from non-political to securitized.

only some actors have the authority and/or means to initiate security measures. This framework provides a spectrum from non-politicized to securitized, and it is an issue's location on this spectrum which determines the urgency and means with which it is addressed (Figure 4.1).

The Copenhagen School does not suggest that securitization is an ideal state, whereby issues are tackled with the urgency that they require. Securitization is a political decision that enables actors to "claim a right to handle something with less democratic control and constraint" (Buzan et al. 1998, 29). Unlike politicization (see Figure 4.1), in which an issue appears in the realm of everyday political choice and decision-making, securitization presents an issue as urgent and "so important that it should not be exposed to the normal haggling of politics but should be dealt with decisively by top-leaders prior to other issues" (Ibid). As such, the Copenhagen School considers securitization as a negative process, "a failure to deal with issues as normal politics" and views "desecuritization" as preferable. In cases of desecuritization, issues are removed from the threat-defence response and put back into the ordinary public sphere (Ibid). This approach offers a useful way to think about the motives behind linking environmental change to security. As reviewed above, many actors that have made this linkage have done so in an attempt to increase the level of urgency given to environmental issues. In response, critics of environmental security have identified many of the same concerns as the authors of the securitization framework (Table 4.2), highlighting the inappropriateness of the threat/defence dichotomy and a militarized response to environmental degradation.

The idea that security is socially constructed can be difficult to grasp, and the securitization framework may, at first, appear abstract. The easiest way to illuminate this process is to provide an illustration – to test the theory by exploring a case of environmental security being constructed in practice. In the following section, I describe the process and speeches whereby the UK government constructed climate change as a threat to international security. This demonstrates how the securitization framework can be used in our research and enables us to explore the interests that different actors have in linking environment and security. Before we do that, however, it is useful to identify some of the security implications of a changing climate.

Climate security and the British government

There are many ways in which climate change can be identified as a threat to the state, individual human beings, the biosphere and life as we know it. The Intergovernmental

Panel on Climate Change (IPCC) is the main source of climate change knowledge for the international community. Scientific knowledge of the causes and effects of climate change has grown exponentially since the first IPCC Working Group I (science) report released in 1990. By the IPCC's Fourth Assessment Report (AR4), warming of the climate system was identified as "unequivocal", and observable in increases in global average air and ocean temperatures, widespread melting of snow and ice and rising global average sea level (IPCC 2007, 2). The impacts of this warming are identified as having a number of global health effects, including increases in malnutrition through shifting agricultural productivity, increased deaths and injuries through heat waves and other extreme weather events and altered spatial distribution of vector-borne diseases (IPCC 2007, 10). These health impacts highlight an important feature of the insecurity arising from climate change; namely, that the effects of climate change are not evenly spread, and at the regional, state and even the community level, there is considerable disparity. As the Stern Review (2007) summarizes, "climate change threatens the basic elements of life for people around the world – access to water, food, health, and use of land and the environment" (65). Despite the serious nature of climate change, it is only in the last decade that climate change has become more routinely identified as a security threat.

In the late 1980s, early 1990s, climate change was largely not identified as a threat in and of itself, but as an issue promising to increase the stress of continuing environmental degradation and population growth (with some exceptions, see Brown 1977; Wirth 1989; Rowlands 1991). Homer-Dixon, for example, emphasized that degradation and depletion of agricultural lands, forests and water would be a more significant contributor to social turmoil than climate change (Homer-Dixon 1994, 1999). There are a number of explanations for this apparent oversight in the literature. As Barnett demonstrates, identifying *which* particular climate risks are security issues is problematic and "has vexed environmental security scholarship" (Barnett 2003, 7). In addition, several features of climate change impacts make conceptualization of **climate security** difficult. Firstly, although today there is greater consensus on the science of climate change, when environment and security literature first emerged in the early 1990s, the scale of change was not well understood, varying from within adaptive capacity to a threat "second only to global nuclear war" (Toronto Conference 1989). Secondly, with greater understanding has come greater awareness of the fact that the impacts of climate change are not evenly spread. For some, the negative effects are significant, for some, minor, and for others, there may even be benefits (O'Brien and Leichenko 2005, 2). Thus, the idea of a global standard for "climate security" has not been appropriate, as the planning and implementation of climate change policies and response measures will create both winners and losers (Paavola and Adger 2003). These two issues combine to make a third, equally problematic issue; namely, what are we attempting to secure? What is the referent object of climate security? A stable climate, human beings or current levels of civilization?

Despite these complexities, the linkage of climate change and security is gaining increasing recognition, as evidenced in the IPCC Fifth Assessment Report, which included a chapter on *Human Security* (Adger et al. 2014). There have also been some successful attempts to highlight the significance and severity of climate change at the international level by linking it to security; the Association for Small Island States (AOSIS) is a particularly important actor in this regard. For many members of AOSIS, climate change is a security threat in conventional national security terms – with rising sea levels threatening national territory and the long-term ability of people to remain living on their islands (Barnett and Adger 2003). AOSIS have actively sought for the parties to the UN Framework Convention on Climate Change (UNFCCC) to acknowledge the threat climate change poses to the survival of small island states and to deepen international mitigation efforts, and have had some success in this regard (Barnett and Campbell 2010; Corneloup and Mol 2014). Another actor that has sought to raise the profile of climate change through security is the UK government. By looking at the British government's usage of security through the securitization framework, it is possible to explore some of the motives underpinning their constructions of climate security.

On 17 April 2007, the UK government used its chairmanship of the UN Security Council to convene the council's first debate on climate change (Beckett 2007). This event was the government's most overt attempt to frame climate change as a threat to international security. In a research project built around the Copenhagen School's securitization framework (Hughes 2007), I examined the change in government's discourse on climate change from 2000 until the above UN Security Council debate in 2007. Analyzing key documents and speeches made by then Prime Minister Tony Blair, foreign secretary Margaret Beckett and environment minister David Miliband, I was able to map the change in government rhetoric over this time period. At first, the government attached climate change to the security object tentatively and did not signify the state as the referent object. For example, in a speech Tony Blair gave in 2000, the prime minister outlined the environmental threats, which included population growth, water resources, soil degradation and dwindling fish stocks, in a list of "environmental challenges" similar to those described in the environment and security literature of the late 1980s and early 1990s. He identified climate change as "the greatest threat to our environment today", stating: "If there is one immediate issue that threatens global disaster, it is the changes in our atmosphere" (Blair 2000).

By 2006, climate security had become one of the government's strategic international priorities, with the prime minister directing the foreign minister to, "put climate security at the heart of her foreign policy responsibilities" (FCO Departmental Report 2006/7). By 2007, the environment minister and the foreign secretary increasingly identified climate change as a threat to national security for its potential to spark conflict, citing Darfur as one such instance: "scarcity of natural resources, in particular water and food, could be a major source of future conflict, as we are already seeing in Darfur" (Miliband 2007a). The government did not confine its definition of climate security to national conceptions, however, it also highlighted the economic and developmental implications for the international community. This is evident in the government's most overt securitizing move: its chairing of a UN Security Council debate on climate change in 2007. The UK's Concept Paper for the debate outlined the government's understanding of the climate issue:

> All members of the international community face a shared dilemma. To ensure well-being for a growing population with unfulfilled needs and rising expectation we must grow our economies. Should we fail, we increase the risk of conflict and insecurity. To grow our economies we must continue to use more energy. Much of that energy

will be in the form of fossil fuels. But if we use more fossil fuels we will accelerate climate change, which itself presents risks to the very security we are trying to build.

(UK Government 2007)

The concept paper focused the debate on "the security implications of a changing climate, including through its impact on potential drivers of conflict (such as access to energy, water, food and other scarce resources, population movements and border disputes)" (Ibid). The UK government constructs climate change as a shared international problem that needs to be addressed collectively through multilateral processes. The question that the securitiza-tion framework leads us to ask is what are their motivations behind the government's secu-ritizing moves? It is clear that the UK government uses the international stage of the UN Security Council to provide an account of the climate change problem and how it should be addressed, and makes a claim for leadership in international climate politics through the process. Chairmanship of the UN Security Council debate enabled the UK government to bring attention to the latest scientific findings of the newly published IPCC reports, and the government commissioned Stern Review of the economics of climate change (Stern 2007). It also focused attention on the climate change problem before the international climate change conference, COP 13, where a post-Kyoto framework was to be negotiated later that year. Despite this role in mobilising international interest in the issue, the UK government's construction of climate security is conservative, promoting a solution that does not challenge prevailing models of economic growth; in fact, it safeguards these by making continued consumption and development possible through "green growth" (Miliband 2007b). This analysis fits with Ole Waever's scepticism of the usage of security; for him, security is a "conservative mechanism" by which social and political elites attempt to retain their position in a particular hierarchical order through invoking security (Waever 1995, 56). The securitisation framework provides a means for us to observe this conservativism in action, and to illuminate the apparent tensions in actor's securitizing moves, which like the UK government, may appear as both progressive and conservative. Through our empirical research, we can shed light on what is at stake for nation states, human wellbeing and the biosphere in competing definitions of environmental security.

Conclusion

Many students of GEP are attracted to the concept of security. Security seems the obvious way to increase the social and political willingness and urgency to tackle our present envi-ronmental crisis. By extension, then, all we as students and researchers need to do is to establish "how" environmental issues constitute a security threat and bring attention to the threat environmental degradation poses. However, as this chapter has aimed to illustrate, a sense of urgency is not the only thing attached to, and carried by, the security term. In order to identify some of the baggage that the concept of security carries, this chapter has provided an account of the historical emergence of the environmental security concept and its popularization in academic and policy circles. This reveals how environmental security was initially constructed through the national security lens, as a non-conventional threat alongside other transnational issues, on a broadened security agenda. This broadened security agenda contributed to the unravelling of the tightly bound mind-set of national security in both academic and policy circles, which accelerated with the end of the Cold War. While this meant that environmental security was given a place in national security strategies, related organizations and research agendas in the United States and within Europe, there was also a move to deepen these definitions and consider human wellbeing and the planet itself as referent objects threatened by global environmental degradation. In order to explore some of the implications of these different ways of knowing and institutionalizing environmental security, the chapter turned to the social constructed nature of security and environmental threats. By exploring the British government's attempt to securitize climate change, I have aimed to demonstrate how particular constructions of environmental security serve particular interests and purposes. It may not be possible to identify these motives as good or bad; after all, many of us want greater attention and global action given to climate change. At the same time, we may not agree that securing the global economy is the right, or most effective, way to protect the planet.

Notes

1 A state is the term used to describe the national government or ruling authority of a particular territory.
2 See Homer-Dixon (1991) for research agenda, Homer-Dixon (1994) for evidence for case studies and Homer-Dixon (1999) for detailed report on successes of project.

Recommended reading

1. It is worth reading some of the early contributions to the environmental security literature and its popularization, for example:
    Kaplan, R. (Feb. 1994) The Coming Anarchy. *The Atlantic Monthly*, 273(2), 44–76.
    Mathews, J. T. (Spring 1989) Redefining Security. *Foreign Affairs*, 68(2), 162–177.
2. For introductions and accounts of environmental security, see:
    Barnett, J. (2001) *The Meaning of Environmental Security: Ecological Politics and Policy in the New Security Era* (1st edition). New York: Zed Books.
    Dalby, S. (2013) *Security and Environmental Change*. Cambridge, UK: Polity Press.
3. For varied contributions to climate change/environmental change and human security, see:
    Matthew, R. A., Barnett, J., Mcdonald, B., Brien, K. O. & Dabelko, G. (2009) *Global Environmental Change and Human Security*. Cambridge, MA: MIT Press.
    Redclift, M. R. and Grasso, M. (2013) *Handbook on Climate Change and Human Security*. Cheltenham, UK and MA, USA: Edward Elgar.

Online resources

Wilson Centre Environmental Change and Security Program (ECSP) Available at: www.wilsoncenter.org/program/environmental-change-and-security-program
ECSP New Security Beat Blog Available at: www.newsecuritybeat.org

References

Adger, W. N., Pulhin, J. M., Barnett, J., Dabelko, G. D., Hovelsrud, G. K., Levy, M., Oswald Spring, Ú. & Vogel, C. H. (2014) Human Security, in Field, C. B., Barros, V. R., Dokken, D. J., Mach, K. J., Mastrandrea, M. D., Bilir, T. E., Chatterjee, M., Ebi, K. L., Estrada, Y. O., Genova, R. C., Girma, B., Kissel, E. S., Levy, A. N., MacCracken, S., Mastrandrea, P. R. & White, L. L. (eds), *Climate Change 2014: Impacts, Adaptation, and Vulnerability. Part A: Global and Sectoral Aspects. Contribution of Working Group II to the Fifth Assessment Report of the Intergovernmental Panel on Climate Change.* Cambridge, UK and New York, NY, USA: Cambridge University Press, 755–791.

Barnett, J. (2000) Destabilizing the Environment—Conflict Thesis. *Review of International Studies,* 26(2), 271–288.

Barnett, J. (2001) *The Meaning of Environmental Security.* London: Zed Books.

Barnett, J. (2003) Security and Climate Change. *Global Environmental Change,* 13(1), 7–17.

Barnett, J., & Adger, W. N. (2003) Climate Dangers and Atoll Countries. *Climatic Change,* 61(3), 321–337.

Barnett, J. & Campbell, J. (2010) *Climate Change and Small Island States: Power, Knowledge and the South Pacific.* New York: Earthscan.

Beckett, M. (2007) Margaret Beckett at UN Security Council Climate Change Debate, UN Security Council Debate on Energy, Climate and Security, New York. Available at: www.fco.gov.uk/servlet/Front?pagename=OpenMarket/Xcelerate/ShowPage&c=Page&cid=1007029391629&a=KArticle&aid=1176454354972 (last accessed 27/06/2007).

Blair, T. (2000) Prime Ministers Speech to CBI/Green Alliance on 24th October 2000. Available at: www.number-10.gov.uk/output/Page10688.asp (last accessed 27/06/2007).

Brown, L. (1977) Redefining National Security, World Watch Paper No. 14, Washington: World Watch Institute.

Buzan, B. (1983) *People, States and Fear; The National Security Problem in International Relations.* Brighton: Wheatsheaf.

Buzan, B. (1991) *People, States and Fear: An Agenda for International Security Studies in the Post-Cold War Era.* 2nd edition. Boulder: Lynne Reinner.

Buzan, B., Waever, O. & de Wilde, J. (1998) *Security; A New Framework for Analysis.* London: Lynne Reinner Publishers.

Corneloup, I. de A. & Mol, A. P. J. (2014) Small Island Developing States and International Climate Change Negotiations: The Power of Moral Leadership. *International Environmental Agreements,* 14(3), 281–297.

Dalby, S. (1999) Threats from the South? Geopolitics, Equity and Environmental Security, in Deudney, D. H. & Matthew, R. A. (eds), *Contested Ground: Security and Conflict in the New Environmental Politics.* Albany: SUNY Press.

Dalby, S. (2000) Geopolitics and Ecology: Rethinking the Contexts of Environmental Security, in Lowi, M. R. & Shaw, B. R. (eds), *Environment and Security Discourses and Practices.* New York: Palgrave.

Deudney, D. H. (1990) The Case Against Linking Environmental Degradation and National Security. *Millennium,* 19(3), 461–476.

Dyer, G. (2011) *Climate Wars: The Fight for Survival as the World Overheats* (Reprint edition). Oxford: Oneworld Publications.

Falk, Richard A. (1971) *This Endangered Planet: Prospects and Proposals for Human Survival.* New York: Random House.

FCO Departmental Report (2006/07) SP6 (Strategic International Priority) Achieving Climate Security by Promoting a Faster Transition to a Sustainable, Low-Carbon Global Economy.

Available at: www.fco.gov.uk/servlet/Front?pagename=OpenMarket/Xcelerate/ShowPage&c= Page&cid=1176454606541 (last accessed 27/06/2007).

Finger, M. (1994) Global Environmental Degradation and the Military, in Kakonen, J. (ed.), *Green Security or Militarised Environment*. England: Dartmouth Publishing Co. Ltd.

Floyd, R. (2007) Towards a Consequentialist Evaluation of Security: Bringing Together the Copenhagen and the Welsh Schools of Security Studies. *Review of International Studies*, 33(2), 327–350.

Homer-Dixon, T. F. (1991) On the Threshold: Environmental Changes as Causes of Acute Conflict. *International Security*, 16(2), 76–116.

Homer-Dixon, T. F. (1994) Environmental Scarcities and Violent Conflict: Evidence from Cases. *International Security*, 19(1), 5–40.

Homer-Dixon, T. F. (1999) Thresholds of Turmoil: Environmental Scarcities and Violent Conflict, in Deudney, D. H. & Matthew, R. A. (eds), *Contested Ground: Security and Conflict in the New Environmental Politics*. Albany: SUNY Press.

Hughes, H. (2007) Climate Change and Securitization. Unpublished master's dissertation, Cambridge University, Cambridge, UK. Available at: www.academia.edu/4591407/Climate_Change_and_ Securitization (last accessed 25/08/2017).

IPCC (2007) Climate Change 2007: Synthesis Report Summary for Policymakers.

Kelley, C. P., Mohtadi, S., Cane, M. A., Seager, R. & Kushnir, Y. (2015) Climate Change in the Fertile Crescent and Implications of the Recent Syrian Drought. *Proceedings of the National Academy of Sciences of the United States of America*, 112(11), 3241–3246.

Krause, K. & Williams, M. (1996) Broadening the Agenda of Security Studies: Politics and Methods. *Mershon International Studies Review*, 40(2), 229–254.

Matthew, R. A. (2002) In defense of environment and security. *ECSP Report* 8, 109–124. Available at: www.wilsoncenter.org/sites/default/files/Report_8_Matthew.pdf (last accessed 19/01/2018).

Miliband, D. (2007a). Let's Make 2007 a Landmark Year for Climate Change. Speech Given to the GLOBE Forum 14 Feb 2007. Available at: www.defra.gov.uk/corporate/ministers/speeches/ default.asp, (last accessed 27/06/2007).

Miliband, D. (2007b). Greening the American dream. Speech given to the Pew Centre, Washington, DC, 6 June 2007. Available at: http://webarchive.nationalarchives.gov.uk/20070814120000/ www.defra.gov.uk/corporate/ministers/speeches/david-miliband/dm070606.htm (last accessed 19/01/2018)

Myers, N. (1989) Environment and Security. *Foreign Affairs*, 74, 23–41.

Myers, N. (1993) *Ultimate Security: The Environmental Basis of Political Stability*. London and New York: W. W. Norton & Company.

O'Brien, K. & Leichenko, R. (2005) Climate Change, Equity and Human Security, Human Security and Climate Change, An International Workshop, Holmen Fjord Hotel, Asker, near Oslo, 21–23 June 2005. Available at: www.cicero.uio.no/humsec/papers/OBrien.pdf, (last accessed, 27/06/2007).

Paavola, J. & Adger, W. N. (2003) Justice and Adaptation to Climate Change, Tyndall Centre Working Paper. Available at: www.uea.ac.uk/env/people/adgerwn/wp23.pdf, (last accessed 27/06/2007).

Page, E. (2002) Human Security and the Environment, in Page, E. & Redclift, M. (eds), *Human Security and the Environment*. UK: Edward Elgar Publishing Ltd.

Rowlands, I. (1991) The Security Challenges of Global Environmental Change. *The Washington Quarterly*, 14(1), 99–114.

Stern, N. H. (2007) *The economics of climate change: the Stern Review*. Cambridge: Cambridge University Press.

Thomas, G. B. (1997) US Environmental Security Policy: Broad Concern or Narrow Interests. *Journal of Environment and Development*, 6(4), 397–425.

Toronto Conference (1989) The Changing Atmosphere: Implications for Global Security, in Abrahamson, D. E. (ed), *The Challenge of Global Warming*. Washington, DC: Island Press.

Trombetta, M. J. (2008) Environmental Security and Climate Change: Analysing the Discourse. *Cambridge Review of International Affairs*, 21(4), 585–602.

UK Government (2007) Energy, Security and Climate. Security Council Open Debate: UK Concept Paper. Available at: https://unfccc.int/files/application/pdf/ukpaper_securitycouncil.pdf (last accessed 25/07/2017).

Ullman, R. H. (1983) Redefining Security. *International Security*, 8(1), 129–153.

United Nations Development Programme (1994) Human Development Report 1994. Available at: http://hdr.undp.org/sites/default/files/reports/255/hdr_1994_en_complete_nostats.pdf (last accessed 24/07/2017).

UNEP (2007) *Sudan: Post-conflict Environmental Assessment*. Nairobi, Kenya: United Nations Environment Programme. Available at: http://postconflict.unep.ch/publications/UNEP_Sudan.pdf (last accessed 25/08/2017).

UN (2009) *Human Security in Theory and Practice: An Overview of the Human Security Concept and the United Nations Trust Fund for Human Security*. New York: Human Security Unit, United Nations. Available at: www.un.org/humansecurity/sites/www.un.org.humansecurity/files/human_security_in_theory_and_practice_english.pdf (last accessed 25/08/2017).

United Nations Millennium Summit & United Nations. (2000) *United Nations Millennium Declaration*. New York: United Nations, Dept. of Public Information.

Waever, O. (1995) Securitization and Desecuritization, in Lipschutz, R. D. (ed.), *On Security*. New York: Colombia University Press.

Walt, S. (1991) The Renaissance of Security Studies. *International Studies Quarterly*, 35(2), 211–239.

Welzer, H. (2017) *Climate Wars: What People Will Be Killed For in the 21st Century*. Cambridge: Polity Press.

Wirth, D. A. (1989) Climate Chaos. *Foreign Policy*, 74, 3–22.

World Commission on Environment and Development (1987) *Our Common Future*. Oxford: Oxford University Press.

Sustainable consumption

5

Doris Fuchs and Frederike Boll

Introduction

The notion of sustainable consumption approaches sustainable development through the lens of consumption. Thereby, it aims to highlight the underlying and most fundamental causes of environmental problems and to attribute responsibility where it is due. Specifically, a huge share of the environmental degradation arising from production processes in developing countries then has to be linked to consumption decisions made by the global consumer class, which predominantly resides in industrialized countries. At the same time, sustainable consumption pinpoints the question of social justice in the use of the world's ecological resources and highlights the enormous asymmetries existing there.

Consumption patterns and levels can therefore no longer be seen as an individual or national problem but become a global political issue. Additional links to global politics arise because various aspects of the global political economy, such as the politics of trade and finance, impact consumption patterns and levels and their environmental (and social) implications (Fuchs and Lorek 2002). Not surprisingly, sustainable consumption has been explicitly present on the global political agenda, in the form of Agenda 21, since the Earth Summit in Rio in 1992 (UN 1992). More recently, it became institutionalized in the Sustainable Development Goals (SDGs, "Goal 12: Ensure sustainable consumption and production patterns") at the United Nations Sustainable Development Summit in 2015 (UN 2015) in New York.

This chapter explores perspectives on, and concepts of, sustainable consumption. It then identifies relevant political actors and traces developments in global sustainable consumption governance, depicts the current state of affairs, discusses obstacles to progress, and explores policy implications. Subsequently, the chapter delineates important new developments in sustainable consumption research. The chapter concludes with a brief summary highlighting that – while progress towards sustainable consumption is still far from satisfactory – two sources of hope can be identified: initiatives pursuing sustainable consumption as a goal are growing in number and reach and promising conceptual developments, such as consumption corridors, are adding new impetus to scientific and policy debates.

What is consumption and why study it?

The *International Encyclopedia of the Social Sciences* (Eglitis 2008: 105) defines consumption as "the personal expenditure of individuals and families that involves the selection, usage, and disposal or reuse of goods and services." In other words, consumption entails all phases of our dealing with goods (and services to some extent): purchase, use, and disposal. As sociologists and psychologists will tell us, such consumption can take place for a variety of purposes. The consumption of food and water, as well as the need for shelter and some way to stay warm, are all requisites for survival. In today's developed societies, however, the purpose of consumption goes beyond this necessary fulfilment of fundamental needs. We consume to entertain ourselves, increase our happiness (even though we sometimes achieve the opposite), define our identity, and/or express status (Røpke 1999).

But why is consumption a topic in environmental politics and policy? The answer to this question becomes highly obvious if we consider the resource use associated with our consumption. In fact, consumption may be identified as the main villain when identifying causes of unsustainable development today.

It is more convenient to attribute responsibility for environmental degradation to production methods and processes, of course. After all, one can argue that the consumer has little information or influence on the environmental degradation caused at that stage. Moreover, the number of companies involved may still be large, but it is certainly smaller than the number of consumers and thus easier to reach and regulate. Finally, and perhaps most fundamentally, it may be politically more acceptable to regulate production than to constrain consumption; as long as we view consumer choice as part of our freedom in the pursuit of happiness and as long as economic growth, which in turn is supposed to depend on consumption, continues to be perceived as the primary and unassailable political goal.

A focus on production is insufficient for a range of reasons. For example, it does not include the environmental degradation caused during the use and final disposal of a product. In order to consider the environmental characteristics of a product in a comprehensive manner, we have to include the whole life-cycle of a product. Based on such ideas, some practitioners and scholars prefer to speak of the concept of "sustainable consumption and production" (SCP, e.g. United Nations 2015).

Most importantly, however, a focus that is limited to production hides the extent to which consumption acts as an extremely powerful driving force behind environmental degradation. It fails to attribute responsibility where it is due. Simultaneously, it obscures a substantial share of potential strategies for intervention, change, and responsibility.

Conversely, a focus on consumption has benefits beyond allowing questions of responsibility and widening the spectrum of potential political reforms. A focus on consumption allows us to ask what the most basic objectives behind resource consumption are and, thereby, shifts the attention to questions of well-being, needs-fulfilment, and justice as well as notions such as sufficiency and limits (Di Giulio et al. 2012, Princen 2005). As a consequence, a focus on consumption creates a real potential for societal transformation towards sustainability.

Indeed, some sustainable consumption scholars shy away from the combined "sustainable consumption" and production label because they fear that the production angle may lead to a constrained focus on improvements in resource efficiency or emission reductions, for example, on the production side, and on improving consumer choices in purchasing, use, and disposal decisions, on the consumption side. In the view of critical sustainable consumption scholars, such a constrained focus may allow for marginal improvements towards sustainability, but does not entail a potential for sustainability transformation.

Of course, these latter sustainable consumption scholars would not argue that the economic actors along the production chain are free from responsibility. Even in the context of global competition, CEOs and large investors have the possibility and responsibility to make environmentally and socially responsible choices. Moreover, the individual consumer is constrained in his or her consumption options by retailers' supply choices and other individual and structural conditions such as information, finances, or time, to name just a few (Akenji 2014, Fuchs and Lorek 2002, Hobson 2003, Maniates 2001). A focus on sustainable consumption, thus, neither relieves economic actors from responsibility nor attributes that responsibility to a large extent to individual consumers. Rather, it highlights the role that the current system of consumption, with its politico-economic, social, and cultural characteristics, plays in the present overstepping of planetary boundaries, as well as the potential for transformation entailed in taking sustainable consumption seriously. The consumption lens, thus, takes the whole supply chain into focus. However, it does so from the end of the chain.

The focus on consumption in global environmental governance originally arose in the context of debates on the main causes of environmental problems. At international conferences, developed countries tended to be concerned about population growth in developing countries, while developing countries pointed out the environmental degradation caused by consumption levels and patterns in developed countries. Indeed, the sustainable consumption debate gained considerable momentum when environmental activists and scholars started to highlight that a single American in his or her lifetime would consume the same amount of environmental resources as a large number of individuals from developing countries together (Durning 1992). Even in today's political debates, we run into these questions of justice again and again. The Chinese or the Brazilians can not only easily challenge demands to reduce their greenhouse gas emissions by juxtaposing their per capita emissions with those of the developed countries, they can also challenge such demands on the basis that a large share of the emissions is caused by production for Western consumers.

Concepts of sustainable consumption

But what is sustainable consumption? The Oslo Roundtable in 1994 defined sustainable consumption as

> the use of services and related products which respond to basic needs and bring a better quality of life while minimizing the use of natural resources and toxic materials as well as the emissions of waste and pollutants over the life cycle of the service or product so as not to jeopardize the needs of further generations.
>
> (Ministry of Environment Norway 1994)

It is important, however, to differentiate between strong and weak sustainable consumption (Fuchs and Lorek 2005). Weak sustainable consumption can result from increases in the efficiency of production and consumption, which are typically reached via technological improvements. In this case, improvements in the sustainability of consumption result from a reduction in resource consumption per consumption unit due to improvements in production processes or, for example, an efficiency-friendly design. Many times, such improvements appear to be win–win scenarios.

However, current trends in resource consumption make it very clear that improvements in the efficiency of consumption will not suffice for achieving sustainable development. Indeed, reductions in resource use achieved via technological innovation have generally been overcompensated by increases in consumption volumes. We may have more energy efficient appliances in households, but we also tend to use bigger ones and more of them. Our cars may have become more fuel efficient, but our mobility in terms of frequency and length of car and plane rides has increased. Scholars have called this effect of (over)compensation of improvements in resource efficiency the "rebound effect" and have identified several forms of it and reasons for its existence (Greening et al. 2000). Most fundamentally, we know today that, after more than 40 years of discussions about "limits to growth" and more than 20 years of sustainable consumption research and policy, income is still the number one predictor of resource use (Boucher 2016, Kuishuang and Hubacek forthcoming).

As a consequence, changes in consumption patterns and reductions in consumption levels of the global consumer class, i.e. strong sustainable consumption, need to be pursued if we want to achieve sustainability. Only strong sustainable consumption is a necessary *and* sufficient condition for sustainable development. It requires questioning of the purpose, drivers, and levels of consumption as well as consideration of consumption contexts in terms of infrastructures and politico-economic institutions. The necessary steps for achieving strong sustainable consumption are, of course, politically highly controversial. Yet, these are the issues that move to the centre of attention when approaching sustainable development from the perspective of sustainable consumption rather than sustainable production. The distinction between strong and weak sustainable consumption is not always clear cut (Hobson 2013). However, it serves as a highly useful tool for critical analyses of global sustainable consumption governance.

Global sustainable consumption governance[1]

Sustainable consumption explicitly appeared on the global governance agenda when the United Nations Conference on Environment and Development (UNCED) called for the adoption of sustainable consumption patterns in Chapter 4 of Agenda 21. Since then, various actors, in particular international governmental organizations (IGOs), have addressed the issue of sustainable consumption. Often, their goals have lacked ambition, however, and actual progress in terms of the sustainability of consumption (by the global consumer class) has yet to be achieved. Global sustainable consumption governance has concentrated almost exclusively on questions of efficiency to date (and even here we find more rhetoric than action). The earliest "global" meetings on sustainable consumption, in particular the Oslo meeting in 1994, adopted a much broader approach. In Oslo, the meeting explicitly noted that a focus on eco-efficiency would not provide a sufficiently comprehensive framework for identifying, understanding, and changing unsustainable consumption patterns. In the following years, however, the focus and ambitions of sustainable consumption governance became much narrower and this more comprehensive understanding disappeared from the political agendas. So far, there is little evidence that the inclusion of "sustainable consumption and production" in the SDGs in 2015 will reverse this trend.

Actors in global sustainable consumption governance

Until 2013, the Commission on Sustainable Development (CSD) was among the most active participants in the sustainable consumption arena. It especially fostered the development of sustainable consumption indicators and the revision of the UN Guidelines on Consumer Protection (UN DESA 2003). This work of the CSD (and, in an institutional context, the Division for Sustainable Development (DSD) of the United Nations Department for Economic and Social Affairs (UN-DESA)) provided sustainable consumption with increased visibility on the global governance agenda. However, it failed to move beyond the debate and indicator stage or to address the dimension of strong sustainable consumption as a governance goal. Questions regarding fundamental changes in consumption patterns and reductions in consumption levels were raised in the context of discussions of "common but differentiated responsibilities" at the CSD, but did not find their way into official reports and documents.

The High-Level Political Forum (HLPF), created at the UN's Rio+20 conference in 2012 as a successor to the CSD, now monitors member states' implementation of the SDGs. For this purpose, it has operationalized the sustainable consumption goal in terms of material footprint and domestic material consumption (HLPF 2016). The first monitoring of Goal 12 in 2018 will have to show if, and how, the HPLF thereby seriously addresses the challenges of the (un)sustainability of consumption.

United Nations Environment Programme (UNEP)

UNEP's Sustainable Production and Consumption Branch (formerly the Sustainable Consumption Programme) is housed in the Division of Technology, Industry, and Economics (DTIE) and started in 1998 with the intention of developing demand-side oriented activities to complement DTIE's supply-side oriented ones. Its stated goals were to understand the forces driving global consumption patterns, to develop appropriate activities for business and other stakeholders, and to look for potential advances for business, governments, and NGOs. In this context, UNEP DTIE also conducted a "global consumer survey" to gain a better understanding of consumer wants and investigated consumption trends and indicators in a variety of fields.

UNEP also serves as the Secretariat for the 10-Year Framework of Programmes on Sustainable Consumption and Production Patterns (10YFP, subsequently elaborated in the Marrakech process), adopted by the United Nations Conference on Sustainable Development (Rio+20) in 2012, and collects country based examples and knowledge as well as facilitating access to technical and financial resources for developing countries (UNEP 2016). Specifically, UNEP has identified strategic areas in which it perceives the greatest need for further work on sustainable consumption, such as public procurement, sustainable tourism, sustainable food systems or providing information for consumers. Yet, NGOs have criticized the 10 YFP strongly, all along, pointing out the weak wording, limited focus, and failure to foster binding commitment.

Overall, UNEP has addressed a substantial range of topics related to sustainable consumption, including a focus on sustainable lifestyles. Yet, a large share of its work has focused on increasing the eco-efficiency of consumption, with a particular interest in innovations for business, which was probably also fostered by the location of its sustainable consumption activities in UNEP DTIE. Except for one publication, UNEP's *Consumption Opportunities Report* (UNEP 2001), which did raise the question of "over-consumption", UNEP had difficulties going beyond a weak sustainable consumption governance focus for a long time. Today, one will find a number of references to "overconsumption" on its website. Yet, such language still tends not to enter official documents. It remains to be seen if more recent activities accompanying the SDG process will allow UNEP to play a more progressive role in global sustainable consumption governance.

OECD

Acknowledging that the OECD (Organisation for Economic Co-operation and Development) countries are home to 19 per cent of the world's population but consume 80 per cent of the world's resources, the OECD addressed sustainable consumption between 1995 and 2008. The core activities included the development of a conceptual framework and indicators as well as reports on trends, policy instruments, and decision-making, especially for tourism, food, energy and water consumption, and waste generation, and, finally, best practices (OECD 2002, 2008). Yet, the framework for its consumption work was clearly set in line with the OECD's traditional focus on economic growth and, as a consequence, failed to go beyond the aim of improving eco-efficiency.

The European Union

In 2001, the European Council adopted a *Sustainable Development Strategy (EU SDS,* revised in 2006 and 2009), which made sustainable consumption and production one of its "key objectives" and "priorities". In this context, the EU and its institutions held meetings with stakeholders, published reports, and introduced its Sustainable Consumption and Production Action Plan in 2008. This led to a number of initiatives focusing on eco-design requirements, energy and environmental labelling, resource efficiency, and green public procurement (European Parliament 2017). In 2016, finally, the EU published a "New European Consensus on Development – 'Our World, Our Dignity, Our Future'" (EU COM 2016).

Despite the considerable number of initiatives and actions the EU took to meet its "leading role" in promoting sustainable consumption and production, however, it has yet to seriously address and support strong sustainable consumption. While the 2007 *Monitoring Report* of the EU SDS mentioned that sustainable development can only be achieved by changing patterns of consumption and production, the subsequent action plan lacked mandatory quantifiable targets and deadlines and weakly promoted cross-sectoral and multi-level relationships instead. Likewise, the "New Consensus . . ." mentions consumption in the context of a sustainable management and reduction of waste, technological innovation also in the context of digitalization, and resource efficiency, for example, but fails to make any reference to questions of sufficiency or levels of consumption. "Overconsumption" still only appears in EU communications today in the context of an overuse of water and other natural resources but is not linked to questions of overall consumption levels and patterns, and normative debates regarding sufficiency, for instance, as a societal objective do not take place. Rather, concepts such as growth, efficiency, and competitiveness continue to remain a pivotal focus of EU policy activities, even in the context of sustainable development and sustainable consumption.

National governments

National governments have also been active in the area of sustainable consumption, both early on and again particularly in the context of the adoption of the SDGs and the associated new international momentum. In this context, the efforts of the Scandinavian and some Western European governments have been particularly noteworthy. These governments have not only sponsored a substantial amount of research on the topic of sustainable consumption but have initiated and pursued specific initiatives to foster global and national sustainable consumption governance. Some countries developed explicit SCP Action Plans. However, these efforts, for the most part, have failed to address and endorse policy measures for fostering strong sustainable consumption, as well, and the popularity of weak instruments (i.e. informational tools) is evident throughout reports and policies.

Today, we still see considerable efforts being made at the national level. Every UN member state is obliged to develop an implementation plan for the SDGs to begin with. Individual governments, such as Germany, have also adopted national programmes for sustainable consumption. Germany's programme posits strengthening and expanding sustainable consumption as its core aim and addresses six areas identified as holding a high potential for improving the sustainability of consumption: mobility, food, housing and household, office and work, clothing, and tourism and leisure (Federal Ministry for the Environment, Nature Conservation, Building and Nuclear Safety 2017). Yet, even this recent effort has been characterized by a lack of attention to levels of consumption and questions of sufficiency, as an open letter by German sustainable consumption scholars highlighted.[2]

Civil society

NGOs and civil society initiatives have always played a strong role in the global campaign to promote sustainable production and consumption. Throughout the many programme cycles of the CSD, the meetings of the HLPF, as well as stakeholder roundtables and such at the national and international level, NGOs working on production and consumption patterns have executed and coordinated advocacy and education efforts, and organized themselves, for instance, into the International Coalition for Sustainable Production and Consumption (ICSPAC). A number of these NGOs do ask the politically sensitive questions regarding consumption patterns and levels. Moreover, civil society contributes to the development of strong sustainable consumption governance by promoting the diffusion of alternative lifestyles and values. Zero waste, voluntary simplicity and "Right to Know" groups, transition towns, local money and social investment groups, eco-labelling, urban gardening, sharing, and fair trade initiatives are all trying to make a difference. Despite the multitude of efforts and initiatives, however, NGOs and civil society have failed to successfully push for political action in the direction of strong sustainable consumption governance to date. While they may clearly aim to induce more-than-marginal change in the sustainability of consumption, their influence at the national, regional, and global levels of governance has proven to be limited thus far.

Scholars have also contributed much to the understanding of sustainable consumption. Fostered by the availability of funding by governments, several studies assess and compare the sustainability characteristics of consumer products, improve consumer choices, or foster product innovation in the interests of resource efficiency. Importantly, critical sustainable consumption scholars have emphasized the need for research on strong sustainable consumption, absolute reductions, sufficiency or related ideas and concepts, explicitly criticizing a limited focus on weak sustainable consumption by most actors (Akenji et al. 2016, Fuchs and Lorek 2005, Princen 2005). Assessments of the willingness and ability of consumers to reduce their consumption, as well as political strategies for reigning global consumption into planetary boundaries, have been the focus of numerous research efforts and collaborations. Unfortunately, few of the ideas and results raised by this research have made it into the official global sustainable consumption discourse.

Business

Business actors have also been active in global sustainable consumption governance. The International Chamber of Commerce and the World Business Council for Sustainable Development (WBCSD) issued a report dealing with the topic of sustainable consumption (WBCSD 2002). The report gave consumers the key role in shaping markets, thus placing responsibility firmly on the demand side rather than the supply side. It identified increasing eco-efficiency as business's contribution to sustainable consumption, but, perhaps not surprisingly, avoided any discussion of the role of business in driving or reducing overconsumption. The only additional responsibility the report attributed to business was to inform consumers about the social and environmental effects of their choices and to offer them appropriate options. Later, reports again analyzed sustainable consumption facts and trends from a business perspective and identified roles for consumers, businesses, NGOs, and governments (WBCSD 2008). Today, the WBCSD focuses primarily on the circular economy, drawing attention to "reinvent how business finds, uses and disposes of the materials that make up global trade" (WBCSD 2017).

Overall, the focus of business on the production, rather than the consumption, side in its global sustainable development initiatives is not surprising. Business influence becomes critical, however, when it weighs in on the global sustainable consumption governance agenda by allocating responsibility solely to the consumer. In this context, the failure of the advertising sector's report (European Association of Communications Agencies & World Federation of Advertisers 2002), prepared at UNEP's request in the context of the World Summit on Sustainable Development in Johannesburg in 2002, to identify any problems with advertising's influence on consumption levels and patterns and its rejection of the notion that the sector could, in any way, have some responsibility for overconsumption is noteworthy.

The current state of affairs

In 2012, the international community reconfirmed their commitment to the 10YFP regarding questions of sustainable consumption. In the Outcome document of Rio+20, §224 states that member states

> recall the commitments made in the Rio Declaration on Environment and Development, Agenda 21 and the Johannesburg Plan of Implementation on sustainable consumption and production and, in particular, the request in chapter 3 of the Plan of Implementation to encourage and promote the development of a 10-year framework of programmes.
>
> (UN 2012: 58)

Within the same paragraph, member states also acknowledge that fundamental changes "in the way societies consume and produce are indispensable for achieving global sustainable development" (Ibid.). As pointed out above, however, critical observers view the 10YFP as a failure.

The central outcome of the last global summit on sustainable development, which took place in New York in 2015, was the SDGs. As indicated, Goal 12 calls on governments to stress and strengthen their commitments regarding their policies of sustainable consumption and production and to develop initiatives to accelerate the shift towards sustainable consumption and production (UN 2015). Given that the SDGs are being operationalized at various levels of governance, one can only hope that the pursuit of Goal 12 will inspire political efforts to seek more than improvements in resource efficiency and technological innovation. So far, however, there is little, if any evidence, justifying such hope.

Barriers to change

In sum, weak sustainable consumption has received attention during the last two years, while strong sustainable consumption is still largely absent from global governance. Strong sustainable consumption only exists in marginal sectors of society and research or as a symbolic reminder in a few official documents. How can this development be explained if strong sustainable consumption is a fundamental precondition for sustainable development? Applying a power lens to global consumption governance can answer this question (Fuchs and Lorek 2005, Fuchs et al. 2016). Such an approach highlights the forces aligned against strong sustainable consumption in the current form of the globalized political economy and consumer society.

Most fundamentally, clear opposition to (strong) sustainable consumption governance exists in the business community. Most business actors tend to reject the notion that they carry any responsibility with respect to consumption levels. According to representatives of the business sector, the latter's role with respect to sustainable consumption is to promote eco-efficiency. Some optimistic scholars and activists point out that business opposition to strong sustainable consumption governance does not necessarily have to be the case. They argue that business may earn profits through, for instance, the selling of fewer, but more sustainable, products with a higher profit margin. However, the globalized economy to a large extent is characterized by a high level of competition in mass markets and cheap products and correspondingly high pressures for externalization of social and environmental costs. Moreover, the ability of products to achieve distinction on the basis of quality, irrespective of price, is limited as only a share of products can be marketed accordingly. Likewise, Corporate Social Responsibility (CSR) and related measures – often proclaimed to signal the ethical turn in business conduct – tend to perform badly when it comes to actual performance improvements (King and Lenox 2000). More importantly, these measures are unlikely to contribute to improvements in strong sustainable consumption.

One specific area in which business may be interested in fostering strong sustainable consumption after all is in the field of eco-efficient services, i.e. the purchase of a service instead of the ownership of a good, which actually involve a reduction in consumption levels (Michaelis 2003). However, one needs to critically assess the actual ecological footprint of services as they still tend to presuppose extensive material provisioning, both on the demand and on the supply side (Cohen 2017). Moreover, eco-efficient services only provide an option in certain areas and are frequently not accepted by consumers.

At the same time, many members of the global consumer class also do not want to engage with questions of consumption levels. Some scholars and practitioners proclaim, and surveys appear to document, a new awareness and interest in the environmental and social effects of consumption by consumers, and the notion of ethical or political consumerism has become somewhat fashionable in scholarly and political circles (Bossy 2014, Dubuisson-Quellier 2013). Yet, environmental, social, or sustainability values are competing with a multitude of criteria in their influence on consumption decisions in real life, and in the sum of communications, "sustainability" messages are overpowered by opposing ones (Jackson 2009, Røpke 1999).

In fact, there is ample evidence that sustainability criteria often rank low compared to competing aims when it comes to action (Fuchs 2017). This is the case even when the question is one of simply consuming a different product. When it comes to consuming less, the hurdle is even higher (Jackson 2005). In addition, even consumers believing in the pursuit of lifestyles emphasizing "experiences" rather than "possessions" tend to have little understanding of the associated size of their ecological footprint or interest in considering it (Bowerman 2014). In other words, some indications of the willingness of consumers to move towards green consumption notwithstanding, there is little evidence today that consumers are willing to fundamentally change or reduce consumption for sustainability objectives. Rather, consumption continues to be proclaimed as an individual right, allowing the expression of self, the pursuit of one's legitimate professional and social goals, or an opportunity for exercising freedom of choice.

Given such opposition by business and a substantial share of consumers, it should not come as a surprise that governmental actors have exhibited little willingness to tackle the real challenges associated with the (un)sustainability of consumption. In addition, governments and IGOs themselves are still attached to the growth discourse and tend to want to foster consumption in order to foster growth. Accordingly, they are much more likely to sign on to continued efforts to increase eco-efficiency than to adopt policies that seriously transform consumption patterns or reduce consumption levels. The SDGs may have opened a new window of opportunity here. However, it remains to be seen if that window can be used by actors aiming to foster societal transformation towards sustainability.

Sources of hope: what is the purpose of consumption?

Taking a power lens on sustainable consumption governance does not only allow the identification of barriers to change but also of forces which may allow the pursuit of the necessary sustainability transformation after all (Fuchs et al., forthcoming). Such forces can be galvanized by asking ourselves why we consume. Consumption is about needs fulfilment; it is about trying to live a good life (Di Giulio et al. 2012). We do not consume in order to use up resources, but in order to fulfil our physical, emotional, social, and cognitive needs. The fulfilment of these needs does require some resource consumption, of course, but not endless amounts of resources. Needs can be satiated. A focus on needs fulfilment can even show that consumption can be too much, i.e. when efforts to fulfil one need start conflicting with the fulfilment of other needs (see also Princen 1999 on overconsumption and misconsumption). It certainly shows that GDP/cap is not a good measure of well-being (Costanza et al. 2007, Jackson 2009).

Asking ourselves what a good life means to us would draw our attention to social relations and creativity, for instance. Scholars speak of "objective" or "protected needs", i.e. needs that we have simply because we are human and that we need to be able to fulfil in order to live a good life, in this context (Di Giulio 2016, Nussbaum 1992, Sen 1993). Philosophers and thinkers have highlighted these conditions of well-being for millennia, and many recent psychological and sociological studies have provided supporting empirical evidence. Being aware of the nature of our needs, in turn, would allow us to distinguish them from both (passing) desires and satisfiers and, on that basis, to question the extent to which we want to fulfil our needs via material consumption. A core characteristic of consumer culture is that we easily and predominantly turn to material consumption when it comes to needs fulfilment. In other words, we tend to use consumer products or consumption related activities to express identity, status, or belonging, for example. Yet, empirical research also shows us that such forms of needs fulfilment frequently tend to be associated with short-term benefits only. For the world's poor, the ability to live a good life and fulfil their objective needs would require more consumption, of course. For the global consumer class, a focus on the good life rather than the ever "better life" promised in advertising and neoliberal thought, however, would imply the ability to consume less and to take questions of sufficiency and satiation seriously (Brand-Correa and Steinberger 2017, Gough 2017). The good life, thus, can provide a powerful and empowering narrative to gather momentum for the sustainability transformation via sustainable consumption (Fuchs et al., forthcoming).

Realizing this potential, however, will require the concerted efforts of actors with relevant ideational and material resources. Given that each member of the global consumer class today is bombarded with a huge number of communications inviting and inducing more consumption, getting through this noise will be a challenge. Yet, the number of civil society initiatives questioning currently dominant definitions of well-being in terms of income or possessions, and pursuing less materially intensive lifestyles, has grown exponentially, as have research and research collaboration on such topics. Connecting these activities and using their synergies provides access to a reservoir of power. Thus, we actually may be achieving the necessary momentum for change, today.

Policy implications

What will the future of global sustainable consumption governance look like? Our analysis of developments to date has shown that political efforts to improve the efficiency of consumption exist, and we can most likely expect more policy proposals promoting efficient technologies for consumer products. However, our analysis has also shown that hardly any progress has been made on questions of consumption levels and that the opposition to such measures will not be easily overcome.

Yet, to seriously combat climate change and other forms of environmental destruction, we clearly require strong sustainable consumption governance, or at least policy approaches targeting the overlapping areas between strong and weak sustainable consumption (Hobson 2013). Proper construction of such policies, moreover, cannot only focus on specific policy issues or narrow environmental targets. Strong sustainable consumption governance has to be designed as an integrated and comprehensive approach, considering consumption across the board, even if key intervention points and consumption clusters with the largest environmental and social burdens (mobility, food, housing) need to be prioritized (Bilharz and Schmitt 2011, Lorek and Spangenberg 2001). Moreover, such governance objectives will have to address and solve conflicts between policy targets. As long as a large share of consumption governance and associated messages focuses on increasing consumption, sustainable consumption governance cannot help but remain symbolic and marginal. Accordingly, strong sustainable consumption governance will have to address advertising and sponsorship, as well as the increasing dependence of public institutions, as well as the media, on business investment and sponsorship (Black et al. 2017).

Ideally, sustainable consumption governance would pursue a global approach, of course. The pitfalls of global sustainable consumption governance to date have been delineated above, however. Moreover, the recent decision of the Trump administration to withdraw from the Paris agreement on climate change further demonstrates the challenges of global sustainability governance. Clearly, we cannot wait for a global agreement on strong sustainable consumption governance. Such governance will have to start at the local and national level, taking global contexts in terms of planetary boundaries as well as intra- and intergenerational governance into account, however.

At the local and national level, a window of opportunity may be opening up, as signalled by the momentum existing in civil society and research described above. Coalitions between these actors and effective strategizing may allow the creation of a real impetus for change here. Part of such strategizing may be the questioning of political venues for relevant political issues. The earlier unfortunate placement of UNEP's sustainable consumption focus with UNEP DTIE was pointed out above. Today, such counterintuitive (from a sustainability perspective) locations for relevant policy debates and targets can still be seen, however. In Germany, for instance, the authority for the implementation, operationalization of the SDGs, and monitoring of Germany's performance, the authority for Germany's climate and energy targets, and the authority for the topic of sustainable consumption are located in three different ministries; the best recipe for ineffective governance.

For governmental actors, only time will determine to what extent the SDGs are able to generate more than rhetoric at the national and international levels. On the one hand, they may be able to draw more attention to sustainability issues, partly thanks to their quantification and monitoring. Moreover, NGOs may use the SDGs as tools to shame governments into compliance efforts. On the other hand, many sustainability related targets have existed for a long time without NGOs managing to get governments to comply. In the absence of environmental organizations with sanctioning power at the national and international levels, then, governmental support for a civil society coalition promoting strong sustainable consumption as delineated above will depend on the willingness and ability of individuals within IGOs and/or national governments to take the sustainability challenges of consumption seriously.

What could concrete policy measures for strong sustainable consumption look like? One promising approach currently receiving significant attention in the literature is the design and implementation of sustainable consumption corridors (Blättel-Mink et al. 2013, Di Giulio and Fuchs 2014, see Figure 5.1). Such consumption corridors allow an integrated pursuit of sustainability and justice in the context of consumption. They start from the idea of the good life and the associated requirement to be able to fulfil one's objective needs. This idea leads to the definition of consumption minima, i.e. the floor of consumption corridors. Needing to ensure access to such consumption minima for all individuals living now and in the future, in turn, means that the existence of planetary boundaries has to lead to consumption maxima, i.e. the ceiling of such consumption corridors. Within these

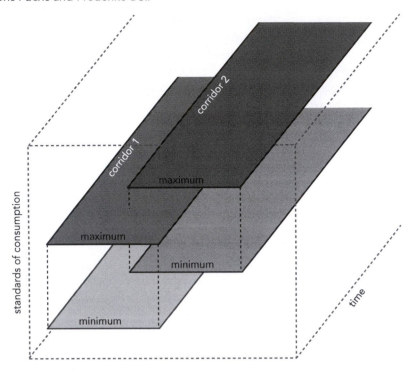

Figure 5.1 Consumption corridors.
Source: Di Giulio & Fuchs 2014, p. 187.

corridors, individuals will be free to make consumption choices according to their life plans. Consumption opportunities below the corridor floors, however, imply restrictions on an individual's ability to live a good life and consumption beyond the ceiling of consumption corridors implies harm for the chances of other individuals to live a good life and thus needs to be considered unethical (see also related concepts such as "living in the doughnut" (Raworth 2012), the safe and just operating space (Rockström et al. 2009), or environmental space (Hille 1997, Spangenberg 2002)).

Of course, such corridors are not easy to develop and implement. They require societal dialogue about objective needs, acceptable satisfiers for these needs, and corridor design, implementation, and enforcement (Fuchs and Di Giulio 2016). Such dialogue, in turn, will require inclusive, fair, and transparent processes, as well as scientific expertise and political initiative and support. Clearly, quite a challenge! The power of the good life as a narrative in combination with the increasing awareness of the shortcomings of, and dangers involved in, business as usual, however, may provide a fertile foundation to enter into such dialogues.

Other research developments

Research on sustainable consumption is thriving in quantity, diversifying in topics, as well as developing and debating new perspectives (Geels et al. 2015). One reason the field of sustainable consumption research is so vibrant and interesting is the truly interdisciplinary nature of the topic. Today, research on sustainable consumption receives contributions from a wide variety of disciplines, including political science, economics, sociology, anthropology, psychology, geography, and philosophy, urban and cultural studies. This research focuses on a broad range of questions. Thus, scholars are still trying to gain a better understanding of the determinants of consumer behaviour. To this end, they attempt to identify different types of consumers and lifestyles in order to develop targeted strategies to reduce and change their patterns of consumption (see Brach et al. 2017, Geiger et al. 2017, Jansson et al. 2017 for some recent examples). The idea of "nudging" has become fashionable in this context.[3] In addition, the potential benefits and challenges of digitalization for the sustainability of consumption are receiving increasing attention.

Fascinating developments, moreover, can be noticed with respect to inquiries into the structural barriers to sustainable consumption as well as potential pathways for transformation. Consumers make their consumption decisions in specific socio-economic, political, and cultural contexts, creating structural opportunities but also constraints (Lorek and Vergragt 2015, Maniates 2014, Schor 1999). In fact, the individualization of the responsibility for sustainable consumption frequently advocated by politicians and business has to be viewed very critically (Maniates 2001). Accordingly, sustainable consumption scholars increasingly explore the role of power and practices, of time and socio-political organization (Fuchs et al. 2016, Hayden 1999, Maniates 2010, Meyer 2015, Pullinger 2014, Schor and Fitzmaurice 2015, Warde 2017). They analyze the role of post- or neo-materialism, the potential for diffusion or upscaling of relevant grassroots initiatives, or new forms of politico-economic organization (Assadourian 2012, Cohen 2017, Jackson 2011, Schlosberg and Coles 2016). Their findings also provide explanations for the rebound effect as well as the value-action and action-impact gaps, which empirical research on sustainable consumption has identified (Csutora 2012, Csutora and Zsóka 2016, Greening et al. 2000, Hertwich 2005, Kollmuss and Agyeman 2002, Lebel et al. 2006). Thereby, research on the structural contexts of sustainable consumption actually pinpoints the insufficiency of inquiries into (the steering of) consumer behaviour. Indeed, given the extent of existing knowledge about consumer behaviour, the investigation of ways to overcome structural barriers to sustainable consumption and the identification of pathways to transformation are probably the areas where additional research is most urgently needed.

Conclusion

Twenty five years after the World Summit in Rio, progression towards the political pursuit of sustainable consumption is still far from satisfactory. This chapter has highlighted more political weaknesses and obstacles than progress, and thereby indicated that the future of sustainable consumption governance may still look bleak. Meanwhile, the urgency with which we need to dramatically improve the sustainability of consumption is bigger than ever because of climate change, environmental destruction, as well as continuing poverty in the world.

However, the chapter also identified sources of hope. Especially, the multitude of sustainability initiatives at the grassroots level pursuing and implementing alternative and reduced forms of consumption provides potential for change. To realize this potential, however, they will have to connect and engage in some form of political activism. Critical sustainable consumption scholarship can provide support here. This scholarship, itself, is gaining further ground, and numerous collaborative efforts are being initiated and pursued. An alliance between sustainability initiatives and science could also try to use the SDGs as an additional source of legitimacy for the pursuit of strong sustainable consumption, as well as provide a critical commentary on the operationalization and pursuit of the SDGs with respect to Goal 12. In other words, such an alliance could employ the political attention the SDGs currently are receiving as an entry point into the political arenas. Via such societal support and pressure, finally courageous and integer members of national governments as well as IGOs could perhaps also be induced to take on a leading role in transformative sustainable consumption governance.

Finally, the chapter introduced the concept of consumption corridors as an instrument to integrate the pursuit of the good life for all individuals living now and in the future, of justice, and of the respect for planetary boundaries. Such consumption corridors would be defined by consumption minima, allowing individuals to live a good life (i.e. provide them with the ability to fulfil their objective needs) and consumption maxima, ensuring that consumption by one individual or group of individuals does not threaten the ability of other individuals to reach their consumption minima. While acknowledging the challenges involved in designing and implementing such corridors, and the need for inclusive, transparent, and fair processes in such efforts, the chapter underlined the transformative potential of this instrument.

Notes

1 For a detailed discussion of the role of the various actors, see Fuchs and Lorek (2005).
2 www.aloenk.tu-berlin.de/menue/offener_brief_np_nk/, last accessed 13/06/2017.
3 For a critical perspective on the "nudging" discourse see Gumbert (forthcoming).

Recommended reading

Dauvergne, Peter (2008) *The Shadows of Consumption*. Cambridge: MIT.
Di Giulio, Antonietta; Fuchs, Doris (2014) Sustainable Consumption Corridors. *GAIA*, 23(S1), 184–192.
Maniates, Michael (2014) Sustainable Consumption—Three Paradoxes. *GAIA*, 23(S1), 200–208.
Princen, Thomas (2005) *The Logic of Sufficiency*. Cambridge: MIT.

References

Akenji, L. (2014) Consumer Scapegoatism and Limits to Green Consumerism. *Journal of Cleaner Production*, 63, 13–23.
Akenji, L., Bengtsson, M., Tukker, A., Bleischwitz, R., Lorek, S., Kojima, S., Vergragt, P., Kuramochi, T. & de Leeuw, B. (2016) Absolute Reductions in Material Throughput, Energy Use and Emissions. *Journal of Cleaner Production*, 132, 1–12.

Assadourian, E. (2012) *The Path to Degrowth in Overdeveloped Countries.* Washington: The Worldwatch Institute, 22–37.

Bilharz, M. & Schmitt, K. (2011) Going Big with Big Matters. *GAIA*, 20(4), 232–235.

Black, I., Shaw, D. & Trebeck, K. (2017) A Policy Agenda for Changing our Relationship with Consumption. *Journal of Cleaner Production*, 154, 12–15.

Blättel-Mink, B., Brohmann, B., Defila, R., Di Giulio, A., Fischer, D., Fuchs, D., Gölz, S., Götz, K., Homburg, A., Kaufmann-Hayoz, R., Matthies, E., Michelsen, G., Schäfer, M., Tews, K., Wassermann, S. & Zundel, S. (2013) *Konsum-Botschaften.* Stuttgart: S. Hirzel.

Bossy, S. (2014) The Utopias of Political Consumerism. *Journal of Consumer Culture*, 14(2), 179–198.

Boucher, J. L. (2016) Culture, Carbon, and Climate Change. *Socijalna ekologija: Časopis za ekološku misao i sociologijska istraživanja okoline*, 25(1–2), 53–80.

Bowerman, T. (2014) How Much is Too Much? *Sustainability: Science, Practice & Policy*, 10(1), 14–28.

Brach, S., Walsh, G. & Shaw, D. (2017) Sustainable Consumption and Third-Party Certification Labels. *European Management Journal*, 36(2), 254–265. Advance online publication. DOI: 10.1016/j.emj.2017.03.005. Available at: www.sciencedirect.com/science/article/pii/S0263237317300506 (last accessed 17/01/2018).

Brand-Correa, L. & Steinberger, J. (2017) A Framework for Decoupling Human Need Satisfaction from Energy Use. *Ecological Economics*, 141, 43–52.

Cohen, M. (2017) *The Future of Consumer Society Prospects for Sustainability in the New Economy.* Oxford: OUP.

Costanza, R., Fisher, B., Ali, S., Beer, C., Bond, L., Boumans, R., Danigelis, N., Dickinson, J., Elliott, C., Farley, J., Elliott Gayer, D., MacDonald Glenn, L., Hudspeth, T., Mahoney, D., McCahil, L., McIntosh, B., Reed, B., Turab Rizvi, A., Rizzo, D., Simpatico, T. & Snapp, R. (2007) Quality of Life. *Ecological Economics*, 61(2–3), 267–276.

Csutora, M. (2012) One More Awareness Gap? *Journal of Consumer Policy*, 35(1), 145–163.

Csutora, M. & Zsóka, Á. (2016) Breaking Through the Behaviour Impact Gap and the Rebound Effect in Sustainable Consumption, in Lorek, S. & Vadovics, E. (eds), *Sustainable Consumption and Social Justice in a Constrained World.* Budapest, Hungary: SCORAI Europe Workshop Proceedings.

Di Giulio, A. (2016) Which Wants? Identifying the Foundations of a New Narrative for the Future. Paper, Degrowth Conference, 30.08.2016–03.09.2016, Budapest.

Di Giulio, A., Bohrmann, B., Clausen, J., Defila, R., Fuchs, D., Kaufmann-Hayoz, R. & Koch, A. (2012) Needs and Consumption—A Conceptual System and Its Meaning in the Context of Sustainability, in Di Giulio, A., Defila, R. & Kaufmann-Hayoz, R. (eds), *The Nature of Sustainable Consumption and How to Achieve it.* Munich: Oekom, 45–66.

Di Giulio, A. & Fuchs, D. (2014) Sustainable Consumption Corridors. *GAIA*, 23(S1), 184–192.

Dubuisson-Quellier, S. (2013) *Ethical Consumption.* Black Point: Fernwood Publishing.

Durning, A. (1992) *How Much is Enough?* Washington: Worldwatch.

Eglitis, D.S. (2008) Consumption, in Darity, W. (ed.) *International Encyclopedia of the Social Sciences.* Detroit: Thomson Gale, 105–109.

European Association of Communications Agencies & World Federation of Advertisers (2002) *Industry as a Partner for Sustainable Development. Advertising.* Brussels: EACA&WFA.

European Commission (EU COM) (2016) *Proposal for a New European Consensus on Development.* Strasbourg: European Commission.

European Parliament (2017) *Sustainable Consumption and Production.* Brussels: European Parliament.

Federal Ministry for the Environment, Nature Conservation, Building and Nuclear Safety (2017) *Nationales Programm für nachhaltigen Konsum.* Berlin: BMUB.

Fuchs, D. (2017) Consumption Corridors as a Means for Overcoming Trends in (Un-)Sustainable Consumption, in Bala, C. & Schuldzinski, W. (eds), *International Conference on Consumer Research 2016. The 21st Century Consumer—Vulnerable, Responsible, Transparent?* Düsseldorf: VZ-NRW.

Fuchs, D. & Di Giulio, A. (2016) Consumption Corridors and Social Justice: Exploring the Limits, in Lorek, S. & Vadovics, E. (eds.) *Sustainable Consumption and Social Justice in a Constrained World.* SCORAI Europe Workshop Proceedings, August 29–30, 2016, Budapest, Hungary. *Sustainable Consumption Transitions Series,* Issue 6.

Fuchs, D., Di Giulio, A., Glaab, K., Lorek, S., Maniates, M., Princen, T. & Ropke, I. (2016) Power: The Missing Element in Sustainable Consumption and Absolute Reductions Research and Action. *Journal of Cleaner Production,* 132, 298–307.

Fuchs, D. & Lorek, S. (2002) Sustainable Consumption Governance in a Globalizing World. *Global Environmental Politics,* 2(1), 19–45.

Fuchs, D. & Lorek, S. (2005) Sustainable Consumption Governance. *Journal on Consumer Policy,* 28(3), 261–288.

Fuchs, D., Lorek, S., Di Giulio, A. & Defila, R. (Forthcoming) Power and Sustainable Consumption, in Isenhour, C., Martiskainen, M. & Middlemiss, L. (eds), *Power, Politics and Ideology in Sustainable Consumption.* London: Routledge.

Geels, F., McMeekin, A., Mylan, J. & Southerton, D. (2015) A Critical Appraisal of Sustainable Consumption and Production Research. *Global Environmental Change,* 34, 1–12.

Geiger, S., Fischer, D. & Schrader, U. (2017) Measuring What Matters in Sustainable Consumption. *Sustainable Development,* 26(1), 18–33. Advance online publication. DOI: 10.1002/sd.1688.

Gough, I. (2017) Recomposing Consumption. *Philosophical Transactions of the Royal Society A,* 375, 20160379. DOI: 10.1098/rsta.2016.0379.

Greening, L., Green, D. & Difiglio, C. (2000) Energy Efficiency and Consumption. *Energy Policy,* 28(6–7), 389–401.

Gumbert, T. (Forthcoming) Freedom, Autonomy and Sustainable Behaviors, in Isenhour, C., Martiskainen, M. & Middlemiss, L. (eds), *Power, Politics and Ideology in Sustainable Consumption.* London: Routledge.

Hayden, A. (1999) *Sharing the Work, Sparing the Planet.* London: Zed.

Hertwich, E. (2005) Consumption and the Rebound Effect. *Journal of Industrial Ecology,* 9(1–2), 85–98.

High Level Political Forum (HLPF) (2016) *Sustainable Development Knowledge Platform.* New York, NY: UN.

Hille, J. (1997) *The Concept of Environmental Space.* Luxemburg: EEA. www.historylab.unina2.it/files/47.pdf (last accessed 17/01/2018)

Hobson, K. (2003) Thinking Habits into Action. *Local Environment,* 8(1), 95–112.

Hobson, K. (2013) 'Weak' or 'Strong' Sustainable Consumption? *Environment and Planning C: Politics and Space,* 31(6), 1082–1098.

Jackson, T. (2005) Live Better by Consuming Less? *Journal of Industrial Ecology,* 9(1), 19–36.

Jackson, T. (2009) *Prosperity without Growth.* London: Earthscan.

Jackson, T. (2011) Societal Transformations for a Sustainable Economy. *Natural Resources Forum,* 35(3), 155–164.

Jansson, J., Nordlung, A. & Westin, K. (2017) Examining Drivers of Sustainable Consumption. *Journal of Cleaner Production,* 154, 176–187.

King, A. & Lenox, M. (2000) Industry Self-Regulation without Sanctions. *Academy of Management Journal,* 43(4), 698–716.

Kollmuss, A. & Agyeman, J. (2002) Mind the Gap. *Environmental Education Research,* 8(3), 239–260.

Kuishuang, F. & Hubacek, K. (Forthcoming) Carbon Inequality in the United States. *Sustainability.*

Lebel, L., Fuchs, D., Garden, P. & Giap, D (2006) *Linking Knowledge and Action for Sustainable Production and Consumption Systems. USER Working Paper WP-2006-09.* Chiang Mai: Unit for Social and Environmental Research.

Lorek, S. & Spangenberg, J. H. (2001) Indicators for Environmentally Sustainable Household Consumption. *International Journal of Sustainable Development*, 4(1), 101–120.

Lorek, S. & Vergragt, P. J. (2015) Sustainable Consumption as a Systemic Challenge, in Reisch, L. & Thogersen, J. (eds), *Handbook of Research on Sustainable Consumption*. Cheltenham: Edward Elgar, 19–32.

Maniates, M. (2001) Individualization. Plant a Tree, Buy a Bike, Save the World? *Global Environmental Politics*, 1(3), 31–52.

Maniates, M. (2010) Cultivating Consumer Restraint in an Ecologically Full World, in Lebel, L., Lorek, S. & Daniel R. (eds), *Sustainable Production and Consumption System*. Dordrecht: Springer, 13–37.

Maniates, M. (2014) Sustainable Consumption—Three Paradoxes. *GAIA*, 23(S1), 200–208.

Michaelis, L. (2003) The Role of Business in Sustainable Consumption. *Journal of Cleaner Production*, 11(8), 915–921.

Ministry of Environment Norway (1994) *Report of the Oslo Ministerial Roundtable*. Oslo: Ministry of the Environment.

Meyer, J. (2015) *Engaging the Everyday*. Cambridge: MIT.

Nussbaum, M. (1992) Human Functioning and Social Justice. *Political Theory*, 20(2), 202–246.

OECD (2002) *Towards Sustainable Household Consumption?* Paris: OECD.

OECD (2008) *Promoting Sustainable Consumption*. Paris: OECD.

Princen, T. (1999) Consumption and Environment. *Ecological Economics*, 31(3), 347–363.

Pullinger, M. (2014) Work Time Reduction Policy in a Sustainable Economy. *Ecological Economics*, 103, 11–19.

Raworth, K. (2012) A Safe and Just Space for Humanity. *Oxfam discussion Paper*. Oxford: Oxfam.

Rockström, J., Steffen, W., Noone, K., Persson, Å., Chapin, F. S., Lambin, E., Lenton, T. M., Scheffer, M., Folke, C., Schellnhuber, H., Nykvist, B., De Wit, C. A., Hughes, T., van der Leeuw, S., Rodhe, H., Sörlin, S., Snyder, P. K., Costanza, R., Svedin, U., Falkenmark, M., Karlberg, L., Corell, R. W., Fabry, V. J., Hansen, J., Walker, B., Liverman, D., Richardson, K., Crutzen, P. & Foley, J. (2009) Planetary Boundaries: Exploring the Safe Operating Space for Humanity. *Ecology and Society*, 14(2), 32.

Røpke, I. (1999) The Dynamics of Willingness to Consume. *Ecological Economics*, 28, 399–420.

Schlosberg, D. & Coles, R. (2016) The New Environmentalism of Everyday Life. *Contemporary Political Theory*, 15(2), 160–181.

Schor, J. (1999) *The Overspent American*. New York, NY: Harper Paperbacks.

Schor, J. & Fitzmaurice, C. (2015) Collaborating and Connecting, in Reisch, L. & Thogersen, J. (eds), *Handbook of Research on Sustainable Consumption*. Cheltenham: Edward Elgar, 410–425.

Sen, A. (1993) Capability and Well-Being, in Nussbaum, M. & Sen, A. (eds), *The Quality of Life*. Oxford: Clarendon, 30–54.

Spangenberg, J. (2002) Environmental Space and the Prism of Sustainability. *Ecological Indicators*, 2(4), 295–309.

United Nations (UN) (1992) *Earth Summit: Agenda 21*. New York, NY: UN.

United Nations (UN) (2012) *The Future We Want*. New York, NY: UN.

United Nations (UN) (2015) *Transforming Our World: The 2030 Agenda for a Sustainable Development*. New York, NY: UN.

UN DESA (2003) *United Nations Guidelines for Consumer Protection (as Expanded in 1999)*. New York, NY: UN.

UNEP (2001) *Consumption Opportunities*. Paris: UNEP.

UNEP (2016) *The 10-Year Framework of Programmes on Sustainable Consumption and Production*. Paris: UNEP.

Warde, A. (2017) *Consumption*. London: Palgrave.

WBCSD (2002) *Sustainable Production and Consumption*. Geneva: WBCSD.

WBCSD (2008) *Sustainable Consumption Facts and Trends from a Business Perspective*. Geneva: WBCSD.

WBCSD (2017) *Announcing Factor10: Delivering innovative, scalable solutions for the circular economy.* Available at: www.wbcsd.org/Clusters/Circular-Economy/News/Announcing-Factor10 (last accessed 17/01/2018).

International environmental and ecological justice

6

*Timothy Ehresman and
Dimitris Stevis*

Models of climate change show that the developing world (the 'South') – already pressed to feed and support growing populations – will likely be impacted the worst by global warming. Yet it is the rich, already industrialized countries (the 'North') who have historically been the highest greenhouse gas (GHG) emitters (see e.g. Ciplet et al. 2015). Consider another scenario: In order to meet the global demand for palm oil – one of the most common tropical vegetable oils produced – large tracts of forest land in developing countries have been, and continue to be, cleared to make way for commercial, large-scale palm oil plantations. The effects of this growing investment in commercially-significant land have included the displacement of indigenous peoples from their land and subsistence forms of agriculture and, in many cases, the diversion of the profits and benefits of commercial activity away from local populations to foreign corporations (see e.g. Schleifer 2016; Vandergeten et al. 2016).

Scholars in the field of international relations have, for some time, raised concerns regarding the fairness and moral urgency of these and other problems in global environmental politics. And, as scholarly work on global environmental issues, initiatives, and institutions has advanced over time, the concept of justice has become central to the broader environmental policy debates. Motivated by this growing significance of justice and equity for global environmental politics, this chapter offers a historical and analytical overview of international environmental justice (IEJ). We start with a brief clarification of the concept of IEJ. This is followed by a historical outline of the treatment of IEJ by international relations scholars. The main part of the chapter then presents an overview of IEJ based on an analytical scheme that we have found useful.

In any consideration of the contours and potential of IEJ as a body of scholarship and source of advocacy, the threshold question that must be asked is 'Why justice?' That is, isn't it enough that we have already identified specific moral values and obligations with respect to the environment that render particular states of affairs and specific dimensions of human activity as arguably good or bad? In fact, as discussed below, justice as a concern and theme accentuates and places in starker relief the urgency of addressing environmental access and effects.

As a general matter, justice is not usually applied to identify an action or inaction as right or wrong per se. As argued by Barry (1989), while we commonly would hold crimes such as murder to be culpable – even insane – we generally would not characterize such actions as 'unjust.' This is because justice involves circumstances imbued with some particular relationship, debt or entitlement between, or among, two or more persons or entities, the violation of which triggers a sense of 'unfairness' to the aggrieved party or parties.

Once we have agreed and determined that the notion of justice is an important and applicable concept in global environmental politics, we need to understand the specific implications of such a move. First, where justice is held to pertain, the weight and depth of obligation on the part of those in a position to extend or withhold justice is measurably intensified (e.g. Baxter 2000). For instance, when national leaders fail to engage pressing issues of environmental degradation within their borders, they can be criticized on the grounds that they 'should' pay more attention to them. But, where their inaction is held to be unjust, they can be criticized for not doing what they 'must' do and, as a result, be accused of failing both a moral *and* quasi-legal obligation.

This leads to the second, and perhaps most important, ramification of applying a justice standard to a particular problem setting. That is, whenever we argue that someone has an obligation to act in accordance with justice, we invest those affected with a specific right and a defensible expectation that the obligation must be respected. This is so even if the recipients cannot themselves defend that right or secure its application by political or legal force. A commonly offered example is that we accord full human rights to children and the infirm, even though they themselves are not able to exercise or defend those rights. Thus, applying a standard of IEJ highlights and strengthens the accountability and responsibility of states, transnational corporations, and other environmental actors in ways that positing only a moral obligation does not.

In this chapter, we use the terms 'environmental justice' and 'environmental equity' interchangeably. Some scholars differ over who is best served by using one term or the other. We note that, in most of the literature surveyed for this chapter and in the conduct of global environmental politics, the terms are used interchangeably, and thus, we have elected to bypass this debate.

Historical overview of international environmental justice

The history of IEJ is best understood as progressing both as part of the global environmental politics literature and as part of the practice of global environmental politics itself. Moreover, while this chapter focuses mostly on international relations scholarship there are also important contributors to the development and debates about IEJ from other disciplines such as economics, sociology, philosophy, and geography.

In 1972, the United Nations (UN) convened a landmark conference on the environment: the UN Conference on the Human Environment, held in Stockholm, Sweden. Observers disagree as to the extent to which Stockholm effectively addressed issues of North–South equity, but it is indisputably the case that the South viewed the proceedings through the lens of justice in identifying the industry and lifestyles of the affluent North as the primary sources of environmental degradation in the South.

Scholarly, and even popular, sentiment regarding a pending global environmental crisis was further propelled at this time by the scarcity discourse, seminally presented in the Club of Rome's 1972 *The Limits to Growth* (Meadows et al. 1972). This report raised the specter of an overpopulated and resource-spent earth no longer capable of sustaining a healthy and satisfactory human existence. The global environmental politics literature and community during this period were not, however, explicitly focused on issues of equity, although as early as 1971, scholars such as Falk (1971) and those associated with the World Order Models Project began raising concern within academic circles regarding the inequality and unsustainability of then-prevailing global environmental practices and proposals. In the decade which followed, the push for equity included the World Commission on Environment and Development (WCED 1987), with its landmark report *Our Common Future*, framing questions of environmental justice as global issues.

At this time, environmental justice also became an important issue nationally and in the USA, in particular. Concern for environmental justice served as the central motivator and organizing driver for the 1974 founding of the Eco-Justice Project and Network at Cornell University, creating a forum and vehicle for action for those whose environmental concerns were significantly founded in the Judaeo–Christian tradition and biblical calls for stewarding the creation (Gibson 2004). Environmental ethics kept growing during that period, leading to the launching of the journal by the same name in 1979. In 1977, the United Automobile Workers organized the first national Environmental Justice Conference, bringing together workers, community activists, and environmentalists. In 1982, the state of North Carolina proposed to construct a PCB disposal site in its Warren County, a move ultimately approved by the US Environmental Protection Agency (EPA). Warren County was primarily poor and African American, and a sense of unfairness mushroomed as local residents took to the streets in protest. Many were imprisoned. Warren County ultimately did get the PCB dump, but the move to expose this sort of environmental 'injustice' was on.

Parallel to the global and national politics of seeking a synthesis between development and environment, a number of political philosophers began to open up notional space for the concept of IEJ. These include Miller (1976) and his book on social justice, Barry's (1989, 1995) work on theories of justice, and Wenz's (1988) treatise on environmental justice. Also of note was the extension by many of the egalitarian approach of Rawls (1971/1999) to the international sphere as a matter of global justice generally (e.g. Barry *supra*). Indeed, the impact of Rawls' work on subsequent developments concerning justice in the international sphere is hard to overstate. These authors continue to be cited as sources of authority and conceptual clarity in formulating the philosophical basis for IEJ (e.g. Dobson 1998; Hurrell 2002). It was not until the late 1980s, however, that international relations scholars addressed IEJ as an important component of global environmental politics; for example, a book by Weiss (1989). Weiss' work can be considered an important turning point but focused on obligations to future generations as distinct from questions of intra-generational justice (on intra-generational justice, see e.g. Agarwal and Narain 1991). As evidence of emerging concerns with power and exploitation, during that same period the newly founded journal *Capitalism, Nature, Socialism* (1988–) provided a forum for addressing issues of environmental equity from a historical materialist point of view. Finally, various environmental ethicists argued that we should move beyond considerations of human rights to also consider the rights of nature, thus providing the foundations for what has been termed 'ecological justice'.

IEJ received focused attention at the 1992 UN Conference on Environment and Development, held in Rio de Janeiro, Brazil ('Rio'). Several of the products of the conference, for example the Convention on Biological Diversity, the UN Framework Convention on Climate Change, The Rio Declaration on Environment and Development, and Rio's sustainable development global action plan – Agenda 21, expressly included formal provisions concerning international environmental equity. Though the end result of Rio was a determined attempt to simultaneously accommodate economic development and environmental protection, the politics associated with it catalyzed a sustained concern for IEJ amongst academics and practitioners. Following Rio, a flurry of attention to the issue ensued (e.g. Shue 1992; Harvey 1996; Wapner 1997; Hampson and Reppy 1996).

The third UN conference on development and the environment – the World Summit on Sustainable Development (WSSD) – was held in Johannesburg, South Africa, in 2002. While some commentators lauded the results of the WSSD, principally for its advances in public/private partnerships for the environment and/or for the Conference's more substantive engagement with questions regarding the 'social' dimension of IEJ, others noted that, by this time, the demands for development were coming to eclipse environmental concerns, blunting somewhat the clarity of vision present at the 1992 Rio Conference (e.g. Conca and Dabelko 2015). Following the WSSD, however, a number of works emerged explicitly dealing with IEJ as a core concept within the global environmental politics literature, including works by Anand (2004), Martinez-Alier (2002), Okereke (2008), and Schlosberg (2007).

The fourth UN conference on the environment ('Rio+20', formally entitled the UN Conference on Sustainable Development) was held in Rio de Janeiro in the summer of 2012. Its goals were to strengthen commitments to sustainable development and to explore the environmental and economic benefits of a shift to a more 'green economy.' However, the conference failed to produce significant outcomes. Indeed, in a public statement shortly after the conclusion of the conference, some UN officials conceded that the intersecting and potentially conflicting interests of economic development, on the one hand, and environmental protection, on the other, may not be fully resolvable in a global, multilateral forum (United Nations 2012).

Despite a sense among some of disillusionment with global initiatives and gatherings, a growing concern and sense of alarm among states and non-state actors regarding the threats presented by climate change have resulted in a noteworthy level of global consensus and commitment. The December 2015 Paris Conference (the 21st Conference of the Parties to the 1992 UN Framework Convention on Climate Change) witnessed an unprecedented level of international cooperation on a shared environmental issue, as over 190 countries – importantly including India and China – committed to the Paris Agreement and its provisions regarding reducing greenhouse gas emissions. While the body of the Paris Agreement does not seek to explicitly promote the issue of environmental justice and fairness among states, a vocal assembly of advocates and scholars continues to press on the centrality and importance of IEJ in the realm of climate change mitigation and adaptation (see e.g. Klinsky et al. 2017). Indeed, the issue of climate change has of late attracted, and continues to attract, a significant amount of scholarly work on 'climate justice' – the fairness question raised at the outset of this chapter. Examples of this coalescence in the justice literature include works authored or edited by Gardiner et al. (2010), Harris (2010, 2011, 2016), Schlosberg (2012), Schlosberg et al. (2017), Ciplet et al. (2015), and Shue (2014). And the prominent journal *Environmental Politics* published a special issue on climate justice in 2013 (Vol. 22/Issue 3).

Attention to IEJ has today expanded into a focus on specific issues such as 'energy justice' (e.g. Heffron and McCauley 2017; Newell and Mulvaney 2013; Farrell 2012), 'food justice' (e.g. Magdoff and Tokar 2010), and 'climate justice', noted above; see also Schlosberg 2013). It is also worth noting that work on IEJ is taken up not only in the international relations literature, but also in other fields such as geography (e.g. Bakker 2010), public health (e.g. Lambert Colomeda 1999), and environmental sociology (e.g. Pellow 2007). Neo-Marxist sociologists such as Ted Benton (1999) and O'Connor (1998) have left their mark on IEJ, as have the more recent works of sociologists Rice (2007), Andrew Jorgenson (2006), Behrens et al. (2007), and Foster et al. (2010). While the terminology may be different, such as the use within sociology of the term 'ecological unequal exchange' to refer to breaches of IEJ in North–South relations, the focus is the same.

The literature on international environmental justice

We now turn to a consideration of the theoretical basis and content of the present state of scholarship, thought, and debate in the field of IEJ. In what follows, we employ a heuristic typology that reflects the diversity of the origins and concerns of the scholarship on IEJ and allows us to present the growing literature in a systematic way. The categories in the typology reflect differences among scholars in political and environmental worldviews, varying foci with respect to the scale and scope of IEJ, and also the impact of differing fundamental ontologies with respect to international relations theory.

One way to categorize thought on IEJ is as intra-generational or inter-generational. That is, intra-generational work on IEJ concentrated on addressing relations and impacts among nation states and peoples today (e.g. Dobson 1998), while the inter-generational literature urged a considered way forward today because of our obligations to future generations (e.g. Wenz 1988). It is not sufficient, however, to stop with this distinction because, over the years, there has emerged significant underlying work that looks at intra-generational and inter-generational justice issues from different theoretical perspectives. We capture this diversity by employing conceptual labels helpfully applied first by Hopwood et al. (2005) to categorize varying approaches to the term 'sustainable development'. These labels are: 'status quo environmental justice', 'reformist environmental justice', and 'transformational environmental justice'. We add a fourth, and perhaps our most inclusive, category:

'ecological justice' (akin to Hopwood's et al. 'eco-centered justice' category) to capture views that accord significant ontological and moral standing to nature (see Table 6.1).

Three caveats are in order: First, while we here identify ecological justice as its own strand of understanding environmental fairness and equity, none of the environmental justice approaches can escape rendering judgments on the human–nature relationship. At a minimum, there is within each environmental justice approach an explicit or implicit view on the relationship between humanity and nature. Second, each of our four approaches accomplishes and represents the fusion of a particular strand of social justice theory with both environmental and ecological justice. Thus, each of the four approaches reflects – also unavoidably – a particular stylized solution to social injustice and inequality (Hopwood et al. 2005). And third, in the text which follows, we employ the terms 'liberal' and 'neoliberal' to identify and differentiate varying perspectives and arguments concerning the human–nature relationship. In so doing, we are not referring to 'liberal' vs 'conservative' distinctions within domestic politics in the United States or UK, for example. Rather, we are referring to a distinctive body of thought and set of perspectives which originated in and spread from Europe from the 18th century onward. In its most basic expression, liberalism advocates for political and economic freedoms, founded significantly in the rightful autonomy of humans as individuals. In its classical form, liberalism calls for democracy in the political realm and free markets in the economic realm, but not without qualification. Many liberals in this strand would contend that some regulation of markets is desirable and necessary, for example in view of the potential environmental impacts of unregulated industry and the possibility that economic liberalism may generate issues of distributive inequity and unfairness. 'Neoliberalism' is a more recent and aggressive promotion of the market model, generating a distinctive strand of liberalism in advocating that, to the maximum extent possible, markets should be allowed to operate free of governmental interference. Arising in the United States and Britain in the 1980s, neoliberalism retains its own set of convictions regarding the positive potential of market freedom to lead to reduced environmental damage over the long haul. We will examine the ramifications of this 'liberal'–'neoliberal' distinction further in the literature review which follows.

Taking each approach separately, then, views in the status quo environmental justice category advance arguments that are founded on deliberative processes that privilege human needs, wants, and ingenuity in the process of securing environmental protection. In this category, environmental concerns are formulated more narrowly – that is, they generally reflect the acceptance of existing national and global institutions and regimes to deal with environmental issues and justice. While not the only conceivable demarcation, our conception of the status quo category centrally includes views that are concerned with the allocation of IEJ.

The reformist environmental justice perspective includes those points of view which contend that appropriate and necessary environmental protections will not be accomplished absent attendant concerns for broader social and economic issues. In particular, the reformist approach looks to ways we can enact reform within prevailing economic systems and structures to achieve a greater level of environmental justice.

The transformational environmental justice approaches contend that a sufficient level of reform will not be attained within the existing system. In this approach, effectively

Table 6.1 The international environmental justice literature

Categories of justice	Views on justice			
	Status quo environmental justice	Reformist environmental justice	Transformational environmental justice	Ecological justice
Environmental injustice	The maldistribution of environmental burdens and benefits, and decision-making authority	Features of and policies within the existing global capitalist system which obstruct a reform-directed distribution of the benefits of economic growth and resource use	Inherent and systemic barriers, distortions, and power disparities which impact environmental effects and access, and which cannot be addressed by internal reform and distribution alone	Privileging human needs and wants with no, or insufficient, regard for the needs of non-human nature
Environmental justice	Fair allocation of environmental benefits and burdens within rules of dominant political economy	The equitable distribution of environmental harms and benefits through reforms	The minimization of environmental harms and a more equitable distribution of harms and benefits through deep changes in political economy	The minimization of harms, and the equitable distribution of harms and benefits amongst humans and nature

addressing environmental concerns must go beyond distributive concerns, must implicate issues of social welfare and capacity, and must also be directed to address structural impediments to these social goods.

Finally, in the ecological justice view, nature must be valued in its own right. The importance of human needs must be counter-balanced by the equally-important needs of non-human nature. While much work within the category of ecological justice finds a real symbiosis with the transformational approach, prioritizing nature may also find a home in less radical thought. By way of illustrating the necessary link between each of our first three approaches and ecological justice, guarding non-human nature may result, in some cases, in deleterious impacts on justice among humans. In particular, making standing for nature paramount may in fact generate social injustices among peoples, including the forcible displacement of indigenous peoples due to the creation of wilderness areas, national parks, game preserves, and even commercial plantations aimed at sequestering carbon (see e.g. discussion in Stevis and Felli 2016).

Plainly, work on IEJ does not always fit so neatly into only one of these categories, and many scholars and issues indeed cross our gridlines in their work. Nonetheless, the categorizations which follow do trace the broad outlines of the different approaches to IEJ. The discussions which follow are not intended to be exhaustive with respect to the literature in each category, but rather provide key examples of the views represented therein.

Status quo environmental justice

The most characteristic approach within this category is the classical liberal (though, as discussed below, not necessarily neoliberal) approach to IEJ (cf. Richardson 2001). The focus is on distributive justice, and the elemental unit of concern is the individual and his or her political and economic rights and liberties. At a system level, this form of liberalism seeks environmental solutions which are largely consistent with support for democratic political structures, free markets, and largely autonomous global economic relations (see also Herman, Chapter 9). Much of the literature surveyed for this chapter supports, to some degree, liberalism so construed (e.g. Beckerman 1999; Achterberg 2001; Lal 2002; Wissenburg 2006; Frankel 2009; Morvaridi 2008). This is due both to principle – the widespread acceptance of the liberal political and economic model – and to practicality – the advocacy of liberal approaches even by those who call for more radical solutions globally, resigned in the belief that deep changes to the global capitalist system will not likely be forthcoming anytime soon.

Scholars in this category call for allocational solutions such as a broader public discourse and a moral consensus on environmental justice – a stronger procedural justice; an attendant increased role for, and decision making access by, civil society; strengthened international institutions; stronger domestic and international law on the environment, including international treaties and agreements to protect humans and the environment; and domestic and international constitutional measures and provisions that will enshrine the rights of humans to a clean and safe environment. In this approach, what is needed is not a rejection of the current global system, but the infusing of current discourse and practice with environmental sensitivities which will drive changes in policies, institutional mandates and operations, and increase stakeholder participation. The ethos of the status quo approach is visible in literature emphasizing the need for emerging environmental perspectives which are substantively 'pragmatic' rather than 'doctrinaire'. In this posited pragmatic approach, our aspirations are tempered by accepting the reality that we have already passed by earlier environmentalists' visions of what a 'sustainable' society would entail and look like. Indeed, the very meaning and content of 'nature' have been altered by the interaction of human society with nature, rendering a wide range of possible visions for a 'sustainable' society, to be debated and considered in societies which are fundamentally democratic (see e.g. Arias-Maldonado 2013; see also discussion of 'post-nature' environmental politics in Wapner 2014).

Some liberals take a highly optimistic approach to global environmental issues, arguing, for example, that the earth's resources will likely be sufficient to meet present and future human needs and that the carrying capacity limits argued for in reports – such as *The Limits to Growth* – are overstated. This is what is termed the 'Promethean' or 'cornucopian' view of the human–nature relationship. We focus on it here, along with the neoliberal economics it propounds, because of the ways in which these views differ from the classical liberal approach, and because of the global dominance of neoliberal views over the past three or so decades (see e.g. discussion in Byrne and Glover 2002).

Where scarcity may impinge on human development, our ever-advancing technological capacities will, in this view, certainly provide answers and tools which permit us to abate harmful environmental effects and extend or replace limited resources. Early advocates of this view include Simon (1984) and Easterbrook (1995). Bjørn Lomborg, who published *The Skeptical Environmentalist* in 2001, is perhaps the best known contemporary advocate. He is the head of the Copenhagen Consensus, a think tank of well-known economists (including a majority of Nobel Laureates), who have met periodically to assign priorities to global initiatives, including environmental concerns. Most controversially, these scholars determine issue priority on the basis of a monetary cost–benefit analysis of the measurable impact of a particular initiative.

As to justice, the growth ethos of the Promethean view matches well with neoliberal economic and political policies to minimize government intervention in the operations of private markets, and to accord individuals the maximum economic liberty and latitude possible. Here, the work of Hayek (1976) and Friedman (1962) is central in founding the arguments that social justice and well-being will be best served not by the intervention of governing authorities, but rather by free market economic development (e.g. Bhagwati 2004; see also discussion in Bernauer and Nguyen 2015 and Chasek et al. 2006). In this view, the main drivers of environmental degradation are poverty, a lack of economic growth, and governmental policies such as subsidies and tariffs which distort the ability of trade dynamism to guide the economy and society towards the most sustainable use of resources (World Trade Organization Secretariat 1997; Organisation for Economic Cooperation and Development 2001; see also discussion in Clapp and Dauvergne 2011).

As to environmental justice, this approach draws on concepts such as the Environmental 'Kuznets Curve'. Applied first to income inequality, this principle is extended by neoliberals and cornucopians to environmental degradation, which is the argument that, while early industrialization will inevitably create harmful environmental externalities, as industrial society advances and matures, the will and resources to address negative environmental effects will strengthen and come to prevail (Desai 1998; see also discussion in Youssef et al. 2016 and in Clapp 2006).

The more classical forms of liberalism do extend the distributive dimension of the environmental justice movement in the United States, described above, into North–South relations. More specifically, much of this literature is concerned with the maldistribution of environmental burdens upon the global poor and economically vulnerable communities (e.g. Shue 1999). By way of illustration, some scholars raise the issue of the justness of transboundary shipment of waste North to South, including electronic waste and hazardous waste in particular (e.g. Lucier and Gareau 2016; Renckens 2015; Pickren 2014; Shrader-Frechette 2002; Pellow 2007).

Reformist environmental justice

In the reformist IEJ approach, we cannot settle for distributive justice alone but must also address the very operation of the contemporary global economic and political system. Social rights and impacts become important as we move away from the more narrow (status quo) neoliberal preoccupation with economic rights and effects (see e.g. discussion in Ioris 2012). However, in the discussion which follows we caution that there is an important risk here; namely that, in the pursuit of social improvements, the environment may be forgotten.

We note here that not all liberals would consider themselves neoliberals, in particular because of the extent to, and means by, which economic neoliberalism (referred to by many as the 'Washington Consensus') has operated over the past 30 or so years (e.g. discussion in Kymlicka 1996; Agarwal et al. 2002; Morvaridi 2008). It is the case that classical liberalism, in its early iteration, reflected a strong moral commitment to the weaker members of society and those who were victims of modernity and progress (Low and Gleeson 2001). Indeed, in its initial formulation, liberalism did not hold private property to be inviolate, but to be defended and upheld only where enough was left in common for others.

Foundational to liberal reform in IEJ, recent scholars such as Amartya Sen, Martha Nussbaum, and Joseph Stiglitz contend for understandings of justice which, while situated in a liberal political and economic structures, shift focus onto elements of existence and flourishing that extend beyond an abbreviated concern with the health of private markets. In the case of Sen, a Nobel Laureate, and Nussbaum, what matters is that the individual has the freedom and liberty to pursue an array of publicly-deliberated (Sen) or specified (Nussbaum) basic capabilities which encompass not only obtaining sustenance needs such as food and shelter, but also higher order capabilities such as being able to earn a sufficient income and the capacity to participate meaningfully in the life of the community (Sen 1999; Nussbaum 2000). This approach goes beyond concern with the distribution of material goods, for – as both Sen and Nussbaum argue – income and economic wealth are not always the best indicators of overall well-being (see also discussion in Marion Suiseeya 2014; Davoudi and Brooks 2014). Income distribution is still important, but it is the possession of, and freedom to exercise, capabilities to make meaningful use of income as well as other resources that should be distributed by government first and foremost.

While it is not above challenge (e.g. Page 2006), the capabilities approach is applied directly to issues of IEJ in works by Schlosberg (2007, 2014) (see also the work of Johnson 2012; Lyster 2017). These scholars, in arguing for liberal reform, assess the issue of IEJ in the context of human capabilities. Schlosberg argues that, in many cases, the environmental impact of the neoliberal global economy directly and unjustly limits the exercise of a full range of not only economic but also social and cultural capabilities by the global poor. In this regard, distributive justice alone – even the redistribution of environmental goods and bads – will not suffice because there may be underlying, and thereby unaddressed, systemic reasons for the maldistribution in the first place.

Stiglitz (2006) is critical of neoliberals who appealed to market forces, privatization, and deregulation to address poverty in the South (see also discussion in Fuentes-George 2013). Stiglitz' proposed 'post-Washington Consensus' retains liberal governance but adds the importance of the role of the state and international consortia in regulating global markets, reforming key international institutions like the IMF, and remedying what he calls the global 'democratic deficit' by developing a broader, more focused, and more inclusive discursive arena, both within and outside international organizations and sovereign states. These and other measures are essential if we are to effectively reform globalization, which among other benefits realized, will in Stiglitz' view facilitate managing and preserving global environmental resources and commons.

Relatedly, while not challenging the importance of free markets and trade at a fundamental level, the 'ecological modernization' approach argues nonetheless that reform of political and economic institutions and relations, and sparing use of regulatory restraints on trade and commercial activity, are necessary to address environmental degradation (e.g. Mol 2002; Payne 2005).

Some authors in this strand provide explicit accountings of the sorts of values and concepts that IEJ requires. These commonly include the employment of precepts such as 'common but differentiated responsibility' as between North and South, state rights to determine their own environmental conditions, including control over their own natural resources, a minimum level of economic, political, and social development, the right to be compensated for environmental damage caused by another state, the precautionary principle, and the polluter pays principle (e.g. Anand 2004).

Transformational environmental justice

Some environmental scholars of a more critical view argue, for example, that if IEJ is to be meaningfully realized, nothing short of a new world order and government will suffice. Others contend that, at a minimum, the drivers of global injustice inherent in the very structure of the global economy must be addressed if we are to impose the burdens of environmental mitigation on those most responsible for environmental degradation (e.g. Parr 2012; Newell 2012; Martinez-Alier 2002). Critical environmental scholars also commonly envision and argue for a more inclusive and democratic global arena and community of discourse and consensus regarding global environmental issues, with a particular emphasis on including the global weak and poor (e.g. Hampson and Reppy 1996; Harvey 1996; Reus-Smit 1996).

Critical scholars may also take on a less apocalyptic approach. Scholars such as de-Shalit (2000) contend instead for the democratic accession of a more pervasive egalitarianism. Capitalist society is, in this view, incapable of dealing with the disparate ecological distribution of benefits and burdens in a manner that moves us towards effective environmental management. For these advocates, neoliberalism is wholly inadequate to address the rapidly expanding universe of global environmental concerns and issues regarding environmental fairness and equity (e.g. Fuentes-George 2013; Böhm et al. 2012; Harvey 1996; Stevis 2005; Parks and Roberts 2006). The environmental Kuznets Curve is challenged in that increased industrial production will inevitably produce increased emissions (e.g. Kütting 2004; see also discussion in Lin et al. (2016) and Dinda (2004)). Indeed, what is needed is not more production but greater social and environmental justice. Global environmental issues and problems are both environmental *and* social (e.g. Agyeman 2013; Taylor and Buttel 1992; Benton 1999; Newell 2007).

Ecological justice

The ecological justice approach argues that what is at stake is not only the impact of negative environmental effects upon humans but also the negative environmental impacts of humans upon nature. This view contends directly with the anthropocentric tendencies of even a more socially progressive environmental discourse, programs, and politics. The term 'ecological justice' is commonly attributed to a 1998 work by Nicholas Low and Brendan Gleeson, but as early as 1948, Aldo Leopold published the *Sand County Almanac*, in which he laid the foundation for the ecological justice movement by arguing that we must expand our moral community to include the natural world (Leopold 1968/1948). And, in 1973, Norwegian philosopher Arne Naess gave formal voice and standing to the contemporary case for ecological justice, advanced in his essay as what he termed 'deep ecology' – an approach ascribing moral status to not only sentient nature but also to the non-sentient (1973).

The questioning of existing structures and hierarchies in this arena of discourse may have the same intellectual roots as the more critical views previously considered, and the following analysis centers on these views. We do note, however, that some liberal scholars, such as Bell (2006), argue that liberal thought can also advocate for an ecological justice understanding. The difference here, for both liberals and critical theorists, is that what is sought is not primarily justice for humans but justice for nature.

As in the arenas we have previously considered, issues such as according rights to other than humans alive today are problematic for some observers (see e.g. discussion in Baxter 2005). For our purposes here, however, we include points of view which contend that there are defensible rational reasons for extending moral standing to non-human nature. We note the importance of a body of related eco-feminist literature, which posits a connection between the domination of women and the deleterious dominance of nature (see e.g. Plumwood 2006; Mies and Shiva 1993). In their focus on the environmental effects of traditional societal norms in the arena of gender, these scholars find a useful symbiosis with other strands of critical theory noted above.

In these perspectives, nature is not only instrumentally, but intrinsically and objectively, valuable. However, while more extreme forms of ecological justice argue that there is absolute moral equivalence between animals and humans, other ecological justice advocates contend for principles to mediate conflicting claims; for example, the conflicting interests of a small sleeping child on the one hand and those of a rattlesnake coiled under the child's bed on the other. These less stringent views allow for a continuum of the strength of moral claims among human and non-human nature (e.g. Low and Gleeson 1998; and discussion in Baxter 2000). Nonetheless, the vision here is that non-human nature will be subject to contemporaneous flourishing in the acceptance of its overall moral significance (e.g. Byrne et al. 2002; Roberts 2003). One can even extend the human capabilities approach to non-human nature, contending that animals, for example, retain a range of entitlements to life and the enjoyment of sentience (e.g. Schlosberg 2007, 2014).

In this approach, the specific activities of global trade and investment are seen by many as principal barriers to ecological justice in the South. Indeed, in the view of such advocates, sustainable development is merely a tool of the North, which uses the concept to perpetuate the hegemony of its corporate interests and markets. Thus, for these scholars, the concerns of ecological justice cannot be addressed in the current capitalist global system (e.g. Faber and McCarthy 2003; Diefenbacher 2006).

Conclusion

We hope it is evident in the foregoing analysis that international environmental and ecological justice have risen to quite high levels of sophistication, conceptual clarity, and visibility among those who would seek to apply the tools and concepts of global environmental politics to particular environmental and ecological problems, issues, and policies. Yet, there is much room for new contributions by scholars and advocates in each of the issue and literature fields we have covered, perhaps most usefully across the various issues we have surveyed. And some of the most important debates and advocacy within IEJ will be found in the emerging work of those in the South, including the efforts of those contending for justice for indigenous peoples.

Our greatest ambition for this chapter, then, is that it serve as the beginning of an ongoing engagement by the reader with the potential of the concept of justice to define and refine our understanding of, and relating with, the human and non-human global 'others'. We include a suggested reading list below, some in addition to the works mentioned in the text, to that end.

Recommended reading

Agyeman, J., Bullard, R. D. & Evans, B. (eds), (2003) *Just Sustainabilities: Development in an Unequal World*. Cambridge, MA: The MIT Press.

Carmin, J. & Agyeman, J. (eds), (2011) *Environmental Inequalities Beyond Borders: Local Perspectives on Global Injustices*. Cambridge, MA: The MIT Press.

Dobson, A. (1998) *Justice and the Environment*. Oxford: Oxford University Press.

Okereke, C. (2008) *Global Justice and Neoliberal Environmental Governance: Ethics, Sustainable Development and International Co-operation*. New York: Routledge.

Schlosberg, D. (2007) *Defining Environmental Justice*. Oxford: Oxford University Press.

References

Achterberg, W. (2001) Environmental Justice and Global Democracy, in Gleeson, B. & Low, N. (eds), *Governing for the Environment: Global Problems, Ethics and Democracy*. New York: Palgrave Publishers Ltd.

Agarwal, A. & Narain, S. (1991) *Global Warming in an Unequal World: A Case of Environmental Colonialism*. New Delhi: Centre for Science and Environment.

Agarwal, A., Sunita, N. & Sharma, A. (2002) The Global Commons and Environmental Justice—Climate Change, in Byrne, J., Glover, L. & Martinez, C. (eds), *Environmental Justice: Discourses in International Political Economy, Energy and Environmental Policy*. New Brunswick: Transaction Publishers.

Agyeman, J. (2013) *Introducing Just Sustainabilities: Policy, Planning, and Practice*. London: Zed Books.

Anand, R. (2004) *International Environmental Justice: A North-South Dimension*. Hampshire: Ashgate Publishing Limited.

Arias-Maldonado, M. (2013) Rethinking Sustainability in the Anthropocene. *Environmental Politics*, 22(3), 428–446.

Bakker, K. (2010) The Limits of 'Neoliberal Natures': Debating Green Neoliberalism. *Progress in Human Geography*, 34(6), 715–735.

Barry, B. (1989) *Theories of Justice, I*. Berkeley: University of California Press.

Barry, B. (1995) *Justice as Impartiality*. Oxford: Clarendon Press.

Baxter, B. H. (2000) Ecological Justice and Justice as Impartiality. *Environmental Politics*, 9(9), 43–64.

Baxter, B. H. (2005) *A Theory of Ecological Justice*. London: Routledge.

Beckerman, W. (1999) Sustainable Development and Our Obligations to Future Generations, in Dobson, A. (ed.), *Fairness and Futurity: Essays on Environmental Sustainability and Social Justice*. Oxford: Oxford University Press.

Behrens, A., Giljum, S., Kovanda, J. & Niza, S. (2007) The Material Basis of the Global Economy: Worldwide Patterns of Natural Resource Extraction and Their Implications for Sustainable Resource Use Policies. *Ecological Economics*, 64(2), 444–453.

Bell, D. R. (2006) Political Liberalism and Ecological Justice. *Analyse & Kritik*, 28(2), 206–222.

Benton, T. (1999) Sustainable Development and the Accumulation of Capital: Reconciling the Irreconcilable? in Dobson, A. (ed.), *Fairness and Futurity: Essays on Environmental Sustainability and Social Justice*. Oxford: Oxford University Press.

Bernauer, T. & Nguyen, Q. (2015) Free Trade and/or Environmental Protection? *Global Environmental Politics*, 15(4), 105–129.

Bhagwati, J. (2004) *In Defense of Globalization*. Oxford: Oxford University Press.

Böhm, S., Misoczky, M. & Moog, S. (2012) Greening Capitalism? A Marxist Critique of Carbon Markets. *Organization Studies*, 33(11), 1617–1638.

Byrne, J. & Glover, L. (2002) A Common Future or Towards a Future Commons: Globalization and Sustainable Development since UNCED. *International Review for Environmental Strategies*, 3(1), 5–25.

Byrne, J., Glover, L. & Martinez, C. (2002) The Production of Unequal Nature, in Byrne, J., Glover, L. & Martinez, C. (eds), *Environmental Justice: Discourses in International Political Economy, Energy and Environmental Policy*. New Brunswick: Transaction Publishers.

Chasek, P. S., Downie, D. L. & Brown, J. W. (2006) *Global Environmental Politics*. Boulder: Westview Press.

Ciplet, D., Roberts, J. T. & Khan, M. R. (2015) *Power in a Warming World: The New Global Politics of Climate Change and the Remaking of Environmental Inequality*. Cambridge, MA: Massachusetts Institute of Technology.

Clapp, J. (2006) International Political Economy and the Environment, in Betsill, M. M., Hochstetler, K. & Stevis, D. (eds), *International Environmental Politics*. New York: Palgrave Macmillan.

Clapp, J. & Dauvergne, P. (2011) *Paths to a Green World: The Political Economy of the Global Environment*, 2nd edition. Cambridge, MA: The MIT Press.

Conca, K. & Dabelko, G. D. (2015) Introduction: Three Decades of Global Environmental Politics, in Conca, K. & Dabelko, G. D. (eds), *Green Planet Blues: Environmental Politics from Stockholm to Johannesburg*. 5th edition. Boulder: Westview Press.

Davoudi, S. & Brooks, E. (2014) When Does Unequal Become Unfair? Judging Claims of Environmental Injustice. *Environment and Planning A*, 46(11), 2686–2702.

Desai, U. (1998) Environment, Economic Growth, and Government in Developing Countries, in Desai, U. (ed.), *Ecological Policy and Politics in Developing Countries: Economic Growth, Democracy, and Environment*. Albany: SUNY Press, 1–17, 39–45.

de-Shalit, A. (2000) *The Environment: Between Theory and Practice*. Oxford: Oxford University Press.

Diefenbacher, H. (2006) Environmental Justice: Some Starting Points for Discussion from a Perspective of Ecological Economics. *Ecotheology*, 11(3), 282–293.

Dinda, S. (2004) Environmental Kuznets Curve Hypothesis: A Survey. *Ecological Economics*, 49(4), 431–455.

Dobson, A. (1998) *Justice and the Environment*. Oxford: Oxford University Press, Inc.

Easterbrook, G. (1995) *A Moment on the Earth: The Coming Age of Environmental Optimism*. New York: Viking.

Faber, D. R. & McCarthy, D. (2003) Neo-Liberalism, Globalization and the Struggle for Ecological Democracy: Linking Sustainability and Environmental Justice, in Agyeman, J., Bullard, R. D. & Evans, B. (eds), *Just Sustainabilities: Development in an Unequal World*. Cambridge, MA: The MIT Press.

Falk, R. A. (1971) *This Endangered Planet*. New York: Random House.

Farrell, C. (2012) A Just Transition: Lessons Learned from the Environmental Justice Movement. *Duke Forum for Law & Social Change*, 4(45), 45–63.

Foster, J. B., Clark, B. & York, R. (2010) *The Ecological Rift—Capitalism's War on the Earth*. New York: Monthly Review Press.

Frankel, J. (2009) Environmental Effects of International Trade. *HKS Faculty Research Working Paper Series RWP09-006*, John F. Kennedy School of Government, Harvard University.

Friedman, M. (1962) *Capitalism and Freedom*. Chicago: The University of Chicago Press.

Fuentes-George, K. (2013) Neoliberalism, Environmental Justice, and the Convention on Biological Diversity: How Problematizing the Commodification of Nature Affects Regime Effectiveness. *Global Environmental Politics*, 13(4), 144–163.

Gardiner, S., Caney, S., Jamieson, D. & Shue, H. (eds), (2010) *Climate Ethics: Essential Readings*. Oxford: Oxford University Press.

Gibson, W. E. (ed.) (2004) *Eco-Justice—The Unfinished Journey*. Albany: SUNY Press.

Hampson, F. O. & Reppy, J. (eds) (1996) *Earthly Goods: Environmental Change and Social Justice*. New York: Cornell University Press.

Harris, P. (2010) *World Ethics and Climate Change: From International to Global Justice*. Edinburgh: Edinburgh University Press.

Harris, P. (ed.) (2011) *China's Responsibility for Climate Change: Ethics, Fairness and Environmental Policy*. Bristol: The Policy Press.

Harris, P. (ed.) (2016) *Ethics, Environmental Justice and Climate Change*. Cheltenham: Edward Elgar.

Harvey, D. (1996) *Justice, Nature & the Geography of Difference*. Oxford: Blackwell Publishers.

Hayek, F. (1976) *Law, Legislation and Liberty: The Mirage of Social Justice*, 2. Chicago: The University of Chicago Press.

Heffron, R. J. & McCauley, D. (2017) The Concept of Energy Justice Across the Disciplines. *Energy Policy*, 105, 658–667.

Hopwood, B., Mellor, M. & O'Brien, G. (2005) Sustainable Development: Mapping Different Approaches. *Sustainable Development*, 13(1), 38–52.

Hurrell, A. (2002) Norms and Ethics in International Relations, in Carlsnaes, W., Risse, T. & Simmons, B. A. (eds), *Handbook of International Relations*. London: Sage Publications.

Ioris, A. A. R. (2012) The Neoliberalization of Water in Lima, Peru. *Political Geography*, 31(5), 266–278.

Johnson, C. A. (2012) Governing Climate Displacement: The Ethics and Politics of Human Resettlement. *Environmental Politics*, 21(2), 308–328.

Jorgenson, A. K. (2006) Unequal Ecological Exchange and Environmental Degradation: A Theoretical Proposition and Cross-National Study of Deforestation, 1990–2000. *Rural Sociology*, 71(4), 685–712.

Klinsky, S., Roberts, J. T., Huq, S., Okereke, C., Newell, P., Dauvergne, P., O'Brien, K., Schroeder, K., Tschakert, P., Clapp, J., Keck, M., Biermann, F., Liverman, D., Gupta, J., Rahman, A., Messner, D., Pello, D. & Bauer, S. (2017) Why Equity is Fundamental in Climate Change Policy Research. *Global Environmental Change*, 44, 170–173.

Kütting, G. (2004) *Globalization and the Environment: Greening Global Political Economy*. Albany: State University of New York Press.

Kymlicka, W. (1996) Concepts of Community and Social Justice, in Hampson, F. O. & Reppy, J. (eds), *Earthly Goods: Environmental Change and Social Justice*. New York: Cornell University Press.

Lal, D. (2002) *The Poverty of 'Development Economics'*. London: The Institute of Economic Affairs.

Lambert Colomeda, L. A. (1999) *Keepers of the Fire: Issues in Ecology for Indigenous Peoples*. Boston: Jones and Bartlett Publishers.

Leopold, A. (1968/1948) *A Sand County Almanac*. Oxford: Oxford University Press.

Lin, B., Omoju, O. E., Nwakeze, N. M., Okonkwo, J. U. & Megbowon, E. T. (2016) Is the Environmental Kuznets Curve Hypothesis a Sound Basis for Environmental Policy in Africa? *Journal of Cleaner Production*, 133, 712–724.

Lomborg, B. (2001) *The Skeptical Environmentalist: Measuring the Real State of the World*. Cambridge: Cambridge University Press.

Low, N. & Gleeson, B. (1998) *Justice, Society and Nature: An Exploration of Political Ecology*. London: Routledge.

Low, N. & Gleeson, B. (2001) Introduction—The Challenge of Ethical Environmental Governance, in Gleeson, B. & Low, N. (eds), *Governing for the Environment: Global Problems, Ethics and Democracy*. New York: Palgrave Publishers Ltd.

Lucier, C. A. & Gareau, B. J. (2016) Obstacles to Preserving Precaution and Equity in Global Hazardous Waste Regulation: An Analysis of Contested Knowledge in the Basel Convention. *International Environmental Agreements*, 16(4), 493–508.

Lyster, R. (2017) Climate Justice, Adaptation and the Paris Agreement: A Recipe for Disasters? *Environmental Politics*, 26(3), 438–458.

Magdoff, F. & Tokar, B. (eds), (2010) *Agriculture and Food in Crisis: Conflict, Resistance, and Renewal*. New York: Monthly Review Press.

Marion Suiseeya, K. R. (2014) Negotiating the Nagoya Protocol: Indigenous Demands for Justice. *Global Environmental Politics,* 14(3), 102–124.

Martinez-Alier, J. (2002) *The Environmentalism of the Poor: A Study of Ecological Conflicts and Valuation.* Cheltenham, UK: Edward Elgar Publishing Limited.

Meadows, D. H., Meadows, D. L., Randers, J. & Behrens III, W. W. (1972) *The Limits to Growth.* New York: Universe Books.

Mies, M. & Shiva, V. (1993) *Ecofeminism.* Halifax: Fernwood Publications.

Miller, D. (1976) *Social Justice.* Oxford: Oxford University Press.

Mol, A. P. J. (2002) Ecological Modernization and the Global Economy. *Global Environmental Politics,* 2(2), 92–115.

Morvaridi, B. (2008) *Social Justice and Development.* New York: Palgrave Macmillan.

Naess, A. (1973) The Shallow and the Deep, Long-Range Ecology Movement; A Summary. *Inquiry,* 16(1), 95–100.

Newell, P. J. (2007) Trade and Environmental Justice in Latin America. *New Political Economy,* 12(2), 237–259.

Newell, P. (2012) *Globalization and the Environment: Capitalism, Ecology, and Power.* London: Polity Press.

Newell, P. & Mulvaney, D. (2013) The Political Economy of the 'Just Transition'. *The Geographical Journal,* 179(2), 132–140.

Nussbaum, M. (2000) *Women and Human Development: The Capabilities Approach.* Cambridge: Cambridge University Press.

O'Connor, J. (1998) *Natural Causes: Essays in Ecological Marxism.* New York: Guilford Press.

Okereke, C. (2008) *Global Justice and Neoliberal Environmental Governance: Ethics, Sustainable Development and International Co-operation.* New York: Routledge.

Organisation for Economic Cooperation and Development (OECD) (2001) *Policies to Enhance Sustainable Development.* Paris: OECD.

Page, E. A. (2006) *Climate Change, Justice and Future Generations.* Cheltenham: Edward Elgar.

Parks, B. C. & Roberts, J. T. (2006) Environmental and Ecological Justice, in Betsill, M. M., Hochstetler, K. & Stevis, D. (eds), *International Environmental Politics.* New York: Palgrave Macmillan.

Parr, A. (2012) *The Wrath of Capital: Neoliberalism and Climate Change Politics.* New York: Columbia University Press.

Payne, A. (2005) *The Global Politics of Unequal Development.* New York: Palgrave Macmillan.

Pellow, D. N. (2007) *Resisting Global Toxics: Transnational Movements for Environmental Justice.* Cambridge, MA: The MIT Press.

Pickren, G. (2014) Political Ecologies of Electronic Waste: Uncertainty and Legitimacy in the Governance of E-waste Geographies. *Environment and Planning A,* 46(1), 26–45.

Plumwood, V. (2006) Feminism, in Dobson, A. & Eckersley, R. (eds), *Political Theory and the Ecological Challenge.* Cambridge: Cambridge University Press.

Rawls, J. (1971/1999) *A Theory of Justice.* Cambridge, MA: Belknap Press of Harvard University Press.

Renckens, S. (2015) The Basel Convention, US Politics, and the Emergence of Non-state E-waste Recycling Certification. *International Environmental Agreements,* 15(2), 141–158.

Reus-Smit, C. (1996) The Normative Structure of International Society, in Hampson, F. O. & Reppy, J. (eds), *Earthly Goods: Environmental Change and Social Justice.* Ithaca: Cornell University Press.

Rice, J. (2007) Ecological Unequal Exchange: Consumption, Equity, and Unsustainable Structural Relationships within the Global Economy. *International Journal of Comparative Sociology,* 48(1), 43–72.

Richardson, J. L. (2001) *Contending Liberalisms in World Politics: Ideology and Power.* Boulder: Lynne Rienner Publishers.

Roberts, D. (2003) Sustainability and Equity: Reflections of a Local Government Practitioner in Southern Africa, in Agyeman, J., Bullard, R. D. & Evans, B. (eds), *Just Sustainabilities: Development in an Unequal World*. Cambridge: The MIT Press.

Schleifer, P. (2016) Private Governance Undermined: India and the Roundtable on Sustainable Palm Oil. *Global Environmental Politics*, 16(1), 38–58.

Schlosberg, D. (2007) *Defining Environmental Justice*. Oxford: Oxford University Press.

Schlosberg, D. (2012) Climate Justice and Capabilities: A Framework for Adaptation Policy. *Ethics & International Affairs*, 26(4), 445–461.

Schlosberg, D. (2013) Theorising Environmental Justice: The Expanding Sphere of a Discourse. *Environmental Politics*, 22(1), 37–55.

Schlosberg, D. (2014) Ecological Justice for the Anthropocene, in Wissenburg, M. & Schlosberg, D. (ed.), *Political Animals and Animal Politics*. Hampshire: Palgrave Macmillan.

Schlosberg, D., Collins, L. B. & Niemeyer, S. (2017) Adaptation Policy and Community Discourse: Risk, Vulnerability, and Just Transformation. *Environmental Politics*, 26(3), 413–437.

Sen, A. (1999) *Development as Freedom*. New York: Anchor Books.

Shrader-Frechette, K. (2002) *Environmental Justice: Creating Equality, Reclaiming Democracy*. Oxford: Oxford University Press.

Shue, H. (1992) The Unavoidability of Justice, in Hurrell, A. & Kingsbury, B. (eds), *The International Politics of the Environment*. Oxford: Clarendon Press.

Shue, H. (1999) Global Environment and International Inequality. *International Affairs*, 75(3), 531–545.

Shue, H. (2014) *Climate Justice: Vulnerability and Protection*. Oxford: Oxford University Press.

Simon, J. L. (1984) *The Resourceful Earth: A Response to Global 2000*. Oxford: Oxford University Press.

Stevis, D. (2005) The Globalizations of the Environment. *Globalizations*, 2(3), 323–333.

Stevis, D. & Felli, R. (2016) Green Transitions, Just Transitions? Broadening and Deepening Justice. *Kurswechsel*, 3, 35–45.

Stiglitz, J. E. (2006) *Making Globalization Work*. New York: W.W. Norton & Co.

Taylor, P. J. & Buttel, F. H. (1992) How Do We Know We Have Global Environmental Problems? Science and the Globalization of Environmental Discourse. *Geoforum*, 23(3), 405–416.

United Nations (UN) (2012) Press Conference on Rio+20's Impact on Future of Development Cooperation, *United Nations Conference on Sustainable Development*. Rio de Janiero, July 5, 2012.

Vandergeten, E., Azadi, H. A., Teklemariam, D., Nyssen, J., Witlox, F. & Vanhaute, E. (2016) Agricultural Outsourcing or Land-Grabbing: A Meta-Analysis. *Landscape Ecology*, 31(7), 1395–1417.

Wapner, P. (1997) Environmental Ethics and Global Governance: Engaging the International Liberal Tradition. *Global Governance*, 3(2), 213–231.

Wapner, P. (2014) The Changing Nature of Nature: Environmental Politics in the Anthropocene. *Global Environmental Politics*, 14(4), 36–54.

Weiss, E. B. (1989) *In Fairness to Future Generations: International Law, Common Patrimony, and Intergenerational Equity*. Dobbs Ferry: Transnational Publishers.

Wenz, P. S. (1988) *Environmental Justice*. Albany: State University of New York Press.

Wissenburg, M. (2006) Global and Ecological Justice: Prioritising Conflicting Demands. *Environmental Values*, 15(4), 425–439.

World Commission on Environment and Development (WCED) (1987) *Our Common Future*. Oxford: Oxford University Press.

World Trade Organization Secretariat: Committee on Trade and Environment (WTO) (1997) *Environmental Benefits of Removing Trade Restrictions and Distortions*. Geneva, Switzerland.

Youssef, A. B., Hammoudeh, S. & Omri, A. (2016) Simultaneity Modeling Analysis of the Environmental Kuznets Curve Hypothesis. *Energy Economics*, 60, 266–274.

Part II
Case studies

Climate change 7

Science, international cooperation and global environmental politics

Paul G. Harris

Among all of the myriad global environmental issues, climate is by far the most complex – scientifically and politically. It presents profound dangers to people, other species and the biosphere in the long term. The politics of climate change have been tortuous and slow, particularly at the international level. Over several decades, climate change has moved from being a minor issue in international relations to being one of the most high-profile global issues. It is by far the most prominent challenge in both the practice and study of global environmental politics.

As climate change has become better understood and more prominent in the media and public discourse, so too have predictions about its impacts on human societies and nature. Major impacts of climate change are already being experienced around the world (IPCC 2014). These range from noticeable sea-level rise along many coastlines to more powerful storms, droughts and spread of deadly pathogens. Climate change is now a significant concern for almost every government, many major international organizations, industries of every variety, thousands of nongovernmental organizations and indeed millions of people around the world. Climate change is now high politics.

Governments have negotiated agreements to study climate change and to start putting in place policies that limit the 'greenhouse gas' pollution that causes it. However, despite the high profile of climate change and actions around the world to address it, the responses of states and other actors, including individuals, have failed to keep up with the increasing pace of change. While policies to address climate change are many and varied, and increasingly these policies are starting to curb greenhouse gas pollution, they are grossly inadequate. Only radical action can avert dangerous climate change (Barkdull and Harris 2015). But such radical action would require changes to the status quo – changes to who wields political influence, changes to who controls economic resources and changes to the way that most people, particularly in the developed world, live their lives. The science of climate change has been disputed, its solutions challenge powerful vested interests, its policy implications mean requiring industries and individuals to do things differently. All of these attributes make it a formidable political challenge. For students of global environmental politics, a fundamental question is whether climate change has become just too difficult to solve – or just too political.

As a case study in global environmental politics, climate change is nothing if not byzantine. This chapter aims to reveal some of the complexity of the problem while also shedding light on several major and recurring attributes of the problem.[1] It summarizes some of the scientific findings on climate change and notes how climate science has been politicized. It describes how governments have negotiated a regime of international agreements and institutions intended to address climate change collectively and individually. It is not possible in a book chapter to find a solution to climate change – after all, such a solution has eluded diplomats, politicians, activists and experts for decades. But this chapter may help to identify some obstacles to more effective action on climate change and some potential pathways that might lead toward such action.

Climate change science: environment and politics

The term 'climate change' is now widely used to refer to unnatural human-caused (anthropogenic) large-scale environmental changes brought on by the emissions of greenhouse gases. The idea that actions by humanity could bring about changes to Earth's climate system is not new. Hypotheses about the 'greenhouse effect' – global warming precipitated by the accumulation of carbon dioxide in the atmosphere – were proposed in the nineteenth century. Much more recently, particularly since the mid-twentieth century, as observed climatic conditions became more noticeably abnormal, the problem gained prominence among both scientists and governments.

Carbon dioxide, the most influential greenhouse gas in aggregate, is produced in massive quantities through the burning of fossil fuels – coal, oil and natural gas – and by the cutting and burning of forests, as well as other land-use changes. Human activities are adding carbon to the environment at unprecedented rates. The most prominent manifestation of climate change is warming of the atmosphere and oceans, from which many of the worst impacts follow. For example, warming of the oceans and atmosphere leads to rising sea levels as seawater expands and glaciers recede, sending their meltwater into the sea. Other changes, such as ocean acidification and the cumulative effects of other forms of pollution and environmental degradation, are among many other effects of climate change arising from greenhouse gas emissions.

Environmental pollution and its consequences

Human-induced global warming was, until quite recently, viewed as an issue of the *future* – a problem for future generations, future governments and future citizens to address. But it is now evident to scientists that *ongoing* environmental changes, such as widespread droughts and extreme warming of the Arctic, are consequences of global warming and contemporaneous climate change. The impacts of climate change on natural ecosystems and on human societies will be increasingly severe, particularly in parts of the world where geographic vulnerability and poverty make adaptation to changes difficult or impossible. Importantly for understanding the global politics of climate change, the problem is intimately connected to nearly all economic activity and is particularly wrapped up with modern lifestyles and consumption habits, thereby connecting the science of the global environment to how people live and work – and to what governments, industries and people care about the most.

Over the last three decades, scientists have radically improved their knowledge of climate change. They have developed a nuanced understanding of how greenhouse gas pollution is affecting the environment on land, in the oceans and in the atmosphere. Very importantly, debates among scientists about climate change are now about the details of the problem; there is no longer significant scientific doubt that human activities are to blame for global warming and myriad manifestations of climate change. The Intergovernmental Panel on Climate Change (IPCC), an international body of experts created by governments in 1988 to study climate change, declared in its latest scientific assessment that

> Human influence has been detected in warming of the atmosphere and the ocean, in changes in the global water cycle, in reductions in snow and ice, in global mean sea level rise, and in changes in some climate extremes. It is *extremely likely* that human influence has been the dominant cause of the observed warming since the mid-twentieth century.
>
> (IPCC 2013: 17)

The IPCC defines 'extremely likely' as 90–100 per cent probability (IPCC 2013: 142) – about as certain as the scientific community can be when making statements about a complex environmental issue.

Sources of scientific information on climate change are ubiquitous, leaving many concerned citizens facing the problem of deciding which sources of information to rely upon. The most authoritative official reports on the causes and consequences of climate change come from the IPCC, most recently its fifth assessment report (IPCC 2013, 2014). The IPCC is an official international body created for, and by, governments, and as such it tends to reach conclusions based on consensus. Consequently, its findings have tended to *under*-estimate the pace and scale of climate change, as well as the resulting adverse impacts. Generally speaking, based on reports from the panel over nearly 30 years, whatever conclusions the panel reaches and warnings it may give about future climate change, things are likely to be worse. Consequently, the panel's assessments are best viewed as a lower baseline for understanding and action. Nevertheless, the IPCC's findings have, for decades, been routinely challenged by 'climate skeptics' and 'climate deniers' as overstating the problem (see below). Politics has often turned scientific reality on its head.

According to the fourth assessment report of the IPCC, after 1970, greenhouse gas emissions increased globally by 70 per cent, with carbon dioxide in particular increasing by 80 per cent, especially after 1995 (IPCC 2007: 37). The panel concluded in its fifth assessment report that 'atmospheric concentrations of carbon dioxide, methane, and nitrous oxide have increased to levels unprecedented in at least the last 800,000 years. Carbon dioxide concentrations have increased by 40% since pre-industrial times, primarily from fossil fuel emissions . . .' (IPCC 2013: 11). The concentration of carbon dioxide in the atmosphere in 2011 reached 391 parts per million (ppm) compared to 280 ppm prior to the Industrial Revolution (IPCC 2013: 11) – and in 2013 it surpassed 400 ppm, the highest in recorded human history (NASA 2013). Plants and the oceans absorb enormous amounts of carbon dioxide; oceans alone absorb about a third of it. This is important to bear in mind because atmospheric warming would be much greater were it not for the environmental 'sinks' of carbon.

Atmospheric warming has become especially pronounced in recent decades: each of the last three decades has been warmer than the prior one, consistently and repeatedly exceeding historical averages (IPCC 2013: 5). The oceans have warmed substantially, too. Indeed, global warming would be much worse were it not for the oceans absorbing much of the 'greenhouse' heat (IPCC 2013: 8), much as they have absorbed the carbon dioxide creating this heat to begin with. Ocean warming results in sea-level rise due to thermal expansion and from the melting of ice on land. Ice around the world has been decreasing markedly, with the glaciers of Greenland warming and sending enormous quantities of meltwater into the sea. Furthermore, Arctic sea ice has been markedly reduced, as has snow cover in many areas, allowing the sun to warm those areas and thereby adding to yet further warming of land and sea (IPCC 2013: 9).

According to the IPCC's fifth assessment report (IPCC 2014: 4–13), every part of the natural world, both on land and sea, has been affected by climate change. Water systems have been particularly affected, for example, with diminished snowfall reducing runoff in some locations while melting glaciers have increased it in others. Species on land and in the sea are shifting their ranges, with, for example, some land animals moving toward higher elevations and fish moving away from areas of the oceans that are unusually warm. Some species have gone extinct, and others are likely to do so. Crop yields are being affected, mostly adversely, thereby reducing food security. Human health is being affected directly by climate change. For example, more people are dying from heat stress and more are being affected by diseases spread by pathogens, such as mosquitoes, that benefit from warming. Extreme weather events have become more common. Increased heat waves, wildfires, droughts, severe storms and floods are causing suffering to humans and other species. These and other climate-related changes are multiplying the dangers posed by existing risks for communities and individuals. In the case of risks to people, they are especially high for those individuals and communities that have limited ability to cope, namely the poor. People in areas of conflict face added vulnerability due to the impacts of climate change. These and similar changes will continue to increase in the future.

Tables 7.1 and 7.2 identify a number of key risks from climate change described by the IPCC.

Table 7.1   Selected sectoral risks

Freshwater resources	• Water scarcity and flooding will increase alongside warming
	• Competition for reduced water resources to increase
Terrestrial and freshwater ecosystems	• Species face increased risk of extinction
	• High chance of 'abrupt and irreversible' changes to these ecosystems
Coastal and marine systems	• Adverse impacts of sea-level rise, such as flooding and erosion
	• Migration and loss of marine species
	• Ocean acidification to adversely affect species, notably in polar and reef ecosystems
Food	• Major crops (rice, corn and wheat) negatively impacted
	• Food security to suffer due to scarcities, rising prices
Rural areas	• Water scarcities, food insecurity and reduced agricultural incomes, especially among the poor
Economics	• Rising costs to cope with climate change
	• Reduced incomes due to climate impacts
	• Losses accelerate with greater warming
	• Reduced economic growth and increased poverty
Security	• Increased displacement and involuntary migration
	• Increased risks of violent conflict
	• Potential threats to national security from territorial changes, boundary impacts, effects on fish stocks and so forth

Source: Adapted from IPCC (2014: 14-20).

Politicization of climate science

The basic science of climate change is straightforward. Observational research confirms scientists' hypotheses and computer models are now quite accurate. (We know this because scientists use their models to go back in time and predict subsequent environmental conditions that have been confirmed by environmental measurements and observations.) This does not mean that uncertainties are gone; far from it: climate change is so complex that details will always be the subject of analysis. For example, there is great uncertainty about potential impacts of 'positive feedback' loops, such as the potential runaway warming that could result from methane emissions from melting tundra (and, worryingly, possibly from melting methane hydrates beneath the sea). What is very clear from the science is that the consequences of many uncertain impacts will be bad. Thus, the scientific uncertainty is not that climate change is happening and is at the root of future hardships, but instead that scientists have not yet determined fully how bad the many bad impacts will be – whether they will be very bad or utterly catastrophic. Many scientists believe the latter, but this is not yet the consensus. In short, the reality of global warming and its basic causes and consequences, along with the same for broader climatic changes, are now established. Questions now are about the details.

Table 7.2 Key risks for individuals and communities

'**death, injury, ill-health,** or disrupted livelihoods' in coastal areas and on islands affected by storm surges, flooding and rising seas

'**severe ill-health** and disrupted livelihoods' for people in major cities due to flooding

'**extreme weather** events leading to breakdown of infrastructure networks and critical services' (e.g., emergency and health services, basic necessities such as water and electricity)

'**mortality and morbidity** during periods of extreme heat', notably among the poor and those who work outdoors

'**food insecurity** and the breakdown of food systems' due to rising temperatures and weather extremes, notably among the poor

'**loss of rural livelihoods** and income' due to falling agricultural output and shortages of water, especially for those most dependent on the land (e.g., farmer workers and pastoralists)

'**loss of marine and coastal ecosystems,** biodiversity, and the ecosystem goods, functions, and services they provide' for coastal and fishing communities

'**loss of terrestrial and inland water ecosystems,** biodiversity, and the ecosystem goods, functions, and services they provide for livelihoods'

Source: Adapted from IPCC (2014: 13).

Climate change is the most complicated scientific problem ever encountered. But climate science has been made much *more* complicated because it has been highly *politicized*. Initially, large industries that profit from heavy use of fossil fuels, such as oil producers, manufacturers and automobile companies, joined together to aggressively lobby governments to prevent international agreements and national policy action on climate science. They used public relations and media campaigns to confuse the public about the realities of climate change.

By politicizing climate science, and specifically by creating doubt about its reality and effects, they clouded understanding of otherwise clear reports from the IPCC and other scientific bodies. This manufactured sense of doubt has been made worse by 'balanced' media coverage, which until recently, reported the skeptic's view alongside that of the scientists, and 'fake news' spread via online social media platforms. Over more than two decades, enough people and politicians were confused by this campaign to greatly restrain action on climate change. Skepticism and doubt about climate change were especially influential in the United States, including within Congress and inside the federal government. Even some US presidents have publicly expressed doubt about climate change, notably George W. Bush and, more recently, Donald Trump.

However, as the science of climate change has become clearer, as the evidence has built to demonstrate the accuracy of past scientific predictions, and as the realities of actual global warming and felt impacts of climate change have become more apparent around the world, publics have become more worried about the problem. It has become almost impossible for most politicians to remain climate skeptics, and many former skeptics now accept the science. That said, a hard core of 'climate deniers' still exists, particularly in the United States – apparently including the Trump administration's head of the US Environmental Protection Agency, not to mention a number of other officials appointed by President

Trump. Consequently, despite being in a minority, climate skeptics and deniers have been disproportionately influential in policy debates about climate change. To be sure, nearly all governments and the vast majority of people globally do not doubt climate science. That said, many people who believe the basic science still do not accept that things will be as bad in the future as scientists are predicting. These people might be referred to as the 'luke-warmers' – they believe that global warming is happening but that temperature rises, and all that they portend, will not be catastrophic. They believe that action is needed, but not major action and certainly not urgent action. They believe that global warming is manageable. The danger of such views is that they help to hold back bold policy actions that are needed to address both the causes and consequences of climate change.

Manufactured climate skepticism and denial have influenced the work of the IPCC. Compared to its early assessments, in its most recent reports it has been more forthright in declaring the consensus. In its fifth assessment report, the IPCC stated that

> [w]arming of the climate system is unequivocal, and since the 1950s, many of the observed changes are unprecedented over decades to millennia. The atmosphere and ocean have warmed, the amounts of snow and ice have diminished, sea level has risen, and the concentrations of greenhouse gases have increased.
>
> (IPCC 2013: 4)

In its previous assessment, the IPCC declared that 'discernible human influences extend beyond average temperature to other aspects of climate, including temperature extremes and wind patterns' (IPCC 2007: 40). These findings are accepted by most governments, and they have informed international negotiations on climate change and related national policies in most states. What comes from this story, however, is that climate science is definitely not just about science per se; it is also very much about politics. It demonstrates profoundly how the global environment and politics are intimately linked, for better or worse.

International cooperation: negotiations, agreements and policies

The work of scientists has stimulated the global politics of climate change, although the latter has often taken on a life of its own. In December 1990, the United Nations General Assembly established the Intergovernmental Negotiating Committee for a Framework Convention on Climate Change. The goal of that committee was to negotiate a 'framework' convention – much as happened in negotiations to address stratospheric ozone depletion – that would form the foundation of subsequent 'protocol' agreements to deal with the problem of climate change.

The framework: the climate change convention

Diplomats from more than 150 states negotiated the United Nations Framework Convention on Climate Change (UNFCCC), which was signed at the 1992 United Nations

Conference on Environment and Development – the 'Earth Summit'. The declared object-ive of the framework convention was, and remains, the

> stabilization of greenhouse gas concentrations in the atmosphere at a level that
> would prevent dangerous anthropogenic interference with the climate system. Such
> a level should be achieved within a time-frame sufficient to allow ecosystems to adapt
> naturally to climate change, to ensure that food production is not threatened and to
> enable economic development to proceed in a sustainable manner.
>
> (UNFCCC 1992: art. 2)

The convention called on the economically developed states to reduce their emissions of greenhouse gases to 1990 levels by 2000 – something that they failed to do. The convention came into force in 1994. In addition to agreeing to reduce their climate pollution, developed states agreed to provide 'new and additional' resources to developing states to help them address climate change. This concession did not come easily; the United States, for example, was very much opposed to taking on new obligations to provide assistance to developing states.

Negotiations for the framework convention were fraught with major disagreements between developed and developing states in particular. This set a precedent for subsequent negotiations for a protocol and other agreements intended to realize the declared aims of the framework convention.

International negotiations on climate change became more or less regularized and recurring. In 1995, the UNFCCC Conferences of the Parties was established. The aim of what would become more or less annual conferences was to act as the overriding author-ity of the convention and to negotiate the details of how greenhouse gas limitations and other aspects of the convention would be achieved. At the first Conference of the Parties, held in Berlin, Germany, in 1995, developed states acknowledged that they had a greater share of the responsibility for causing climate change and should therefore act to address it first. This acknowledgement became known as the 'Berlin Mandate', central to which was the recurring demand of developing states that affluent states take on greater com-mitments to reduce their greenhouse gas emissions and to assist the poor states in achiev-ing environmentally sustainable development. The Berlin Mandate was an affirmation of the importance of 'common but differentiated responsibilities' in global environmental politics. According to this concept, all of the world's states have common responsibility to address climate change, but the developed states have differentiated – that is, much greater – obligation to do this.

Top-down: negotiating the Kyoto Protocol

At the 1996 second Conference of the Parties in Geneva, Switzerland, diplomats called for a legally binding protocol to the UNFCCC that would have specific targets and timetables for limiting greenhouse gas pollution coming from developed states. That conference's Geneva Declaration would become the foundation for the Kyoto Protocol, the first formal protocol to the UNFCCC. The 1997 Kyoto Protocol was negotiated in December 1997 at the third Conference of the Parties in Kyoto, Japan. It required most developed states collectively to reduce their greenhouse gas emissions by 5.2 per cent below 1990 levels by 2012. However, not all developed states agreed to be bound by the protocol. Much as developed states failed to do what they promised in the UNFCCC, history shows that collectively they did not actually do what the Kyoto Protocol required.

While the Kyoto Protocol was a 'top-down' instrument – that is, by agreement it imposed negotiated greenhouse gas limitations on states – it was designed to provide flexibility in implementing its objectives. This flexibility was to be achieved through three related market-based mechanisms: emissions trading (a 'carbon market'), joint implementation and the Clean Development Mechanism. Emissions trading enabled developed states to barter emissions credits among themselves. If a particular state could limit its emissions more than required by the protocol, it would have unused 'emissions reductions' that it could sell to other states failing to achieve their own reduction targets. The price of the unused emissions reductions was to be determined by market demand. One contentious issue among all states was whether the use of carbon sinks, such as planting forests and making other land-use changes to remove greenhouse gases from the atmosphere, should be counted alongside concrete reductions in greenhouse emissions. The effectiveness of such an approach is still subject to debate.

Another market-based mechanism under the Kyoto Protocol was joint implementation. Under this mechanism, developed states could earn emissions credits when investing in one another's emissions-reduction projects. The aim was to allow developed states to join forces to use the least expensive means of reducing their joint greenhouse gas pollution. The Clean Development Mechanism is similar in that it was designed to allow developed-state parties to the Kyoto Protocol to achieve their emissions limitations, or receive saleable emissions credits in the carbon market, by supporting emissions-reduction projects in developing states not subject to emissions limitations themselves. From a climatic perspective, it makes little difference where the emissions cuts are made (provided that they are actual cuts and not simply accounting tricks). The Clean Development Mechanism quickly resulted in an expanding market for emissions credits from projects in China, India and other developing states (although China took the vast bulk of the projects in the early years) (Ruthner et al. 2011). The intention was for these states, with assistance from the Clean Development Mechanism, to build less polluting factories and other facilities than they might have done or to clean up existing factories that might not have been cleaned up otherwise.

The argument made in favor of these projects was that they were good for everyone: developed states would be able to reduce their greenhouse gas pollution at lower cost by paying for projects in developing states, and the developing states with the projects would benefit from new investment. Furthermore, cleaner facilities in these states could also reduce local air pollution. However, these projects were not without their critics. One argument was that many of the projects would go ahead anyway, and another was that many projects were created simply to profit from the mechanism's financial transfers. What addressing climate change effectively really demanded was cuts from both developed and larger developing states.

Realizing the objectives of the Kyoto Protocol became a major subject of discussions in subsequent Conferences of the Parties to the UNFCCC. For example, some of the means by which the protocol could be implemented were codified at the 1998 fourth Conference of the Parties, held in Buenos Aires, Argentina. At the fifth Conference of the Parties in Bonn, Germany, in October 1999, a timetable for completing outstanding details of the Kyoto Protocol was agreed. The sixth Conference of the Parties was held in November 2000 at The Hague, the Netherlands, and in Bonn, Germany, in July 2001. Around this time, ratification of the Kyoto Protocol by signatories was put into doubt with the election of George W. Bush to be president of the United States. He subsequently withdrew US support for the protocol. Nevertheless, the sixth conference resulted in agreement on emissions trading, carbon sinks, compliance mechanisms and aid to developing states. The seventh Conference of the Parties met in Marrakech, Morocco, in 2001. Diplomats formulated the Marrakech Accords, a complex set of proposals for implementing the Kyoto protocol, largely designed to garner ratification from enough states to allow the protocol to enter into force. Diplomats also agreed to increase funding for the Global Environmental Facility.

The latter fund, focusing on adaptation, served as recognition that efforts to mitigate climate change would not be enough to prevent painful impacts, notably in poor states. Not surprisingly, therefore, at the eighth Conference of the Parties in New Delhi, India, in October 2002, diplomats shifted focus away from preventing climate change by cutting greenhouse gas pollution toward adapting to unavoidable climate change. At the conference, developed states agreed to help developing states adapt to impacts. This approach would enable wealthy states to avoid having to undertake as many costly actions to reduce greenhouse gas emissions as would be required if mitigation of climate change were to remain the overriding priority. Assuming that poor states would be hit by the effects of climate change anyway, the shift toward adaptation had some practical merits, specifically that they might benefit from additional assistance. Because greenhouse gas concentrations in the atmosphere have already reached the point where dangerous climate change is inevitable, adaptation is an obvious near-term priority for those most affected.

At the eighth and ninth Conferences of the Parties, diplomats discussed ways to implement the Marrakech Accords and to prepare for the ratification of the Kyoto Protocol, but adaptation was once again a priority at the December 2004 tenth Conference of the Parties in Buenos Aires, Argentina. That conference was called the 'Adaptation COP' because discussion focused more on adaptation to climate change than the mitigation goals of the Kyoto Protocol. Reflecting what had been, and remains, a trend in climate negotiations, the Buenos Aires conference resulted in pledges of additional assistance to aid poor states most affected by climate change, but there were no clear commitments to making access to adaptation funds possible. Importantly, it was also in 2004 that Russia ratified the Kyoto Protocol, allowing the agreement to finally enter into force in February 2005.

The eleventh Conference of the Parties, and the 'First Conference of the Parties Serving as the Meeting of the Parties' to the Kyoto Protocol, met in Montreal, Canada, in late 2005. The conference began to formalize implementation of the protocol: rules for emissions trading, joint implementation, crediting of emissions sinks and penalties for non-compliance. It also took steps to strengthen the Clean Development Mechanism and establish guidelines for an Adaptation Fund. Several developing states, albeit still opposed to binding obligations to limit their own greenhouse gas emissions, expressed interest in undertaking *voluntary* measures to do so. It would be a full decade before this approach, whereby *all* states would take some sort of action (thus satisfying persistent US demands for this), would be codified in a formal agreement (see below on the Paris Agreement).

Subsequent climate negotiations resulted in incremental steps toward action on climate change, in the process highlighting recurring differences among states about how best to achieve the objectives of both the UNFCCC and the Kyoto Protocol. For example, much as at other conferences before it, differences among states were apparent at the thirteenth Conference of the Parties in Bali, Indonesia, in 2007. European states argued for deeper international commitments for greenhouse gas cuts, revealing their more or less consistent willingness to take greater action compared to the United States. In contrast, the United States strongly opposed adding new commitments – even as developing states argued that they ought to receive more financial and technological assistance.

The discussions at Bali were pushed to a substantial degree by the IPCC's fourth assessment report (IPCC 2007), which removed any remaining doubt about the main causes and consequences of climate change – at least in the minds of diplomats and other officials who were willing to accept the facts. One significant aspect of the Bali conference was widespread opposition to efforts by US diplomats to prevent negotiation of a new agreement that might require developed states to go substantially further to reduce their greenhouse gas pollution and to provide assistance to developing states to help them cope with the impacts of climate change. The conference resulted in the so-called Bali Roadmap, which was intended to guide negotiations toward a new agreement for the Conference of the Parties to be held in Copenhagen, Denmark, at the end of 2009.

A step on the way to Copenhagen was the 2008 fourteenth Conference of the Parties held in Poznan, Poland. The Poznan conference was noteworthy because, amidst the global financial crisis, even European states that had previously pushed for action on climate change were less supportive of deeper greenhouse gas cuts. Nevertheless, by this point in the climate change negotiations – two decades since they began – there was realization that more needed to be done. This realization was reflected in the level of participation at the Copenhagen conference: it involved 192 states and 119 state leaders (IISD 2009). The most important result of the conference was the Copenhagen Accord. The accord was agreed on the last day of the conference by a small number of diplomats and leaders (including US President Barrack Obama), meeting behind closed doors. It reaffirmed the science of climate change, acknowledged the need to stop increasing global greenhouse gas pollution and declared that global warming should be limited to not more than 2 °C. Importantly for developing states, the accord promised to mobilize $100 billion per year by 2020 and establish a Green Climate Fund to help them deal with climate change (UNFCCC 2009).

At first glance, the Copenhagen Accord seemed to be significant. On closer inspection, it looked to be something less: like the original pledge of governments at the Earth Summit, the accord's provisions were voluntary. States revealed a continued unwillingness to accept internationally mandated robust cuts in their greenhouse gas pollution. Consequently, at the December 2010 sixteenth Conference of the Parties in Cancun, Mexico, diplomats yet again agreed that more effort was needed, but they were unable to agree on what to do when the Kyoto Protocol would expire in 2012.

The tortuous diplomatic process to negotiate the Kyoto Protocol and work toward its implementation revealed a problem with climate change politics and, to some extent, global environmental politics more generally: like any collective action problem, those who are called upon to take action will often do all that they can to avoid doing so. Looked at over the first two decades of climate diplomacy, the United States – until early in this century the largest national source of greenhouse gas pollution (since overtaken by China) – never really wanted to address climate change. It used its diplomatic muscle to water down the Kyoto Protocol – nobody seriously thought that cutting greenhouse gas emissions by 5.2 per cent among some states would do much to solve the problem – and then used its influence to see that the agreement remained weak in implementation. The top-down approach to climate negotiations, whereby pollution standards would be set at the international level, proved not to work very well. The Americans argued for what would be a more bottom-up approach: individual states setting their own pollution-reduction targets based on their own capabilities and circumstances. Given the failure of the Kyoto process, the Americans got their way. This bottom-up approach would guide the next major step in climate politics: the Paris Agreement.

Bottom-up: the Paris Agreement

The seventeenth Conference of the Parties took place in Durban, South Africa, in late 2011. Perhaps recognizing that more action was needed, diplomats at the conference agreed to the Durban Platform for Enhanced Action. While the title of the platform suggested additional action, the contents were mostly unambitious pledges to implement previously negotiated agreements. For example, the platform called for implementing the Green Climate Fund and finding new sources of financing for developing states, but then it did not identify the actual sources of funding. Diplomats at Durban agreed to keep the Kyoto Protocol alive, but far more importantly, they made a commitment to negotiate an entirely new climate agreement, no later than 2015, that would include pledges for limitations in greenhouse gas pollution from *all* states. At the Durban conference, the European Union called for the new agreement to include legally binding emissions commitments from large developing states – essentially making the same argument that the United States had been making for years. Meanwhile, China and India argued that developed states should first implement past agreements. China's chief diplomat at the conference suggested that China would consider accepting new commitments after 2020, but only if developed states fulfilled their obligations under existing agreements.

The Durban action plan reaffirmed the objective of keeping global warming below 2° C. At the same time, negotiators acknowledged that twice that much global warming was likely without new national commitments to cut global emissions of greenhouse pollution much more aggressively. However, as the Durban conference closed, there was little prospect that governments would agree to those essential cuts. The Durban Conference of the Parties exposed a basic flaw in climate change politics (and often global environmental politics in other issue areas); namely, that states normally put their own perceived short-term interests before common long-term environmental objectives (see Harris 2013).

Negotiations continued at the eighteenth Conferences of the Parties, held in Doha, Qatar, in 2012, and the nineteenth conference, held in Warsaw, Poland, in 2013. The outcomes were consistent with past conferences: agreement to continue negotiations and to resolve the perennial problem of developed states failing to meet their obligations and developing states (particularly China) quickly becoming major sources of greenhouse gas pollution. Shortly before the twentieth Conference of the Parties in Lima, Peru, in December 2014, the IPCC released its latest assessment reports (IPCC 2013, 2014), therein reaffirming that climate change would have devastating environmental and social impacts (see above). The United Nations Environment Programme argued that urgent action would be required to stem the growth in greenhouse gas emissions – meaning halving them almost immediately and eliminating them completely later in the century (UNEP 2014).

At the Lima conference, several developed states offered to contribute substantial new money to the Green Climate Fund. No doubt this was meant to help nudge developing states to take on emissions limitations of their own. Indeed, at a China–US summit that nearly coincided with the Lima conference, the Chinese president said that China's carbon emissions would level off no later than 2030, and the US president pledged that US emissions would fall by a quarter or more by 2025 (but both of them used 2005 as their base year for these pledges, meaning that they were not nearly as impressive as they might have been had they used the 1990 base year of the UNFCCC and the Kyoto Protocol). The agreement that emanated from the Lima conference – the Lima Accord – was significant in that, for better or worse, it began the shift away from the traditional differentiation between developed and developing states, which required action by the former before asking it of the latter, and moved toward more common responsibility to act, albeit still expecting historical polluters of the developed world to take on greater responsibility. Developing states would not be expected necessarily to promise future emissions *cuts*, as would be expected of developed states, but they would be expected to pledge emissions *limitations* (at least reducing their increases) of some kind in the future. However, the Lima Accord did not include any new pledge from states to cut their greenhouse gas pollution. That was to come the following year in the run up to the twenty-first Conference of the Parties in Paris, France, in 2015.

The Paris conference was the culmination of efforts to move international climate regulation away from top-down collective mandates to bottom-up national pledges. The Paris Agreement on climate change for the first time required developing states to limit their greenhouse gas pollution alongside developed states (United Nations 2016). To be sure, the requirements were to be self-made: all states would pledge to take action to contribute to the common goal of limiting global warming to less than 2 °C, and the agreement nominally calls for warming to not exceed 1.5 °C. Each state pledged to limit national emissions in some way, although not necessarily to *reduce* them. The idea was that these pledges would become baselines for more robust action in the future. The great advantage of this approach is that it garnered nearly universal participation; almost every state in the world joined. The associated disadvantage is that this bottom-up, nationally determined approach does not necessarily go far beyond what states would do anyway – and, so far, the pledges have been far too limited. Even if all of the national pledges to implement that Paris Agreement are fully implemented by almost every state, global warming would likely surpass 3 °C (UNEP 2016). That is double the nominal objective of the agreement.

It is still early days to assess the bottom-up approach. Whether the Paris Agreement is ultimately successful will be determined by whether it is a catalyst for states to take much more aggressive steps in the near future to collectively reduce global greenhouse gas pollution and to move quite rapidly to a global economy that does not rely on fossil fuels. Initial indications have been mixed. The United States has had a shifting position on the Paris Agreement. It was embraced by President Barack Obama, who put in place national policies to help nudge the United States away from heavy reliance on coal. But his successor, Donald Trump, declared in 2017 that the United States would withdraw from the agreement, and his administration worked to promote the use of coal and undo environmental policies of the Obama administration. Nevertheless, other states, including the Europeans and major developing states, notably China and India, pledged to continue working to limit their greenhouse gas emissions. Even within the United States, sub-state actors, including several US states (e.g., California), municipalities, businesses and nongovernmental organizations pledged to make up for Trump's anti-climate policies. It is conceivable that Trump's dislike for the Paris Agreement will make it more likeable by almost everyone else. As with the top-down approach, we see that climate change is very much a question of politics (see Table 7.3).

Global politics of climate change: selected key themes

Climate change has a prominent place on the international environmental agenda because its causes and consequences have become so evident and prudentially important. The driving force behind climate change has been material consumption, modern lifestyles and associated industrial pollution – and especially the world economy's reliance on fossil-based

Table 7.3 International climate policymaking: top-down vs. bottom-up

	Top-down	Bottom-up
Major international agreement under the 1992 Framework Convention on Climate Change	1997 Kyoto Protocol	2015 Paris Agreement
Emissions mitigation expectations for developed states	Reduce collective greenhouse gas emissions as internationally agreed[a]	Reduce national greenhouse gas emissions as nationally determined
Emissions mitigation expectations for developing states	No obligation to reduce emissions	Limit national greenhouse gas emissions as nationally determined
Support for implementation and adaptation	Joint implementation, Clean Development Mechanism, Global Environment Facility, etc.	Green Climate Fund to increase assistance to developing states to $100 billion per year by 2020, etc.

[a]Some developed states were allowed to increase their emissions within agreed limits.

fuels for most of its energy. Transnational actors have played a central role in highlighting the problem (as in the case of scientific groups and communities), in pushing for government action (by environmental nongovernmental organizations) and – especially in the United States – in using domestic political processes to prevent or delay action (as in the case of a number of American business and industry groups). These roles have routinely been premised on maintaining the economic status quo: energy-intensive, and specifically carbon-intensive, economic development and growth. But they have been politically juxtaposed against growing concerns about the many ways in which climate change will undermine national and human security in coming decades. All of these themes have been wrapped up in disparate conceptions of how to achieve fair agreements and action to address climate change – how to achieve ecological justice.

Consumption

The underlying force that has propelled climate change is material consumption (see Fuchs and Boll, Chapter 5). Nearly everything that people consume leads to the emission of greenhouse gases, whether directly, as with the burning of fossil fuels for transportation, or indirectly, as when fossil fuels are burned to produce electricity and material 'goods' that people consume by necessity or for pleasure, or when other greenhouse gases are emitted from human behaviors, such as methane that comes from animals (e.g., cattle) that are consumed for food. The vast bulk of the historical consumption of material goods and energy occurred in the developed, industrialized world. This has changed as people in developing states have increasingly adopted lifestyles and consumption habits similar to those in the West, although average per capita energy use and consumption in Western states is many times that in most (but not all) of the developing world. The developed world's disproportionate impact on the global environment, manifested in its greater historical pollution and higher average per capita greenhouse gas emissions, explains why many developed states were the first to commit to start reducing their emissions. However, trends are shifting, and quite rapidly so. China has overtaken the United States to become the largest national source of greenhouse gas emissions. Many millions of people in China and several other developing states have moved into the global middle class, thereby enabling them to consume and pollute as much as Westerners have done for a century or more. Per capita carbon emissions in China are now about the same as in many European states. Consequently, the globalization of modern lifestyles is having a profoundly damaging impact on the earth's atmosphere. A key question for global environmental politics will be whether these trends can be tempered, both by limiting the amount of 'stuff' that people consume and by deploying new technologies, such as alternative sources of energy, that allow consumption without exacerbating climate change.

Transnational actors

As holds true with other cases of global environmental politics, climate change demonstrates the importance of transnational actors, particularly groups of scientists but also myriad environmental nongovernmental organizations. As noted previously, the underlying scientific understanding of climate change, which feeds into national policy and international negotiations on climate change, was developed by scientists collaborating internationally. Their findings have been disseminated for the use of national policymakers and for diplomats involved in the climate change negotiations. Sometimes scientists serve on national delegations at Conferences of the Parties. They also work in collaboration with nongovernmental organizations, which in turn, attempt to influence public opinion and government officials. Nongovernmental organizations active in pushing for stronger action on climate change include those in favor of more robust action to cut back on greenhouse gas emissions and to help poor states and people cope with climate change, such as Greenpeace, Oxfam and WWF.

These and similar organizations have been prominent and visible in their public relations and direct-action campaigns to persuade developed-state governments and members of their national legislatures to support greenhouse gas emissions cuts, subsidies for green programs and industries, and international aid for climate change-related projects in the developing world. Many of these groups have large memberships that garner the attention of national legislators, expertise that can be brought to bear in climate change debates and the moral high ground as news about the impacts of climate change becomes more prominent and widespread. Environmental nongovernmental organizations work at both the grassroots level to muster public support and with like-minded groups in other states to pool resources and expertise. Many of these groups routinely show up at Conferences of the Parties to publicly shame diplomats and governments for not doing more to address climate change.

Other nongovernmental organizations, such as the American Chamber of Commerce and the former Global Climate Coalition, have lobbied legislators and governments to avoid climate-related laws, particularly those that would require businesses to comply with new regulations or that would lead to 'green taxes' or 'carbon taxes' on activities that result in greenhouse pollution. Industries that have been most opposed to action on climate change have included petroleum companies, electric utilities and automobile manufacturers. By appealing to legislators' concerns about jobs and economic growth, and through their donations of money to politicians' election campaigns (common in the United States), these industries have been able to foster skepticism of climate science (see above) and thereby block robust regulations and laws to bring about reductions in greenhouse gas pollution. In recent years, however, as climate science has become more robust and more people have become concerned about the environment, many industries have shifted positions, slowly reducing their opposition to climate change-related laws while looking for new economic opportunities in energy savings, alternative energy sources and 'green' products. These more environmentally inclined businesses have diluted the political influence of industries that continue to support carbon-intensive economic activity.

Environmental security and justice

In the last few years, there has been a tectonic shift in the global politics of climate change away from scientific skepticism to recognition that it is a real problem requiring action by governments and other actors. One reason for this shift is realization among officials and publics that climate change presents very real challenges to their prudential interests. Put another way, climate change is a matter of *security*, although there has been some hesitation in calling climate change a *national* security threat in the traditional sense. Some experts will debate whether climate change is an existential threat to states, but for small-island states most vulnerable to sea-level rise, there is certainly no doubt about this. What is more, there is no longer doubt that climate change is a major threat to human and economic security, especially in the developing world. The environmental changes that result from climate change leave people who are already vulnerable to drought, storms and pestilence even more vulnerable than before. For many of them, climate change is now a matter of life or death.

This impact on those who are vulnerable raises profound questions of justice. Concerns about international justice have been expressed by developing states from the beginning of the climate change negotiations. As they argue, it is the developed states of the world that are most responsible for historical emissions of greenhouse gases, and it is the developing states that will suffer the most from the environmental changes brought on by those emissions. The developed states are therefore responsible for reducing emissions of greenhouse gases and helping developing states to adapt to the inevitable changes that cannot be avoided. This is an unassailable argument: at its most basic level, justice demands that those causing harm to others stop that harm and meet reasonable demands of those who have been harmed.

Consequently, as noted above, early in the climate negotiations, governments agreed upon the principle of common but differentiated responsibility. It followed from this principle that the Kyoto Protocol would not require developing states to reduce their emissions of greenhouse gases. But, as we have seen, the actual cuts in emissions by developed states have barely matched their obligations, and the amount of funding that affluent states have given to poor states for adaptation to climate change has been tiny compared to the need. Climate change also presents potentially even more profound questions of *global* justice. As millions of people in developing states join the world's affluent classes, calls will grow for them to join Americans, Germans and Japanese to limit and eventually reduce their greenhouse gas pollution (see Harris 2016).

Conclusion

News about climate change, or about the most recent 'natural' disaster that may be a manifestation of global warming, is now daily fare for most people who spend much time reading newspapers, watching television or getting news via the Internet. The science has improved to the point where it is now impossible for policymakers to credibly deny the reality of the problem or its seriousness for most of the world. Consequently, climate change has become one of the most prominent issues in global politics, now routinely garnering the attention of presidents and prime ministers. Nevertheless, despite the heightened pace of international negotiations that have resulted from the growing amount of high-level and public attention to climate change, greenhouse gas pollution remains far too high to avert dangerous climate change (the stated objective of the Framework Convention on Climate Change). While it is very likely that governments will be able to agree to more action, and specifically more cuts in atmospheric pollution at the root of the problem, currently there is not a high prospect for the scale of cuts globally that scientists say are needed. Global warming will continue throughout our lifetimes and beyond. Even if the developed world cuts back substantially on its greenhouse gas emissions, the developing world's emissions will likely grow, or at least continue, for some decades more. Without radical changes in government policies and rapid deployment of environmentally friendly technologies, the best we can expect in the near- and medium-term is modest limitations on pollution and, thus, somewhat lesser impacts later this century and beyond.

Climate change exposes the difficulties and limits of global environmental politics. Fundamentally, climate change and its various painful manifestations are inevitable. It is imperative that states work toward agreements and policies that are vastly more aggressive in cutting global greenhouse gas pollution. If they can do that, some of the worst impacts of climate change might be avoided in the future. In the meantime, the history of climate politics demonstrates the great need for all capable individuals to do whatever we can to reduce our pollution and, ideally, to help those people who suffer the most from climate change – the world's poor.

Note

1 Parts of this chapter are adapted from Harris (2007a, 2007b, 2008a, 2008b, 2009a, 2009b, 2010a, 2010b, 2013, 2016, 2017, 2018) and works cited therein.

Additional reading

Harris, P. G. (2013) *What's Wrong with Climate Politics and How to Fix It*. Cambridge: Polity.

Harris, P. G. (2016) *Climate Change and American Foreign Policy*. Updated paperback edition. New York: Palgrave Macmillan.

Harris, P. G. (2016) *Global Ethics and Climate Change*. 2nd edition. Edinburgh: Edinburgh University Press.

Hulme, M. (2009) *Why We Disagree about Climate Change: Understanding Controversy, Inaction and Opportunity*. Cambridge: Cambridge University Press.

Vogler, J. (2016) *Climate Change in World Politics*. New York: Palgrave Macmillan.

Useful websites

Climate Home News: www.climatechangenews.com/

Intergovernmental Panel on Climate Change: www.ipcc.ch/

International Institute for Sustainable Development Reporting Services, Climate and Atmosphere: http://enb.iisd.org/process/climate_atm.htm

Skeptical Science: https://skepticalscience.com/about.shtml

United Nations Framework Convention on Climate Change: http://unfccc.int/

References

Barkdull, J. & Harris, P. G. (2015) Climate Change and Transformationalism. *Journal of Diplomacy and International Relations*, 16(1), 119–130.

Harris, P. G. (2007a) Collective Action on Climate Change: The Logic of Regime Failure. *Natural Resources Journal*, 47(1), 195–224.

Harris, P. G. (ed.) (2007b) *Europe and Global Climate Change: Politics, Foreign Policy, and Regional Cooperation*. Cheltenham: Edward Elgar.

Harris, P. G. (2008a) Constructing the Climate Regime. *Cambridge Review of International Affairs*, 21(4), 671–672.

Harris, P. G. (2008b) The Glacial Politics of Climate Change. *Cambridge Review of International Affairs*, 21(4), 455–464.

Harris, P. G. (2009a) Climate Change in Environmental Foreign Policy: Science, Diplomacy and Politics, in Harris, P. G. (ed.), *Climate Change and Foreign Policy: Case Studies from East to West*. London: Routledge.

Harris, P. G. (ed.) (2009b) *The Politics of Climate Change*. London: Routledge.

Harris, P. G. (2010a) Climate Change, in Kuetting, G. (ed.), *Global Environmental Politics*. London: Routledge, 107–118.

Harris, P. G. (2010b) *World Ethics and Climate Change: From International to Global Justice*. Edinburgh: Edinburgh University Press.

Harris, P. G. (2013) *What's Wrong with Climate Politics and How to Fix It*. Cambridge: Polity.

Harris, P. G. (2016) *Global Ethics and Climate Change*. 2nd edition. Edinburgh: Edinburgh University Press.

Harris, P. G. (2017) China's Paris Pledge on Climate Change: Inadequate and Irresponsible. *Journal of Environmental Studies and Sciences*, 7(1), 102–107.

Harris, P. G. (2018) *Pathologies of Climate Governance: International Relations, Domestic Politics and Human Nature*. Cambridge: Cambridge University Press.

Intergovernmental Panel on Climate Change (IPCC) (2007) *Climate Change 2007: Synthesis Report*. Cambridge: Cambridge University Press. Online. Available at: www.ipcc.ch/pdf/assessment-report/ar4/syr/ar4_syr.pdf (last accessed 17/01/2018).

Intergovernmental Panel on Climate Change (IPCC) (2013) *Climate Change 2013: The Physical Science Basis*. Cambridge: Cambridge University Press. Online. Available at: www.ipcc.ch/report/ar5/wg1/ (last accessed 17/01/2018).

Intergovernmental Panel on Climate Change (IPCC) (2014) *Climate Change 2014: Impacts, Adaptation and Vulnerability*. Cambridge: Cambridge University Press. Online. Available at: www.ipcc.ch/report/ar5/wg2/ (last accessed 17/01/2018).

International Institute for Sustainable Development (IISD) (2009) *A Brief Analysis of the Copenhagen Climate Change Conference*. New York: IISD Reporting Services. Available at: www.iisd.org/pdf/2009/enb_copenhagen_commentary.pdf (last accessed 17/01/2018).

NASA (2013) NASA Scientists React to 400 ppm Carbon Milestone. *Global Climate Change*. Online. Available at: https://climate.nasa.gov/400ppmquotes/ (last accessed 17/01/2018).

Ruthner, L., Johnson, M., Chatterjee, B., Lazarus, M., Fujiwara, N., Egenhofer, C., du Monceau, T. & Brohe, A. (2011) *Study on the Integrity of the Clean Development Mechanism (CDM)*. London: AEA. Available at: https://ec.europa.eu/clima/sites/clima/files/ets/markets/docs/final_report_en_0.pdf (last accessed 17/01/2018)

United Nations (2016) Paris Agreement. Available at: http://unfccc.int/paris_agreement/items/9485.php (last accessed 17/01/2018).

United Nations Environment Programme (UNEP) (2014) *Emissions Gap Report 2014: The UNEP Synthesis Report*. Nairobi: UNEP. Available at: https://issuu.com/unep/docs/the_emissions_gap_report_2014 (last accessed 17/01/2018).

United Nations Environment Programme (UNEP) (2016) *Emissions Gap Report 2016: A UNEP Synthesis Report*. Nairobi: UNEP. Available at: http://web.unep.org/emissionsgap/ (last accessed 17/01/2018).

United Nations Framework Convention on Climate Change (UNFCCC) (1992) Online. Available at: http://unfccc.int/resource/docs/convkp/conveng.pdf (last accessed 17/01/2018).

United Nations Framework Convention on Climate Change (UNFCCC) (2009) *Copenhagen Accord*. UN Doc. FCCC/CP/2009/L.7. New York: United Nations. Available at: http://unfccc.int/resource/docs/2009/cop15/eng/l07.pdf (last accessed 17/01/2018).

As China goes, so goes the planet

8

The environmental implications of the rise of China

Judith Shapiro

The Chinese superpower has arrived, its environmental footprint extending to the far reaches of the globe, from the Amazon to the Arctic, from Australia to the Americas. China's domination of Asia is all but assured, its investments in new infrastructure integrating the region and pulling it into the orbit of the "Middle Kingdom." But there are enormous uncertainties about the environmental implications of China's newfound economic and political power. On the one hand, the accelerated pace of globalization, with the extraction of raw materials and resources needed to fuel China's growth, will leave environmental degradation in its wake in the form of deforestation, biodiversity loss, scarred landscapes, and toxic chemicals. On the other hand, China is quickly emerging as the global leader in the fight against climate change, and much of this new investment is welcomed by recipient countries seeking to attract Chinese capital and develop their economies. The Chinese regime has incorporated "ecological civilization" into its major policy platforms, and it claims that its international lending criteria are green, minimizing environmental damage while bringing prosperity through new railways, highways, and deep water ports. How should we think about the environmental promises and pitfalls represented by the rise of China? Why does China merit a chapter on its own, when other major countries, from the United States to India to Brazil also have enormous environmental footprints? Is there something special about the breadth and speed of China's impact that cries out for close examination by anyone concerned about the future of the planet? China epitomizes the importance of global economy and political development, as Hickmann and Lederer describe in their chapter (Chapter 3). China's meteoric rise is transforming the way resources are extracted in the farthest reaches of the globe.

The rapidity of China's transformation is unprecedented. In the mid-19th century, China was known as "the sick man of Asia," colonized by imperial powers, forced to accept opium in trade for tea and other valuables. When the dynastic system collapsed in 1911 with the end of the Qing, the country faced seven decades of upheaval involving the Japanese invasions and World War Two, civil war between the Communists and the Nationalists, and then seemingly endless internal political campaigns and conflict during the Mao years (1949–1976), all of which crippled China's economy and limited its international dealings. When the reformist leader Deng Xiaoping launched the Four Modernizations in 1978 and opened up China's door, he needed to reassure traumatized citizens that it was "glorious to get rich," so afraid were they of anything that hinted of capitalism or private ownership.

Today, China is not merely "rich" but a global superpower, buying natural resources around the globe, claiming the oil and fisheries-rich South China Sea with its critical transport channel in the Straits of Malacca, and leaving the recipients of its largesse in terms of grants, loans, and investment both delighted with the influx of capital and apprehensive about its implications and how to manage relations with their new friend. China has launched its own development banks to rival the Bretton Woods institutions of the World Bank and International Monetary Fund, arguing that a "Beijing Consensus" which emphasizes the value of social harmony and hierarchy, with China at the core, is a valid alternative to the "Washington Consensus" that sees globalization, free trade, democratic elections, and privatization as bringing benefits to all. There is even talk of a "China Dream" of national renewal, prosperity, and social stability offered as a counterweight to the American Dream of individual rights and social mobility.

This chapter begins with an overview of the international impacts of China's domestic environmental challenges, including ground-level air pollution, carbon emissions, and water pollution. It then turns to China's stunning assumption of leadership in international environmental governance after President Trump announced the United States' intention to withdraw from the Paris Agreement on climate change mitigation. It then offers a snapshot of how China's quest for resources is being felt around the world, where the taste for shark fin is decimating fisheries off Africa, the extraction of minerals is creating conflicts in countries as far-flung as Peru and Ghana, and the purchase of agricultural lands is leading nervous communities from Africa to Canada to accuse China of "land-grabbing." We then focus more deeply on China's green governance efforts and two major new initiatives, the Asian Infrastructure Investment Bank (AIIB) and the One Belt, One Road initiative (OBOR), which together with the China Development Bank, are promoting China's economic and political interests overseas. Finally, we explore how China's domestic environmental groups (ENGOs) are working to help the country solve its environmental problems despite the tight social and political controls on civil groups in recent years. I hope that this brief chapter will inspire readers to explore this critical moment in China's rise. The international order is being reorganized at a moment of intense crisis for the future of the planet, and how China handles its newfound power will be critical for us all.

Air and water: international environmental impacts

Although, for many readers of this book, China may lie halfway around the globe, what happens within the country has an impact far beyond national borders. Take air pollution, for example. China's particulate air pollution, a product of its reliance on coal for manufacturing and of its heavy automobile emissions, has not only affected the health of millions of its own citizens but is a deep concern for its neighbors, particularly Japan and Korea, whose forests and lakes have mightily suffered from China's acidic air (Wilkening 2004). The mercury in China's air pollution has even affected regions across the Pacific, in California and Western Canada. The truism that environmental issues do not carry passports is particularly obvious for air pollution.

Challenges relating to emissions are not only regional but global, affecting the very infrastructure of the planet. As Paul Harris underlines in his chapter on climate change (Chapter 7), global environmental problems threaten the very infrastructure that supports life on the planet. China's carbon emissions are now the largest aggregate emissions in the world, and they have overtaken those of the European Union (the United States is still number one in *per capita* emissions). China has an enormous need for energy and, despite efforts to reduce coal consumption, is rapidly adding power plants, not only within China but beyond. As the manufacturing hub of the world, it is bearing the brunt of the world's air pollution as other countries displace the environmental harm of their own consumption patterns onto China, essentially exporting their pollution to a less developed, more vulnerable population. (Also known as "dirty migration," this phenomenon now sees the wealthy coastal areas of China shifting their industrial pollution toward the less developed West and to poorer countries in Southeast Asia and Africa.) We cannot separate China's carbon from the carbon that is driving temperatures up across the globe. Climate change is melting Arctic and Antarctic ice, causing sea levels to rise and oceans to become too acidic to support coral reefs, and exacerbating extreme weather events like hurricanes, tornadoes, floods, and droughts.

China's water challenges, too, often have international impacts. As China seeks to shift its energy mix away from coal, government agencies are building hydropower dams, particularly in the Western part of the country where rivers rush downstream from the high elevations of the Himalayan Plateau, which has been called the water tower of Asia, or the "third pole." Many of the rivers that are being dammed flow downstream from the headwaters in China into other countries, and the diminished flow of these rivers affects the livelihoods of millions of people. The Mekong River (in China, the Lancang), for example, flows through six countries to the delta in Vietnam, where reduced flow is affecting farmland and fisheries. Contention over dams built either within China or across the border in Laos, Cambodia, Myanmar, and Thailand with Chinese investment is deeply affecting relations among these states. Concern has also been expressed about China's plan to dredge and deepen parts of the Mekong to facilitate shipping. Other rivers that have their headwaters on the Tibetan Plateau, and are thus controlled by China, include the Indus, Ganges, Salween, and China's own two major rivers, the Yellow and Yangzi. India has expressed deep concern over potential damming of the Brahmaputra (Tsangpo in China), a mother river which nurtures hundreds of millions of people. (Tilt 2014, Chellaney 2013).

Another aspect of China's water challenges that sometimes has international implications is chemical pollution. According to established principles of international environmental law, states have a "duty to notify" and a "duty not to cause harm" when an industrial accident occurs. But when benzene contaminated the Songhua River in Jilin city in Heilongjiang province near Russia in 2005, local officials tried to keep the spill secret and were slow to notify their own citizens, much less Russia. As we see from this example, transboundary watercourses deserve special attention and sensitivity as their management can deeply influence downriver states. Similarly, coastal water pollution from fertilizer and pesticide runoff causes algae blooms known as red tides that can imperil fisheries and migratory birds, having an impact beyond China's borders.

China on the world stage: environmental leadership

Although China has signed and ratified most of the major environmental treaties and participated in global conferences since the United Nations Conference on the Human Environment (UNCHE) in Stockholm in 1972, the country was long seen as a laggard on climate change. China often led a bloc of developing nations (the G77 plus China) that asserted their "right to development" and negotiated strongly on the basis of "common but differentiated responsibilities" at global forums. Understandably, they argued that the developed countries had enjoyed the benefits of fossil fuel emissions since their industrial revolutions and were now in a phase of "luxury emissions," while developing countries' emissions were for basic survival needs of food and heat. There was a stalemate, since the developed countries, especially the United States, refused to change their economic models: at the Rio Earth Summit in 1992, the elder George Bush stated, famously, "the American way of life is not up for negotiation."

However, China no longer claims to be a developing country, and there are strong constituencies in the United States to address climate change, particularly at the state and local levels. In November 2014, President Xi Jinping and then-President Barack Obama jointly issued a historic bi-lateral climate deal at the APEC summit meeting, essentially breaking the stalemate. Both leaders committed to reducing their country's carbon footprint and China became a strong supporter of the Paris climate negotiations, committing the country to increase its renewable energy portfolio, cap coal consumption, and build an "ecological civilization" that would combine economic development with green values. After Donald Trump was elected, promising to dismantle environmental regulations and reject the Paris agreement, all eyes were on China to see whether the country would renege on its own commitments. Instead, however, China stepped into the leadership vacuum and asserted its ongoing support of the treaty. The country has continued its aggressive efforts to deal with its domestic carbon output, strengthening environmental laws, increasing funding for environmental inspections, making violations more costly and subject to punishment, and opening the courts to a broader range of environmental cases and actors. The implementation challenges are huge, but there seems to be strong resolve at the central level to deal not only with carbon emissions but with the myriad other air, water, and soil pollutants that are causing great public dissatisfaction. China has also asserted strong leadership in cracking down on domestic markets for shark fin and elephant ivory as a way to curtail the global trade governed under international environmental law by the Convention on International Trade in Endangered Species (CITES), of which more is discussed in the next section of the chapter.

The resources quest: biodiversity

The environmental impacts of China's rise are not only spillovers from domestic activity. China's "going out" policy, launched in 1999, actively encourages international investment so as to help guarantee a secure supply of the resources needed to maintain the country's economic growth and take advantage of its massive foreign currency reserves. One of China's fundamental insecurities concerns the supply of grain.

China has one quarter of the world's population and is a huge country, but relatively little of that land is good arable land, and even that is being converted to urban use, causing alarmed policymakers to declare a "red line" to protect minimal acreage for agricultural use. Devastating famines have punctuated Chinese history, most recently in 1959–1961 when the "three hard years" after the ill-advised Great Leap Forward caused as many as 30 million unnecessary deaths. Anxiety over grain supply has been a theme of China's governance for centuries (Wemheuer 2014). Unsuccessful campaigns to increase arable land by filling in wetlands and terracing steep mountains marked the Mao years (Shapiro 2001). Since the post-Mao reform and opening policy, however, China has discovered it can both buy grain on the open market and legally purchase arable land around the globe. While many would argue that this sort of land acquisition is no different from that pursued by other corporate investors, others accuse China of "land-grabbing," and in July 2011, a German official caused a scandal by accusing China of causing the famine in the Horn of Africa (Hofman and Ho, 2011).

Biodiversity loss is another key environmental concern where China exerts a disproportionate influence. Parts of endangered species are valuable ingredients for Traditional Chinese Medicine (TCM), as the consumption of certain animals is believed to impart the characteristics of the animal, and China's newfound wealth is putting pressure on tigers, consumed for their bones (strength), rhinoceroses, killed for their horns (sexual stamina), and turtles (believed to promote longevity), along with a long list of less well known creatures like pangolins. As Doris Fuchs and Frederike Boll (Chapter 5) and Wendy Godek (Chapter 12) indicate in their respective chapters on consumption and on the politics of food, purchasing power greatly affects the degree and nature of resources extraction.

The most prominent example of China's impact on global biodiversity is the plight of the African elephant. Chinese traditional culture has always placed great value on ivory; some intricate carvings collected by emperors and high officials span an entire tusk. Thus, although the Chinese arts have long cherished ivory, it has only been since China established a major presence in Africa that illegal trade networks formed alliances with African militias and corrupt elites, bringing African elephant poaching to crisis levels. China now boasts many of the wealthiest people in the world along with a middle class able to afford life's luxuries and interested in displaying their wealth, propelling market demand. Fortunately, the Chinese government is taking steps to ban the import and sale of ivory products, as have other governments like the United States, where the market for ivory is second largest in the world. Civil society groups like WildAid, with the help of basketball star Yao Ming, are adding pressure from below with the slogan "When the Buying Stops, the Killing Can Too." Whether this will have a rapid enough effect is unclear. Many observers fear that the African elephant will become extinct in the wild within a few decades (Orenstein 2013).

The oceans' declining shark populations present another urgent case attracting global concern. Chinese demand for shark fin, used in soup at banquets and fancy hotels, is decimating sharks world-wide. As an "apex predator," sharks play a critical role in ocean ecosystems. But shark fins are often "harvested" to supplement the meager incomes of impoverished fishermen and also fished on an industrial scale on the high seas, where it is easy to evade international laws protecting endangered species. Also through the efforts of Yao Ming and WildAid, shark fin is becoming unfashionable and the government has banned it from official banquets. This drop in demand gives hope that similar efforts to reduce demand for ivory will be effective.

Elephant ivory and shark fins are but two examples of Chinese pressure on global biodiversity. The Convention on International Trade in Endangered Species (CITES) seeks to govern the illegal trade in wildlife and other biodiversity (including plants) and to establish which species are in need of protection. The list of affected species is long, and the drivers of biodiversity loss are complex and often indirect. For example, China's use of imported timber to manufacture furniture (often for export to developed countries) results in habitat loss and ecosystem destruction. The group TRAFFIC, which monitors the trade in endangered species and works on finding substitutes for TCM ingredients, is a great source of additional information about this urgent problem.

The resources quest: minerals and other raw materials

China's resources quest is marked not only by the consumption of grain and other food products but also by the need for raw materials for manufacturing. Among the most contentious of these is the extraction of minerals like copper, iron, gold, and rarer materials, and its pursuit of fossil fuels like oil, coal, and natural gas. While many countries are delighted by the infusion of cash, grants, and loans that this quest involves, China is a relatively inexperienced global player. Unaccustomed to consulting with communities affected by big infrastructure and extraction projects, Chinese project managers have often found themselves surprised by public protests and resistance campaigns, relying on the fact that government elites in the given country have given the project the green light. In Peru, for example, which describes itself as open for business and is a mining nation, strife around labor and environmental issues in copper and iron mines has marked Chinese investment projects even as the government works to attract more of them. China tends to invest more freely in countries that have weaker property rights and rule of law than other countries, so the Chinese percentage of investments in such places is comparatively large, creating, if nothing else, an image problem (Chen et al. 2015). Fortunately, China is learning quickly that social and environmental considerations will ultimately determine a project's success and has a better track record on recent investments than in early ones (Gallagher 2016).

Development finance: green governance?

Much information about China's complex international investment institutions and activities is not publically available. Financial arrangements of interest to those concerned about environmental impacts include so-called "debt for oil" swaps, as structured in Ecuador, where China has been granted concessions to drill for oil in rainforests in exchange for low-interest loans. Also of interest are the major grants and gifts given in exchange for a country's recognition of China rather than Taiwan as the sole legitimate government of China, as occurred in 2017 in Panama, one of the last hold-outs, where financial incentives and the promise of maritime cooperation around the Panama Canal shipping lanes proved overwhelming emoluments. China's "going out" policy involves a complex mix of direct investment and joint ventures; favorable loans with repayment conditions; and direct grants. The initiatives getting the most attention are the Asian Infrastructure Investment Bank (AIIB) and One Belt, One Road (OBOR) economic plan, which intends to bind a huge swath of Asia to China economically via new land infrastructure and consolidated control of the seas.

The AIIB was initiated to facilitate infrastructure construction in the Asia-Pacific region and to give China a great voice as compared with that in established lending institutions like the World Bank, IMF, and Asian Development Bank, where China has long felt frustrated by the domination by Western countries. The AIIB extends the depth and heft of the soft loans and investments that the China Eximbank and China Development Bank were already making to developing country governments and institutions. Proposed in 2013 over the strenuous objections of the United States, the AIIB became operational in late 2015 with capital of about 100 billion USD and draws membership from 80 approved countries, including Australia, which was a founding member, and the UK. The Bank will help support the OBOR initiative, announced at around the same time, which intends to develop six overland corridors and one maritime "belt" to bring a wide swath of Asia into China's political and economic sphere. With investments in deep-water ports, railroads, highways, pipelines, and bridges, OBOR is being promoted as bringing prosperity to the region while binding it closer through trade (see Figure 8.1).

We can understand the AIIB and OBOR initiatives as China's way to reassert economic and political dominance in a region that, in historical and cultural terms, it felt it lost unfairly during the centuries of humiliation at the hands of foreign powers. As Howard French has written, China's historical and cultural legacy governs its conduct of international relations and sits uncomfortably with the Westphalian notion of equality among states. China's relations with its neighbors in Japan and Southeast Asia were, for millennia, governed by the concept of *tianxia*, which held that everything "under the heavens" belonged to the empire. If we use the lens of historical anthropology, we can understand the symbolic context much better: China's goal is to displace the US barbarians and correct historic humiliations imposed by those who dethroned China from its rightful position at the center of the world (French 2017).

Despite this historical context, the new investments have a 21st century feel to them. Great care has been taken to promise that these institutions will make "green" investments, with low environmental impacts and strong social screenings. But, for many

Figure 8.1 The Silk Road routes of China. Map courtesy of Alyson Hurt/NPR.

environmentalists skeptical about whether economic globalization is accelerating our reckoning with the limits of the planet's resources, there are major questions. Can major infrastructure projects be built in an environmentally friendly way, without displacing vulnerable populations and without altering ecosystems? Even if they can, will increased transport and human activity inevitably promote the over-extraction of raw materials and continue an environmentally destructive cycle of extraction, manufacturing, consumption, and disposal? This debate illustrates fundamentally different philosophical differences, theoretical perspectives, and attitudes toward the world. The cheery public information videos issued by the Chinese government about OBOR demonstrate little awareness of the debate whether globalization means "a rising tide lifts all boats" or if it is more of a "race to the bottom," in which poor countries are pressured to weaken their environmental and social standards in an effort to compete against one another for foreign investment. If nothing else, OBOR bears close watching in the years to come to see whether China can keep its promises of international investment in development coupled with sustainability.

Shifting strategies and tactics of Chinese ENGOs in uncertain times

We turn finally to a discussion of how Chinese citizens' groups, commonly known as non-governmental organizations (NGOs) are responding to the environmental challenges outlined above. Chinese environmental non-governmental organizations (ENGOs) must deal with uncertainty and change under a fundamentally authoritarian regime (Shapiro 2017). Such ENGOs must try to keep within boundaries of what is permissible when such limits are often shifting and unclear. In China, in an age of contracting public space under President Xi Jinping and new regulations governing the conduct of social organizations, ENGOs must play a delicate game. Lucy Ford's chapter on transnational actors (Chapter 2) provides important background for understanding China's special situation.

Chinese citizens have responded to their intensifying environmental crisis with increasing sophistication and maturation of activist strategies. Although much attention focuses on intensified controls over the Internet and civic association, over recent decades there has been a remarkable expansion of political space, albeit punctuated by contractions in level of trust between NGOs and government and marked by regional variations. The politics of information surrounding the poaching of the Tibetan Antelope in the mid-1990s, pioneered by Friends of Nature, has blossomed into the social media-driven accountability and transparency politics of today, with thousands of officially registered environmental "social organizations" (as the Chinese government prefers to call them) and new powers for environmental groups to bring public lawsuits and to expose corporate illegal behavior and corruption. Much of this activism is supported by a central government that must enforce environmental laws and regulations if it is to retain legitimacy (Shapiro 2016).

The new foreign NGO registration laws which took effect January 1, 2017, shifted oversight over foreign environmental groups from the Ministry of Civil Affairs to the Public Security Bureau, via a governmental entity called a Professional Supervisory Unit. The official justification was to provide foreign NGOs with more clarity about legal frameworks and give China information about their funding sources, but the message conveyed to worried international groups is that they can more easily be expelled from the country if they transgress. Similar concern is being paid to a new campaign to strengthen the Great Firewall which limits Internet access to websites and social media tools within China. VPNs (virtual private networks) which allow groups and citizens to evade the firewall are being banned, and controversial blog posts disappear ever more quickly.

There is another trend under way, however, that observers tend to miss when they predict the coming Chinese "environmental authoritarianism" (Beeson 2010). Life has become somewhat easier for domestic ENGOs since the implementation of the new Charity Law in September 2016. The requirement to find a government sponsor has been removed, such that NGOs can now register directly with the Ministry of Civil Affairs. Even as foreign NGOs are becoming more restricted in their abilities to fund Chinese domestic groups, domestic NGOs are developing new funding sources, including foundation support, government grants, and small donations.

Conversations with activists reveal a remarkable determination to continue to push the envelope on such issues as information transparency, environmental public interest litigation, and even public protest, albeit of a kind intended to avoid labels of creating public disturbances. Hard-hitting environmental reportage continues, in the powerful alliance between journalists and environmental civil society that has characterized such efforts since the mid-1990s.

ENGO confidence lies primarily in their strong alliance with central government forces that are also urgently attempting to curb China's intense pollution and crack down on provincial and local governments and enterprises that flout and ignore laws and regulations. The "war on pollution" involves the ENGOs as allies, if often uneasy ones, in trying to bridge the implementation gap between China's excellent environmental laws and what happens on the ground. The Chinese government understands clearly that it must deal with the country's environmental crisis if it is to retain a semblance of legitimacy. The December 2016–January 2017 air pollution "red alert" event, for example, resulted in 720 arrests of polluters and the announcement that in 2017 the Chinese government would cancel construction of 103 planned coal plants. Beijing announced a 2017 expenditure of 18.2 billion RMB on pollution controls and the creation of a new "environmental police."

Many scholars have chronicled the Gramscian-style penetration of Chinese civil society by the state. Teets (2014), for example, calls the relationship "consultative authoritarianism." Given this context, there is a special need to appreciate the fluid nature of the relationship between environmental activists and the Chinese government so as to avoid oversimplification. There are unusual freedoms available for ENGOs despite the particular political landscape. On the one hand, such groups could not exist without the tacit, or in some cases active, approval of government agencies. ENGOs are sometimes seen as strengthening the hand of the weak Ministry of Environmental Protection, as occurred when journalist Chai Jing's documentary "Under the Dome" was widely available in March 2015 before it was excised from the Chinese Internet. On the other hand, as has been the case for civil society groups beginning with the first new freedoms after Mao, the boundaries are not clear. There are reports of arrests of local activists who pushed too hard. In northern Hunan, an environmentalist investigating heavy metals in Lake Dongting was seized for "revealing state secrets." In Yunnan, activists who successfully fought dams on the Nu and other rivers with the help of foreign activists have found their relationships with local government officials increasingly tense.

Nevertheless, the strategies and activities available to these groups have expanded from tree-planting and recycling in the mid-1990s, with the formation of the initially very cautious and courageous Friends of Nature, to the current trends toward aggressive pressure toward information transparency and supply chain investigations, public interest litigation not only targeting factories but even sometimes government agencies, nimble on-the-ground investigations and exposes of environmental crimes, and sophisticated use of social media to "name and shame" polluters, to use crowd-funding techniques to support themselves, and to promote web apps that will empower people not only with information about pollution sources and levels but also with mechanisms to upload their own pollution readings as citizen scientist-monitors. Direct action against illegal poachers by dismantling bird snares, for example, and waging "symbolic politics" through street theater, are risky activities but common even under the current regime. A major factor in the expansion of strategies and tools has been the proliferation of social media tools, even in their paler Chinese expressions behind the Great Firewall in the form of Sina Weibo, WeChat, Tencent, and other platforms. International ENGOs such as Greenpeace East Asia have used both Chinese and Firewall-free "naming and shaming" campaigns against international and Chinese apparel brands to force them to stop dumping chemicals into Chinese waterways. The "Detox" campaign has met with outstanding results, as the threat of consumer boycott has led one brand after another to commit to change its practices.

These examples indicate a more positive future for domestic Chinese environmental NGOs than the concern about an invigorated authoritarianism might initially indicate. Chinese ENGOs do not operate outside the government; they are in many ways allies of the government and supporters of the government, even as they occasionally name the government as a defendant in a lawsuit. The trend toward information transparency and rule of law, coupled with the government's urgency about dealing with China's environmental calamities, has placed Chinese ENGOs in a somewhat favorable position. That said, the successful ENGO knows where the red lines are. It shares information with government when asked and actively volunteers information about its activities and intentions. It cultivates friends in high places, and it avoids embarrassing the government or transgressing into what might be perceived as public disturbance. It wields social media carefully for its ability to pressure violating companies and to raise funds, but avoids using it for advocacy that might seem to be creating a social movement. Having internalized potential barriers and roadblocks such that caution comes to feel like common sense, the successful ENGO focuses on mobilizing the public to do good work that supports the government's own goals to create a cleaner, more harmonious society that is part of the "China dream."

Conclusion

This chapter has provided a snapshot of the international impacts of China's domestic challenges, the country's changing and increasingly positive leadership role in global environmental governance, the direct impacts of China's quest for resources, and the promises and pitfalls inherent in the emergence of new financial institutions likely to intensify some of these impacts even as they promise "green" development. We have also seen how China's domestic citizens' groups must seek to support the country's efforts to green itself rather than adopt the confrontational methods common among ENGOs in the West. It remains to be seen to what extent Chinese citizens will become internationally aware and empowered such that they can help to monitor and critique the impacts of China's Foreign Direct Investment and other activities that have an impact beyond China's borders.

As so many chapters in this book underline, however, it is essential for the future of the planet that concerned citizens around the world adopt a global view. Environmental harm can be displaced for only a short time. Ultimately, we have only one planet. Pollution in one place becomes pollution elsewhere. A warming atmosphere affects the infrastructure that supports all life. Loss of biodiversity is a loss for all human beings, no matter where they live. And the acceleration of extraction of raw materials supports a global lifestyle and aspirations that may ultimately prove unsustainable. China's ability to handle its newfound power will play a pivotal and very special role in our global future.

Internet resources

China Dialogue. www.chinadialogue.net. An important on-line clearing house for China environment issues, with text in both English and Chinese.

China Environment Forum. www.wilsoncenter.org/program/china-environment-forum. The website of an important think tank in Washington, DC, based at the Woodrow Wilson International Center for Scholars.

www.traffic.org. The civil society organization that supports and monitors the Convention on International Trade in Endangered Species (CITES).

Further reading

Evan Osnos (2014) *Age of Ambition: Chasing Fortune, Truth, and Faith in the New China*. New York: Farrar, Straus, & Giroux. An excellent introduction to China today.

Judith Shapiro (2016) *China's Environmental Challenges* (2nd Edition). Cambridge: Polity Books. A deeper exploration of many of the issues introduced in this chapter, including broad trends, governance, national identity, civil society, and environmental justice.

Jonathan Watts (2010) *When a Billion Chinese Jump: How China Will Save Mankind – Or Destroy It*. New York: Scribner. A readable account of China and the environment, with particular attention to biodiversity, by a former *Guardian* reporter.

References

Beeson, Mark (2010) The Coming of Environmental Authoritarianism. *Environmental Politics*, 19(2), 276–294.

Chellaney, Brahma (2013) *Water: Asia's New Battleground*. Washington, DC: Georgetown University Press.

Chen, Wenjie; Dollar, David; Tang, Heiwai (2015) *Why is China Investing in Africa? Evidence from the Firm Level*. Washington, DC: Brookings Institution. Available at: www.brookings.edu/wp-content/uploads/2016/06/Why-is-China-investing-in-Africa.pdf (last accessed 02/07/2017).

French, Howard W. (2017) *Everything under the Heavens: How the Past Helps Shape China's Push for Global Power*. New York: Alfred A. Knopf.

Gallagher, Kevin (2016) *The China Triangle: Latin America's China Boom and the Fate of the Washington Consensus*. Oxford: Oxford University Press.

Hofman, Irna; Ho, Peter (2011) Rethinking China's 'Land Grabs': Chinese Land Investments in Central Asia, *International Institute for Asian Studies Newsletter*, No. 58, Autumn/Winter 2011. Available at: http://iias.asia/sites/default/files/IIAS_NL58_21.pdf (last accessed 02/07/2017).

Orenstein, Ronald (2013) *Ivory, Horn and Blood: Behind the Elephant and Rhinoceros Poaching Crisis*. Richmond Hill, Canada: Firefly Books.

Shapiro, Judith (2001) *Mao's War against Nature: Politics and the Environment in Revolutionary China*. Cambridge: Cambridge University Press.

Shapiro, Judith (2016) *China's Environmental Challenges* (2nd Edition). Cambridge: Polity Books.

Shapiro, Judith (2017) "Threats are Unseen: Shifting Strategies and Tactics of Chinese ENGOs in Uncertain Times" *China Policy Institute*. Available at: https://cpianalysis.org/2017/03/16/threats-are-unseen-shifting-strategies-and-tactics-of-chinese-engos-in-uncertain-times/ (last accessed 28/09/2017).

Teets, Jessica C. (2014) *Civil Society under Authoritarianism: The China Model*. New Jersey: Routledge.

Tilt, Bryan (2014) *Dams and Development in China: The Moral Economy of Water and Power*. New York: Columbia University Press.

Wemheuer, Felix (2014) *Famine Politics in Maoist China and the Soviet Union*. New Haven: Yale University Press.

Wilkening, Kenneth E. (2004) *Acid Rain Science and Politics in Japan: A History of Knowledge and Action toward Sustainability*. Cambridge, MA and London: MIT Press.

The role of technology in the global environment

9

Kyle Herman

This chapter takes a detailed look at how global environmental policies are becoming increasingly more efficient at directing and inducing green technologies. Environmental, or green, technology means products or processes that either control or completely prevent avoidable pollution. These technologies play a crucial role in sustainable development because they are considered more efficient and less polluting but do not require an entirely different global economic model. This chapter first traces the role of technologies in global sustainable development and climate change, under the guidance of the UNDP (United Nations Development Programme) and UNFCCC (United Nations Framework Convention on Climate Change). This is referred to as the Global Environmental Regime, and is slightly more broad than its closely associated Global Climate Change Policy Regime. The chapter then looks at green technology more closely from the perspective of the Global Climate Change Policy Regime, spearheaded by the UNFCCC, which has a clearly defined focus of limiting emissions from conventional energy systems. Last, the chapter aims to highlight some of the "glass half full" outcomes we've witnessed in climate policy geared towards successful environmental technology innovation.

Situating technology in sustainable development

Sustainable development deals with population growth, food security, eco-system destruction, or transition to sustainable energy technologies (Shrivastava 1995). The most common definition, echoed in other chapters throughout this book, is the Brundtland Report's definition: "Sustainable development is development that meets the needs of the present without compromising the ability of future generations to meet their own needs" (Keeble 1988: 21). Broadly, what is meant by sustainable development is continued human development with minimal impact on our shared environment.

Technologies for sustainable development range anywhere from water-purification technologies to solar cookstoves or even green building materials. More efficient and cleaner technologies allow more productivity using the same amount of energy as older technologies (Shrivastava 1995), thereby limiting the impact on our environment. For example, renewable energies emit no greenhouse gases while electric cars do not require oil which, when burned, causes harmful climate change emissions such as hydrocarbons, nitrogen oxides, and carbon monoxide. Another example is highly energy efficient sky-scrapers. These are environmental technologies helping to achieve sustainable development. Their increasing penetration into all sectors of society is, by and large, considered a good thing, and such successes can partly be attributed to long-term global environmental policies.

Acid rain to climate change: evolution in science and technology

Scientists discovered acid rain in the 1970s. It was attributed mostly to coal power-plants, and policies were quickly developed to "clean" the air pollution emitted from the production of electrical energy from coal. Unfortunately, the technologies were developed in a way that did not lead to long-term solutions, but rather short-term quick fixes. Due to the ad hoc nature of these technological bandages, and what were seen as short-term policies that led to these technologies, the notion of technological lock-in, or "Newtonian", environmental policies was coined (Kütting 2004). Newtonian scientific policy prescriptions to stymie the release of sulfur into the atmosphere (from coal plants or other sources) resulted in affixing coal power-plant scrubbers (Adams and Kütting 1995), which turned out to be a short-term fix with longer term negative consequences.

The technological changes such policies induced "locked-in" technologies that turned out not to be sustainable because both the policies and the technologies didn't stand the test of time. Some have referred to such technologies as "end-of-pipe" innovations (Nill and Kemp 2009; Geels 2011) because they clearly deal with the Newtonian, or linear, notion we can fix large scale pollution at the end of a coal smokestack. Below, we will review exactly why such technologies are not well equipped to deal with global environmental problems. Either way, end-of-pipe technologies later entered the lexicon of global environmental policy under the guise of "best-available-technologies" (BATs), and to this day, maintain a strong following in corporate and big government circles.

BAT is first mentioned in the Nitrogen Oxides Protocol (1979), originally called *Protocol to the 1979 Convention Long-Range Transboundary Air Pollution Concerning the Control of Emissions of Nitrogen Oxides or Their Transboundary Fluxes* (apparently the policy-makers in those days did not ascribe to brevity). The flurry of policy and BATs to prevent acid rain was indeed remarkable, especially considering global environmental policy did not even exist until midway through the 20th century. Since 1970, no fewer than eight

Protocols have been signed by the international community to prevent nitrogen pollution (Selin and Vandeveer 2003). However, the BATs involved in stemming acid rain are evidence global environmental policy has, for some time now, relied on technological fixes.

BATs precipitated in end-of-pipe technological "fixes" rather than diagnosing the real environmental–economic issue at source, namely the burning of fossil fuels (Adams and Kütting 1995). This alarming trend continued through the 1980s as coal-fired power-plants were given the option to install "scrubber" technologies (read: end-of-pipe) intended to render the emissions less noxious. In reality, scrubbers only lengthened the lifetime of harmful coal plants while not actually providing any long-term solution. Thus, we see in the early years of environmental technology, buttressed by environmental policy, some of the detracting factors of building policies based on science and technologies that are not yet entirely understood. Likewise, it is evident solving the problems of pollution must be tackled at source rather than after the fact.

Beginning in the 1970s, science and scientists played a central role in identifying causes of environmental problems (Berkhout et al. 2006), and therefore the techno-scientific end-of-pipe solutions seemed appropriate. For instance, the fact that scrubbers were mandated in some countries appeared to be an environmental policy win in the 1980s. Suffice to say, in these earlier days, the views of scientists were much more respected than they are today. In the 1980s, global environmental policy, led by world-renowned scientists, began in earnest to deploy environmental technologies to deal with growing environmental threats. Therefore, considering the many unknowns at the time, end-of-pipe technologies still should be considered a good first approach to dealing with global environmental problems.

After acid rain and the ozone hole were identified as existential threats to human existence, another, much more alarming and ubiquitous environmental problem, took center stage. In the mid-1980s global greenhouse gases (GHGs) were identified as being partly responsible for global climate change because these gases increasingly trapped heat in the earth's atmosphere. At the Villach Conference (1985), scientists unanimously declared GHG emissions as a serious global environmental threat that was perhaps twice as harmful as previously thought. Importantly, the Villach Conference warned emissions of other gases aside from carbon were largely overlooked but probably just as critical. Today, we often hear only of carbon emissions, a result of policy framing that continues to cause confusion to citizens and politicians.

However, in the 1980s, politicians around the world, even the US republican president Reagan, reacted to the alarm set off by climate change scientists. In 1986, we witnessed the first Emissions Trading Policy, seen as a move away from the command-and-control regime (Praetorius and Schumacher 2009), with the explicit purpose of promoting environmental technologies through a market-based mechanism. No longer did it seem acceptable to police and promote end-of-pipe technologies; market policies in line with the neo-liberal agenda were promoted to encourage innovations to solve seemingly endless environmental problems mounting each year. A market for environmental technologies was born. Many years later, global emissions trading policies are still not viable (Hill, 2001). Yet, while climate change policies in the 1980s did not immediately gain traction, experts and scientists definitely made the global environmental issues stand out as real problems in need of long-term, global solutions (ibid).

The crystallizing of expert opinion on options to avert climate disaster marked a trend towards a new Global Climate Regime (GCR) which would evolve into the UNFCCC in 1992, a global political regime tasked with building global climate policy. Several years prior, the IPCC (Intergovernmental Panel on Climate Change) was initiated, considered the scientific arm of the UNFCCC. A strict upper limit for emissions led to the creation of an advisory Group on Greenhouse Gases. Importantly, technologies were considered critical to solving GHGs as most air pollutants were indeed caused by conventional energy technologies such as coal, oil, and natural gas. As such, the UNFCCC, from the very beginning, promoted the development and diffusion of "environmentally sound technologies" (Haites et al. 2006). The Kyoto Protocol, crafted in 1997 and still the strongest agreement to emerge from UNFCCC, specifically addresses the central role of technology innovation and diffusion (see Kyoto's article 4.5). For example, Kyoto's "Co-Development Mechanism" (CDM) explicitly aims to diffuse environmental technologies from developed to lesser-developed countries. Furthermore, three other documents from the Global Environmental Regime demonstrate the underlying importance of environmental technology innovation and diffusion:

- The IPCC: "Achieving the UNFCCC goal of stabilizing GHGs [. . .] will require technological innovation and rapid and widespread transfer and implementation of technologies."
- Article 1.9 of the UNFCCC (1992): "A subsidiary body for scientific and technological advice [. . .] to identify innovative, efficient and state-of-the-art technologies and know-how and advise on the ways and means of promoting development and/or transferring such technology."
- Agenda-21: "Governments [. . .] should provide economic or regulatory incentives [. . .] to stimulate industrial innovation towards cleaner production methods."

Clearly the UNFCCC intended, from the very beginning, to fully support the development of technology and innovation for green technologies. This is also evident in Figure 9.1 below.

However, the idea of using technology to solve GHGs is partly, and not illogically, guided by the overwhelming success of the United Nation's (UN) Montreal Protocol (MP) in 1987.

The MP, although predating the UNFCCC, is unique because it represents the world's first predominantly successful environmental treaty. In about a decade, the MP effectively halved global production of CFCs (chlorofluorocarbons) (although they might persist in the atmosphere until at least 2040). The MP, which was signed by Member States in 1987, developed over the years following the Stockholm Conference (1972), the former sounding the alarm on the hole in the ozone layer. Hydrofluorocarbons (HFCs), sulfur dioxide (SO_2), nitrogen oxides (Nox), and volatile organic compounds (VOCs) were mainly produced from usage of aerosols; products that were not as completely embedded in the world's socio-economic system as energy or automobiles are.

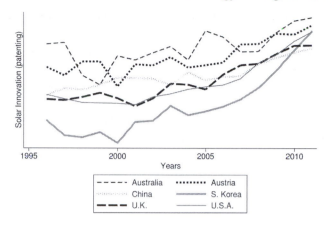

Figure 9.1 Innovations with respect to own country innovation.

One critical issue that appears to cause confusion with researchers, however, is the transfer of policy successes experienced in the MP over to the UNFCCC. It is important to understand these policy regimes deal with entirely different environmental issues, and therefore, the solutions are not transferable.

What will forever set the MP apart from the UNFCCC is technological variety and implementation. Only a few technologies were understood to be causing the majority of ozone-hole destruction (Rowland 1989): for example, aerosol sprays such as hair spray. The solution for the ozone layer, and thus the MP, was therefore to enforce the switching of these few technologies into BATs that were immediately available. In fact, companies having trouble switching were simply paid for their now-illegal products. In contrast, global climate change is the result of thousands of independent power producers, millions of oil-powered cars, and hundreds of different technologies. There is not a BAT for climate change, and as we have found out, there are no great end-of-pipe solutions either. The UNFCCC has shown it is able to induce a switch away from conventional energies, towards a long-term vision of sustainable development, but these changes will not occur overnight due, in large part, to the immense scale and breadth of the destructive technologies mostly responsible for climate change.

Still, it is evident the UNFCCC and emissions policies have impacted the development of sustainable energy technologies over the past three decades (Johnstone et al. 2010). For example, in both developed and developing countries, we are witnessing incredible innovations in clean technologies (Dechezleprêtre et al. 2011). Europe leads the way in renewable energy installations, but even in developing countries and so-called post-Soviet republics, there is remarkable progress. For example, nearly 50% of Tajikistan's energy is renewable while Albania boasts 27% (the same as the once world leader, Denmark); Kyrgyzstan has 30% (on par with Finland) (REN21). Even Kazakhstan, a poor country with an economy dependent on fossil fuels, was able to introduce its very first utility solar plant in 2015. The introduction of renewable energy to all corners of the world therefore should be seen as a policy success, even though there remains a lot of work to be done.

Building long-term sustainable policies for climate change technology

Well-drafted environmental policies are capable of maintaining a link between environmental technologies, their development, and their diffusion into society. Such links act as intermediaries between environmental policy constraints and technological opportunities (Nill and Kemp 2009). In other words, as technologies for the environment become better, policies for climate change gain legitimacy. This leads to a snowball effect whereby policies and technologies mutually support each other's development. Policies guide innovators and decision-makers, opening up windows of opportunity by exposing environmental destruction and pointing towards technological solutions. That is to say, once regulatory pressure exists or becomes likely, the search begins for the competitive edge in the direction of cleaner technology (Adams and Kutting 1995). We are not seeing this search being carried out by people all around the world.

For example, in the case of the Kyoto Protocol, a reasonable assumption by firms, regardless of which signatory country they are from, would have been that regulatory stringency will increase in the coming years (Hoffmann 2011). Thus the Kyoto Protocol induced innovators to begin searching for technological solutions for the environment. The result was an enormous amount of environmental technology innovation, evidenced by a huge spike in patenting for these technologies from 2004–2010 (the Kyoto Protocol was signed and ratified by most between 2000–2002). The fact that global climate policies induced technological innovations for clean technologies leaves open the possibility that increasingly stronger and resilient climate policies can significantly impact the further development and diffusion of these much needed technologies. Evidently, stringent climate policies are already expediting the diffusion of environmental technologies to low-income countries (Costantini and Crespi 2008), which is one critical pillar of Kyoto. By the time the Kyoto Protocol was introduced in 1997, climate technologies were embedded in the treaty to promote the invention, development, and transfer of critical environmental technologies, especially clean energy (Solomon et al. 2007; Ockwell and Mallett 2012; Williams et al. 2012). In the absence of such policies, we might speculate, there is no telling how long it would have taken to deliver such critical climate technologies. Now, with Kyoto and the UNFCCC, off-grid solar energy has become a reality for poor countries which never before had access to electricity.

Technology therefore takes center stage within the UNFCCC (Botcheva and Martin 2001). Even though uncertainty in climate modeling, and therefore climate policy, was a persistent feature of the UNFCCC in the early 1990s (Bosetti et al. 2013), the moderate success of the Kyoto Protocol legitimized the UNFCCC as an agenda-setter for action on climate change (see Harris, Chapter 7 of this volume). Consequently, the support for climate technologies by both scientists and politicians experienced a marked increase in the late 1990s (particularly in countries such as Denmark, Germany, and Spain). Armed with the evidence that the Montreal and Kyoto Protocols were able to, at a minimum, induce reactions around the world in terms of technology development, the UNFCCC reached an important milestone in Paris, 2015. In Paris, for the very first time, all countries agreed that, in order to keep global average temperature increases below two degrees Celsius, we must develop and implement evermore clean technologies.

Technology for environment: a double-edged sword?

Despite the moderate success of climate technology, it is important to remember technologies have, throughout history, been both a source and a solution for environmental problems. In particular, there remain several key drawbacks to technological development for sustainability. Some new technologies, such as natural gas, at first appear to save energy or emit less GHGs, but later are found to emit only slightly less or even more than previous technologies. To give a prime example, when automobiles were first introduced around the end of the 19th century, they solved an impending environmental crisis: horse manure was piling up in the streets of major cities so fast as to make London very close to becoming uninhabitable (Geels 2005). If not for gas-powered cars, horse manure would have utterly destroyed the environments of many cities worldwide (Ibid). Similarly, the invention and diffusion of electricity producing technologies (i.e. fossil-fuel power-plants) was seen as clean and environmental technology around the turn of the 19th century because it replaced horse power with fossil fuel power: "In the city culture [. . .] based on the horse economy, electricity presented itself as a nervous (as it destroyed the night), but *clean technology*" (Mom 2012: 9). The science in the 19th century was not equipped to deal with global climate change (even though, interestingly, global emissions were identified as a problem as early as 1896 by Svante August Arrhenius). Yet the science did identify horse manure as a major environmental and societal issue. Fossil fuel electricity and automobile technologies at once solved these environmental problems.

In this way, environmental technologies have always been somewhat of a double-edged sword. The timing of policies and innovations in technologies are a consequence of expert opinions on what classifies as environmental destruction at a certain point in time. As such, these technologies often solve the environmental crises of the present while only later are understood to be environmentally damaging themselves, and sometimes even worse than the vintage technologies. Therefore, it is critical to maintain the definition of Sustainable Development as defined by *Our Common Future* because it forces us to always think of the long-term potential consequences of technology and policy.

We can thus see how the double-edged sword applies both politically and conceptually. First, environmental technologies are not always so "green"; at least not as green as they are purported to be. What appears to at first be a clean or green innovation often turns out later to be even worse than what the green innovation replaced. A prime example is automobiles replacing horse-drawn carriages; the former are now understood to be much more polluting, in terms of a global scale, than horse manure, which caused only local and temporary pollution, or nuclear power replacing steam power-plants. Yet powerful actors (see Chapter 4 actor-network theory) are sometimes able to construct a story of a "green" innovation that should be supported by policy because it is a BAT. These powerful actors are in government, industry, and even sometimes, unfortunately, identified as being part of the Global Environmental Regime. That is how we sometimes end up with short-sighted policies leading to short-term green technology fixes. This turns out to naturally permeate through global corporations but also global non-governmental organizations (NGOs). The latter are supposedly very concerned with environmental destruction but perhaps unaware of the short-term goals they seek while ignoring more harmful long-term effects of such goals; NGOS are seen as being very concerned with environmental destruction but perhaps only aware of the short-term goals they seek while ignoring more harmful long-term effects of such goals. This leads some, more short-sighted NGOs, to promote ad-hoc solutions such as Carbon Capture. Ultimately, this kind of short-termism is not much better than short term planning put forward by corporations in terms of the environment.

The ambiguity in technology for environment

While climate technologies come in all shapes and sizes, widespread support and encouragement of these differentiated technologies are not always forthcoming. It follows that, politically speaking, environmental technologies frequently land in the cross hairs of environmental non-governmental organizations (ENGOs) because environmental technologies only partially, or not at all, solve the environmental problem at hand. For example, Bird Life International, one of the strongest ENGOs in the world, is vehemently against wind energy because wind turbines kill thousands of migratory bird species (Driessen 2007). We might ask, however, how many birds were killed in the Gulf Oil Spill? ENGOs often prioritize environmental issues according to their own narrow interests. Other NGOs fully support nuclear power as a "clean-burning" energy (Drewitt and Langston 2006), even though, if taking a long-term view, it is by far the most destructive form of electricity production because the waste it produces remains for over 10,000 years (Buessler et al., 2011; Macfarlane & Ewing, 2006). Nuclear waste is estimated to last around 10,000 years (in comparison, carbon emissions remain in the atmosphere for around 100 years, and methane emissions around 25 years, implying emissions from fossil fuels are actually a much more manageable pollutant than the nuclear waste produced from nuclear energy power-plants).

Perhaps the single greatest contradiction of technologies for the environment is embodied in the technology "Carbon-Capture and Storage", or CCS. CCS works by affixing an end-of-pipe technology to prevent carbon from escaping into the atmosphere (Haszeldine, 2009). This technology can, hypothetically, be used with coal, oil, natural gas, or biofuel energy production. It remains commercially unviable except in the richest countries in the world (Norway has the only CCS for oil in the world). Not only is CCS a fledgling technology, responsible for eating up billions of government-funded research money without coming up with any affordable solution, it also does not offer a reasonable long-term solution. It merely serves short-term political and economic motives to continue polluting-as-usual for oil and gas companies, or countries reliant on revenue from these industries (see Vogler, Chapter 1 for more on oil companies and their ties to state regimes).

CCS technology is meant to capture emissions at source and "safely" transport them underground for "permanent" storage (Scott et al. 2013). These ideas are "techno-fixes" (Lucy Ford, Chapter 2) and almost sound like science fiction, considering any geologist will tell you the ground underneath us is changing all the time. Yet the technology is supported by many national governments. There is still insufficient thought as to how it might be safely stored for many generations into the future, or even to considering that the earth's geology is in flux, which may very well precipitate in widespread GHG leakage in the future. It is alarming to think we can "safely" store carbon underground for an extended period (hundreds or thousands of years) into the future. Unsurprisingly, in the 2015 Paris Climate Convention many of the world's top oil companies supported the rapid development of CCS as a technology to curb "carbon" emissions; this gives them a free pass to continue to sell conventional energy and shifts the funding of CCS onto governments. CCS does not attempt to solve the problem of emissions at source but rather kick the problem down the road for future generations to deal with (Haszeldine, 2009). It is, therefore, not an environmental technology for sustainable development. Arguably, it is even worse than the response to horse manure-filled streets with GHG-emitting automobiles.

Difficulty in developing clean technologies

Even though CCS is not a viable sustainable development technology, it does reveal an important issue at stake in climate policy for environmental technology. For example, at first CCS and other similar environmental technologies such as ethanol biofuels did appear very promising. Many scientists supported, and even promoted, such solutions. But ethanol from corn, now commonplace in the United States, is currently seen as both economically wasteful and grossly inefficient. Indeed, corn biofuels appear to use more energy in their entire lifecycle production than they offer by the time these fuels are used in our vehicles (Pimentel 2003), meaning their net benefit to society is negative. Another problem with corn-ethanol is its reliance on food resources for energy production. This has an adverse effect on the price of food around the world. Sustainable development is meant to consider developed and developing countries at the same time. Developing inefficient biofuels at the expense of the developing world's food supply seems both unsustainable and unethical. As such, both corn-ethanol and CCS are not environmental technologies for sustainable development. Policies promoting such technological fixes are severely misguided.

Evidently environmental technologies face strict developmental criteria. They must be socially acceptable and politically feasible, while also being economically sound. This involves economic, political, and social factors, all dynamically related to each other (Jänicke 2008). In other words, new environmental technologies should be more efficient in comparison to the vintage technologies; they must offer some cost reduction, if not immediately then predictably in the near future; and, they must be accepted by politicians, policy-makers, and society at large. Lastly, environmental technologies must stand up to the test of time. Thus, there is a hard bargain to be won, often leading to innovative environmental technologies being shelved long before they are commercially produced and widely available.

This makes policies for environmental technologies very difficult to develop, especially at the global level. At the same time, *politics* for environmental technologies also becomes very polarized, in particular around differentiated technologies. In fact, politics and policies operate on vastly different timelines. While the former, environmental policies, should hypothetically last for many decades, the latter, politics for the environment, is a direct outgrowth of politics in general. Politicians sometimes take environmental policies hostage in order to promote their short-term political visions; this is referred to as political capture (Ashford and Hall 2011). Hence, while policy-makers at the UNFCCC worked for over 20 years to patch together the Paris Climate Convention in 2015, President Trump withdrew from it after only several months in office; indeed, this move is quite similar to President Bush's withdrawal from the UNFCCC's Kyoto Protocol in 2001, shortly after being elected into office. This type of political flux puts pressure on environmental policies aiming to induce new environmental technologies while decreasing the likelihood of sustained political support for expensive but innovative technologies.

If a cleaner technology emerges, it can only enhance sustainable development pathways if its costs are reasonable and not increasing over time. Consequently, it is nearly impossible to "scale" a technology which is not yet widely available or acceptable. Therein lies the dilemma: if an environmental technology is determined, with high confidence, to be beneficial to society but is not yet commercially available, governments should theoretically step in to subsidize the early development and commercialization of these technologies. Without such government support, innovative environmental technologies are rendered prohibitively expensive. The result is that new environmental innovation is not successfully deployed throughout society.

Cost reductions, even from policy support or rapid innovation, are therefore seen as critical for the survival of new environmental technologies. We have witnessed enormous solar and wind energy cost reductions over the past decade, which invariably led to increased support for climate policies. As mentioned above, increasing innovations in clean technologies further legitimize climate policies. Therefore, cost reductions for clean energies, in comparison to conventional energy technologies, mutually reinforce international agreements under UNFCCC (Barrett 2003; Catenacci et al. 2013; Skea 1995). Thus, environmental technology innovation is not only needed to lower emissions but also to mutually reinforce the legitimacy of climate policy at the highest levels: firms and people are responding as global environmental policies are becoming more stringent and more coordinated. As global conferences such as UNFCCC Paris (2015) unfold, we must be careful not to be fooled by firms not interested in climate technologies at all, but instead seeking to capitalize on the appearance of "going green" and promoting misleading technologies such as CCS.

"Greenwashing" is a corporate practice of marketing as "green" while remaining "dirty" and it is closely related to political manipulation of environmental technologies (Laufer 2003). Common examples are multinational corporations claiming to "go green" even though they are in the oil business (Shell and BP). These companies would need to switch industries if they were in actuality "green", because they have no desire nor do they have the innovative capacity to develop clean energy technologies. Another example is "clean coal." Clean coal promised to save the coal industry because of a new technology enabling coal to burn in a "cleaner" way. The catch is the coal supplied to clean-coal power-plants is typically much dirtier than conventional coal, resulting in zero net benefit as compared to older coal plants (Goodell 2007). Ironically clean coal, which employs a few thousand workers in West Virginia, is the primary reason the United States pulled out of the Kyoto Protocol (Schiermeier 2012). From a cost–benefit perspective, putting a few thousand people ahead of the entire world's future population seems grossly unethical. This is a perfect example of political capture: clean coal technologies aligned well with short-term politics, with the negative result of sacrificing long-term climate policy for short-term political wins. Thus we can see how corporate greenwashing is quite similar to political capture by certain interest groups.

The role of policies for sustainable technology

Short-term politics, or populism, can derail long-term climate policies. Canada and the United States withdrawing from the Kyoto Protocol, and of course the now infamous withdrawal from the Paris Agreement by the Trump Administration, serve as salient points. The United States and Canadian withdrawals serve as conspicuous examples of such short-termism. We have witnessed two UNFCCC climate change treaties, Paris (2015) and Kyoto (1997), be temporarily shocked by populist forces. With Kyoto, the effect of Bush withdrawing only led to increased innovation for environmental technologies in China, Japan, and several key players in Europe, while American environmental technologies for climate largely stayed flat. Will a similar effect occur yet again after Paris? Are there short-term technological consequences in countries taking short-term climate policy withdrawal decisions?

While environmental policy requires long-term planning and steadfast policy-making, the latter is often captured by politicians intent on capitalizing on short-term populism. This leads not only to ad hoc policy-making but also adds to uncertainty in environmental industries. A high amount of uncertainty in policy can effectively deadlock innovation. This is especially the case concerning development of new and innovative environmental technologies. Examples abound in not only the United States but also European countries such as Spain, which installed the most renewable energy in the early 2000s, employing hundreds of thousands of people, only to see the industry nearly collapse due to austerity in the aftermath of the 2007/2008 financial crisis (Mallon 2006).

As polarizing as politics may be, in terms of environmental policies, it is not completely responsible for delaying or eliminating promising new climate and environmental technologies. Long-term policies can also severely distort the industry inadvertently. For example, the aforementioned policies to develop CCS over many years of cooperation among researchers around the world, who at first mostly agreed it was a technology worth deploying, were only later seen to be a misguided long-term climate goal. Only much later did it become clear the idea is flawed, not to mention extremely expensive. Some policies are simply not pliable enough to change under emerging evidence that the past conceptions were plain wrong. Thus, while short-term political capture is certainly a problem for environmental technology development, we also must be keenly aware of long-term development goals for climate technologies resting on assumptions that turn out to be wrong in the near future.

One pitfall of environmental policies is the mistaken assumption that technologies remain static and unchanging. In this way, climate policies often do not embody dynamic technological change into their models; in other words, they do not adequately incorporate the effect of innovation on environmental technology development. As new innovations come online, "vintage" innovations become, relatively speaking, less efficient. In a similar vein, emerging "green" technologies are not always so green or cost-efficient (e.g. nuclear fission). Nuclear fission may not even benefit from a global agreement to develop it in every country at once – it might simply be impossible for humans to develop because it is "just out of reach" forever. Other obvious examples include vintage solar and wind energy technologies, overwhelmingly supported by "feed-in-tariffs" (subsidies for installations), which come at the expense of new and emerging solar and wind technologies which are likely to be both more efficient and less expensive. By favoring older technologies, climate policies are guilty of stifling innovation. Often, the result is we become locked into older, vintage environmental technologies while sidelining new, innovative technologies. This is a huge challenge for long-term environmental policy and planning.

How are we to properly interpret global environmental policy in terms of technological change? Should policies attempt to support and invent these technologies? Indeed, there is no straightforward answer to these questions. Many of the researchers included in this book have devoted their entire careers to some aspect of this, but each policy and each region of the world is vastly different in terms of environmental technologies needs and capacity to fill those needs. Likewise, each technology is different. This makes the subject so difficult to pin down and calls for a new generation of researchers and policy-advocates to carry the torch.

Other long-term policies are sometimes continued even in the face of new knowledge showing the technologies are simply not viable. Above, government support for CCS is mentioned. CCS is well-known to be a fledgling technology but, for some reason, continues to receive even more funding than development of new renewable energy technologies. While renewable energy technologies are viable, and are now installed throughout nearly every country on the planet, CCS only works in a few countries. The former are categorized as a point of source innovations, while CCS is clearly an end-of-pipe innovation. Another example, even though it is considered renewable energy in many areas of the world, is large hydropower, which is not really beneficial to the environment because these stations are so massive that they deplete a nation's water resources and fish stocks. Sustainable hydropower is, accordingly to experts, any hydro power-plant less than 25 megawatts (Neij 1997), sometimes referred to as (Anderson et al. 2015).

Clean-burning public buses using natural gas are also the result of either poor or slightly misinformed public policy. Indeed, a city's air is cleaner using these buses but, outside the city where the natural gas is drilled for, citizens are often unable to access safe drinking water and experience man-made earthquakes due to hydraulic fracturing ("fracking") to dig for unconventional natural gas. Should we consider natural gas-powered city buses as a sustainable development? Are such environmental technologies leading us to a more sustainable future? Probably not: in the near future, these technologies are likely to lead to even more environmental problems because of short-sighted environmental policies, political jockeying, and patchwork environmental technologies.

Static views, static results

Probably the biggest pitfall of environmental policy for technology development lies in a perfectly human assumption of a static world. Environmental policies, perhaps even more than other long-term government policies such as healthcare or social security, speak to generations in the future. For example, in the UNFCCC, policy-makers frequently refer to mean global temperature by the end of the 21st century; in other words, these policy-makers are concerned with building policies for the next 80 plus years.

An important new line of research attempts to distance itself from earlier, static models of interpreting environmental technology change (Kemp 1997). Static environmental policies are not well equipped to deal with rapid technological development for environmental-saving technologies or clean energy technologies. Promoting today's technology at the expense of even better technology will leave us ill-equipped to deal with future environmental issues. The aim of technology development for the environment needs to be more incubative and dynamic, for example, by providing supportive and adaptive apparatus for developing, testing, demonstrating, installing, and updating technologies as they come online. This creates "dynamic efficiencies" in the market for climate technologies. Here, we can borrow some of the things we've learned from business innovation theory and merge these ideas with the growing field of eco-evolutionary transition theory (Kemp 1997).

Scholars have recently called for a more adaptive and evolutionary plan for environmental technologies (Nill and Kemp 2009). An adaptive and dynamic policy instrument can successfully integrate technological needs and induce climate technology innovations at lower costs (Nill 2003).

In this manner, policies are tweaked ever so slightly to draw in new technologies, while keeping online vintage technologies until they've been mostly exhausted. Those vintage technologies might then be delivered to lesser-developed countries unable to access or develop new environmental technologies. By having a more global vision of the eco-technology pipeline, for example that vintage solar technologies insufficient in a developed country might be sought after in a developing country, we might build a more dynamic ecosystem for harvesting and diffusing environmental technologies on a global scale. This is easier said than done, and will require increasing coordination of global climate policies. Nevertheless, technological change for the environment has experienced such rapid innovation rates over the past decade it is now beginning to appear human invention actually is able to solve some of the worst environmental crises.

Over the past two decades, we have witnessed enormous growth in worldwide development and installation of wind and solar energy technologies. Renewable energies now make up nearly 20% of all energy consumptions worldwide, up from about 2% in 1995 (IRENA 2017). In 2015, 61% of all new power installed worldwide came from renewables (IRENA 2017), with over $ 348.5bn invested in new clean energy developments (Bloomberg New Energy Finance 2017). Wind turbine costs have fallen to one third the price since only 2009, while solar photovoltaics have fallen by over 80% (IRENA 2017). In terms of climate policy initiatives, it is remarkable that, in 2016, 176 countries had renewable energy targets. These statistics belie the incredible trends, in part due to policies, but perhaps even more due to innovative reactions from intuitive, forward-looking companies. As of 2017, renewable energy technology development and installations around the world are growing rapidly. This process has taken nearly 30 years and is one direct consequence of ongoing UNFCCC conferences, raising awareness by key policy-makers, and in-depth research studies by some of the world's top academics. This is evident in Figure 9.2 below.

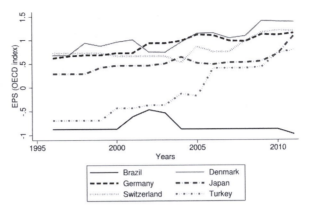

Figure 9.2 Increase in environmental policy stringency over time.

These are all very positive environmental technology improvements for the environment. But, at some point, the question of cost arises. This is certainly an important question and, as discussed above, critical to the success of environmental technology development. A related question asks if other, perhaps more affordable, climate technologies are sidelined in favor of the market needs of only the developed world? Also, are developed world clean technologies, considering the costs and their high-tech components, really right for developing countries? Can developing countries develop their own climate technologies? For example, instead of West African countries importing Chinese and German solar panels, might they be able to build simple solar cookstoves, thereby providing their citizens with both clean air *and* jobs? By the same token, do some solar and wind technologies favor the most profitable opportunities, which in fact usually do not yet exist in developing countries? Again, these questions have no simple and straightforward answers. These are examples of forward-looking, dynamic environmental policies able to respond to rapid changes in the industrial landscape. This evolutionary policy perspective helps build environmental policies with future generations in mind, with the result being lasting environmental protection. Indeed, our great public lands are national monuments in need of the highest level of protection, now and into the future (see more in the final chapter by Humphreys (Chapter 13) on protection of forests).

Global institutions and technology development for the environment

The Global Climate Policy Regime is not entirely composed of only the UNFCCC and the IPCC. Even though the UNFCCC carries the torch, the climate regime is buttressed by other global organizations such as the World Trade Organization, the World Bank, the International Energy Agency, and the Organisation for Economic Cooperation and Development. Indeed, global institutions have a special role to play in changing the perceived costs and risks of environmental technologies (Ibid). They are able to legitimize the policies and the technologies. They can help diffuse and induce new innovations (Stern 2013). Technology for climate change is now overwhelmingly supported in organizations making up the global institutional regime, and the relations between these global institutions are becoming increasingly more important for successful technology diffusion. This is sometimes referred to as "institutional interplay" (Young 2002) or "regime interaction" (Gehring and Oberthur 2004) and is of particular importance to global environmental policies. It reconstitutes the unique responsibility global institutions have in supporting environmental technologies to mitigate what are, by their very nature, global problems. These "institutional links" are able to mediate between environmental requirements and "technological opportunities and constraints" (Kemp 1997). Importantly, the global climate regime can encourage invention, innovation, and diffusion of environmental technologies.

These institutional linkages are evidently critical to development and diffusion of environmentally friendly technologies (Ibid). Such links act as intermediaries between environmental policy constraints and technological opportunities (Ibid). Innovation has always been embedded in the Global Environmental Regime, even though it has only recently been seen as being a dynamic aspect of the policy. For example, Tews (2005) investigated innovative activities in environmental technologies following important global environment conferences, including Stockholm (1972) and the Earth Summit (Rio de Janeiro 1992). He found that, indeed, environmental technology innovations surged after these two UN conferences. In other words, after attention is drawn to environmental catastrophes and policies are discussed at the global level, people and transnational corporations (TNCs) are seen to respond by redoubling efforts to invent and market cleaner technologies. In the context of internationally regulated environmental directives and policies "industry has begun to recognize that cleaner technologies can offer not just environmental but also economic benefits." (Adam and Kütting 1995: 5).

Policy-induced environmental technologies

Such rapid advances in clean technologies lead many researchers to focus on the causes of such innovations. Lately, there is a newfound emphasis on "policy-induced" technological change for the environment (see Popp 2006; Verdolini and Galeotti 2011; Herman 2018). Simply stated, policy-induced innovation for environmental technologies implies environmental policies directly spur firms to innovate. The result is firms provide needed environmental technologies at lower cost, while satisfying some of the central pillars of climate policies. Although the field is still quite new, there have been many empirical investigations supporting the theory of climate policy induced innovations in environmental technologies.

It is perhaps surprising to learn that automobile technology had been induced by policies for well over 100 years, at least as far as technology transfer is concerned. Around 1900, American companies dominated the electrical vehicle market, while the Europeans specialized in gas-powered engines. Electric car technology subsequently transferred from the USA to Europe while gas vehicle technology transferred the other way. Before World War I, for example, between 20,000–30,000 electric cars existed in the United States (Mom 2012).

This fact is quite remarkable and, in some ways, mirrors the transfer of climate technology from the global North to the global South.

North vs. South environmental technology development

As the developed world finally begins in earnest to limit its emissions of GHGs, economic growth in developing countries is leading to increased emissions, on balance, worldwide. This is no more evident than in India and China, which together now account for a third of global GHG emissions. Reducing these emissions, while still enabling developing countries to prosper, requires the use of climate-friendly technologies in these countries, even though often the reverse is argued for (i.e. developing countries should be allowed to pollute as the West did during its industrial revolution). Logically speaking, even if emissions in the United States and the European Union were driven down to zero, emissions in India and China, among other developing countries, need to be dealt with by climate policy-makers because eventually, it seems, these two countries alone, if we stick with business as usual, will emit nearly half the world's GHGs. Thus, we see how global capitalism, together with its inbuilt capacity to organize the world's resources rather efficiently, is by its very nature, intricately interwoven with the overall functioning of global climate policy.

Indeed, both capitalism and environmental protection need the same things to function smoothly and effectively: regulatory oversight; entrepreneurial support (in the form of acceptance of failure); rules; trust; some form of monetary exchange; institutional support, and institutional separation of powers (i.e. not autarky, monarchy); and lastly capitalism and environmental policy require at least a basic judiciary system able to support the afore-mentioned characteristics. Capitalism also craves new and innovative technologies, some-thing which is clearly needed to help solve some of the worst global environmental problems, such as GHG emissions from conventional energy sources. An entirely new global system called for by some scholars, in particular throughout this book, is sometimes not a viable option. The capitalist "system", for all its faults, presently organizes the world and is expected to remain for at least the near to medium future. Combatting climate change needs to happen now and cannot afford to wait for monumental changes to the global capitalistic system. That is why calls for an entirely new system to confront environ-mental destruction may not be warranted. At any rate, innovative change needs to happen now, while we still have time to overcome the limits of the conventional energy systems at the heart of the capitalistic model.

In most cases, environmental technologies are first created in high-income countries. This is due to the technological supremacy of northern countries. Emerging environmen-tal technologies are usually, though not always, comprised of advanced technologies. Yet, it is interesting to see China and India rapidly develop their own fleet of companies able to deliver first-world environmental technologies. Indeed, these developments are very prom-ising for the future of environmental technologies. China now accounts for over half the world's solar photovoltaic production. Nevertheless, both Chinese and Indian climate tech-nologies are still mainly exported to developed countries, the result being developing countries continue to be undersupplied with much needed clean energy technologies.

Thus, an additional challenge is to ensure developing economies have access to these technologies and are able to import at least some of the new technologies. If countries such as India and China are unable to access and install climate technologies, the products we buy from them will contribute significantly to global warming because all products require energy inputs. Recent studies suggest "carbon-embodied goods" are simply moving to countries with less stringent environmental policies, while these goods are then exported back to countries with very strict policies (Sato 2014). In other words, countries such as Denmark actually have done nothing to lower their "carbon" footprint, even though nearly half the country is powered by renewable energy. Shifting carbon emissions to lesser developed countries does nothing, in terms of a global scale, to stem GHG emissions. This is a major problem because it, in a sense, counteracts any productive climate policies in the developed world. For example, European countries could hypothetically be 100% renewable energy-powered but, if they continue to import goods from China, these same countries continue to contribute the same, or even more, to climate change in comparison to when they had limited renewable energy installed.

From this example, it becomes clear how interconnected global environmental policy and technologies really are. Climate change is not only a global issue because it affects, and is caused by, countries and people around the world; it is also a global issue in terms of cooperation because significant gains in some countries (i.e. creation and use of new environmental technologies) could at once be offset by massive increases in GHGs elsewhere. Since some of the most sophisticated clean technologies are first developed in the world's leading economies, international trade and foreign investments provide access to these technologies. The newest renewable energies are designed in the West, built in factories in Asia, then exported mostly back to Europe.

Domestic to international and vice versa

Even though some scholars contend the global capitalistic model will not be able to provide adequate measures to stem climate change, it remains the model in place. Furthermore, it is hard to deny the organizational capacity of TNCs, in concert with capitalism. Together they organize the world's resources quite well; something that is definitely needed if we are to continue deploying evermore clean technologies. The capitalistic model, in contrast to a communist model, reacts well to consumer preferences; we can hope that, as citizens around the world become more aware of climate change, they will increasingly demand cleaner technologies. Therefore, until another model is proven to be capable of both distributing and organizing the world's resources, and at the same time able to respond to demands of, for example, greener goods and healthier products, we are stuck with the global capitalist model. TNCs typically develop new environmental technologies, are well equipped to diffuse these, and also must, by default, be cognizant of varying climate policies throughout the world, in particular, where their businesses operate.

Capitalism is probably not the cleanest way to organize the world, but history suggests it is better than Communism. Case in point are the countries of the Soviet Bloc that were, after 1989, shown to be some of the world's most polluted. Evidently the communist model in China is not able to properly mitigate harmful pollution either. At heart, consumers in communist countries have no voice or accountability, leaving companies unaccountable to their customers, both ecologically and technologically. Likewise, in the Soviet countries, innovation did not exist apart from what the government said was needed. There is no such thing as serendipitous innovation in countries that fail to reward individual innovations, and therefore an eco-transition is all but impossible. Therefore, we must not completely downplay the fact that TNCs retain a tacit ability to, very effectively, organize the world's resources, including people, raw materials, and products. This means TNCs are equipped with quickly understanding that environmental technologies will be rewarded. In a similar vein, TNCs represent a large part of the global system upholding our livelihoods and make it easier for humans to work, live, trade, and prosper. This allows talented people to develop environmental technologies and scale promising renewable energies. Indeed, some of the world's largest private corporations have led the way in sustainable technology since the 1970s, including 3M, Proctor and Gamble, and others. It is also TNCs (transnational coroprations) and MNCs (Sanyo, LG, Samsung) who have been predominantly responsible for innovation in clean energy technologies over the past two decades. (Kyocera, Sharp, Mitsubishi) That does not mean, however, that TNCs are free from error.

Of course, some have argued, TNCs are responsible for much destruction of climate systems; but it is probably misguided to issue a blanket statement that all TNCs are polluting and destructive. Interestingly oil companies, which suffer the ire of environmentalists the world over, are not truly TNCs in the sense that they are strictly private companies. Indeed, by identifying oil companies as the most responsible for climate change, it is at the same time impossible to ignore that oil companies worldwide are predominantly *still owned by nation-states*. (examples here are Saudi, BP, Shell, Total). Therefore, it is shortsighted to simply blame the capitalist model and corporations, or even oil companies still owned by governments. We must hold states accountable for state-owned companies causing much of the worldwide pollution. This is perhaps as important as holding states accountable for formulating strong environmental policies.

The question then becomes, is it the corporate system we should be blaming or national governments?

Global renewable energy development is happening

Some of the chapters in this book have painted a slightly gloomy picture of global environmental policy. In particular, some chapters have exposed faults in the global capitalistic model partially (see Chapters 3 and 4), if not entirely, responsible for some of the worst environmental problems we now face. Indeed, there is much work to be done, and at times, power and greed (in governments, people, and corporations) appear insurmountable. How can we overcome the power of oil companies? How can we slow the progress of global trade to produce more things closer to home, and not ship expensive products to every corner of the globe by air? These problems leave us feeling helpless and hopeless. With each advance, it appears we as a human race take two steps back.

The good news is, over the past 20 years or so, clean energy technology development and diffusion have actually spread rapidly and do not appear to be abating (Sawin et al. 2010). This is, in large part, due to the work of the Global Climate Regime spearheaded by the UNFCCC and the IPCC, and the thousands of researchers at the helm of this effort. Likewise, these technological milestones are also, in large part, the result of innovations by "well-attuned" businesses reacting wisely to new developments in environmental policies (Porter and van der Linde 1995). And, while some of the earlier environmental technologies were innovated and developed in the North, we are witnessing a rapid transfer of know-how and usage of clean technologies in the South and throughout the developing world.

This is now truly a global phenomenon: in 2014 alone, 34.3 GW of solar photovoltaics were installed. Total worldwide capacity reached 303 GW in 2017 (IRENA 2017). To put that in perspective, 303 GW of electricity is about 150 Hoover Dams. We can confidently declare renewable energy is here to stay, and it is the most promising technology for climate change mitigation. Renewable energy also provides vast job opportunities. In 2014, the United States employed 174,000 people in solar photovoltaics while Japan boasted 126,000. Keep in mind, solar photovoltaics is just one of over a dozen commercially available renewable energy technologies.

In 2016 alone, China installed 23.4 GW of wind energy, enough electricity to power at least *15 million homes*. Another amazing aspect of China's renewable energy industry is its development and innovation in the field of solar energy technologies. It is now, by far, the world leader in the production of solar panels. China is largely responsible for driving the cost of solar down to levels that were unthinkable only ten years ago. In 2016, China, colloquially speaking, installed about five Hoover Dams worth of solar photovoltaic energy. These technology developments and installments, in tandem with cost reductions, in turn inspired policy-makers to continue strengthening climate policies. Just as the early success of wind energy in countries such as Denmark, Spain, and Germany influenced the legitimacy of the technology (Walz 2007), China has now fully legitimized solar technology as a viable innovation and a cost-effective alternative to polluting conventional energy technologies. Indeed, we are increasingly witnessing incredible innovation coming from developing countries, including, in particular, India and China but also Brazil and Mexico. These countries are in a good position to innovate because, by being in a more precarious position economically, they are forced to think about the extra cost of each additional unit of energy.

Unlike in the West, where we mostly take for granted flicking the light on and off, in the developing world lights are turned off all day and the refrigerator is opened once or twice within a 12 hour period. In consumption of energy per person (energy per GDP), developing countries are much more energy efficient. Over the past few years, solar energy has allowed countries such as India, Bangladesh, Peru, and Honduras to give their citizens access to energy for the first time. In this way, they can also access the internet and the world's vast knowledge resources. At once, millions of citizens in developing countries now have at least some opportunity to advance up the social ladder. Their children can study with solar-powered lights, parents can research skills needed for a new job opportunity and learn how to be more productive in their agricultural methods. What is remarkable is both the rapid development of renewable energy technologies and their globally dispersed installments. Both sides of this phenomenon are, in many ways, the result of carefully constructed environmental policy parallel to the rapid innovative responses of certain countries to the challenges at stake. It also relates to the innovativeness of industry and the risks taken by certain entrepreneurs to help build a lower carbon economy.

Conclusion

The main part of this chapter is dedicated to highlighting how the global climate policy regime, despite the apparent lack of action from year to year, has actually made a huge difference over past decades in promoting environmental technologies. There are some things governments cannot provide, and even less is expected of international governance. Global citizens need action on global climate change, but action is very hard when myriad problems exist at source. These problems are exacerbated by the fact that thousands of different actors are stuck between each of these problems, each with their own idea of how to change society for the future. Innovation is a critical component in climate change policy because it effectively reduces the overall cost of climate change mitigation while also improving our resilience to these changes (Bosetti et al. 2013). These systemic changes concern two pillars: technological innovation in process and products, and socio-economic innovation in policy and economic tools. Clearly, both interact symbiotically with one another. Likewise technological advancements in clean technology lead to both wider dispersion (diffusion) of such technologies and precipitous fall in their costs (Ibid). The 21st century will be won by those actors and countries able to respond with climate policies that are malleable and promote social development along with equitable, forward-looking policies.

Further reading

Dechezleprêtre, A., Glachant, M., Haščič, I., Johnstone, N. & Ménière, Y. (2011) Invention and Transfer of Climate Change–Mitigation Technologies: A Global Analysis. *Review of Environmental Economics and Policy*, 5(1), 109–130.

Geels, F. W. (2005) The Dynamics of Transitions in Socio-Technical Systems: A Multi-Level Analysis of the Transition Pathway from Horse-Drawn Carriages to Automobiles (1860–1930). *Technology Analysis & Strategic Management*, 17(4), 445–476.

Nill, J. & Kemp, R. (2009) Evolutionary Approaches for Sustainable Innovation Policies: From Niche to Paradigm? *Research Policy*, 38(4), 668–680.

Verdolini, E. & Galeotti, M. (2011) At Home and Abroad: An Empirical Analysis of Innovation and Diffusion in Energy Technologies. *Journal of Environmental Economics and Management*, 61(2), 119–134.

Bibliography

Adam, B. & Kütting, G. (1995) Time to Reconceptualize 'Green Technology' in the Context of Globalization and International Relations. *Innovation: The European Journal of Social Science Research*, 8(3), 243–259.

Anderson, D., Moggridge, H., Warren, P. & Shucksmith, J. (2015) The Impacts of 'Run-of-River' Hydropower on the Physical and Ecological Condition of Rivers. *Water and Environment Journal*, 29(2), 268–276.

Ashford, N. A. & Hall, R. P. (2011) The Importance of Regulation-Induced Innovation for Sustainable Development. *Sustainability*, 3(1), 270–292.

Barrett, S. (2003) *Environment and Statecraft: The Strategy of Environmental Treaty-Making: The Strategy of Environmental Treaty-Making.* Oxford: OUP.

Berkhout, F., Hertin, J. & Gann, D. M. (2006) Learning to Adapt: Organisational Adaptation to Climate Change Impacts. *Climatic Change*, 78(1), 135–156.

Bosetti, V., Carraro, C., De Cian, E., Massetti, E. & Tavoni, M. (2013) Incentives and Stability of International Climate Coalitions: An Integrated Assessment. *Energy Policy*, 55, 44–56.

Botcheva, L. & Martin, L. L. (2001) Institutional Effects on State Behavior: Convergence and Divergence. *International Studies Quarterly*, 45(1), 1–26.

Buesseler, K., Aoyama, M. & Fukasawa, M. (2011) Impacts of the Fukushima nuclear power plants on marine radioactivity. *Environmental science & technology*, 45(23), 9931–9935.

Catenacci, M., Verdolini, E., Bosetti, V. & Fiorese, G. (2013) Going Electric: Expert Survey on the Future of Battery Technologies for Electric Vehicles. *Energy Policy*, 61, 403–413.

Costantini, V. & Crespi, F. (2008) Environmental Regulation and the Export Dynamics of Energy Technologies. *Ecological Economics*, 66(2), 447–460.

Dechezleprêtre, A., Glachant, M., Haščič, I., Johnstone, N. & Ménière, Y. (2011) Invention and Transfer of Climate Change–Mitigation Technologies: A Global Analysis. *Review of Environmental Economics and Policy*, 5(1), 109–130.

Drewitt, A. L. & Langston, R. H. (2006) Assessing the Impacts of Wind Farms on Birds. *Ibis*, 148(s1), 29–42.

Driessen, P. (2007) *Eco-Imperialism Green Power, Black Death*. New Delhi: Academic Foundation.

Geels, F. (2011) The Role of Cities in Technological Transitions. *Cities and Low Carbon Transitions*, 3e28.

Geels, F. W. (2005) The Dynamics of Transitions in Socio-Technical Systems: A Multi-Level Analysis of the Transition Pathway from Horse-Drawn Carriages to Automobiles (1860–1930). *Technology Analysis & Strategic Management*, 17(4), 445–476.

Gehring, T. & Oberthür, S. (2004) *Exploring Regime Interaction. In Regime Consequences* (pp. 247–279). The Netherlands: Springer.

Goodell, J. (2007) *Big Coal: The Dirty Secret behind America's Energy Future*. Boston: Houghton Mifflin Harcourt.

Haites, E., Duan, M. & Seres, S. (2006) Technology Transfer by CDM Projects. *Climate Policy*, 6(3), 327–344.

Haszeldine, R. S. (2009) Carbon Capture and Storage: How Green can Black be? *Science*, 325(5948), 1647–1652.

Herman, K.S. (2018) Can Foreign Environmental Policies Induced Clean Technology Innovation at Home? *Working Paper. Submitted to Environmental and Resource Economics*.

Hill, M. R. (2001) Sustainability, Greenhouse Gas Emissions and International Operations Management. *International Journal of Operations & Production Management*, 21(12), 1503–1520.

Hoffmann, M. J. (2011) *Climate Governance at the Crossroads: Experimenting with a Global Response after Kyoto*. Oxford: Oxford University Press.

IEA/IRENA. *Perspectives for the Energy Transition (IEA/IRENA, 2017)*. Available at go.nature.com/2pgfwd

Jänicke, M. (2008) Ecological Modernisation: New Perspectives. *Journal of Cleaner Production*, 16(5), 557–565.

Johnstone, N., Haščič, I. & Popp, D. (2010) Renewable energy policies and technological innovation: evidence based on patent counts. *Environmental and resource economics*, 45(1), 133–155.

Keeble, B. R. (1988) The Brundtland Report: 'Our Common Future'. *Medicine and War*, 4(1), 17–25.

Kemp, R. (1997) *Environmental Policy and Technical Change*. Cheltenham: Edward Elgar.

Kütting, G. (2004) Globalization and the Environment: Greening Global Political Economy. Albany, NY: SUNY Press.

Laufer, W. S. (2003) Social Accountability and Corporate Greenwashing. *Journal of Business Ethics*, 43(3), 253–261.

Macfarlane, A. & Ewing, R. C. (Eds.) (2006) *Uncertainty underground: Yucca Mountain and the nation's high-level nuclear waste*. MIT press: Massachusetts.

Mallon, K. (ed.) (2006) Renewable Energy Policy and Politics: A Handbook for Decision-Making. Oxford: Earthscan.

Mom, G. (2012) *The Electric Vehicle: Technology and Expectations in the Automobile Age*. Baltimore: JHU Press.

Nepstad, D., McGrath, D., Stickler, C., Alencar, A., Azevedo, A., Swette, B. & Armijo, E. (2014) Slowing Amazon Deforestation through Public Policy and Interventions in Beef and Soy Supply Chains. *Science*, 344(6188), 1118–1123.

Neij, L. (1997) Use of experience curves to analyse the prospects for diffusion and adoption of renewable energy technology. *Energy policy*, 25(13), 1099–1107.

Nill, J (2003) Instrumentation of Time Strategies for an Ecological Innovation Policy: A New Role for Subsidies?

Nill, J. & Kemp, R. (2009) Evolutionary Approaches for Sustainable Innovation Policies: From Niche to Paradigm? *Research Policy*, 38(4), 668–680.

Ockwell, D. G. & Mallett, A. (eds) (2012) *Low-Carbon Technology Transfer: From Rhetoric to Reality*. Routledge: New York.

Pimentel, D. (2003) Ethanol Fuels: Energy Balance, Economics, and Environmental Impacts are Negative. *Natural Resources Research*, 12(2), 127–134.

Popp, D. (2006) Innovation in Climate Policy Models: Implementing Lessons from the Economics of R&D. *Energy Economics*, 28(5), 596–609.

Porter, M. E. & Van der Linde, C. (1995) Toward a New Conception of the Environment-Competitiveness Relationship. *The Journal of Economic Perspectives*, 9(4), 97–118.

Praetorius, B. & Schumacher, K. (2009) Greenhouse Gas Mitigation in a Carbon Constrained World: The Role of Carbon Capture and Storage. *Energy Policy*, 37(12), 5081–5093.

Rosenzweig, R. & Blackmar, E. (1992) *The Park and the People: A History of Central Park*. Ithaca, NY: Cornell University Press.

Rowland, F. S. (1989) Chlorofluorocarbons and the Depletion of Stratospheric Ozone. *American Scientist*, 77(1), 36–45.

Sato, M. (2014) Embodied Carbon in Trade: A Survey of the Empirical Literature. *Journal of Economic Surveys*, 28(5), 831–861.

Sawin, J. L., Martinot, E., Barnes, D., McCrone, A., Roussell, J., Sims, R., . . . & Riahi, L. (2010) *Renewables 2011-Global Status Report*. REN21: Paris.

Schiermeier, Q. (2012) Hot Air. *Nature*, 491(7426), 656.

Scott, V., Gilfillan, S., Markusson, N., Chalmers, H. & Haszeldine, R. S. (2013) Last Chance for Carbon Capture and Storage. *Nature Climate Change*, 3(2), 105–111.

Selin, H. & VanDeveer, S. D. (2003) Mapping Institutional Linkages in European Air Pollution Politics. *Global Environmental Politics*, 3(3), 14–46.

Shrivastava, P. (1995) Environmental Technologies and Competitive Advantage. *Strategic Management Journal*, 16(S1), 183–200.

Skea, J. (1995) *Acid Rain: A Business-as-Usual Scenario.* In: Gray, T.S. (ed.) *UK Environmental Policy in the 1990s* (pp. 189–209). Basingstoke, UK: Palgrave Macmillan.

Solomon, S., Qin, D., Manning, M., Chen, Z., Marquis, M., Averyt, K. & Miller, H. (2007) *IPCC fourth assessment report (AR4). Climate change.*

Stern, N. (2013) The Structure of Economic Modeling of the Potential Impacts of Climate Change: Grafting Gross Underestimation of Risk onto Already Narrow Science Models. *Journal of Economic Literature,* 51(3), 838–859.

Tews, K. (2005) The diffusion of environmental policy innovations: cornerstones of an analytical framework. *Environmental Policy and Governance,* 15(2), 63–79.

Verdolini, E. & Galeotti, M. (2011) At Home and Abroad: An Empirical Analysis of Innovation and Diffusion in Energy Technologies. *Journal of Environmental Economics and Management,* 61(2), 119–134.

Von Weizsäcker, E. U. (1994) *Earth Politics.* Chicago: Zed Books.

Walz, R. (2007) The role of regulation for sustainable infrastructure innovations: the case of wind energy. *International Journal of Public Policy,* 2(1–2), 5–88.

Williams, J. H., DeBenedictis, A., Ghanadan, R., Mahone, A., Moore, J., Morrow, W. R. & Torn, M. S. (2012) The Technology Path to Deep Greenhouse Gas Emissions Cuts by 2050: The Pivotal Role of Electricity. *Science,* 335(6064), 53–59.

Young, O. R. (2002) *The institutional dimensions of environmental change: fit, interplay, and scale.* MIT press: Massachusetts.

The politics of energy and the environment

10

Bridging the divide

Maria Julia Trombetta

Access to energy services is a fundamental aspect of contemporary life. We rely on energy for transport, production, communication. Energy empowers. Access to energy sources is a strategic priority for many nation states and the provision of energy services is essential for the economy and for development. Yet, even if energy is fundamental to fulfil human potential, 1.2 billion people have no access to electricity.[1] At the same time, without a radical transformation of existing energy systems, ensuring existing consumption and allowing for growth and broadening access to energy services will have catastrophic consequences for the environment. Contemporary energy systems are unsustainable. They rely on fossil fuels, which contribute to climate change. Globally, the energy sector is responsible for more than two-thirds of all greenhouse gas (GHG) emissions (IEA 2015). Global warming is not the only environmental impact of energy production, distribution and consumption. Burning coal contributes to acid rain and local pollution, and air pollution has reached apocalyptic levels in many Chinese cities. Fracking – the recent technological breakthrough that unlocked unconventional oil and gas, postponing concerns for declining reserves – has severe environmental impacts and requires large amounts of water. At a global level, energy politics is confronted with the triple challenge of ensuring energy supply, protecting the global environment and reducing energy poverty (Dubash and Florini 2011; Falkner 2014: 192).

The link between climate change and energy choices is well known, and yet, energy and environmental politics have ignored each other for decades, as they were considered two distinctive and separate domains, characterized by different actors, approaches and priorities. Only recently, as the sustainability of existing energy systems has been questioned, has the need for an integrated approach emerged, both in academic and political debates. Focusing on climate change, this chapter deals with the relations between energy politics and the environment and explores how an integrated approach has been slowly emerging. It does so by exploring two developments: the first one is the renewed interest for energy security and the incorporation of environmental sustainability in energy security considerations, the second one is the emergence of global energy governance, both as a process and as an analytical tool.

The chapter proceeds as follows. The first section of the chapter illustrates the three challenges of energy politics: ensuring security of supply, protecting the global environment and reducing energy poverty. In doing so, it points at their synergies and tensions. The second section shows that these challenges are determined by the characteristics of contemporary energy systems, which rely on fossil fuels, are unsustainable and need to be governed not only at national but also at global level. Yet, global energy governance is fragmented and it lacks legitimacy. Using the changing conceptualization of energy security as an analytical tool and drawing on insights from the global governance literature, the chapter will then analyze the transformation of energy politics, the emergence of forms of global energy governance and the main actors involved in it.

Dealing with a triple challenge: geopolitical dimension

Access to energy sources is a priority for states and they try to ensure it through both cooperative and competitive measures, often in the name of national security. Not only does the military require energy, the provision of energy services is relevant for economic development and social stability. As energy systems became more and more reliant on oil imported from distant places, energy politics gained an international dimension and access to oil and gas started to shape international politics. Yergin (2003) provides an intriguing account of how the scramble for oil transformed the Middle East. More recently, the assertive Chinese oil diplomacy has fuelled the perception of a Chinese threat (Campion 2016). Klare (2009) warns about the possibilities of future oil wars and shows how the geopolitics of energy is shaping the new world order. The extent of the issue is evident when considering that, in 2014, more than half (53.5%) of the European Union (EU) energy consumption came from imported sources (DG Energy 2016). Traditionally, these concerns have characterized the study of energy politics within the discipline of international relations, mainly from realist perspectives, even if security of supply is often ensured through markets and international institutions (Correlje and Van der Linde 2006).

Concerns for security of supply at affordable prices can downplay environmental considerations. An example is provided by the enduring reliance on coal, even if it is more polluting than other fossil fuels. While oil and gas resources are concentrated in a few countries, coal is distributed more evenly across the globe, making it cheaper and more secure to access. The industrialization and electrification in China, which have provided millions of people with access to modern energy services, have been based on domestic coal. Coal, however, not only contributes to global warming more than other fossil fuels, it is also highly polluting locally. High concentrations of PM2.5,[2] which make air noxious in many Chinese cities, are caused by coal combustion. Renewable energy can provide the solution to both security of supply and sustainability, as it is more evenly distributed and sustainable.

Several actors, including the EU and, recently, the International Energy Agency (IEA), have been vocal advocates of how renewables can solve both environmental and supply issues. Yet, they face opposition from not only oil producing countries but also from states prioritizing economic development based on cheap energy and by those advocating clean fossil fuels or nuclear energy.

Environmental dimension

The threat of climate change played a major role in questioning the sustainability of energy systems but global warming is not the only relevant impact energy systems have on the environment. Energy choices are relevant to several aspects of environmental politics and their implications are global. Production, distribution and consumption of energy services have relevant impacts on the environment. Oil spills have caused serious environmental accidents. Production of non-conventional gas and oil has high environmental impacts: it transforms landscape, uses toxic chemicals, needs large amounts of water and produces massive amounts of waste. Problems are not limited to fossil fuels and need to be considered when decarbonification of the economy is suggested as the way to achieve sustainability. For example, hydropower, considered by many to be a renewable energy source, contributes to deforestation, impacts on fisheries and ecosystems. Nuclear energy, considered to be a viable solution for reducing GHG emissions, poses the problem of the safe storage of waste and its acceptability is problematic. In 2011, the Fukushima accident once again questioned its safety, with global ripple effects on energy policy. German closure of nuclear plants after the Japanese accident required the opening of new coal (lignite) power plants and resulted in higher emissions and higher energy prices in Germany, despite the country's success in promoting renewable energy sources (Helm 2014: 32).

Finally, there is the trade-off between environmental and other dimensions of energy policies, which is evident, for instance, in the debate on biofuels: on the one hand, they are renewable and do not release carbon dioxide that has been stored in fossil fuels; on the other, they subtract land from agricultural production and increase food insecurity. The water–energy–food nexus has become central to discussions regarding sustainable development (UN 2012).

Energy poverty dimension

Access to modern energy services is essential for human well-being and for economic development. Yet, as the IEA reports, across the globe, 1.2 billion people have no access to electricity and more than 2.7 billion people do not have clean and safe cooking facilities (IEA 2016). Rural areas in Sub-Saharan Africa and in developing Asia are the most problematic. A satellite image of the Earth at night clearly shows the extent and location of energy poverty.

These people suffer consequences for their health, due to indoor pollution, opportunity cost, due to the hours spent collecting fuels, and they can contribute to deforestation and

soil degradation (Dubash and Florini 2011: 9). Hodgson (2010: 24) identifies a striking correlation between energy consumption and life expectancy:

> People in the poorer countries, especially in Africa and Asia, have an average energy
> consumption between 0.01 and 0.1 tons of coal equivalent per person per year and
> have an average life expectancy of between 35 and 45 years. At the other end of the
> scale, people in the rich well-developed countries in Europe, North America and
> Japan use between five and ten tons of coal equivalent per person per year and have
> an average life expectancy between 70 and 75 years.

Providing universal access to modern energy services is a huge challenge, which was only
included in sustainable development goals in 2015. To meet the challenge, however, world
energy production will have to be increased at least fourfold (Hodgson 2010: 3). Without a
radical transformation of existing energy systems, the consequences for the climate will be
catastrophic.

Reliance on fossil fuels and the late emergence of the energy–climate nexus

The nature and extent of the challenges outlined above depend on the characteristics of
contemporary energy systems. Since the industrial revolution, energy services have been
provided by burning carbon reserves that have been accumulated in geological eras: coal
first, as it was relatively abundant and easy to access, oil later, as it is easier to transport and
more energy intensive, which is relevant for mobility. The shift from coal to oil meant that
many countries had to import it as reserves are concentrated in a few regions. More recently,
natural gas has partially replaced coal, especially for domestic consumption and electricity
production, as it is less polluting.

Fossil fuels are either burnt directly, in the industrial, domestic and transport sectors,[3] or
burnt to produce electricity. Electricity provides most of the energy services for modern
society. While biofuels can replace oil for transport, it is in the production of electricity
where renewable and nuclear play a relevant role. Electricity is distributed through the
power grid and, as electricity cannot be stored,[4] it has to be produced and consumed. It is
the grid operator that needs to make sure that different power plants are connected and
disconnected to maintain balance and avoid blackouts. Traditionally, centralized and interconnected power grids have ensured the flow of electricity from power plants producing
electricity to the customers. As the production of electricity from renewable sources has
been incentivized, with solar panels on house roofs and small wind turbines, smart grids
have been introduced to allow consumers to also become producers of electricity, lowering
their energy bills in return.

Even if the energy mix varies from country to country, according to domestic resources
and political choices, the extent of reliance on fossil fuels is evident if we consider global
data. In 2015, more than 80% of the global primary energy supply was based on fossil fuels,
a category which includes oil (31.8%), natural gas (21.6%) and coal 28.1%. The remainder

was ensured by nuclear (4.9) and renewables (13.5), which include hydroelectric (2.5), biofuel and waste (9.5) and solar, wind and tide (1.5) (IEA 2017).

Energy systems based on fossil fuels are not sustainable, both in terms of existing resources and due to their contribution to global warming. Despite early concerns prompted by the oil crisis in the 1970s, which brought energy into the political debate for a few years, and increasing awareness of climate change since the 1990s, the extent of the problem only emerged in the early 2000s. Rising and volatile oil prices showed that the crisis was a structural one, related to increasing consumption from emerging economies like China, India and Brazil. Concerns over peak oil and growing demand characterized the debate. At the same time, increasing awareness of climate change questioned the environmental sustainability of the system, while the growing influence of emerging economies questioned its justice, calling for action on energy poverty. Renewable energies, but also nuclear energy, were considered as solutions to both the security of supply and environmental problems. The debate was prompted mainly by considerations of security of supply but it started to question the assumptions behind energy security and the means to provide it (Dyer and Trombetta 2013).

While concerns for peak oil characterized the early 2000s, the recent unlocking of vast reserves of unconventional oil and natural gas in North America – the so-called shale revolution – suggests that, in terms of sustainability, the main issue is not the scarcity of reserves but rather their abundance. There is three times more carbon in the existing reserves of fossil fuels than can be burnt without global warming exceeding 2 degrees celsius, the target agreed on in Paris in 2015 to avoid climate calamities (Goldthau 2017). A shift toward renewables will provide energy that is abundant and effectively free and "energy assets will move further up the value chain, from commodities to technologies" (Goldthau 2017: 204). Such a transition will have a deep effect on the economy and on geopolitical equilibrium. On the one hand, countries with technology and capital will benefit most, while those lacking them, mainly in the global South, will lose out. On the other hand, as burning existing reserves would release more carbon dioxide than the Paris Agreement allows, a large part of them will need to be left in the ground, as commentators have started to point out (McKibben 2012, Goldthau 2017). These reserves are assets worth up to 100 trillion US dollars, about five times the GDP of the United States in 2016, and they are owned by a variety of stakeholders (Goldthau 2017: 204). There will be winners and losers, as Goldthau stated.

The challenge of decarbonizing the economy involves transforming existing infrastructures and institutional designs. It is a challenge that involves the ideational more than the technological dimension. If, at a global level, the challenge involves ensuring security of supply, environmental protection and energy poverty reduction, individual players, mainly states, face the challenge of ensuring the provision of energy services, their acceptability, which includes the environmental dimension, as well as their competitiveness. Here, the debate can be framed along the divide between realist or economic nationalist perspectives, interested in maximizing national interest and relative gains, and liberal positions, which consider absolute gains and the possibility of cooperation.

National energy choices have a global effect, as climate change demonstrates, and economists point to the existence of externalities to call for international action (Van de Graaf 2013: 34–36) or consider sustainable energy as a global public good (Karlsson-Vinkhuyzen and Jollands 2013). Part of the problem is that competitiveness is affected by subsidies and other economic incentives, and fossil fuels are largely subsidized. While there are subsidies for green technology, in 2012 the IEA reported that subsidies for fossil fuels amounted to 523 billion US dollars, six times the amount of subsidies for renewable sources (Van de Graaf 2013: 24). Subsides exist because governments decide to support economically relevant energy sectors or to exempt others from energy taxes. Governments promote economic growth and stability with cheap energy. In China, gasoline and electricity prices are controlled and subsidized. Oil producing countries rely on low energy prices to ensure social stability. Besides, technological breakthroughs are often the result of specific incentives. As Van de Graaf explains, the unlocking of unconventional oil and gas, thanks to hydraulic fracturing and horizontal drilling, is considered as an example of a successful technological breakthrough, which has been made possible by subsidies. Innovation was determined by specific circumstances as "oil companies were forced to move to more technically difficult, economically costly, environmentally risky, and politically sensitive sources due to global market circumstances" (Van de Graaf 2013: 25).

According to the United Nations (UN), energy is "perhaps the topmost sector on the agenda of issues in need of global management" (UN-Energy 2006: 1) but energy governance lacks legitimacy; it is fragmented and characterized by overlapping institutions, representing different interests and sectors (Florini and Dubash 2011). Part of the problem is that the coordination between environmental and energy policy has been a long-overlooked issue. Despite the long-recognized link between the use of fossil fuels, energy consumption and climate change, only recently have the two issues been considered together, recognizing that "climate policy is energy policy" (Scrase et al. 2009: 3). This is a division that characterized not only politics and institutions but also academic inquiry.

At the domestic level, responsibilities for energy and climate policies have been prerogatives of separate ministries, often with different priorities. Only in the early 2000s did a few countries start to create ministries incorporating both environmental and energy competencies. The division has impacted on international negotiations and agreements. As Heubaum and Biermann noticed, the United Nation Framework Convention on Climate Change (UNFCCC) negotiations and annual meetings are attended by environment and foreign ministry representatives, not by energy ones (2015: 230).

The difficulties of integrating environmental and energy perspectives reflect the different priorities assigned to energy and environmental politics; the former is often prioritized as a strategic issue, even when aspects of it are left to the market, the latter is not. At international level, discussions on energy cooperation in multilateral settings and as part of environmental negotiations have been resisted by states concerned about the possibility of having their sovereign prerogatives on energy issues limited by environmental and other agreements. Global energy governance lacks legitimacy (Karlsson-Vinkhuyzen 2016: 115).

Even in the academic literature on global environmental politics, energy has been quite a marginal and recent topic. Part of the problem is that the politics of energy itself tends to be under-explored in social science literature. On the one hand, energy experts, with access to data, are practitioners and are not particularly interested in academic publishing; on the other hand, energy politics requires a relevant amount of technical knowledge and interdisciplinarity. As Strange states, energy is "a classic case of the no man's land lying between the social sciences, an area unexplored and unoccupied by any of the major theoretical disciplines" (quoted in Van de Graaf et al. 2016: 8). The result is an artificial, problematic separation of politics and economics in dealing with energy issues, which, in turn, contributes to the marginalization of environmental ones.

Some aspects of energy politics have been considered in the research on environmental impacts and ecological limits, and in the literature on sustainable development (Falkner 2014: 190). The first was relevant in the 1960s and 1970s and was informed by neo-Malthusian concerns about limited resources and gained momentum in the wake of the oil crisis. The second emerged later. It emphasized the importance of sustainability and contributed to analyzing the complexity of the issues involved in transitions toward environmentally sustainable energy systems (Bradshaw 2014). Only recently, however, two different but interrelated approaches have provided new perspectives to incorporate energy in global environmental politics. The first is the literature on global environmental governance and the parallel, even if more recent, debate on global energy governance. The second is the literature on the transformation of security, which has been informed by the debate on environmental security but has acquired new dimensions when energy is involved.

In the literature on global environmental governance, the concept of global governance is used to analyze a range of formal and informal arrangements in which states and other actors engage. The concept points at the existence of forms of steering and governing that are not necessarily based on formal authority but can arise from private or hybrid sources of global authority. By focusing on processes it cuts across disciplines and levels of analysis (see also Chapter 1), and this approach is quite relevant for both environmental and energy governance. However, the very topic of global energy governance is relatively new in the literature, with the first works dating back to the early 2010s. Dubash and Florini (2011) provide one of the first attempts to map the literature and the challenges of global energy governance.

Within this framework, scholars have outlined the challenges of integrating energy and environmental politics (Falkner 2014) and called for "holistic thinking across traditional policy fields" (Goldthau 2012: 182). While some scholars are pointing at the solutions available within existing systems, optimizing climate policy instruments, like emission trading permits, financing energy transitions and strengthening institutional arrangements (Falkner 2014: 192–193), others emphasize the need to transform the system and point at the limits of neo-liberal approaches and ecological modernization. Kuzemko, in her analysis of the "Energy Security-Climate nexus," shows how concerns for climate change are providing a new energy policy paradigm that challenges both the strategic, geopolitical approach and the market-oriented, liberal one, but she warns that the relevance of this paradigm is limited by the resilience of the neo-liberal approach that "has not been understood to be at fault in creating energy crises" (Kuzemko 2013: 7) (see also Ehresman and Stevis, Chapter 6).

The other relevant approach is provided by the literature on the transformation of security, which has questioned the traditional understanding of security focused on the state and on a realist, zero sum approach. The literature on environmental security has contributed to the debate about broadening, deepening and transforming security (see also Hughes, Chapter 4). The debate has been characterized by a divide between those supporting the framing of environmental problems in security terms to prioritize them and those opposing the idea for the problematic practices security evokes and allows.[5] Even if quite late, a similar debate emerged over energy. Here, the opposition is between energy security, often understood as geopolitics of energy, informed by realism, and an approach based on markets and institutions to govern energy. Some commentators stick to a traditional understanding of energy security as security of supply and warn that considering energy as a security issue, rather than an economic one, can limit cooperation and prompt conflict (McGowan 2011, Radoman 2007). Others argue that energy security means different things to different actors and that different approaches are associated with different disciplines concerned with the provision of energy services (Cherp and Jewell 2011; Chester 2010); not all of them are associable with the realist, zero sum approach to security. Analyzing the transformation of energy security discourses can contribute to understanding the evolution of energy politics.

Research focused on the tensions and synergies between environmental and energy security (Vogler 2013; Umbach 2012) and on how the meaning of energy security evolved. Inspired by critical security studies, the latter literature explores whose security is considered in energy security discourses, what threats are considered and what means can be legitimately employed. It has shown how environmental considerations have been incorporated in energy security discourses and how the meaning of energy security has shifted from security of supply to a broader understanding that includes security of demand, sustainability and justice considerations (Dyer and Trombetta 2013, Sovacool et al. 2014).[6]

The energy governance and the energy security debate provide the most promising approaches to provide an account of the evolution in the politics of energy. They will be used in the remainder of the chapter to analyze the evolution of energy politics and the actors involved in energy governance.

Reading the evolution of energy politics through security lenses

A fundamental divide characterizes energy policy. On the one hand, the neo-liberal approach considers energy a commodity like many others and leaves the provision of energy services to the market, as the most efficient mechanism to allocate resources.[7] On the other, those who consider energy a strategic commodity argue that the functioning of societies depends on energy and call for state intervention in energy policies, from subsidies to oil diplomacy. The presumptive divide ignores that, even within the neo-liberal perspective, markets need to be regulated and energy remains a political and security concern even if it is assumed that markets more adequately address political and security concerns. Actually, states tend to combine elements from these two perspectives and energy policies oscillate between the two, in the conceptualization of energy security and in the means to provide it. A focus on the construction of energy security allows an analysis of the evolution of energy politics, bringing together the economic and the (geo)political perspectives and overcoming a problematic divide for policy making and academic inquiry.

The years after the Second World War were characterized by states' intervention in the energy sector with the nationalization of oil reserves, the creation of large national oil companies and integrated energy utilities. These measures consolidated centralized, integrated energy systems based almost exclusively on fossil fuels.[8] Energy services were considered public goods and provided by a few state-owned companies. Prices were controlled, even in the United States, which traditionally adopted market principles more easily than other OECD (Organisation for Economic Co-operation and Development) countries (Goldthau 2012: 201), limited environmental regulations were introduced to limit the environmental impact of the energy sector. In Western countries, energy security was security of supply and states were seen as a guarantor of this supply.

The oil crises in the 1970s questioned this approach. The OPEC (Organization of the Petroleum Exporting Countries) embargo, and the shortage it created, led to economic disruption in Western countries. Western responses to the crisis promoted the creation of a global oil market, with emergency mechanisms to deal with short term supply disruptions (the strategic oil reserves). The success of this approach contributed to an apparent depoliticization of energy, which was left to the market and considered as an economic rather than a political or strategic issue. The great interest for the politics of energy that characterized the 1970s disappeared and a liberal approach that considered energy as an economic issue rather than a strategic issue emerged.

The 1980s and 1990s were characterized by a process of privatization and liberalization. Against the backdrop of an over inflated public sector and economic recession, a neo-liberal approach emerged. In the United States, price control and most environmental provisions were cancelled; in the UK, BP, the state-owned behemoth, was privatized.[9] The state became a regulator rather than an owner or a service provider. The EU championed this approach, promoting the introduction of competition to promote efficiency, even if liberalization in the energy sector was slow and integration difficult as many states were still considering energy as a matter of national security and wanted to protect their national champions. Sustainability was not a primary concern in a market based approach to energy politics. Within this approach, the emerging issue of climate change was considered as a market failure and mechanisms to internalize externalities were introduced, like emission trading permits. These measures reflected the trust in the market to provide incentives to reduce emissions and global warming.

The situation changed again in the early 2000s when concerns for the growing demand of fossil fuels, especially by emerging economies like China and India, and climate change started to dominate political agendas. Energy security was back. Even if the threat posed by global warming had already been acknowledged by the late 1980s, it was only after 2005 that the link between climate change and energy was clearly established. The Stern Review, in 2006 (Stern 2007), and the Intergovernmental Panel on Climate Change IPCC Fourth Assessment Report, in 2007, made scientific data available to a broader public and refocused attention on the climate–energy nexus (IPCC 2007). Not only was the consensus on climate change growing but the need for a holistic rethinking of energy systems to tackle climate change also emerged. Climate and energy, traditionally two separate policy areas started to merge (Goldthau 2012: 204). At the same time, two other issues emerged: the awareness that it was no longer possible to leave the provision of energy security to the market and that new forms of global governance were called for.

The responses to the crises were rather different. Within the EU, concerns over increasing energy dependency and environmental considerations prompted an ambitious plan to decarbonize the economy and achieve a "secure, sustainable and competitive energy". In 2007, the European Council adopted ambitious energy and climate change objectives for 2020 – to reduce GHG emissions by 20%, to increase the share of renewable energy to 20% and to make a 20% improvement in energy efficiency. These objectives were followed by a long term commitment to decarbonization with a target of 80 to 95% cuts in emissions by 2050. The European Commission's 2011 Energy Roadmap set out four main routes to a more "sustainable, competitive and secure" energy system in 2050: energy efficiency, renewable energy, nuclear energy and carbon capture and storage.

The European conceptualization of energy security has been quite influential; it suggested that security of supply, environmental security and competitiveness can be achieved together. Yet, European choices and leadership in promoting renewable energy have been determined not only by the strong European commitment to sustainability but also by a specific vision of future developments in the oil and gas markets. Europe was gambling on increasing energy prices and hoping to acquire a competitive advantage in clean energy. Europe's expectations have not materialized yet. Shale gas has provided the United States with cheap energy and energy independence, making renewables less attractive (Helm 2014: 31–32). The lack of agreement in Copenhagen and in Durban on the future of the Kyoto Protocol made clear the difficulties of implementing explicit carbon caps and the weakness of the European leadership. The transformation of the international context, with declining fossil fuel prices and political instability threatening security of supply, have challenged the European vision. Commentators (Szulecki and Westphal, 2014, Helm 2014) have questioned the sustainability of the approach and recent developments suggest greater concerns for security of supply and competitiveness (Youngs 2014: 66–71).

Despite a strong preference for domestic energy sources, demonstrated by the reliance on coal, and despite being the world's fifth largest oil producer, since 1993 China has been a net oil importer, and it is now relying on imports for more than half of its consumption (BP 2016). As imports grew, so did concerns over security of supply. In the early 2000s, China developed a rather aggressive oil diplomacy, supporting acquisitions by its national oil companies and prioritizing security of supply to ensure economic growth. However, by 2006, China started to call for a "depoliticized" approach to energy security[10] and became more involved in global energy governance (He 2016). Domestically, it promoted energy efficiency and invested in renewable energy. The 2005 Renewable Energy Law set ambitious targets and called for 15% of China's energy to be coming from renewable sources by 2020. The 12th Five Year Plan (2011–2015) set the goal of installing 100 GW of on-shore wind power and 34 GW of solar photovoltaics; having achieved this ambitious goal, the 13th Five Year Plan (2016–2020) doubled and tripled the respective targets. China is leading the way in solar and on-shore wind power installations; in 2015 "half of all wind power capacity and almost one third of all solar PV capacity installed globally was in China".[11] This is quite relevant for global energy and environmental politics as China is the number one GHG emitter in the world. Yet, the country remains reliant on coal, which accounts for about 66% of its energy mix (BP 2016), and it is causing noxious air pollution. Despite a reluctance to consider climate change as a security issue, China has started to develop an integrated approach to energy security, which considers energy efficiency and renewables as a way to ensure economic growth, broaden access to energy services and tackle pollution and climate change. The announcement, in November 2014, by President Xi that emissions would peak by 2030 and his signature on the Paris agreement are relevant signals, even if security of supply remains a relevant concern for China.

In North America, growing concerns over security of supply created incentives to develop domestic sources and promote innovation in that direction. The "Blueprint for a Secure Energy Future" in 2011 called for reductions in foreign oil import, expansion of domestic drilling and increased energy efficiency (Umbach 2012: 378). The Obama administrators had pushed for clean energy, suggesting that the United States risked falling behind in new technologies and calling for investments in clean energy and new fuel efficiency standards. Yet, the development of Canadian tar sand and of the so-called non-conventional oil and gas unlocked new resources, ensured energy independence for North America and questioned the scarcity narrative associated with peak oil. A fundamental shift has occurred with the US switch to shale gas and oil, which has implications for both geopolitical and environmental aspects. Shale gas is more evenly distributed across the globe and other countries could follow the American path (Youngs 2014: 69). Environmentally, it has made renewables less competitive, and yet the "switch to shale gas has given the US its lowest emissions in 20 years" (Youngs 2014: 69) as gas emissions are lower than those produced burning oil or coal. However, IEA Executive Director Fatih Birol has warned: "A golden age of gas is not necessarily a golden age for the climate" (Umbach 2012: 380) as a shift to gas will not be sufficient to meet the two degree Celsius target set in climate agreements. Having achieved energy independence, relying on non-conventional oil and gas rather than on renewable sources, competitiveness remains dominant in the US energy security agenda. The Trump administration has emphasized that aspect, downplaying environmental concerns and even denying climate change. However, among political elites, awareness of the security implications of climate change remains relevant and the business sector is worried about the implications of a re-carbonification of the economy for American competitiveness and technological leadership (Stiglitz 2017).

Renewed concern over geopolitical aspects of energy supply in Europe and Asia, but also increased concerns over climate change and the way energy has been mainstreamed into fighting poverty, suggest a growing consensus that energy cannot be left to private actors. The neo-liberal free market model has been questioned and various forms of state intervention have re-emerged to ensure energy security (Goldthau 2012: 204). The interventionist approach is characterizing not only countries like China, used to state intervention in key sectors of the economy, but also Western ones. Increased state intervention in the energy sector to fix perceived shortcomings in energy security goes hand in hand with the development of forms of global governance. The transformation of global energy governance involves both the incorporation of environmental considerations as part of a holistic approach and the transformation and multiplication of the actors involved in energy governance. Two dynamics characterize the transformation and multiplication of actors: on the one hand, emerging economies are gaining importance and the ability to shape global energy governance and its agenda; on the other hand, new actors, like public–private partnerships and global networks are emerging. These developments are discussed in the next section.

Global energy governance: actors, organizations and their evolution

This section explores the actors and institutions involved in global energy governance, and outlines how they contributed to promoting more sustainable energy systems by including environmental and energy access considerations in energy politics and by challenging a narrow understanding of energy security.

Energy policy is still decided by states, even if decisions impact beyond their borders and call for coordinate actions. Over the years, some institutional arrangements were created, often as a response to crises, even if the energy sector remains one in which governance is weak and fragmented. The actors and institutions that emerged have played a relevant role in shaping ideas and transforming the understanding of energy security. At the same time, they represent an institutional design that emerged with little consideration for the environment and with an emphasis on fossil fuels, and in turn, they contribute to the resilience of that system.

The IEA is emblematic in this respect. The IEA plays a relevant role in collecting information on energy trends and, more recently, on emissions and renewable energy. Its reputation and influential role make it the most authoritative voice in a context characterized by the lack of a world energy organization. Yet, its role and capabilities reflect its origin and membership. The IEA was created in 1974 as an independent organization within the OECD framework to respond to the oil crisis prompted by the OPEC's embargo. It brought together consumer countries to increase their resilience to crises determined by short term supply shortage.[12]

Since the 1970s, the IEA has contributed to developing a global liquid oil market and promoting energy liberalization. It ensured energy security by supporting the smooth working of the oil market, providing reliable information, ensuring cooperation with oil companies and developing mechanisms to deal with short term crisis, such as the strategic oil reserves. The success of these mechanisms contributed not only to the success of an energy system based on fossil fuels but also to "de-securitizing" energy, transforming energy into an economic rather than a strategic issue.[13]

As concerns for energy security re-emerged in the early 2000s, the capability of the IEA to ensure the smooth working of the system, as well as the relevance of a narrow conceptualization of energy security and of the mechanisms to ensure it, were questioned. The authoritative status of the IEA played a relevant role in incorporating environmental concerns in energy security strategies. While during the 1980s and 1990s the IEA's definition of energy security focused on availability of energy at all times, in different forms, in sufficient quantities and at affordable prices, since 2001 the IEA has adopted the following definition of energy security: "the uninterrupted physical availability at a price which is affordable, while respecting environmental concerns" (IEA, quoted in Umbach 2012: 376) and it has started to collect information on CO_2 emissions and on GHG emission policies. Since 2008, the *World Energy Outlook* (WEO), the IEA's flagship publication, has had a section on climate change (Heubaum and Biermann 2015: 233). In 2012, the IEA signed a memorandum of understanding with the UNFCCC Secretariat promoting a mutual effort to combat climate change and support clean energy. This is contributing to an integrated framework in which the UNFCCC is providing the governance structure and the IEA is contributing its expertise and data (Heubaum and Biermann 2015: 234). Before the 21st Conference of the Parties of the UNFCCC (COP 21) in Paris in 2015, which led to the signing of the Paris Agreement, the IEA published a special WEO report on climate change "explicitly emphasizing energy use and climate change as inextricably linked" (Heubaum and Biermann 2015: 233).

Critics, however, have argued that the IEA has been entangled with the oil industry and supported energy systems based on fossil fuels, adopting a cautious position on renewable energy sources, which has downplayed expectations and discouraged investments (Van de Graaf 2013: 9, Van de Graaf and Lesage 2009). The issue is relevant as it reflects not only different commitments to act on climate change but also different strategies to do so, opposing, for instance, those promoting renewable energy and the advocates of clean coal. The debate has contributed to the successful creation, in 2009, of the International Renewable Energy Agency (IRENA).

As energy security reappeared in the international arena, the G8 and, more recently, the G20 have started to discuss the climate–energy nexus and promote a more comprehensive approach to energy security. The 2005 Gleneagle G8 summit issued the Plan of Action on Climate Change, Clean Energy and Sustainable Development; one year later, in St Petersburg, the G8 produced a statement on global energy security calling for "sufficient, reliable and environmentally responsible supplies of energy at prices reflecting market fundamentals" and stating that "neither global energy security, nor the Millennium Development Goals can be fully achieved without sustainable access to fuels for the 2.4 billion people and to electricity for the 1.6 billion people currently without such access in developing countries" (G8 2006). These statements are relevant because they signal changing perspectives in energy politics; however, the G8's renewed concern for energy and the environment translated not only in a set of grand pledges, but also in specific initiatives like the International Partnership for Energy Efficiency and Cooperation, established at the Hokkaido summit in 2008 (Zelli et al. 2013: 346). As emerging economies are playing a greater role in the energy field, it is the G20 rather than the G8 that is considered by commentators (Goldthau 2017) as the most appropriate forum to coordinate action, share information and promote energy transitions, as the G20 includes not only many members of the IEA but also the main GHG emitters and emerging economies, whose energy consumption is growing fast. The G20 set several working groups on energy and debated the issue of abolishing subsidies on fossil fuels.

The UN have started to address issues related to energy, sustainability and development. The marginal role of the UN in the field points at the main problem of energy politics: states do not consider it justified that the UN exerts authority on energy issues (Karlsson-Vinkhuyzen 2016: 115). Yet, several UN bodies have been involved in shaping norms about energy poverty and environmental protection. Since the early 2000s, energy issues have been discussed by the Commission for Sustainable Development. The 2001 annual meeting of the Commission was the first time energy was specifically discussed, considering economic, social and environmental dimensions (Karlsson-Vinkhuyzen 2016: 117).[14] The link between energy and the environment was discussed in 2002 at the UN World Summit on Sustainable Development (WSSD), where the EU pushed for the end of subsides for fossil fuels and time bound targets for renewables but was opposed by China and G77 whose concerns were for ensuring universal energy access. No targets were agreed, even if the text on energy that emerged represents a relevant enhancement in developing global norms as it provided extensive reference to renewable energy and energy efficiency (Karlsson-Vinkhuyzen 2016: 17). In 2004, UN-Energy, a mechanism for inter-agency collaboration in the field of energy, was established "to help ensure coherence in the United Nations system's multidisciplinary response to the World Summit on Sustainable Development (WSSD)" and to support countries in their transition to sustainable energy (UN-Energy 2006: 2). Yet divisions remained, especially as climate change rose on the agenda. Proponents of fossil fuels called for clean "end of pipe" technologies, such as carbon capture and storage (see Chapter 7) while renewables were advocated by countries asking for strong action on climate change and by those facing high costs to import fossil fuels.

Energy has also been brought to the UN Security Council. On April 17, 2007, the UN Security Council had the first meeting ever on Climate Change and Security, which can be read not only as an attempt to promote action on climate change but also as a way to emphasize the link between climate and energy politics.[15] Yet the debate demonstrated the reluctance to consider climate change as a security issue.

The debate within the UN has contributed to framing access to energy as a human security issue.[16] In 2012, the UN Conference on Sustainable Development linked energy to human well-being, with a pledge for "sustainable, modern energy services for all" (UN 2012). The same year, the UN Secretary General launched the "Sustainable Energy for all initiative", a partnership between governments, the business sector and civil society, with the vision of achieving sustainable energy for all by 2030, and the UNGA (United Nations General Assembly), despite the resistance of governments to institutionalizing energy governance, established the UN Decade for Sustainable Energy for All. In 2015, access to "Affordable, Reliable Sustainable and modern energy for all" was included in the sustainable development goals.

As Karlsson-Vinkhuyzen points out, the universal membership of the UN provides legitimacy that the IEA or other club arrangements, like the G8 or the G20, will never have. The incorporation of access to energy in the sustainable development goals and the emphasis on sustainability represent relevant steps in increasing the legitimacy of global energy governance and in making the energy sector subject to multilateral agreements, monitoring and accountability (see Karlsson-Vinkhuyzen 2016). It also signals a transformation of the norms governing energy and a shift of the conceptualization of energy security to include environmental and humanitarian aspects.

A final aspect that needs to be considered is the impact of climate agreements on energy politics. Even if the international climate agreements have not been created with the view of governing energy, the UNFCCC, with the Kyoto Protocol, has been relevant in shaping states' energy choices and compliance with the Paris Agreement is going to influence future energy choices. Back in 2011, Dubash and Florini noted that a "comprehensive global climate agreement organized around explicit national carbon caps would be transformative and become a de facto global energy governance regime" (Dubash and Florini 2011: 14). Yet, states' resistance to interference in their energy policies resulted in the lack of specific references to energy in climate agreements. Two main critiques have been moved to the UNFCCC in terms of influence on energy policies (see Zelli et al. 2013: 342). First, the approach adopted by the Kyoto Protocol, requiring emission reduction targets for developed countries only, did not impact on the energy policy decisions of developing ones. Second, with the Paris Agreement, the regime is moving toward a bottom up approach (Falkner 2016), which leaves the choice of actions to mitigate climate change to individual countries, as commitments are voluntary. While this approach proved to be successful in getting the Paris Agreement signed, it might hinder the development of global energy governance.

The growing relevance of transnational governance networks involving non state actors is another aspect of the development and of the transformation of energy governance. Many involve partnership between the business sector and other actors that can be both state and civil society groups. These initiatives are particularly relevant in promoting transparency and the disclosure of data on carbon emissions by the energy sector. They include the Carbon Disclosure Project, the Global Reporting Initiatives, the Extractive Industries Transparency Initiative (Falkner 2014: 194).

Since the early 2000s, a combination of concerns over the sustainability of energy systems and a governance structure to ensure energy security have contributed to combining energy and environmental policies. On the one hand, there is a re-conceptualization of energy security that sees energy security and environmental security as complementary rather than antagonistic. On the other, there is an approach that is focusing on carbon governance which brings together consideration of energy efficiency, carbon intensity with global warming but also local pollution.

Conclusions

This chapter has considered the evolution of energy politics and the emergence of the triple challenge of ensuring the provision of energy services at affordable prices, broadening access to energy services and ensuring sustainability. Contemporary energy systems, largely based on fossil fuels, are not sustainable and are highly unequal. Decarbonizing the economy and moving toward renewable energy sources would allow GHG emissions to be reduced, broaden access to energy services and increase security of supply. Yet, energy transitions face a variety of challenges and obstacles. On the one hand, there is the resilience of existing energy systems and infrastructures. On the other, there are vested interests and competing priorities.

The challenges of promoting transitions toward more sustainable energy systems are complicated by the way energy politics has traditionally been conceptualized, as a very specific, highly technical sector governed by states that – while willing to delegate the provision of energy services to the market and private actors – have been reluctant to legitimize forms of global energy governance. The result has been a marginalization of energy politics within social science, a division between geopolitical aspects and economic ones and a marginalization of environmental considerations.

Promoting sustainability requires a holistic approach, and yet energy and environmental politics have traditionally been considered as two separate fields, governed by different structures and actors, often with competing priorities. The need for an integrated approach has emerged only recently. The transformation is evident not only in the creation of ministries with responsibilities for both energy and climate change but also in the adoption of an integrated approach that sees increased energy efficiency as a way to tackle both security of supply and pollution or in the emerging concerns for the energy–climate–water nexus. Even more relevant is the shift from an approach that considers the provision of energy services and environmental protection as two competing objectives to one that regards them as compatible or even complementary. The incorporation of sustainability into energy security suggests a move that is similar to the conceptual shift that allowed the conceptualization of "sustainable development" as a way to merge two objectives: environmental protection and development, which were previously considered incompatible. The shift is implicit in the European discourse about a "secure, competitive and sustainable energy", even if different actors have different priorities and tend to prioritize different aspects of energy security.

The other problematic aspect in promoting transitions toward sustainable energy systems is the lack of legitimacy for global energy governance, as testified by the marginality of energy within the UN system. Yet, global issues like climate change have contributed to the awareness that energy needs to be governed globally. The debate within the UN has contributed to legitimizing forms of multilateral governance and transforming norms governing energy, introducing considerations for sustainability, access and energy justice. The shift characterizes not only the issues to be governed and their complementarity but also the actors involved as more and more actions are brought forward by private actors and transnational networks.

These transformations point to the relevance of ideas and accepted norms for energy politics. Developments in the literature, both on energy governance and energy security, largely inspired by constructivist approaches, have provided the instrument to analyze them.

Notes

1 IEA, World Energy Outlook 2016 (Paris: IEA, 2016). The 2016 energy access database is available at www.worldenergyoutlook.org/media/weowebsite/2015/WEO2016Electricity.xlsx (accessed on October 2, 2017).

2 The term PM 2.5 refers to fine particulate matter with a diameter of 2.5 micron or less. These microscopic particles suspended in the air are extremely dangerous for health as they can penetrate deeply into the lungs and in the blood stream.

3 Crude oil needs to be refined and transformed into usable fuels such as gasoline, fuel oils, and into petroleum-based products.

4 Electricity itself cannot be stored, but it can be transformed to other energy forms which can be stored and, when needed, reconverted to electricity. The most common form of storage is batteries but compressed air and pumped hydro storage can be used.

5 This is an aspect that has been fleshed out by securitization theory, which, drawing on a specific political tradition, identifies security with a specific form of social practice that refers to governing issues as emergencies and allows for exceptional measures, breaking with ordinary politics and democratic procedures (Buzan, Wæver and de Wilde 1998).

6 Within this literature, Cherp and Jewell (2014) provide an interesting approach. They show that, when discussing energy security, what needs to be secured is not access to oil or gas but the

working of specific critical energy systems, which deliver energy services. These systems are complex socio technical systems that incorporate not only material and technological aspects but also values about what needs to be protected.

7 This approach gained relevance after the oil crises in the 1970s in order to "secure supply" for the West, see section 'Reading the evolution of energy poltiics through security lenses' below for an historical account of the evolution of the energy security discourse and of the ways to provide it.

8 The centralized approach involved megaprojects, including gigantic dams and hydroelectric power stations, like the Hoover Dam in the United States, whose sustainability has been questioned.

9 British Petroleum's privatization started in 1977 and continued with Thatcher's governments. By 1987, the government had sold all its shares in the company (BP website: https://www.bp.com/en/global/corporate/who-we-are/our-history/late-century.html) accessed on January 24, 2018.

10 Hu Juntao, speaking at the G8 Summit in St. Petersburg, proposed a "new energy security concept" based on "sustainable development of human society" (http://www.fmprc.gov.cn/mfa_eng/wjdt_665385/zyjh_665391/t264261.shtml).

11 http://energydesk.greenpeace.org/2016/09/08/china-six-little-known-facts-countrys-solar-wind-boom/

12 The creation, in the 1970s, of two international organizations, IEA and OPEC, representing consumer and producer countries, respectively, had a long term impact on energy governance.

13 Over the years, the antagonistic approach that characterized the divide between the IEA and OPEC countries diminished and it became clear that security of supply requires security of demand for producer countries to ensure investments; the International Energy Forum was created to promote dialogue.

14 The choice of the Commission, while suggesting a rather marginal role for energy issues, indicates an attempt to bring together environmental sustainability, access and development issues and adopt an integrated approach. Within the Commission, access to "affordable supply of modern energy" has been presented as an energy security issue, not only by developing countries but also by the EU and China. Yet the debate within the Commission was characterized by opposition between the EU, promoting renewable energy sources, and the coalition of G77 and China that emphasized the importance of affordable energy and fossil fuels for economic development (Karlsson-Vinkhuyzen 2016: 121–122).

15 It was a few days before the 15th meeting of the Commission on Sustainable Development which had energy on the agenda and concluded with no agreement ENV/DEV/938 11 May 2007.

16 Access to energy impacts on several dimensions of human security as defined by UNDP, such as economic security, food security, health security and environmental security. Yet, access to energy has not been included in the UNDP definition or in millennium development goals, agreed in 2000, which testifies to the difficulties of including energy in international negotiations and the slow process of creating norms considering the environmental and social aspects of energy.

Recommended reading

Cherp, A. & Jewell, J. (2014) The Concept of Energy Security: Beyond the Four As. *Energy Policy*, 75, 415–421.

Hodgson, P. (2010) *Energy, the Environment and Climate Change*. London: Imperial College Press/World Scientific Publishing Company.

Kuzemko, C. (2013) *The Energy Security-Climate Nexus: Institutional Change in the UK and Beyond*. Basingstoke: Palgrave Macmillan.

Websites

UN-Energy. Available at: www.un-energy.org/.
IEA. Available at: www.iea.org.
IRENA. Available at: www.irena.org.

References

BP (2016) *Country Insights: China*. Available at: https://www.bp.com/en/global/corporate/energy-economics/energy-outlook/country-and-regional-insights/china-insights.html (last accessed 12/03/2017).

Bradshaw, M. J. (2014) *Global Energy Dilemmas: Energy Security, Globalization, and Climate Change*. Cambridge: Polity Press.

Buzan, B., Wæver, O. & De Wilde, J. (1998) *Security: A New Framework for Analysis*. Boulder, CO: Lynne Rienner.

Campion, A. (2016) *The Geopolitics of Red Oil: Constructing the China Threat Through Energy Security*. Abington: Routledge.

Cherp, A. & Jewell, J. (2011) The Three Perspectives on Energy Security: Intellectual History, Disciplinary Roots and the Potential for Integration. *Current Opinion on Environment and Sustainability*, 3(4), 1–11.

Cherp, A. & Jewell, J. (2014) The Concept of Energy Security: Beyond the Four As. *Energy Policy*, 75, 415–421.

Chester, L. (2010) Conceptualising Energy Security and Making Explicit Its Polysemic Nature. *Energy Policy*, 38(2), 887–895.

Correlje, A. & Van der Linde, C. (2006) Energy Supply Security and Geopolitics: A European Perspective. *Energy Policy*, 34(5), 532–543.

DG Energy (2016) EU Energy in Figures: Statistics Pocketbook. Available at: https://publications.europa.eu/en/publication-detail/-/publication/c3d179b2-9a82-11e6-9bca-01aa75ed71a1 (last accessed 10/08/2017).

Dubash, N. & Florini, A. (2011) Mapping Global Energy Governance. *Global Policy*, 2(s1), 6–18.

Dyer, H. & Trombetta, M. J. (2013) The Concept of Energy Security: Broadening, Deepening, Transforming, in Dyer, H. & Trombetta, M. J. (eds), *International Handbook of Energy Security*. Cheltenham: Edward Elgar.

Falkner, R. (2014) Global Environmental Politics and Energy: Mapping the Research Agenda. *Energy Research & Social Science*, 1, 188–197.

Falkner, R. (2016) The Paris Agreement and the new logic of international climate politics. *International Affairs*, 92(5), 1107–1125.

Florini, A. & Dubash, N. (2011) Introduction to the Special Issue: Governing Energy in a Fragmented World. *Global Policy*, 2(s1), 1–5.

van de Graaf, T. (2013) *The Politics and Institutions of Global Energy Governance*. Basingstoke: Palgrave.

van de Graaf, T. & Lesage, D. (2009) The International Energy Agency after 35 years: Reform Needs and Institutional Adaptability. *The Review of International Organizations*, 4(3), 293–317.

van de Graaf, T., Sovacool, B., Ghosh, A., Kern, F. & Klare, M. (2016) States, Markets and Institutions: Integrating International Political Economy and Global Energy Politics, in Graaf van de, T., et al. (eds), *Palgrave Handbook of International Political Economy of Energy*. Basingstoke: Palgrave.

G8 (2006) 'Definition of Global Energy Security', for the G8 Summit 2006, St Petersburg. Available at: www.g8.utoronto.ca/summit/2006stpetersburg/energy.html (last accessed 26/01/2017).

Goldthau, A. (2012) From the State to the Market and Back: Policy Implications of Changing Energy Paradigms. *Global Policy*, 3(2), 198–210.

Goldthau, A. (2017) The G20 Must Govern the Shift to Low-Carbon Energy. *Nature*, 546(7657), 203–205.

He, X. (2016) *China and Global Energy Governance under the G20 Framework*. Centre for International Governance Innovation Papers No. 98, Waterloo, ON Canada.

Helm, D. (2014) The European Framework for Energy and Climate Policies. *Energy Policy*, 64(1), 29–35.

Heubaum, H. & Biermann, F. (2015) Integrating Global Energy and Climate Governance: The Changing Role of the International Energy Agency. *Energy Policy*, 87, 229–239.

Hodgson, P. (2010) *Energy, the Environment and Climate Change*. London: Imperial College Press/ World Scientific Publishing Company.

IEA (2015) *Energy and Climate Change. World Energy Outlook Special Report*. Paris: OECD/IEA.

IEA (2016) *World Energy Outlook*. Paris: OECD/IEA.

IEA (2017) *Renewables Information*. Paris: OECD/IEA

IPCC (2007) *Climate change 2007*. Cambridge: Cambridge University Press.

Karlsson-Vinkhuyzen, S. (2016) The EU, Energy and the Sustainable Development Goals, in Graaf van de, T., et al. (eds), *Palgrave Handbook of International Political Economy of Energy*. Basingstoke: Palgrave.

Karlsson-Vinkhuyzen, S. & Jollands, N. (2013) Human Security and Energy Security: A Sustainable Energy System as a Public Good, in Dyer, H. & Trombetta, M. J. (eds), *International Handbook of Energy Security*. Cheltenham: Edward Elgar.

Klare, M. (2009) *Rising Powers, Shrinking Planet: The New Geopolitics of Energy*. New York: Metropolitan Book.

Kuzemko, C. (2013) *The Energy Security-Climate Nexus: Institutional Change in the UK and Beyond*. Basingstoke: Palgrave Macmillan.

McGowan, F. (2011) Putting Energy Insecurity into Historical Context: European Responses to the Energy Crises of the 1970s and 2000s. *Geopolitics*, 16(3), 486–511.

McKibben, B. (19 July 2012) Global Warming's Terrifying New Math. *Rolling Stones*. Available at: https://www.rollingstone.com/politics/news/global-warmings-terrifying-new-math-20120719.

Radoman, J. (2007) Securitization of Energy as a Prelude to Energy Security Dilemma. *Western Balkans Security Observer*, 4, 36–44.

Scrase, I., Wang, T., MacKerron, G., McGowan, F. & Sorrell, S. (2009) Introduction: Climate Policy is Energy Policy, in Scrase, I. & MacKerron, G. (eds), *Energy for the Future: A New Agenda*. Basingstoke: Palgrave Macmillan.

Sovacool, B. Sidortsov, R. & Lones, B. (2014) *Energy Security, Equality and Justice*. Abingdon: Routledge.

Stern, N. H. (2007) *The Economics of Climate Change: The Stern Review*. Cambridge: Cambridge University Press.

Stiglitz, J. (2017) Trump and the Truth about Climate Change. *Project Syndicate* 2nd July 2017. Available at: www.project-syndicate.org/commentary/trump-climate-change-fairness-argument-by-joseph-e--stiglitz-2017-07 (last accessed 20/07)

Szulecki, K. & Westphal, K. (2014) The Cardinal Sins of European Energy Policy: Nongovernance in an Uncertain Global Landscape. *Global Policy*, 5(Suppl.1), 38–51.

Umbach, F. (2012) The Intersection of Climate Protection Policies and Energy Security. *Journal of Transatlantic Studies*, 10(4), 374–387.

UN-Energy (2006) *Energy in the United Nations: An Overview of UN-Energy Activities*. New York: United Nations.

United Nations (2012) The Future We Want. Outcome Document of the United Nations Conference on Sustainable Development, Rio De Janeiro 20–22 June 2012. New York: United Nations. https:// sustainabledevelopment.un.org/content/documents/733FutureWeWant.pdf. In: Resolution 66/288. Rio + 20 United Nations Conference on Sustainable Development. (A/RES/66/288).

Vogler, J. (2013) Changing Conceptions of Climate and Energy Security in Europe. *Environmental Politics*, 22(4), 627–645.

Yergin, D. (2003) *The Prize: The Epic Quest for Oil, Money, and Power*. New York: Free Press.

Youngs, R. (2014) *Climate Change and European Security*. Abingdon: Routledge.

Zelli, F., Pattberg, P., Stephan, H. & van Asselt, H. (2013) Global Climate Governance and Energy Choices, in Goldthau, G. (ed.), *The Handbook of Global Energy Policy*. Hoboken: Wiley-Blackwell.

Endangered species, biodiversity and the politics of conservation

11

Alice B. M. Vadrot

Compared to climate change, the loss of biological diversity is less visible and popular in global environmental politics. However, for the last decade, the study of international biodiversity politics has received new impetus, *inter alia* because of the increased recognition that biodiversity and climate change must be tackled together. Another important factor – and this is the main focus and argument of this chapter – is the particular role science has played in reconfiguring biodiversity conservation as a relevant parameter for economic development and human well-being. In this vein, the politics of conservation are increasingly characterized by struggles over the kinds of values attributed to nature, the forms of knowledge suitable to understand the drivers and causes of biodiversity loss, and the appropriate regulatory frameworks for the equal distribution of the costs and benefits related to the protection of biodiversity.

In order to develop a better understanding of the underlying dynamics at the intersection between science, politics and policy, this chapter examines the historical, conceptual and institutional conditions of the emergence of "biodiversity" as a global environmental concern and a policy issue. Subsequently, the regulatory framework, which has been established to tackle what is increasingly conceived to be the "sixth mass extinction", will be described and emerging power struggles between the Global North and the Global South discussed. The chapter closes with a tentative outlook and a description of hegemonic patterns and trends visible in the politics of conservation of the 21st century.

From species extinction to biodiversity loss and the emergence of a new policy field

> In the term biodiversity, subjective preferences are packaged with hard facts; eco-feelings are joined to economic commodities; deep ecology is sold as dollars and sense to more pragmatic, or more myopic, policy makers and members of the public.
>
> (Takacs 1996: 99)

Biodiversity loss goes beyond what is broadly understood as an increase in "endangered species" (EN), often represented by the decimation of charismatic mammals such as tigers, elephants, lions, and rhinos.[1] Since 1758, approximately 1.8 million species have been described, of which 1.3 million are animals (Ceballos et al. 2015, Mace et al. 2012). The *London Convention*, a multilateral treaty on wildlife preservation signed in 1900 by the European colonial powers, aimed at protecting 43 of them. In the 1950s and 1960s, and particularly after political decolonization, international conservationists feared the implications for wildlife, particularly in Africa, where hunting was steadily growing in importance (Adams 2013). At the beginning of the 1960s, the International Union for Conservation of Nature (IUCN),[2] together with the United Nations Educational, Scientific and Cultural Organization (UNESCO), the Food and Agricultural Organization (FAO) and other organizations, advised several African governments, under the umbrella of the African Special Project, on how to develop and implement conservation policies. National parks were established, non-governmental organizations (NGOs) founded and manifold conservation and development projects started (Adams 2013).

This was a time when several initiatives for regulating nature conservation globally were initiated. The *Convention on International Trade in Endangered Species of Wild Fauna and Flora* (CITES) was drafted by the IUCN in 1963. Throughout the 1960s, governments and NGOs negotiated the *Ramsar Convention on Wetlands* (RAMSAR) to protect wetland habitats for migratory water birds. In 1964, IUCN established the *Red List of Threatened Species,* which is still considered to be the authoritative global assessment of the conservation status of animal and plant species (McCormick 1989). In 1975, IUCN began to develop its categorisation system for species. Together with the United Nations Environment Programme (UNEP), based in Nairobi, Kenya, the IUCN created a database on protected areas, published in 1981. In 1994, a "scientifically rigorous approach" to increase the credibility of assessing the conservation status of a species and its risk of becoming extinct was presented. Six categories were identified and distinguished. According to this categorization scheme

> a taxon is Endangered when the best available evidence indicates that it meets any of the criteria A to E for Endangered [. . .] and it is therefore considered to be facing a very high risk of extinction in the wild.
>
> (IUCN 2012: 14)[3]

Since its establishment, the IUCN red list has assessed more than 77,300 species, estimating that 41% of amphibians, 25% of mammals and 13% of birds are currently threatened (Ceballos et al. 2015).

At least since the mid-1980s, the species approach has been criticized, in particular because nature conservation was seen as entailing not only the maintenance of species diversity, but the maintenance of all processes and patterns of organization in nature (Boitani et al. 2015). Hence, whilst the species approach has been helpful to communicate conservation to policy-makers and the broader public, it was increasingly conceived as incomplete with regard to the conservation of ecosystems as a whole and the societal dimensions of environmental problems more specifically. The same is true for trade-related aspects which, particularly after the emergence of modern biotechnology in the 1970s, had to embrace patent law and access and benefit-sharing (ABS) issues to cope with expanding life science industries and the exploitation of natural reservoirs in the Global South (Rosendal 2011). Another issue concerns what has slightly been addressed at the beginning of this paragraph: The practices and self-concept of botanists and overseas collectors of plants, which formed the largest scientific network worldwide, were considerably put in question (Mackay 1985). Political decolonization evidently contributed to fears among conservation-ists that wildlife might not be sufficiently addressed or protected by the newly established governments (Adams 2013).

Insecurities also emerged with regard to the legal frameworks for doing field work in the tropics and, related to this, the conditions for studying, commodifying and trading plant and animal products. The notion of a "common good" associated with nature has steadily been threatened by the concept of natural heritage and the idea that its protection is bound to the territory where it is situated and, thus, of national concern. State sovereignty over all kinds of natural resources extended the areas where nation states compete in terms of economic and symbolic power and performance. The global political economy of species diversity increased the dual difficulties faced by pure academic research and more industri-al-oriented scientists working for the steadily expanding life science industries.

Against this background "by the late 1980s and early 1990s scientists [. . .] began to find their way toward a revived environmentalism" (Worster 1994: 417). A "new conservation ethic" emerged together with a "broader intellectual and moral community" for which the preservation of "biological diversity became a unifying imperative" (Ibid. 419).

The rise in interest in "biodiversity" as a scientific object and a global resource

From a scientific point of view the concept of "biodiversity" was introduced to re-frame the issue at hand and to replace the established terms "species diversity" and "species richness". The term "biodiversity" itself was coined at the "The National Forum on Bio-Diversity" held in Washington, DC, in September 1986 under the auspices of the American National Academy of Science and the Smithsonian Institute. One of the objectives of this forum was to shed light on the necessity to develop global regulatory and scientific frame-works, within which the perceived loss of species and habitats could be understood and addressed. Edward O. Wilson, who edited the famous book *Biodiversity* (1988), where the results of the forum and the state of the art of research on biological diversity were pre-sented, argued that the rise in interest in biodiversity – which coincided with the forum and the foundation of the Society for Conservation Biology – was due to two more or less independent developments. Wilson describes the reasons for the rise in interest in biodiversity as follows:

> I believe that this increased attention, which was evident by 1980 and had steadily picked up momentum by the time of the forum, can be ascribed to two more or less independent developments. The first was the accumulation of enough data on deforestation, species extinction, and tropical biology to bring global problems into sharper focus and warrant broader public exposure. [. . .] The second development was the growing awareness of the close linkage between the conservation of biodiversity and economic development.
>
> (Wilson, 1988, v)

Data and evidence on species extinction

Firstly, the availability of a sufficient amount of data on species extinction, deforestation and tropical biology "[brought] global problems into sharper focus and warrant broader public exposure" (Wilson 1988 v). In 1988, about 1.4 million living species had been described, and estimations indicated that the absolute number would be somewhere between five and 30 million species, each being "the repository of an immense amount of genetic information" (Wilson 1988: 7). Even though scientists acknowledged that no precise estimate of the numbers of species being extinguished could be made, the observed permanent clearing of rainforest and its conversion into the shifting-cultivation cycle indicated that "extinction is proceeding far faster than it did prior to 1800" (Wilson 1988: 10). The ongoing extinction of species began approximately 11,700 years ago and is mainly due to human activity. Current estimates reveal a remarkably rapid loss of biodiversity over the last few centuries, which is increasingly likely to compromise the capacity of ecosystems to sustain their current functioning (Rockström et al. 2009). The authors of the famous study on planetary boundaries identified "tipping points", which – as soon as they are reached – instantiate a disproportionately rapid destruction of the earth (Rockström et al. 2009). This assumption is based on earth system science and the idea that "planetary boundaries" demarcate "safe operating space for humanity", within which current natural resource and land use practices can be continued without causing irreversible and abrupt environmental change. Estimates indicate that three of these boundaries, including biodiversity loss, climate change and the biogeochemical flow, are likely to already have been crossed. Recent data support the hypothesis that a sixth mass extinction – sometimes also referred to as Holocene or Anthropocene extinction – is already under way (Seddon et al. 2016; Ceballos et al. 2015).

Biodiversity conservation and economic development

The second development that had contributed to the rise of interest in biodiversity in the 1980s is the increased awareness among scientists and policy-makers that the conservation of biological diversity is closely tied to economic development. The global political economy of biodiversity has three dimensions which, in many aspects, are interrelated and particularly relevant for understanding current dynamics in international biodiversity politics, described in section three of this chapter.

Economic development invariably led to new industries reliant on materials from the tropics, leading to further demand for biodiversity products integral to pharmaceuticals, new foods, petroleum substitutes and fibres (Wilson 1988: vi). For example, from the 250,000 to 750,000 plants described in the 1980s, 119 plant-derived drugs used worldwide were obtained from less than 90 plant species (Farnsworth et al. 1985). Today, more than 70,000 different plant species are used in modern and traditional medicine (IUCN 2012).[4] In the 1980s, the search for new plant drugs increased significantly and anticipated the development of NAPRALERT[5], a global database on natural products based on scientific and historical literature, including indigenous knowledge of the medical use of plants (Farnsworth et al. 1985). Optimistic estimates of the economic value of plant species for the pharmaceutical industry increased the commercialization of new drugs based on activities of bioprospecting, predominantly in the Global South (Boisvert and Vivien 2012).[6] A similar increase in interest in particular components of biodiversity could be observed with regard to agricultural and industrial plant products. In the 1980s, a yearlong expedition and three years of follow-up research on tomato seeds – costing the US National Science Foundation only around 21,000 US dollars – led to the production of a new hybrid, worth more than 80 million US dollars over a decade (Iltis 1988: 102). The economic benefits of native indigenous plants – and indigenous knowledge related to these plants – for industry, particularly if developed on a large scale, had also raised expectations with regard to the substitution of fats, fuels and oils (Plotkin 1988: 112).

In other words, the discovery of new plant products and the rapid development of biotechnology as both a scientific instrument and an industrial tool has benefited some parts of the world but also created new challenges and conflicts over the rights to access and use natural resources. Governments from the Global South became increasingly suspicious of "biopiracy" by scientists conducting research on their territory.[7] Conflicts inevitably emerged, particularly in cases where indigenous plants, local knowledge or cultural practices form the basis of new plant products; likewise, GMO seeds developed and patented by the life science industry, which refused to share the benefits resulting out of the commodification and marketization of plant material collected in countries of the Global South (Dutfield 2000, Brand et al. 2008). Even though successful products, especially in the area of pharmaceuticals, are relatively rare, diverse benefits can be developed (Rosendal 2006). Over the years, however, the interest in bioprospecting by the pharmaceutical industry has significantly decreased and has partly been transferred to other sectors, such as cosmetics, nutraceutics and the agribusiness (Boisvert and Vivien 2005).

While biodiversity has been framed in terms of a "common good", to be conserved for the sake of local economic development, the constituents are not clearly defined. As such, the promotion of the commoditization of biodiversity is the key for both its conservation and the development of frameworks within which the benefits of nature can equitably be shared. The underlying "environmental–economic paradigm", also described in terms of "Green Development Theory" (Adams 1995) or "Green Developmentalism" (McAfee 1999), draws on the assumption of win–win situations, in which nature conservation creates syn-ergetic effects in terms of economic development and poverty eradication. The combina-tion of conservation and development goals for poverty eradication ideally implies prior informed consent by locals and, likewise, integration into conservation projects, such as in the planning of protected areas or the development of new commodities based on local and traditional knowledge. Related measures are expected to create new sources of income and labour through conservation initiatives and sustainable forms of using and commodi-fying biodiversity, such as in the case of eco-tourism (Kütting 2010). McAfee has called this practice "selling nature to save it", meaning that conservation projects are financed by new sources of income and business models, such as admission charges for protected areas in tourism or new forms of natural resource use and commodification (McAfee, 1999). The regulation of access to natural habitats and of natural resource use creates several chal-lenges, particularly in those areas and communities where people depend on particular types of biodiversity valuation and related cultural practices. This often implies that local commu-nities participating in related conservation projects have to change the way they govern themselves and their relationships with the natural environment they live in; a process which is accompanied by multiple conflicts and challenges related to land use rights and the equal distribution of goods and services (Escobar 1998, Dauvergne 2016). In the past two decades, several "parks versus sustainable use" arguments have been emerging and preoccupying conservationists and political ecologists, raising doubt with regards to solving both conser-vation and poverty issues (Adams et al. 2004).

The third way in which biodiversity is tied to economic development is less evident, but increasingly relevant. Early on in the biodiversity debate, instruments were developed for economically valuing those aspects of nature which have traditionally not been commodi-fied. A prominent example is pollination, which is of critical importance for healthy ecosys-tems and food production. The "work" of pollinators such as bees, butterflies and other insects had, for a long time, been taken for granted. In order to increase awareness of the value of these "ecosystem services", i.e. services provided by nature for free, scientists have tried to estimate the monetary value of pollination. To this end, you can either measure how much it would cost to replace the act of pollination by human labour or – as recently done – estimate the annual market value directly attributable to animal pollination worldwide, which ranges between 235 billion and 577 billion US dollars (Hrabranski and Pesche 2016: 8).

In the 1980s, research on how to put a value on nature began to rise. In 1987, Jacquemot and Filion tried to measure the economic value of birds in Canada. They identified 100,000 persons involved in bird-related activities and calculated the related expenditure, which amounted to $2.4 billion of Canadian GDP in 1986. Pearce (1993) combined three different types of values to estimate the value of plant-based pharmaceuticals. He combined the actual market value of the plants when traded, the market value of the drugs for which they are the source material and the value of the drugs in terms of their life-saving prop-erties, using the monetary value of a "statistical life" (Pearce 1993). The assessment of the value of biodiversity has many different dimensions. Norton has differentiated between what he refers to as ordinary concepts, namely *commodity, amenity* and the *moral value* of biodiversity (Norton 1988: 201): the *commodity value* is the value attributed to the species when they are made into a product that can be traded, i.e. bought and sold on the market.[8]

The *amenity value* of the species is the contribution of the species to the improvement of human well-being in a non-material way. The amenity value is associated with the contribution of the species to recreation and aesthetics, i.e. to human experiences and activities with, and in, nature, such as hiking, hunting or fishing. These activities create huge market opportunities. The *moral value* is more controversial. Norton takes the position that "species have a moral value even if that moral value depends on us". This rather anthropocentric view is often used as an argument for convincing policy-makers to engage in the conservation of biodiversity. However, here the moral argument is mostly combined with estimates of the monetary value of biodiversity and related "ecosystem services"[9]; a concept which has significantly increased in importance in the past 20 years. Ecosystem services are not the same as biodiversity, but are often used interchangeably or in terms of "biodiversity and ecosystem services" to underpin the centrality of biodiversity for human well-being and economic development. Furthermore, the parallel use of biodiversity and ecosystem services also stems from the assumption that the notion of "services" might facilitate the communication of the impact and value of biodiversity loss to policy-makers and the broader public (Vadrot 2014, 2018).

In 1997, Robert Costanza et al. had already calculated the total value of the world's ecosystem services, with an average of US$33 trillion per year (Costanza et al. 1997). Estimating the monetary value of ecosystem services has been conceived as a promising path to solve conservation related trade-offs by packing the actual effects of biodiversity loss into numbers. The idea was, and is, simple: if the "real" value of nature could be represented in terms of numbers, the costs emerging from the destruction of nature and from political inaction could be calculated and the environmental impact of different policy options and business activities evaluated. Furthermore, the "natural capital" of a local community or a nation could be balanced and the real dependence upon natural resources and their sustainable use and conservation displayed.

From today's perspective, the three described ways by which the rise in interest in biodiversity is tied to economic development are, in many ways, interrelated. Conservation projects in countries of the Global South, as for example, in the case of The Economics of Ecosystems and Biodiversity (TEEB), increasingly rely on ecosystem service valuation and new modes of commodifying and financializing biodiversity supported, for example, by funds of the Global Environmental Facility (GEF), itself an outgrowth of the World Bank. Two decades ago, scientists such as Edward O. Wilson could not even have foreshadowed what is, today, a common term: "for-profit biodiversity conservation" (Dempsey and Suarez 2016: 654). At this stage, the rise in interest in *biodiversity* as "a global resource, to be indexed, used, and above all, preserved" (Wilson 1988: 3) had contributed to the formation of a new global scientific community, which evolved in the 1980s and 1990s around a "new conservation ethic" and the unifying imperative of protecting biodiversity, regardless of existing scientific uncertainties involved in estimations of species extinction and a missing definition of what biodiversity actually means (Takacs 1996, Escobar 1998).

> But does "biodiversity" actually exist? Is there a discrete reality of "biodiversity" different from the infinity of living beings, including plants, animals, microorganisms, homo sapiens, and their interactions, attraction and repulsion, co-creation and destructions?
>
> (Escobar 1998: 54)

Defining "biodiversity"

In the late 1980s, the research community around biodiversity grew significantly. The different kinds of knowledge and data needed to better understand the effects and causes of biodiversity loss called for a definition encompassing past and present understandings of species diversity. By the beginning of the 1990s, biodiversity research increased unsystematically and 14 different definitions of biodiversity were circulating (Jutro 1993). As the two quotes from David Takacs, author of the book *The idea of biodiversity* (1996), and Arturo Escobar (1998) suggest, biodiversity means many different things to different people (Vadrot 2014). Should biodiversity be framed in terms of its global totality, natural communities, its role in providing society with 'free services' or by mapping the regions where biodiversity is most concentrated? (Lovejoy 1997: 7 ff.).

Overlapping interests, normative standpoints and scientific paradigms anticipated the need for defining and conceptualizing biodiversity for the purpose of both science and policy. From a scientific point of view, a definition was needed to develop research programmes targeted towards the systematic development of knowledge on the decline of biodiversity, its drivers, indicators and causes, and on the parameters for appropriate conservation concepts and measures. From a political point of view, a definition was needed to structure global regulatory frameworks for orchestrating the different national priorities in biodiversity conservation and tackling the sharpening conflicts between the Global North and the Global South over the access to, and the benefits from, the use of the different aspects of biodiversity.

In 1991, the International Union of Biological Sciences (IUBS) launched DIVERSITAS[10], a cooperative scientific programme on biodiversity (di Castri and Younès 1996: 5). This initiative was supported by the Scientific Committee on Problems of the Environment of The International Council for Science (ICSU) and UNESCO. UNESCO was entitled to support this process for two reasons. Firstly, UNESCO is a specialized agency of the United Nations (UN) and the natural sciences are one of its main programmes. Secondly, UNESCO was already, by then, hosting two conventions related to conservation: the *World Heritage Convention* protecting natural and cultural heritage and the RAMSAR Convention (see the next section). The definition that DIVERSITAS had been developing was taken up at the *United Nations Conference on Environment and Development* (UNCED), where the CBD, which was drafted under the auspices of the UNEP and a small group of experts – *inter alia* from IUCN – was opened for signature. According to the CBD definition:

> 'Biological diversity' means the variability among living organisms from all sources including, inter alia, terrestrial, marine and other aquatic ecosystems and the ecological complexes of which they are part: this includes diversity within species, between species and of ecosystems.
>
> (CBD 1992)

The emergence of the term biodiversity and its expanded definition, including the three levels of genes, species and ecosystems, had contributed to a reconfiguration of biodiversity as both a policy issue and an object of research by the late 1980s. The recognition of the level of ecosystems has accounted for the critique on species focussed conservation. The integration of the genetic level acknowledged the need to respond to developments in biotechnology and their impact on how diversity is described, measured and commodified. And, last but not least, the emphasis of ecosystems and their "services" has created a new entry point for studying and demonstrating the economic value of biodiversity for society. According to Arturo Escobar, there is a close link between the scientific framing of biodiversity, which has been emerging since the 1980s and the political framework, which has emerged to deal with the new cause at the global level of policy making:

> In fact, the current scientific approach to biodiversity is geared not toward "theorizing biodiversity" per set but towards assessing the significance of biodiversity loss to ecosystem functioning, and to ascertaining the relation between biodiversity and the "services" ecosystems provide. Established definitions of biodiversity do not create a new object of study that is outside of the existing definitions in biology and ecology. Rather, "biodiversity" is the response given to a concrete situation that is certainly preoccupying but which goes well beyond the scientific domain. As critical studies of science have shown, the act of naming a new reality is never innocent. What views of the world does this naming shelter and propagate? Why has this new way of naming been invented at the end of a century that has seen untold levels of ecological destruction? From a discursive perspective, then, biodiversity does not exist in an absolute sense. Rather, it anchors a discourse that articulates a new relation between nature and society in global contexts of science, cultures, and economies.
>
> (Escobar 1998: 55)

Several global scientific and political initiatives, working groups and negotiation rounds have led to this specification, steering the emergence of a complex institutional landscape on biodiversity, composed of multilateral environmental agreements, intergovernmental organizations, regional groups, transnational alliances and a myriad of NGOs, actors and groups. In the following, the institutional dimension of global environmental politics will be described and the most relevant multilateral environmental agreements addressing biodiversity loss presented.

Global biodiversity politics and the politics of conservation

The rise in interest in the protection of biodiversity and the increased emphasis on its economic value have led to the establishment of several fora wherein negotiations among nation states exist. This complexity is the result of the varied targets assigned to biodiversity: (1) conservation and protection of the natural world, (2) sustainable use of natural resources and (3) a fair distribution of the benefits resulting from different forms of use (LePrestre 2002, Hufty and Muttenzer 2002).

From an institutional and governance perspective, this development can be viewed as a way by which nation states try to cope with the perceived loss of biodiversity by realizing common interests and goals (e.g. Keohane 1989, Young 1994). This necessitates particular forms of international cooperation and "principal modalities of global rule-making and implementation" (Held and McGrew 2002: 11). Some scholars describe related processes in terms of "regime building", "regime complexes" or "regulation". Studying and understanding the role of actors in global biodiversity politics, and the kinds of power and strategies they use to pursue their interests, depend on two decisions: firstly, the empirical focus of the research and, secondly, the theoretical framework guiding the understanding of international relations and global environmental politics. The latter significantly benefits from theories that allow an understanding beyond global environmental politics as fine-tuning of existing agreements (Kütting and Lipschutz 2009: 4) (see Chapter 1 in this book).

Multilateral Environmental Agreements (MEAs) are important objects of research for studying the politics of biodiversity conservation. The regularly performed *Conferences of the Parties* (COPs), the governing bodies of MEAs, are of increased interest among scholars of global environmental politics (e.g. Dimitrov 2010, Campbell et al. 2014, Sending 2015). They are field sites, where nation states come together to review and advance the implementation of the particular convention, through amending or further developing text through decisions taken at its periodic meetings. These meetings offer the possibility to empirically examine the performance of different forms of power, authority and hegemony within a highly regulated and structured setting of international relations and diplomacy. Hence, instead of viewing these fora as facilitators for international cooperation to solve global environmental problems, they need to be described as what they are: historically grown negotiation sites, where nation states consensually agree on sentences, numbers and words by employing different forms of argumentative power and authority to increase the likeliness that the decisions taken do not dissent or hamper national interests. The rules and procedures established by the negotiating states structure the interaction between governments and non-state actors and contribute to the particular distribution of power and influence within and beyond these negotiation settings.

The seven biodiversity-related conventions

To date, seven international conventions or multilateral environmental agreements (MEAs) have been established to address biodiversity related issues: the CITES, the CBD, the *Convention on Conservation of Migratory Species (CMS)*, the *International Treaty on Plant Genetic Resources for Food and Agriculture* (ITPGRFA), the RAMSAR Convention, the *International Plant Protection Convention* (IPPC), and the *Convention Concerning the Protection of the World Cultural and natural Heritage* (World Heritage Convention). Table 11.1 lists all seven conventions and gives an overview of the year of their signature and entry into force, the number of signatures and current members, the location of the secretariats, the organization administering the convention and the subsidiary bodies established to govern the work of the agreements.

The conventions are administered by different UN organizations: the UNEP, FAO and UNESCO. Administering means that the organizations in charge support the secretariat, for example, by seconding staff or by hosting the secretariat, as for example, in the cases of the IPPC and the World Heritage Convention. In cases where the location of the secretariat differs from the location of the administering organization, diplomatic or strategic reasons

Table 11.1 Overview of biodiversity related conventions

Name and abbreviation	Year of signature/ entry into force	Parties in 2017	Location of secretariat	Administered by	Convention Bodies/Subsidiary Bodies

Convention on International Trade in Endangered Species of Wild Fauna and Flora (CITES)	1973/1975	183	Geneva/ Switzerland	UNEP	• Conference of the Parties (COP)
					• Standing Committee (StC)
					  ○ Animals committee
					  ○ Plants committee
					• Secretariat

Convention on the Conservation of Migratory Species of Wild Animals (CMS)	1979/1983	124	Bonn/ Germany	UNEP	• Conference of the Parties (COP) • Standing Committee (StC) • The Scientific Council (ScC). • The Secretariat • Working groups (regional, species specific, thematic)
Convention on Biological Diversity (CBD)	1992/1993	196	Montreal/ Canada	UNEP	• Conference of the Parties (COP) • Subsidiary Body on Scientific, Technical and Technological Advice (SBSTTA) • Subsidiary Body on Implementation (SBI) • Secretariat • Working Group on Article 8(j)
Ramsar Convention on Wetlands	1971/1975	169	Gland/ Switzerland	UNESCO	• Conference of the Parties (COP) • Standing Committee (StC) The Scientific and Technical Review Panel (STRP) • Secretariat
Convention Concerning the Protection of the World Cultural and natural Heritage	1972/1975	193	Paris/France	UNESCO	• The Committee • The General Assembly • Statutory Meetings • Advisory Bodies (e.g. IUCN)

(Continued)

Table 11.1 continued

Name and abbreviation	Year of signature/ entry into force	Parties in 2017	Location of secretariat	Administered by	Convention Bodies/Subsidiary Bodies
The International Plant Protection Convention (IPPC)	1951/1952	183	Rome/Italy	FAO	• Commission on Phytosanitary Measures (CPM) • CPM Bureau • Standards Committee (SC) • Subsidiary Body for Dispute Settlement (SBDS) • Capacity Development Committee (CDC) • National Reporting Obligations Advisory Group

International Treaty on Plant Genetic Resources for Food and Agriculture (ITPGRFA)	2001/2004	139	Rome/Italy	FAO	• Governing Body
					  ○ The Bureau
					  ○ Chairs of the GB
					• Secretariat

might play a role. The CBD COP, for example, established an interim secretariat in 1993 located in Geneva, Switzerland, where RAMSAR, CITES and the IUCN Headquarters are located. Three years later, the Government of Canada, which was the first country of the Global North signing and ratifying the convention, won a bid, by which the secretariat was moved to Montreal, Québec, in 1996. In such cases, national governments contribute to the budget of the convention by means of in-kind contributions reflecting the willingness to be an influential and powerful actor within the particular agreement. Administering can also mean that the rules and procedures of UNEP, or UNESCO, are applied to the way in which the conventions work and, for example, organize the negotiations in the framework of their COPs, which take place regularly and assemble national government delegations, representatives of NGOs, IGOs and other stakeholders (Biermann and Siebenhüner 2010). The fact that the seven biodiversity-related conventions are administered by three different organizations is also testimony of the particular focus the conventions assert themselves and of the specific framing of biodiversity they are committed to.

UNESCO uses the framework of natural heritage to designate that biodiversity is inherited from past generations and that it needs to be maintained in the present and for the benefit of future generations. Natural heritage is bound to cultural practices and a particular state territory. More recently "biocultural diversity" emerged as a concept linking biological and cultural diversity in order to better grasp the contribution of local and indigenous communities to the preservation of ecosystem services (Maffi 2001). The FAO addresses conservation issues in relation to food security, agriculture and plant protection (see also Chapter 12 in this book). CITES and CMS, which are administered by UNEP, have a clear focus on species protection and species-related trade regulations. To some extent, these two conventions represent the IUCN approach to conservation.

The adoption of the CBD, which is also administered by UNEP, has significantly increased the overlap between the different topics addressed by UNEP, UNESCO and FAO and the aims and objectives of the conventions (see Table 11.2). The CBD was signed at the *UN Conference on Environment and Development* in Rio de Janeiro in 1992, more than 20 years after CITES. CITES, which was signed in Washington in 1973 and drafted a decade earlier by members of the IUCN, is often referred to as the most successful and effective agreement (Fuchs 2010). The reason for this judgement stems from the fact that CITES is not only a conservation treaty but also a trade instrument balancing the conservation of endangered species and the economic interest in these species.

In turn, the CBD is often seen as the most important forum, where negotiations on the protection and the sustainable and equitable use of biodiversity in all its facets take place (Le Prestre 2002, Brand and Görg 2008). The multiple goals of the CBD and the other conventions indicate several overlaps and potential redundancies. In order to prevent duplication between the seven conventions, several efforts were made to identify and tackle these overlaps. In 2016, official representatives of the parties of the seven conventions met at the United Nations Office in Geneva to explore ways to strengthen synergies among the conventions.[11] Furthermore, representatives of the secretariats participate in the COPs of the respective other conventions in order to ensure that information on the state of affairs is communicated and issues of overlap are identified and recorded into agreed text. The issue of overlap is, however, not only a matter of written and agreed text or responsibilities.

Table 11.2 Aims of the seven biodiversity related conventions

Convention	Aims
Convention on International Trade in Endangered Species of Wild Fauna and Flora (**CITES**)	• the protection of wild plant and animal species for current and future generations (Art. II CITES); • the regulation of trade in species that the convention is intending to regulate (listed in three appendices).
Convention on the Conservation of Migratory Species of Wild Animals (**CMS**)	• avoid any migratory species becoming endangered; • promote co-operation and support research relating to migratory species; • the conservation and management of migratory species (listed in two Appendices) (Art II CMS).
Convention on Biological Diversity (**CBD**)	• the conservation of biological diversity; • the sustainable use of the components of biological diversity; • the fair and equitable sharing of the benefits arising from the utilization of genetic resources (Art 1 CBD).
Ramsar Convention on Wetlands (**RAMSAR**)	• work towards the wise use of all their wetlands; • designate suitable wetlands for the list of Wetlands of International Importance (the "Ramsar List") and ensure their effective management; • cooperate internationally on transboundary wetlands, shared wetland systems and shared species.
World Heritage Convention	• ensuring the identification, protection, conservation, presentation and transmission to future generations of the cultural and natural heritage referred to in Articles 1 and 2 [of the conventions] and situated on its territory, belongs primarily to that State.
The International Plant Protection Convention (**IPPC**)	• secure coordinated, effective action to prevent and to control the introduction and spread of pests of plants and plant products.
International Treaty on Plant Genetic Resources for Food and Agriculture (**ITPGRFA**)	• recognizing the enormous contribution of farmers to the diversity of crops that feed the world; • establishing a global system to provide farmers, plant breeders and scientists with access to plant genetic materials; • ensuring that recipients share benefits they derive from the use of these genetic materials with the countries where they originated

The signatories of the conventions, which are the national governments, send national delegates to COPs, where the negotiations take place. Particularly small delegations, such as the delegation of Bolivia or Ghana, tend to be composed of only one person, covering several conventions and attending several meetings at the same time. The size of delegations varies significantly and reflects the economic and institutional ability of a nation state to perform successfully in those settings.

Other actors and overlapping issues

The institutional landscape of international biodiversity politics is, however, broader than the listing of the seven conventions suggests. Biodiversity is increasingly an issue in the *United Nations Framework Convention on Climate Change* (UNFCCC), the *United Nations Convention to Combat Desertification* (UNCCD), and the *United Nations Convention on the Law of the Sea* (UNCLOS). Furthermore, topic-specific treaties and intergovernmental organizations address biodiversity issues and play important roles within the various negotiation settings: the *United Nations Development Programme* (UNDP), the *International Maritime Organisation* (IMO), the *Global Environmental Fund* (GEF), the *Intergovernmental Science-Policy Platform on Biodiversity and Ecosystem Services* (IPBES), the *Intergovermental Group on Earth Observation*, the *World Health Organization* (WHO), the *World Trade Organization* (WTO) and the *World Bank*. Furthermore, there are regional actors such as the *North American Free Trade Agreement* (NAFTA), the EU, or the *Association of Southeast Asian Nations* (ASEAN) performing within the international fora where biodiversity politics take place.

This listing is far from being complete and is case dependent. Nation states and other global, transnational, national or local actors, such as NGOs, business actors, scientific organizations, representatives of local and indigenous communities, the media and, increasingly, representatives of cities and regions, have been using different fora within this institutional landscape to pursue their own interests in biodiversity. In order to further clarify the way in which different actors interrelate, and for the purpose of understanding the different roles the conventions play in regulating the conservation and use of biodiversity at a global scale, the CBD, which is regarded as the most relevant and overarching biodiversity convention, will be described in more detail.[12]

The case of the CBD

As described above, the CBD is often conceived as the most relevant biodiversity related convention. At the same time, it remains the most complex convention in this field. Its focus on conservation as an agent of economic development and poverty eradication, which is in line with the general theme of the *Earth Summit*, where the CBD was opened for signature, enrols the convention into the gradually expanding "environmental–economic paradigm". *Article 1* of the CBD refers to the three goals of the agreement: firstly, the preservation of biodiversity, secondly, the sustainable use of the components of biological diversity and, thirdly, the fair and equitable sharing of the benefits arising out of the utilization of genetic resources (Art. 1 of the CBD; www.cbd.int/intro). Hence, the CBD deals with issues of biodiversity conservation, use and trade pertaining to all three levels of biodiversity. The decision to address conservation *and* use has expanded the scope of the convention to intellectual property rights, technology transfer and access and benefit sharing, which has created tensions with other international negotiation sites such as the WTO and its *Agreement on Trade-Related Aspects of Intellectual Property Rights* (TRIPS) (Rosendal 2006, Oberthür and Rosendal 2013, Brand and Görg 2008). The issues, which fall under the convention, are constantly renegotiated within its *Subsidiary Body on Scientific, Technical and Technological Advice* (SBSTTA), established under Art 25 and the CBD COPs. The scientific and technological intensity of both the preservation and the use of biodiversity anticipates negotiations on new items to be dealt with under the CBD, such as, for example, biofuels and bioengineering.

The convention's text and the several issues addressed express the plurality of national interests entering the agreement on how to govern biodiversity at a global scale. Its establishment in 1992 followed the exploration of the need of a new environmental agreement by several experts involved in the *Ad Hoc Working Group of Experts on Biological Diversity* from 1988 onwards. The process was coordinated by UNEP and involved experts from IUCN and other conservation organizations. In order to link this kind of expertise to the formal requirements of an international legal instrument, the *Ad Hoc Working Group of Technical and Legal Experts*, known as the *Intergovernmental Negotiating Committee*, started its work in 1989. At this stage, it was clear that a new conservation treaty, addressing the multiple dimensions of biodiversity, would only be accepted by countries of the Global South if issues of *environmental justice* (see Chapter 6 in this book) and "ways and means to support innovation by local people" were part of it.[13] This conflict line is virulent in CBD-related negotiation settings, where technology transfer and a fair sharing of the costs and benefits of the conservation and use of biodiversity are claims by countries of the Global South and a large number of NGOs, and the avoidance of global regulations on trade and intellectual property rights characterize the positioning of countries of the Global North.

During the process of drafting the convention, IUCN, the World Wide Fund for Nature (WWF), Switzerland, and the United States argued in favour of an umbrella convention encompassing existing conservation treaties and protocols only (MacGraw 2002, Andersen 2008). Particularly the United States aimed at avoiding issues of distribution and equity *inter alia* in relation to plant genetic resources, which in the end, were nonetheless recognized and integrated into the scope of the convention. The United States, which intended to protect a growing domestic biotechnology industry, has still not ratified the CBD and is participating in COPs with the status of an observer.

In May 1992, regardless of the conflict lines described above, the text of the CBD was adopted and, one month later, at the *Earth Summit*, opened for signature. The recognition of access and benefit sharing issues into the CBD was partly the result of orchestrated bargaining of countries of the Global South, supported by global NGOs and ENGOs (environmental NGOs), and the increasingly successful conception of win–win situations, which lowered suspicions towards western science conceptions on how to protect and use biological diversity.

The first *Ordinary Meeting of the Conference of the Parties to the Convention on Biological Diversity* took place in the Bahamas in 1994. At that meeting, several decisions were taken, such as on the rules and procedures of the COPs (including the consensus principle), the financial mechanism, the location of the secretariat, a Clearing-House mechanism for technical and scientific cooperation and the establishment of the SBSTTA. The SBSTTA was established to provide the COPs and the negotiating parties with expertise on different aspects of biodiversity. However, and as described above, the lack of global knowledge on biodiversity was conceived as a challenge for the implementation of the CBD, also, because an assessment producing body such as the IPCC, established in 1988, even before the UNFCCC was established (see Chapter 7 in this book), was not available.

Initially, the SBSTTA was conceptualized as the body where national experts are expected to inform decisions to be taken at COP meetings. Particularly in the early 1990s, little knowledge was available among national bureaucracies on how to address biodiversity-related issues at a global scale. At one of the first SBSTTA meetings, Brazil sent a diplomat instead of an expert in order to increase its strategic positioning within a body dominated by western scientists and their views on how to protect biodiversity. Other parties quickly did the same. SBSTTA rapidly became politicized and turned into a "mini COP" or a "pre-COP", where decisions are drafted and pre-negotiated before the actual negotiations within COPs take place (LePrestre 2002, Koetz et al. 2008). The deficient character of the SBSTTA was often conceived as major reason for the severe implementation deficits of the CBD, which partly explains the establishment of IPBES in 2012 and the *Subsidiary Body on Implementation* (SBI), a successor of the *Ad Hoc Open-ended Working Group on the Review of Implementation of the Convention* (WGRI) in 2014. An earlier response to the lack of scientific knowledge was the call of COP 2 for the preparation of the *Global Biodiversity Outlook* (GBO). GBO is a periodic report summarizing the status of biodiversity and the possible steps to be taken to ensure that the goals of the CBD are met.

Figure 11.1 gives an overview of the development of the CBD from 1992 to today. The figure lists the subsidiary bodies and working groups, the locations and years of the COPs, the two protocols to the CBD, the strategic plans and the assessments conducted as a response to, and in accordance with, the needs identified by the parties to the CBD and to some of the other biodiversity-related conventions.

Besides SBSTTA and the SBI, several working groups were established to address particular items, such as intellectual property rights and the protection of local and indigenous knowledge (Working group on Art. 8j established in 1998) and protected areas (established in 2004). In two cases, ad hoc working groups resulted in the adoption of a protocol. In 2000, the *Cartagena Protocol on Biosafety* was adopted with the aim of ensuring the safe handling, transport and use of living modified organisms (LMOs) resulting from modern biotechnology and affecting biodiversity. Parallel to the CBD COPs, the Biosafety COP-MOPs take place to advance the negotiations in this particular subfield of the CBD.

In 2010, COP 10 adopted the *Nagoya Protocol on Access to Genetic Resources and the Fair and Equitable Sharing of Benefits Arising from their Utilization*, which entered into force in October 2014. The Nagoya Protocol has been described as a major success within global environmental politics; however, several issues regarding the actual impact of the protocol and its contribution to supporting fairness and equity remain uncertain (Oberthür and Rosendal

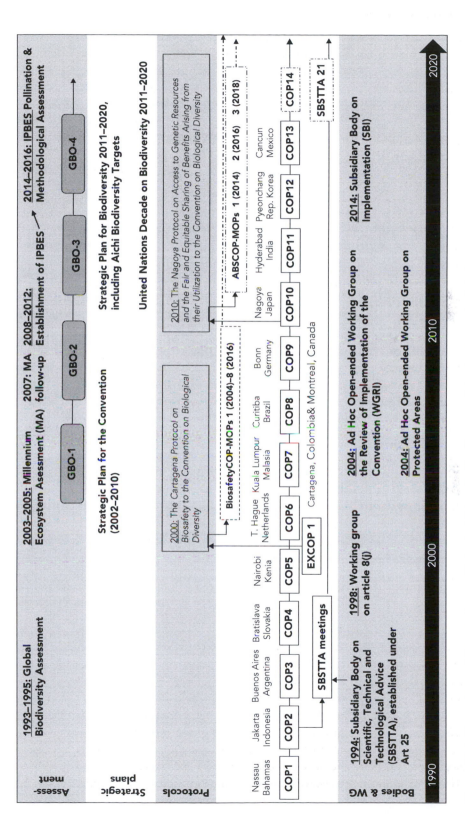

Figure 11.1 Chronology of Convention on Biological Diversity Conference of the Parties and related events.

2013, Brand and Vadrot 2013). In 2014, the first ABS COP-MOP was conducted *inter alia* with the aim to overview the progress made in implementing the protocol.

To sum up, since its establishment, the CBD COPs have adopted several decisions and identified a diverse range of emerging issues to be dealt with under the convention. In the 1990s, negotiations centred on developing the concepts and frameworks for cooperation (Art. 5), general measures for conservation and sustainable use (Art. 6), in situ (Art. 8) and ex situ conservation (Art. 9), access to genetic resources (Art. 15) and handling biotechnology and distribution of benefits (Art. 19). More recently, synthetic biology became an emergent issue under the convention and a new field of conflict, comparable to the debate over LMOs in the early days of the CBD. At COP 13, which took place in Mexico in December 2016, 33 decisions were taken, covering issues such as "biodiversity and climate change", "invasive alien species: addressing risks associated with trade, experiences in the use of biological control agents, and decision support tools", "digital sequence information on genetic resources", or "climate-related geoengineering".

The scope of the CBD is expanding, together with the number and the backgrounds of participants. Fifteen to twenty thousand people participate in CBD COPs. Representatives of the business sector are steadily increasing, particularly after the Rio + 20 conference, which took place in 2012. At this conference, the notion of the "Green Economy" was introduced and expanded the framework of the politics of biodiversity conservation. "Green Economy", together with new modes of valuing and commodifying biodiversity, as described, have been introduced as a way to increase the availability of alternative financial sources and mechanisms for global and local environmental programmes and initiatives framed within a revived "economic–environmental paradigm" (see also Hickmann and Lederer, Chapter 3).

The politics of conservation in the 21st century: patterns and trends

In the following, developments reproducing these selective views on how to address biodiversity loss, both scientifically and politically, will be retraced; and the emergence of global biodiversity knowledge, "international for profit biodiversity conservation" and "essential biodiversity variables" (EBVs) contextualized.

From the global biodiversity assessment to the "IPCC for biodiversity"

An important reference point in global biodiversity politics and policies has always been the attempt of the scientific community to contribute to intergovernmental efforts by providing global assessments on the state of global biodiversity. After the establishment of the CBD, a group of more than 300 scientists conducted the Global Biodiversity Assessment (GBA), published in 1995 (Heywood 1995). The assessment started from the assumption of a total figure of 13 million species, out of which only 13% had been scientifically described.

Besides remaining scientific uncertainties, the authors came to the conclusion that a major part of biodiversity conservation must involve local communities and take place outside of nature reserves and protected areas. The contribution of small-scale farming and indigenous agricultural practices had been recognized for its contribution to sustainable food production, agrobiodiversity conservation, sustainable use and the protection of biodiversity. The GBA has also pointed to the economic and societal consequences of transforming global biogeochemical cycles and the reduction of biomass worldwide. Compared to the regular assessments on climate change, the GBA has not had the effect which was expected by many scientists. It was criticized for not being relevant to policy-makers and giving the impression of a textbook on biology (Vadrot 2016). Compared to IPCC reports, the GBA did not rely on modelling exercises (Guay 2002: 225), which may be another reason why the CBD and its SBSTTA had been reluctant to systematically use or endorse the GBA (LePrestre 2002: 106).

Ten years later, in 2005, the *Millennium Ecosystem Assessment* (MA) was published, receiving far more attention than the GBA. The MA was intended to be policy relevant, which is exemplified by the fact that it was launched on the World Environment Day of the United Nations by UN Secretary-General Kofi Annan in 2001. A simplified version of the IPCC procedure was used to conduct, structure and organize the work of more than 1500 scientists representing 95 countries. The MA cost more than 24 million US dollars and was financed by a number of international organizations and private donors. The assessment, as such, was organized in five chapters addressing the link between ecosystems and human well-being with regard to five different areas: biodiversity, desertification, opportunities and challenges for business and industry, wetlands and water, and health. One important aim of the MA was to analyze and, as much as possible, quantify the importance of ecosystems to human well-being. On this basis, better decisions regarding the sustainable use and management of ecosystem services – a concept central to the MA – were expected. The MA differentiates between different ecosystem services, including provision services (e.g. water and food), regulatory services (pollination and water regulation), cultural services (e.g. aesthetics and recreation) and services required for the production of all other services (MA 2005).

The question, which has been preoccupying scientists particularly after the publication of the MA, is how to move non-traditional resources that are unbound from material essences through global circuits of finance commodities and credit (e.g. Banzhaf 2005). Whilst it has been said that related efforts remain within the intention to develop communication metaphors (intending to design environmental management programmes), more and more efforts are being made to develop models and markets for environmental or ecosystem services (e.g. Gómes-Baggethun and Ruiz-Perez 2017). One expected benefit of valuing ecosystem services and related policy instruments, such as "Payment for ecosystem services" (PES), is that they could provide a framework within which trade-offs between different political priorities could be solved on the basis of numbers and balances. This trend is, however, not new and reflects, in part, long-standing debates among conservation scientists and ecologists on the usefulness and feasibility of measuring the monetary value of nature.

More recently, the *Intergovernmental Platform on Biodiversity and Ecosystem Services* (IPBES), established as an "IPCC for Biodiversity" in 2012, published its first thematic assessment, concluding that the annual market value directly attributable to animal pollination worldwide ranges between 235 billion and 577 billion US dollars (Hrabranski and Pesche, 2016, p. 8). IPBES draws on the concept of ecosystem services and has been criticized for reproducing a narrow understanding of nature and the kinds of knowledge required to represent and study biodiversity (Vadrot 2014).

Between ecosystem services and Mother Earth: diverse knowledge forms

Tensions over the concept of ecosystem services are inherent in, as well as characteristic for, past and present disputes among ecologists and conservationists over the strategic use of "money talk", which has gained so much momentum over the last decade (Blanchard et al. 2016, 122).

> While so called 'market-based instruments' (MBIs) such as ecotourism, taxation and subsidies have existed in conservation practice for quite some time, new instruments such as payments for ecosystem services (PES), biodiversity derivatives and offsets,[14] and mitigation banking have recently become more widespread.
>
> (ibid. 112)

"Biodiversity and ecosystem services" became a new buzzword used by a diverse range of scholars with different ontological, institutional and normative positions, and literature where "ecosystem services" and "biodiversity" are simultaneously used seemed to have exploded (Vadrot 2018).

A similar increase in significance of the ecosystem services approach is visible in litera- ture addressing the neoliberalization of nature, whereat neoliberalism is understood as "a complex and variable assemblage of ideologies, institutions, discourses, actors, and related practices that seek to broaden and deepen processes of financialisation, privatization, mar- ketisation, decentralisation, and/or commodification in society" (Holmes and Cavanagh 2016: 201). Hence, the incorporation of values of biodiversity into decision-making using economic methods is both "rapidly gaining momentum – as well as opposition" (Seddon et al. 2016: 1).

At the same time, and as the Conceptual Framework (CF) of the IPBES suggests, diverse knowledge forms and the recognition of non-monetary values of nature are increasing in importance. Studies interested in the role of science and expertise within intergovernmen- tal negotiation settings illustrate how scientific concepts, numbers and new terminologies are contested by governments through influencing final negotiated texts (Hughes, 2015; Sending, 2015). Whilst references to "scientific, technical and legal knowledges" were pre- dominantly made by government representatives of the Global North, southern countries increasingly contest "northern" positions by making their own claims related to science, data and technology (Scott et al. 2014). Examples from my own research also demonstrate that countries from the Global South contest the authority and legitimacy of scientific knowledge by making their own knowledge claims and introducing concepts such as

"Pachamama" and "Buen Vivir" (Vadrot 2014). At the same time, concepts increasing the legitimacy of non-scientific knowledge (e.g. biocultural diversity) are rejected, specifically by the United States, who question their saliency and credibility (Hughes and Vadrot forthcoming). Many researchers have identified a shift in the politics of knowledge in the field of biodiversity politics towards an increased competition between different knowledge forms and methodologies (Scott et al. 2014, Vadrot 2014). The concepts of "Buen vivir" and of "Mother Earth" are increasingly recognized as ways of approaching and assessing nature. This is the result of several attempts by countries from the Global South, particularly Bolivia and other Latin American countries, to oppose hegemonic views on nature and related scientific concepts and narratives reproducing the valorization paradigm of the 1980s (Vadrot 2014, Borie and Hulme 2015).

Biodiversity big data and the emergence of "essential biodiversity variables"

Another issue has been gaining importance: biodiversity big data. The systematic coordination and management of biodiversity data corresponds to several questions: How can the implementation of the CBD in individual countries be monitored and compared? How can policy options be formulated against the background of partial data? How can the diversity of existing types of data be combined and turned into suitable policy instruments? And, how can scenarios for predicting the future of biodiversity and the impact of policy measures be supported by robust data? Such questions have existed for a while but only recently increased in significance after the IPBES was established with the mandate to produce global biodiversity assessments.

Furthermore, new technologies enable the collection and storage of vast amounts of different types of data and their integration (Bowker 2000). Examples include the integration of data stemming from satellites, drones, robots and citizen science into more traditional data sets. This development has anticipated the constitution of new scientific disciplines such as "biodiversity informatics" or "bioinformatics". Linking field observations to remote sensing and increasing efforts in streamlining, integrating and disseminating biodiversity data are expected to contribute to tackling uncertainty and, more specifically, overcoming the taxonomic impediment "by liberating the taxonomic scientists from the clerical labour of locating comparative materials, both specimens and literature" (Hardisty and Roberts 2013: 8). Emerging scientific and technological issues are also visible in the global politics of environmental data orchestrated by the *Intergovernmental Group on Earth Observations* (GEO), established in 2005.

In 2008, GEO launched the idea of a *Global Earth Observation System of System* (GEOSS), which connects a multiplicity of actors involved in prediction. In the same year, the *Global Biodiversity Observation Network* (GEO-BON), a flagship project of GEO, was formed by actors involved in the GBA, the MA, IPBES, NASA, ESA and other relevant scientific organizations and networks. The CBD became a member of GEO-BON and a representative of its SBSTTA participates in its meetings. Efforts to further develop and harmonize related methodologies, datasets and indicators by "the data and scenarios communities" and

GEO-BON are conceived as contributions to the challenges of the CBD in monitoring the implementation of its strategic goals (Pereira et al. 2010; 2013). In 2011, the CBD requested the development of *Essential Biodiversity Variables* (EBV), which were introduced in 2013 by people involved in GEO-BON as a way to address uncertainties in relation to biodiversity loss and the use of scenarios (Pettorelli et al. 2016).

In recent years, EBVs have been further developed and the concept of *satellite remote sensing essential biodiversity variables* framed (e.g. Pettorelli et al. 2016). In parallel, an IPBES expert group worked on the first methodological assessment of the platform, focussing on models and scenarios for biodiversity and ecosystem services. In February 2016, the Summary for Policy Makers (SPM) of the methodological assessment was approved by the members of the platform. The assessment identifies "large gaps in the availability of data for constructing and testing scenarios and models, and significant barriers to data sharing [. . .]" (Hrabranski and Pesche, 2016). Subsequently, COP 13 of the CBD invited governments, scientific communities and other stakeholders "[. . .] to contribute to the further development of scenarios and models". At the same time, controversies over the scientific credibility of the sixth mass extinction intensified after Ceballos et al. (2015) published their paper on *Accelerated modern human–induced species losses*. Besides all global political and scientific efforts described earlier, the elephant in the room remains the question how to scientifically underpin the loss of biodiversity and measure its effects.

Conclusion

In the first section of this chapter, I described the emergence of biodiversity as a scientific object and a global concern. Biodiversity emerged in relation to new scientific findings and three different conceptions of how biodiversity is linked to economic development. I argued that the global political economy of biodiversity is closely tied to scientific discoveries, new emerging industries, shifting understandings of intellectual property rights, state sovereignty over particular aspects of biological diversity and related challenges and conflicts between different groups of actors, including nation states, local communities and different groups of scientists. Section 2 examined the parallel development of an international landscape of multilateral environmental agreements and related negotiation settings, which have been created, designed and strategically used by nation states to govern biodiversity at a global scale and within the United Nations framework. The seven biodiversity related conventions were described and the CBD, as the most relevant biodiversity convention, examined in more detail.

The triple objective of the CBD, addressing the protection, use and equitable sharing of benefits related to biodiversity, continues to nourish conflicts between the Global North and the Global South over the just distribution of the costs and benefits related to the conservation and use of biological diversity. The establishment of two protocols to the CBD addressing biosafety and ABS have not resolved the tensions in place and are a testimony of persistent patterns on how the political economy of biodiversity has been structuring the relationship between modern societies and their natural environment: in terms of commodification, marketization and financialization of diverse aspects of nature under the umbrella of local development, poverty eradication and scientific evidence on how to better understand and solve trade-offs between biodiversity conservation and use. The current trend of "international for profit biodiversity conservation" is visible in both global environmental politics and in the way in which conservationists frame and communicate their research *inter alia* by relying on the market-environmentalist rhetoric and discursive successors of "selling nature to save it" of the late 1980s.

However, this does neither mean that a diffusion in terms of investments and "big big money" for conservation can be observed nor that this trend is uncontested. It has been possible for diverse knowledge systems, including indigenous knowledge, and alternative views on the value of nature (e.g. Mother Earth) to enter the international scene. But, scientific concepts developed to monitor the implementation of the CBD, such as the concept of "essential biodiversity variables" favour particular scientific theories, methods and concepts over others. They enable the strategic use of scientific knowledge but also contribute to the maintenance of "selling nature to save it", which remains the main conflict point in the politics of conservation today.

Notes

1 In conservation biology, individual (charismatic) species are understood as flagship species, umbrella, keystone, or indicator. Conserving one species goes hand in hand with conservation efforts related to the habitat, where the species lives, as a whole (e.g. Simberloff 1998).

2 www.iucnredlist.org

3 e.g. Area of occupancy estimated to be less than 500 km^2 (criteria B), population size estimated to number fewer than 250 mature individuals (Criteria D) (IUCN 2012, 18ff).

4 www.iucn.org/content/facts-and-figures-biodiversity

5 www.napralert.org/

6 From today's perspective, the interest of the pharmaceutical industry in plant resources in the Global South and in bioprospecting can be described as relatively low (Boisvert and Vivien 2005)

7 The Brazilian Government is still one of the most protective states and highly regulates access to research sites in the tropics, even if it concerns Brazilian researchers working for Brazilian research institutions.

8 Norton distinguishes between *direct* and *indirect* commodity values as some products might be copies of the original one. A typical example is the synthetic reproduction of biologically evolved chemicals, i.e. the production of pharmaceuticals. Norton provides another typical example: '[. . .]alligators have potential value in the manufacture of shoes, but they may also have indirect commodity value if it turns out that vinyl shoes stamped in an alligator pattern sell for more than plain vinyl shoes' (Norton 1988: 201).

9 The Millennium Ecosystem Assessment's classification of ecosystem services contains four categories: provision services (e.g. water and food), regulatory services (pollination and water regulation), cultural services (e.g. aesthetics and recreation) and services required for the production of all other services (MA 2005).

10 DIVERSITAS was merged into Future Earth.

11 www.cbd.int/doc/?meeting=BRCWS-2016-01

12 For other biodiversity related conventions see the following chapters of this book: Chapter 7 for the UNFCCC, Chapter 13 for forest related aspects, Chapter 13 for forests and Chapter 9 for issues related to technology.

13 www.cbd.int/history/

14 Biodiversity offsetting "seeks to compensate for losses to biodiversity in one place (and at one time) by creating equivalent gains elsewhere" (Apostolopoulou and Adams 2017: 23).

Recommended reading

Adams, W. M. (2013) Against Extinction: The Story of Conservation, in *Against Extinction: The Story of Conservation*. 1–311.

Escobar, A. (1998) Whose Knowledge, Whose nature? Biodiversity, Conservation, and the Political Ecology of Social of Social Movements. *Journal of Political Ecology*, 5(1), 53–82.

Rosendal, G. K. (2011) Biodiversity Protection in International Negotiations: Cooperation and Conflict, in *Beyond Resource Wars: Scarcity, Environmental Degradation, and International Cooperation*. 59–86.

Vadrot, A. B. M. (2014) The Politics of Knowledge and Global Biodiversity, in *The Politics of Knowledge and Global Biodiversity*. 1–303.

Internet resources

www.cbd.int/
www.millenniumassessment.org/en/index.html
www.ipbes.net/

References

Adams, W. M. (1995) *Future Nature: a vision for conservation*. London: Earthscan.

Adams, W. M. (2013) Against Extinction: The Story of Conservation, in *Against Extinction: The Story of Conservation*, 1–311.

Adams, W. M., Aveling, R., Brockington, D., Dickson, B., Elliott, J., Hutton, J., Roe, D., Vira, B. & Wolmer, W. (2004) Biodiversity Conservation and the Eradication of Poverty. *Science*, 306(5699), 1146–1149.

Andersen, R. (2008) Governing Agrobiodiversity: Plant Genetics and Developing Countries, in *Governing Agrobiodiversity: Plant Genetics and Developing Countries*. 1–420.

Apostolopoulou, E. & Adams, W. M. (2017) Biodiversity Offsetting and the Reframing of Conservation: A Reply to Ten Kate & von Hase and Dempsey & Collard. *Oryx*, 51(1), 40–42.

Banzhaf, H. S. (2005) Green price indices. *Journal of Environmental Economics and Management*, 49(2), 262–280.

Biermann and Siebenhüner (2010) *Managers of Global Change: The Influence of International Environmental Bureaucracies*. Cambridge, MA: MIT Press.

Blanchard, L., Sandbrook, C., Fisher, J. & Vira, B. (2016) Investigating consistency of a pro-market perspective amongst conservationists. *Conservation and Society*, 14(2), 112–124.

Boisvert, V. & Vivien, F.-D. (2005) The Convention on Biological Diversity: A Conventionalist Approach. *Ecological Economics*, 53(4), 461–472.

Boisvert V. & Vivien F.-D. (2012) Towards a political economy approach to the Convention on Biological Diversity. *Cambridge Journal of Economics*, 36(5), 1163–1179.

Boitani, L., Mace, G. M. & Rondinini, C. (2015) Challenging the Scientific Foundations for an IUCN Red List of Ecosystems. *Conservation Letters*, 8(2), 125–131.

Borie, M. & Hulme, M. (2015) Framing Global Biodiversity: IPBES between Mother Earth and Ecosystem Services. *Environmental Science & Policy*, 54, 487–496.

Bowker, G. C. (2000) Biodiversity Datadiversity. *Social Studies of Science*, 30(5), 643–683.

Brand, U. & Görg, C. (2008) Post-Fordist Governance of Nature: The Internationalization of The State and the Case of Genetic Resources—A Neo-Poulantzian Perspective. *Review of International Political Economy*, 15(4), 567–589.

Brand, U., Görg, C., Hirsch, J. & Wissen, M. (2008) Conflicts in Environmental Regulation and the Internationalisation of the State: Contested Terrains, in *Conflicts in Environmental Regulation and the Internationalisation of the State: Contested Terrains*, 1–263.

Brand, U. & Vadrot, A. (2013) Epistemic Selectivities and the Valorisation of Nature: The Cases of the Nagoya Protocol and the Intergovernmental Science-Policy Platform for Biodiversity and Ecosystem Services (IPBES). *Law, Environment and Development Journal*, 9(2), 202–220.

Campbell, L. M., Corson, C., Gray, N. J., MacDonald, K. I. & Brosius, J. P. (2014) Studying global environmental meetings to understand global environmental governance: Collaborative event ethnography at the Tenth Conference of the Parties to the Convention on Biological Diversity. *Global Environmental Politics*, 14(3), 1–20.

CBD (1992) *Convention on Biological Diversity*, United Nations. Available at: www.cbd.int/doc/legal/cbd-en.pdf

Ceballos, G., Ehrlich, P. R., Barnosky, A. D., García, A., Pringle, R. M. & Palmer, T. M. (2015) Accelerated Modern Human–Induced Species Losses: Entering the Sixth Mass Extinction. *Science Advances*, 1(5), e1400253, doi: 10.1126/sciadv.1400253.

Costanza, R., d'Arge, R., de Groot, R., Farber, S., Grasso, M., Hannon, B., Limburg, K., et al (1997) The Value of the World's Ecosystem Services and Natural Capital. *Nature*, 387(6630), 253–260.

Dauvergne, P. (2016) Environmentalism of the Rich, in *Environmentalism of the Rich*, 1–218.

Dempsey, J. & Suarez, D. C. (2016) Arrested Development? The Promises and Paradoxes of "Selling Nature to Save It". *Annals of the American Association of Geographers*, 106(3), 653–671.

di Castri, F. & Younés, T. (1996) *Biodiversity, science and development: towards a new partnership*. Wallingford: CAB International in association with the International Union of Biological Sciences.

Dimitrov, R.S. (2010) Inside UN climate change negotiations: The Copenhagen conference. *Review of Policy Research*, 27(6), 795–821.

Dutfield, G. (2000) *Intellectual property rights, trade and biodiversity: Seeds and plant varieties*. London: Earthscan Publications and IUCN.

Escobar, A. (1998) Whose Knowledge, Whose Nature? Biodiversity, Conservation, and the Political Ecology of Social of Social Movements. *Journal of Political Ecology*, 5(1), 53–82.

Farnsworth, N. R., Akerele, O., Bingel, A. S., Soejarto, D. D. & Guo, Z.-G. (1985) Medicinial plants in therapy. *Bull. WHO*, 63(6), 965–981.

Fuchs, C. (2010) Convention on International Trade in Endangered Species of Wild Fauna and Flora (CITES) – Conservation Efforts Undermine the Legality Principle, in von Bog-dandy, A., Wolfrum, R., von Bernstorff, J., Dann, P. & Goldmann, M. (eds) The Exercise of Public Authority by International Institutions. *Beiträge zum ausländischen öffentlichen Recht und Völkerrecht, 210*. Berlin and Heidelberg: Springer.

Gómes-Baggethun, E. & Ruiz-Perez, M. (2011) Economic valuation and the commodification of ecosystem services. *Progress in Physical Geography*, 35(5), 613–628.

Guay, L. (2002) The Science and Policy of Global Biodiversity Protection, in Le Prestre, P. (ed) *Governing Global Biodiversity. The Evolution and Implementation of the Convention on Biological Diversity*. Burlington, VT: Ashgate.

Hardisty, A. & Roberts, D. (2013) A Decadal View of Biodiversity Informatics: Challenges and Priorities. *BMC Ecology*, 13(1), 16.

Held, D. & McGrew, A. G. (eds) (2002) *Governing Globalization: Power, Authority, and Global Governance*. Cambridge, UK: Polity Press.

Heywood, V. H. (1995) *Global biodiversity assessment*. Cambridge & New York, NY: Cambridge University Press.

Holmes, G. & Cavanagh, C. (2016) A review of the social impacts of neoliberal conservation: Formations, inequalities, contestations. *Geoforum*, 75, 199–209.

Hrabranski, M. & Pesche, D. (eds) (2016) *The Intergovernmental Platform on Biodiversity and Ecosystem Service (IPBES): Challenges, Knowledge and Actors*. London & New York: Routledge Earth Scan.

Hufty, M. & Muttenzer, M. (2002) Devoted Friends: The Implementation of the Convention on Biological Diversity in Madagascar, in Le Prestre, P. (ed) *Governing Global Biodiversity*. Burlington, VT: Ashgate, 279–309.

Hughes, H. (2015) Bourdieu and the IPCC's symbolic power. *Global Environmental Politics*, 15(4), 85–104.

Iltis, H. H. (1988) Serendipity in the Exploration of Biodiversity: What Good are Weedy Tomatos, in Wilson, E. O. (ed) *BioDiversity, National Academy of Sciences*. Washington, DC: National Academy Press, 98–105.

IUCN (2012) *Facts and Figures*. Available at: https://www.iucn.org/content/facts-and-figures-biodiversity (accessed 30 January 2018).

Jutro, P. R. (1993) Human influence on ecosystems: dealing with biodiversity, in McDonnell, M. J. & Pickett, S. T. A. (eds) *Humans as Components of Ecosystems. The Ecology of Subtle Human Effects and Populated Areas*. Berlin: Springer-Verlag, 246–256.

Keohane, R. O. (1989) *International institutions and state power: Essays in international relations theory*. Colorado: Westview Press.

Koetz, T., Bridgewater, P., van den Hove, S. & Siebenhühner, B. (2008) The role of the Subsidiary Body on Scientific, Technical and Technological Advice to the Convention on Biological Diversity as science–policy interface. *Environmental Science & Policy*, 11, 505–516.

Kütting, G. (2010) The Global Political Economy of the Environment and Tourism, in *The Global Political Economy of the Environment and Tourism*. 1–193.

Kütting, G. & Lipschutz, R. (eds) (2009) *Environmental Governance, Power and Knowledge in a Local-Global World*. London & New York: Routledge.

Le Prestre, P. G. (ed) (2002) *Governing Global Biodiversity. The Evolution and Implementation of the Convention on Biological Diversity*. Burlington, VT: Ashgate.

Lovejoy, T. E. (1997) Biodiversity: what is it? In Reaka-Kudla, M. L., Wilson, D. E. & Wilson, E. O. (eds) *Biodiversity II. Understanding and Protecting Our Biological Resources*. Washington, D.C.: Joseph Henry Press, 7–15.

MA. (2005) *Millennium Ecosystem Assessment. Ecosystems and Human Well-being: Current State and Trends*. Volume 1. Washington, Covelo and London: Island Press.

MacGraw, D. M. (2002) The story of the Biodiversity Convention from negotiation to implementation, in LePrestre, P. (Ed.). Governing Global Biodiversity. *The Evolution and Implementation of the Convention on Biological Diversity*. Burlington, VT: Ashgate, 7–38.

Maffi, L. (2001) *On Biocultural Diversity: Linking Language, Knowledge, and the Environment*. Washington, D.C.: Smithsonian Institution Press.

Mace, G., Norris, K. & Fitter, A. (2012) Biodiversity and ecosystem services: A multilayered relationship. *Trends in Ecology & Evolution*, 27(1), 19–26.

Mackay, D. (1985) *In the Wake of Cook: Exploration, Science and Empire, 1780–1801*. London: Croom Helm.

McAfee, K. (1999) Selling Nature to Save It? Biodiversity and Green Developmentalism. *Environmental Planning and Development*, 17(2), 133–154.

McCormick, J. (1989) *The Global Environmental Movement. Reclaiming Paradise*. London: Belhaven Press.

Norton, B. (1988) Commodity, Amenity, and Morality. The Limits of Quantification in Valuing Biodiversity, in Wilson, E. O. (ed) *BioDiversity, National Academy of Sciences*. Washington, DC: National Academy Press, 200–205.

Oberthür, S. & Rosendal, G. K. (2013) Global Governance of Genetic Resources: Background and Analytical Framework, in *Global Governance of Genetic Resources: Access and Benefit Sharing after the Nagoya Protocol*. 1–17.

Pearce, D. W. (1993) *Economic Values and Natural World*. London: Earthscan.

Pereira, H. M., Ferrier, S., Walters, M., Geller, G. N., et al (2013) Essential Biodiversity Variables. *Science*, 339(6117), 277–278.

Pereira, H. M., Leadley, P. W., Proenca, V., et al (2010) Scenarios for Global Biodiversity in the Twenty-First Century. *Science*, 330(6010), 1496–1501.

Pettorelli, N., Wegmann, M., Skidmore, A. et al. (2016) Framing the Concept of Satellite Remote Sensing Essential Biodiversity Variables: Challenges and Future Directions. *Remote Sensing in Ecology and Conservation*, 2(3), 122–131.

Plotkin, M. J. (1988) The Outlook for the New Agricultural and Industrial Products from the Tropics, in Wilson, E. O. (ed) *BioDiversity, National Academy of Sciences*. Washington, DC: National Academy Press, 106–118.

Rockström, J., Steffen, W., Noone, K., Persson, A., Chapin III, F. S., Lambin, E., Lenton, T. M., Scheffer, M., Folke, C., Schellnhuber, H. J., Nykvist, B., de Wit, C. A., Hughes, T., van der Leeuw, S., Rodhe, H., Sörlin, S., Snyder, P. K., Costanza, R., Svedin, U., Falkenmark, M., Karlberg, L., Corell, R. W., Fabry, V. J., Hansen, J., Walker, B., Liverman, D., Richardson, K., Crutzen, P. & Foley, J. (2009) Planetary Boundaries: Exploring the Safe Operating Space for Humanity. *Ecology and Society*, 14(2), 32.

Rosendal, G. K. (2006) The Convention on Biological Diversity: Tensions with the WTO TRIPS Agreement over Access to Genetic Resources and the Sharing of Benefits. In Ober-thür, S. & Gehring, T. (eds) *Institutional Interaction in Global Environmental Governance – Synergy and Conflict among International and EU Policies*. Cambridge (MA): MIT Press, 79–103.

Rosendal, G. K. (2011) Biodiversity Protection in International Negotiations: Cooperation and Conflict, in *Beyond Resource Wars: Scarcity, Environmental Degradation, and International Cooperation*. 59–86.

Scott, D., Hitchner, S., Maclin, E. M. & Dammert B., J. L. (2014) Fuel for the fire: Biofuels and the problem of translation at the Tenth Conference of the Parties to the Convention on Biological Diversity. *Global Environmental Politics*, 14(3), 84–101.

Seddon, N., Mace, G. M., Naeem, S., Tobias, J. A., Pigot, A. L., Cavanagh, R., Mouillot, D., Vause, J. & Walpole, M. (2016) Biodiversity in the Anthropocene: Prospects and Policy. *Proceedings of the Royal Society B: Biological Sciences*, 283(1844), 20162094.

Sending, O.J. (2015) *The politics of expertise: Competing for authority in global governance*. Michigan: University of Michigan Press.

Simberloff, D. (1998) Flagships, Umbrellas, and Keystones: Is Single-Species Management Passe in the Landscape Era? *Biological Conservation*, 83(3), 247–257.

Takacs, D. (1996) *The Idea of Biodiversity: Philosophies of Paradise*. Baltimore: Johns Hopkins University Press.

Vadrot, A. B. M. (2014) The Politics of Knowledge and Global Biodiversity, in *The Politics of Knowledge and Global Biodiversity*. 1–303.

Vadrot, A. B. M. (2016) The birth of a science-policy interface for biodiversity: The history of the IPBES, in Hrabranski, M. et al. (eds) *The Intergovernmental platform on biodiversity and ecosystem service (IPBES): Challenges, knowledge and actors*. London & New York: Routledge Earth Scan, 41–76.

Vadrot, A. B. M. (2018) Big data and money talk: conceptions of scientific uncertainty in the institutionalisation of IPBES. *Environmental Science & Policy* (forthcoming).

Wilson, E. O. (1988) *BioDiversity, National Academy of Sciences*. Washington, DC: National Academy Press.

Worster, D. (1994) *Nature's Economy: A History of Ecological Ideas*. Cambridge: Cambridge University Press.

Young, O. R. (1994) *International Governance: Protecting the Environment in a Stateless Society*. Ithaca, NY: Cornell University Press.

The global politics of food system sustainability

12

Wendy Godek

Introduction

The importance of enhancing the sustainability of food systems[1] is an issue that continues to be on the top of global agendas. This is attributed to the deepening of multiple environmental, social, and economic challenges that have compromised the ability of food systems to ensure food security, or when "all people, at all times, have physical, social and economic access to sufficient, safe and nutritious food that meets their dietary needs and food preferences for an active and healthy life for all" (FAO 1996). While hunger has declined over the last decade, global food insecurity continues to be a significant problem, with an estimated 795 million hungry people worldwide (FAO 2015) or about 11% of the world population, most of whom live in poverty in the Global South. One of the biggest food security myths is that there is not enough food to feed the world's population. On the contrary, current production supersedes demand, pointing to the fact that current hunger is not the consequence of food scarcity, but rather political in nature and a question of access. However, the question remains as to whether current production levels can be sustained and increased over the long-term given projected population growth in coming years (more mouths to feed) and the myriad of challenges to food security – including population demographics (growth, aging, and urbanization), economic inequality, increasing concentration of power over different food system components among fewer stakeholders, and, perhaps most pressing, environmental degradation and climate change (FAO 2017a).

Given the challenges mentioned above, among others, the global community is largely in agreement about the need for sustainability in food systems; however, the point of contention lies in how to achieve sustainability. There are clear divergences in the ideas, beliefs, and approaches of different food system stakeholders on how to accomplish this. The aim of the present chapter is to explore these perspectives in an effort to map out the global politics of food system sustainability, paying particular attention to the environmental dimensions of this debate. The discussion begins with an overview of the evolution of contemporary food systems followed by an overview of the major recent debates over how to achieve food system sustainability. The chapter continues with a discussion of critical environmental issues related to food system sustainability, including a discussion of the politics of seeds and also of food security and climate change. The chapter ends with some remarks on the future of food system sustainability.

A brief history of the evolution of contemporary food systems

Historically, the nature of food systems has always been shaped by socio-cultural, environmental, economic, and political factors, as well as technological advances. However, over the last 200 years, industrialization has, by far, produced the most dramatic changes in the nature of food systems. Europe and the United States were the first regions to industrialize agriculture, backed by new scientific methods and chemical and mechanical advances that revolutionized the agrarian sector. Characteristics of this period of food system growth were territorial expansion, largely carried out through colonialism, cheap labor, and trade openness (Friedmann 2005). Food and agricultural goods were increasingly sourced from farther distances. Agrochemicals, including fertilizers and pesticides, were developed to increase yields and control for pests and diseases.

Industrial agriculture, however, was not seen as the panacea for all. In the late 1800s, new movements emerged that challenged ideas about industrialization, and in doing so, critiqued the techniques and values of modern agriculture (Vogt 2007). In particular, these groups advocated methods and approaches that were more in synergy with the natural environment, thus at odds with attempts by modern agriculture to control or manipulate the environment. As such, two distinct frames emerged – one that was amenable to modern technology applied to agriculture and food (henceforth, agrifood), referred to as the "industrial" or "conventional" paradigm, and another that aimed to work with nature to produce food and other agricultural products, known as the "sustainable" or "alternative" paradigm (Beus and Dunlap 1990; Dahlberg 1986). At the very heart of the debates between these two paradigms were differences in opinion over human values and ethics, human–nature relations, and the use of science and technology in food systems. These are reflected in the different goals of advocates of each of the paradigms, which are described in Table 12.1.

In the early 20th century, as a result of World War I and World War II, there was an increased demand for food in war-torn nations unable to produce their own. This led to intensified production and agricultural expansion in the United States and elsewhere, which, coupled with periods of drought, left soils eroded and vulnerable. War also led to disrupted manufacturing of agricultural inputs. By the end of World War II, there was a worldwide food shortage. This was a critical moment for the modern food system. Faced with the challenges created by the World Wars, coupled with several indicators of the

Table 12.1   Goals held by conventional and alternative groups

Group/level involved	Goals of conventional (professed and/or operative)	Goals of alternative (professed and/or operative)
Farmers	Family support Make money/have a high standard of living Produce more through specialization by crop/commodity Stewardship of the land Fight world hunger	Family and community support Diversified farming Conservation of energy, soil, and local species Social justice
Agriculture as a sector	Increased production Stable prices and markets domestically Expand foreign markets Profitable operation Specialization by commodity	Have healthy, nutritious food Sustainable production More local and regional markets (formal and informal) More small farms Farm and regional diversity
National	Increased production Inexpensive food Foreign exchange and industrialization of agriculture and urbanization	Have nutritious/healthy food Rural revival and decentralization
International	Eliminate of hunger through trade and aid Agricultural development Economic development	Elimination of hunger through local production Rural and ecodevelopment Cultural development
Global	Balance between food, population, and resources (Western approach)	Balance between food, population, and resources (recessive Western approach plus non-Western) Conservation of genetic and biological diversity

Adapted from: Dahlberg (1986).

ecological limits of aggressive agricultural intensification, actions were taken by the international community.

The dominant response to the food shortage crisis in the post-World War II period by governments, agrifood research organizations, agribusiness and agrochemical industries, and international organizations was the strengthening of the industrial paradigm to meet the challenge of food shortages. The strategy of this group of powerful actors was to increase the global food supply through further industrialization while adopting nationalist agricultural policies. The United States was at the center of this constellation of powerful actors and adopted policies to protect its domestic markets while at the same time generously subsidizing agricultural exports, a pattern that was replicated by other nations

(Friedmann 2005). Developing countries, unable to compete with the cheap prices of food imports, especially grains, became dependent on often non-traditional food imports (like wheat) (Friedmann and McMichael 1989).

A key pillar of the post-World War II food regime was the deepening of scientific advances in chemical fertilizers and pesticides, seed breeding and hybridization, and mechanized labor, coupled with practices such as monocultures to scale agriculture and produce ever greater supplies of food. In the 1950s and 1960s, this approach began to be applied to developing countries in what was termed the "Green Revolution," guided by notable scientists such as the Nobel Peace Prize Winner, Norman Borlaug, and agricultural research institutes that would later become integrated into a global umbrella organization, the Consultative Group on International Agricultural Research (CGIAR). Research initiatives were largely funded by powerful foundations and had strong links to the private sector, especially chemical companies. For example, Norman Borlaug was a scientist with DuPont Chemical when he was hired by the Rockefeller Foundation to work on agriculture in developing countries.

Meanwhile, a small group of relatively unknown agricultural researchers and farmers began to veer in a different direction. Concerned about the changes in soil fertility and erosion that they linked to the use of agrochemicals, this group began to develop and advocate farming practices that worked to recycle waste products back into soils to improve fertility – a foundational principle of organic agriculture (Heckman 2006). Influenced by the late 19th century movements mentioned above and sustainable techniques used in Asian farming cultures for centuries, early pioneers of organic agriculture in Europe and the United States developed what became known as "biological agriculture" in the 1960s (Vogt 2007). They strongly rejected the dependence on chemical inputs, mechanized labor, and monocultures characteristic of the productivist approach to agriculture, a cornerstone of the industrial paradigm. Also embedded in their discourses were strong opinions about human–nature relations and the connections between environmental and human health.

In the decades that followed, both the industrial and alternative food paradigms continued to evolve and were shaped by important developments. In particular, the publication of Rachel Carson's *Silent Spring* in 1962 led to intense questioning of the use of agrochemicals and their effect on the environment. This conversation deepened in the early 1970s with the consolidating of the environmental movement and the publication of the famous 1972 report by the Club of Rome, *Limits to Growth*, which raised the issue of long-term sustainability given the current nature and trajectory of growth at that time (see also Chapter 1 by John Vogler). It was during this turbulent decade of the 1970s that the effects of the Green Revolution were also increasingly scrutinized by scholars and international institutions concerned with the effects of the approach on the social and economic well-being of, especially, smaller farmers who were unable to compete with farmers implementing Green Revolution techniques, as well as the ecological effects of industrialized agriculture (Pearse 1980). Given these grievances and spurred by the environmental movement, alternative approaches to agriculture were gaining momentum. Attesting to the strengthening of this paradigm was, for example, the founding of the International Federation of Organic Agriculture Movements (IFOAM) in 1972, which grew to include 50 member organizations from 17 countries by 1975 and continued to expand from there (Geier 2007, p. 178).

These developments have to be viewed against the backdrop of the World Food Crisis of the early 1970s and the beginning of the end of the state-led development model that had characterized the post-World War II period, including the accompanying post-war food regime. The cause of the crisis can be traced to four converging factors: first, growing dependence of Global South nations on food imports while prices for traditional colonial exports (e.g., tropical oils and sweeteners) plunged; second, corporate agriculture's takeover of commodity chains that pushed family farmers out and limited their political representation; third, the limitations posed by protectionism for the growth of corporate agriculture, thus leading to initiatives to liberalize agricultural trade; and finally, after years of embargo between the capitalist and communist world, the famous grain deals between the Soviet Union and the United States during the period of détente that resulted in creating grain scarcity in world markets, driving up grain prices and creating a global food crises that occurred in parallel to the Oil Crisis (Friedmann 2005, p. 244). In 1974, the United Nations convened the World Food Conference at which the concept of "food security" was introduced and food supply was identified as the culprit behind the food crisis, even though the cause of the crisis was far more complex. Rather than address the underlying causes of the crisis, the solution was to increase the food supply and loan "petrodollars" to countries with food insecurity so that they could buy food, echoing the onslaught of neoliberalism discussed in Chapter 3 by Thomas Hickmann and Markus Lederer.

The 1980s and 1990s ushered in a new period as a result of several interconnected developments that directly implicated agrifood systems. First, there were important changes in the international political economy. Neoliberalism and market-led development emerged in the 1980s as the favored economic development model, reflected in the trade policies of the United States and other powerful nations as well as in the "Washington Consensus" policies that guided the restructuring of crisis-ridden nations in the developing world. A cornerstone of this approach was trade liberalization, and the General Agreement on Trade and Tariffs (GATT) was the vehicle for the negotiation of trade liberalization. Agriculture had generally been treated as a "special case" in GATT negotiations, as member nations did not agree on its liberalization (McCalla 1993). But this changed in the Uruguay Round of GATT talks, which spanned from 1986 to 1995. The United States, which had been in favor of eliminating protectionism in agricultural markets, called for this round of trade talks and the issue of trade reform in agriculture was at the top of the agenda (McCalla 1993). Besides the founding of the World Trade Organization (WTO), which was created in 1996, other outcomes of the Uruguay Round included a series of new agreements that specifically pertained to food agriculture, such as the Agreement on Trade-Related Aspects of Intellectual Property (TRIPS), the Agreement on the Application of Sanitary and Phytosanitary Measures (SPS), and the Agreement on Agriculture (AoA), which served as the initial move towards the liberalization of agrifood markets. Despite opposition to these agreements by civil society group and farmer organizations due to concerns for small and medium farmers and the privatization of agricultural technology (including the patenting of life) proposed by TRIPS, these agreements went into effect in 1996. In addition to the liberalization of trade under the neoliberal approach was the increased liberalization of financial markets and agriculture was not immune to this. By the early 1990s, Goldman Sachs opened up a commodities trading index that included food commodities (Patel 2012).

Restrictions on the trade of agricultural futures were reduced (Ghosh 2010; Patel 2012). All of this illustrated the onset of the financialization of food and agriculture in this period (see, for example, Clapp and Helleiner 2012).

Second, bearing in mind the rising power of transnational corporations (TNCs) in the agrifood sector over the previous decades, the shift towards market-centered growth gave greater leverage to these firms. The ease with which TNCs could proceed in a global environment characterized by freer trade and fewer regulations allowed for the restructuring of global agrifood supply chains through both vertical (increased control over all aspects of the supply chain) and horizontal integration (increasing the size of TNCs through mergers and acquisitions) across nations, thereby concentrating ownership, resources, and power into the hands of fewer TNCs (Heffernan 1998). Referred to by some as the "globalization" of the food system (e.g., Heffernan and Constance 1994), this process occurred across various sectors, including production and retail sectors. Concerning production, a significant development was that the life sciences industry became more integrated. With strengthened regulations on intellectual property rights as a result of TRIPS, pharmaceutical and chemical companies began to invest more in developing agricultural biotechnology, particularly genetically-modified seeds, and selling and marketing their product, thus integrating the research and development (R&D), seed production, and seed marketing components of supply chains (Murphy 2008; Williams 2009). With regard to the retail sector, as Clapp and Fuchs (2009, p. 5) point out, the deregulation of foreign direct investment (FDI) has enabled the global expansion of supermarket retailers (e.g., Walmart) and other food retailers (e.g., Starbucks, McDonalds, etc.) in the Global South (see also Reardon et al. 2003). This often occurred through the purchasing of local or national outlets or chains, thereby reducing competition and concentrating power and ownership over the sector. The effects of this process for small and medium-sized farmers, food processors, and retailers was to drive them out of business as they were unable to compete with TNCs (Murphy 2008).

Amidst the Uruguay Round negotiations and growing corporatization of the agrifood sector, a third development was underway, which was the heightened importance of the natural environment and issues of sustainability. The Brundtland Report paved the way for the Rio Earth Summit in 1992, when heads of state convened to adopt a set of agreements to deepen commitments to sustainable development, called on the United Nations to create a Commission on Sustainable Development, and opened up two important binding conventions, the United Nations Framework on Climate Change and the Convention on Biodiversity, for signatures. It is important to highlight the presence of over 2,000 global civil society organizations at the Rio Conference, thus reinforcing a growing trend in this period towards enhanced calls for governance from below. All of this served to reorient the discourse around development to not only consider economic factors but also social and environmental dimensions. Moreover, it underscored tensions that were emerging more forcefully in the 1990s between civil society movements, which were advocating for sustainability and human rights, and the dominant market-based approach, which was closing spaces for democratic participation in governance and policy making via international trade agreements that required states to relinquish their sovereignty over certain aspects of the economy.

The final development was the re-emergence of the issue of food security on the global agenda in response to rising rates of food insecurity in the mid-1990s after almost two decades of improved worldwide indices of hunger and malnourishment (FAO 2006). The renewed importance of food security was particularly evident by the convening of the 1996 World Food Summit (WFS). It was at this event where tensions between civil society activists and nations and institutions promoting market-led growth resurfaced again. Heads of state from some 185 countries and the European Community convened to address the protracted crisis of worldwide hunger and malnutrition, and a parallel NGO Forum on Food Security was held with the participation of over 800 organizations from 80 countries, representing both established nongovernmental organizations (NGOs) and grassroots "people's" organizations (McKeon 2010, p. 23). The outcomes of the 1996 WSF were two main documents, the Rome Declaration on World Food Security and the World Food Summit Plan of Action, in which nations committed to trade-based approaches to achieving food security, building on the reorientation in the approach to dealing with food insecurity that emerged during the Uruguay Round at the behest of the United States (McMichael 2005, p. 277).

The results of the WFS highlighted two important developments with respect to food security: First, the discourse of food security had become multidimensional, representing a shift from a primary focus on food supply, access to food, and nutrition to broader issues and debates over food system sustainability, the effects of trade liberalization, intellectual property rights, the right to food, and the global governance of food. Second, there were profoundly different visions of how to achieve food security and guarantee the right to food. In the NGO Forum's Final Statement (1996), civil society organizations widely contested the trade-based approach to food security, the industrial agrifood paradigm, and intellectual property rights, among other issues, as contributing towards environmental degradation, food insecurity, and impoverishment of agriculturally-dependent family farmers and rural people. Instead, they offered a set of measures to implement a new approach that put human rights, agroecological production, and citizen participation and democracy at the center of its model, citing the need for food sovereignty, a new term introduced by the transnational peasant movement, La Vía Campesina, to ensure that states have the ability to make decisions about their own food security without the interference of market forces (NGO Forum to the World Food Summit 1996; McKeon 2010).

Thus, given the developments outlined above, the nature of food systems was categorically different by the mid-1990s. While challenges like hunger and ecological limitations that were noted in the early 1900s were not resolved – and had rather become even more serious – different ways of addressing these problems emerged in response to the application of advances in science and technology and changes to the broader political economy. The two paradigms that had emerged in the late 1800s, the industrial paradigm and the alternative paradigm, evolved substantially in response to changes during the post-World War II period, but each transformed in a unique way and each offered its own recipe for fostering food system sustainability amidst the emerging complexities and contradictions that characterize food systems in the early 21st century.

Twenty-first century approaches to achieving food system sustainability

By the end of the 20th century, sustainability had become the buzzword in discussions about agrifood systems and international development more broadly. Moving into the 21st century, agrifood systems were characterized by a unique set of conditions, including growing uncertainty of the effects of climate change, natural resource degradation and depletion, projected population increases, and the expansion of Western patterns of consumption to the Global South via the globalization of the agrifood trade (Lang 2010). In particular, this last factor resulted in new challenges, like increased waste from packaging and transport, higher demand for processed foods, and growing public health concerns resulting from increased rates of obesity and other nutrition-related, non-communicable diseases (Young 2004). There was a growing consensus that measures had to be taken to ensure the sustainability of agrifood systems. It was also increasingly acknowledged and accepted – even by its own supporters – that the Green Revolution model had substantially contributed to environmental degradation and pollution, and thus new measures to increase productivity would be needed to foster environmental sustainability (Conway 1997; IFPRI 2002).

Despite agreeing on the need for food system sustainability, agrifood system actors were divided over how to achieve it. Influenced by the developments of the 1980s and 1990s outlined above, the industrial and alternative agrifood paradigms that had characterized most of the 20th century began to shift. On the one hand, the industrial paradigm transformed in response to the weaknesses of the Green Revolution model and the rise and promise of biotechnology, which was cited by advocates as being a more environmentally sustainable solution for intensifying agricultural production. Often called the "Doubly Green Revolution" (Conway 1997) or the "Second Green Revolution" (Lynch 2007), this post-productivist industrial approach sought to mediate the ecological woes of the Green Revolution by applying biotechnology to engineer varieties that are adapted to a variety of climactic conditions (e.g., drought resistant), display certain traits that are desirable to retailers and consumers (e.g., longer shelf life), and require less agricultural inputs (e.g., pesticides or fertilizers), thus having less negative environmental impact. Unlike the productivist approaches of the post-WWII period that were state-centric, the post-productivist industrial approach was guided by *neoliberal* principles, with intellectual property rights protections for the biotechnology industry and promotion of market-based food security solutions that emphasize trade and linking farmers to markets. Proponents of this frame initially included many of the same advocates of the Green Revolution, including governments, especially the United States; international agricultural research organizations, including the CGIAR; leading agricultural research universities; international development organizations; powerful philanthropists, particularly the Gates Foundation and Rockefeller Foundation (the latter of which had played a key role in the first Green Revolution); and large agribusinesses and – the newest set of players – life sciences corporations, like Monsanto, Syngenta, and others.

On the other hand, the alternative agrifood paradigm deepened in response to strong concerns over ecological health, biotechnology, and corporate dominance over food.

It remained predicated on organic agriculture techniques, especially and increasingly agro-ecology, which sought as a scientific practice to use ecological concepts and principles to design sustainable agriculture systems (Altieri 1995). The alternative paradigm was generally opposed to the globalization of agrifood systems in favor of more locally-based systems. The notion of "food democracy" and the desire for transparency about how food is grown and processed became an important part of this paradigm. Advocates of food democracy saw the marketization/corporatization of food and agriculture as having compromised the democratic, bottom-up control over agrifood systems and their components and outputs. They looked to national and international public policy and states and international governance institutions to offer solutions to grievances caused by the productivist/post-productivist industrial paradigms. The major actors supporting this frame included social movements focused on food and agriculture (known as "food movements"), including the food sovereignty, organic agriculture, fair trade, Slow Food, and agroecology movements; nongovernment and civil society organizations; academics and researchers; and some local and national governments.

Political support for the alternative paradigm was weak in the early 2000s (Lang and Heasman 2004); however, this began to change by the early 2010s following two important events that further influenced agrifood systems discourses. The first of these was the global food price crisis of 2007–2010. The crisis began with moderately rising food prices in 2006 and then intensified with the rapid price increases throughout 2007 to mid-2008. Prices began to lower after this point, but still remained high into 2009. The FAO (2010, p. 9) estimated that, in the period 2007–2009, the number of undernourished people in the world rose by 175 million, or almost 25%, with the crisis disproportionately affecting the rural and urban poor who spend a greater percentage of their income on food. The causes of the crisis were determined to be the result of multiple factors creating something of a "perfect storm." One of the most significant of these was increased financial investment via speculation in food commodity futures in 2007 and 2008, which was directly linked to broader financial dynamics leading to the Global Financial Crisis in 2008. As Ghosh (2010, p. 78) explained

> As the global financial system became fragile with the continuing implosion of the US housing finance market, large investors, especially institutional investors such as hedge funds and pension funds and even banks, searched for other avenues of investment to find new sources of profit.

The end result of food commodities speculation was extreme fluctuation in the price of food.

While speculation certainly did drive prices up, it was not the sole cause of higher prices. Another factor was the increasing costs of agricultural production, which was attributable to several factors: decreasing public investment in agriculture and agricultural research over the previous several decades (which led to falling agricultural efficiency and productivity) and rising oil prices in 2007 and 2008. The increase in oil prices created another dynamic that contributed to the food price crisis: new policies introduced in the European Union and the United States in the early 2000s to diversify the energy sector and invest in biofuels.

These policies were particularly important in the United States, where a significant proportion of corn production – upwards of 30% in 2007 – previously intended for food was diverted for agrofuel/ethanol production (Ghosh 2010, p. 73). A final factor that some analysts have noted is the changing demand for food with the rise in economic power of countries like China and India, and particularly demand for livestock products, which are dependent on cereal and oilseed supply for animal feed (FAO 2009). Unlike previous food crises, several features of the food price crisis made it historically unique: first, unlike the World Food Crisis in the early 1970s, the cause of the crisis was demand oriented and not a result of insufficient supply; second, nearly all major food and feed commodities rose in price with the potential of remaining high in price for the long-term; and, third, inflated prices were coupled with high price volatility of cereals and oilseeds (FAO 2009).

Against the background of the unfolding food crisis, the second event, the International Assessment of Agricultural Knowledge, Science and Technology for Development (IAASTD) Global Report, was published in 2008. The IAASTD process was initiated by the FAO and the World Bank in 2004 with the purpose of "assess[ing] the impacts of past, present and future agricultural knowledge, science and technology on the reduction of hunger and poverty, improvement of rural livelihoods and human health, and equitable, socially, environmentally, and economically sustainable development" (McIntyre et al. 2008, p. vi). The report was the product of a four-year, multi-stakeholder consultation process with hundreds of participants from different agrifood sectors, and the report was written by 400 experts nominated by governments, NGOs, producer and consumer groups, private sector organizations, and international organizations. In essence, it was a strategy for reshaping agricultural research. At the center of the IAASTD's analysis was the recognition that agriculture is multifunctional, meaning that "agriculture is a multi-output activity producing not only commodities (food, feed, fibers, agrofuels, medicinal products and ornamentals, but also non-commodity outputs such as environmental services [the activities or processes that nature provides to sustain life], landscape amenities and cultural heritage," with the term used by IAASTD to "express the inescapable interconnectedness of agriculture's different roles and functions" (McIntyre et al. 2008, p. 4).

The IAASTD thus took a much more comprehensive and integrated approach to understanding the crisis of food systems, food security, and rural development. The recommendations broadly emphasized enhancing rural livelihoods; promoting equity and empowerment of marginalized stakeholders; acknowledging the value of local and formal knowledge; achieving food security while strengthening environmental sustainability; increasing investment in public goods and multi-stakeholder partnerships to foster and share knowledge; taking more participatory approaches to introducing innovations and new technology, including biotechnology; and adopting reforms to make markets and international trade more just. The report called for a new role for agricultural knowledge, science, and technology in development that reflected a "shared approach to sustainability" to replace the former approach under the Green Revolution that namely functioned with expert-led innovation and state-led implementation of agricultural technology designed to increase productivity while externalizing environmental costs (McIntyre et al. 2008, p. 3). In short, the report stated, "Business as usual is no longer an option" (McIntyre et al. 2008, p. 3), and a paradigm shift away from the productivist industrial model was necessary.

The findings of the study were unsurprisingly controversial. The report squarely questioned core elements of the productivist and post-productivist industrial approaches to food and agriculture. Among the most controversial points made by the IAASTD was its cautious take on biotechnology, which pointed out a lack of consensus on productivity gains of genetically-modified varieties as well as concerns over the impact of privatizing knowledge via patents on genetically-modified organisms (GMOs) and the negative implications this can have for local farmers and food systems (see below). Ultimately, two prominent life sciences companies, Syngenta and Monsanto, withdrew from the IAASTD process in its final days and the United States, Canada, and Australia ultimately did not sign the report, expressing that a number of claims in the report required further analysis, especially concerning biotechnology. Many international research and development institutions were reluctant to engage with the IAASTD due to the contentious findings of the report, notably the prominent global actors that were behind the assessment like the FAO, the World Bank, and the CGIAR centers. On the other hand, some supporters of the alternative agrifood paradigm did not believe the IAASTD went far enough. While the need for fairer trade was included in the recommendations, the emphasis on market solutions was prominent enough in the report that it attracted the attention of critics for not going far enough to critique the neoliberal, market-based approach that served to create impediments to food security and food system sustainability.

The shifts in the alternative and industrial paradigms that had begun in the early 2000s – the strengthening of the alternative paradigm and the reorientation of the industrial paradigm – deepened after the food price crisis and the release of the IAASTD. On the one hand, the alternative paradigm found greater legitimacy as a result of these developments: the food price crisis had illustrated the kinds of risks that market liberalization could give rise to, while the findings of the IAASTD resonated with major core tenets of the alternative paradigm, including the multifunctionality of agriculture and the need for environmentally sustainable approaches to production, among others. As a result, political support for the alternative paradigm has increased in recent years, and especially for agroecology, food democracy, and the importance of local knowledge. For example, Olivier De Schutter, who served as the second Special Rapporteur to the Right to Food for the United Nations from 2008–2014, was a notable and powerful advocate for small-scale farmers, agroecology, and food democracy. His work continues to be instrumental in bringing these ideas, as well as the discourse of food sovereignty, to the forefront of global food policy debates as a framework for achieving the right to food for all (Sage 2014). As mentioned above, the concept of food sovereignty was introduced at the 1996 World Food Summit, and the movement gained traction throughout the 2000s attracting the attention and support of a wide array of civil society organizations, farmer organizations, and academics, among others. Described by some as an umbrella approach (e.g., Windfuhr and Jonsén 2005), the food sovereignty approach provides a framework for achieving food security, strengthening rural livelihoods, and promoting sustainable and equitable development. It has increasingly become the new face of the alternative paradigm, as it resonates with multiple other movements and ideologies belonging to the alternative paradigm, including those of agroecology, fair trade, and environmental justice. Food sovereignty policies were approved in seven nations by the end of 2009. Its comprehensive rights-based approach to achieving food security and ensuring the right to food has become a powerful and sophisticated alternative to the market-based discourse of the Second Green Revolution.

On the other hand, the industrial paradigm continued to shift, maintaining a fundamental commitment to market-based development but with a new orientation towards enhancing productivity, especially among small producers, through "integrated" approaches to agriculture that were more environmentally sustainable. Such integrated approaches were predicated on the early discourse of the "Doubly Green Revolution" that argued for the use of the wide variety of available agricultural production techniques – from biotechnology to agroecology – in order to ensure productivity and sustainability (Conway 1997). More recently the FAO has used the term "integrated" to refer to systems that combine crop, livestock, and/or tree systems together to foster efficiency, productivity, and environmental sustainability (FAO 2013). Recent initiatives like the Alliance for a Green Revolution in Africa (AGRA) and the Global Agriculture and Food Security Program (GAFSP) are hallmark examples of the integrated approach in action. AGRA focuses on small farmers and aims to increase production and strengthen markets to generate economic development and is funded by a wide variety of private foundations, corporations, international cooperation, and development organizations and banks, and works alongside CGIAR centers and other university and research partners.[2] GAFSP is a multilateral initiative with support from the Group of 20 (G-20) and funded by both private and public sources, established in 2009, that seeks to meet global food security and poverty reduction targets through different country projects (Sustainable Development Network 2009). Interestingly, despite their critique of the findings of the IAASTD, prominent supporters of these market-friendly, integrated approaches, like the World Bank, FAO, and CGIAR centers, have increasingly adopted the language of the IAASTD into their work while maintaining loyalty to the neoliberal market paradigm (Feldman and Biggs 2012).

In sum, despite growing agreement around the salience of the environment for the future of food systems, food system actors remain divided about how best to foster sustainable food systems. But the interesting point is the extent to which the industrial, post-positivist approach has increasingly been appropriating elements of the alternative approach, either directly or indirectly. This has either occurred through the adoption of language, like sustainability itself or livelihoods, or the adoption of concepts or practices but using different names. One example of this is the FAO's "integrated approach," which can be argued to be equivalent to the concept of diversification on farms that has been an important part of the discourse of the alternative paradigm for years. In recent years, this appropriation of terms and practices characteristic of the alternative agrifood paradigm has deepened and will be seen in the discussion that follows of several key issues facing contemporary agrifood systems and how the two competing paradigms have approached these issues.

Critical issues in building sustainable agrifood systems

As Lang (2010) observed, ". . . only sustainable food systems can offer food security" (p. 95). Building on the common definition of sustainability as posited by the Brundtland Report

(1987), the High Level Task Force on Global Food and Nutrition (2015b) defined a sustainable food system as one that "delivers food and nutrition security for all in such a way that the economic, social and environmental bases to generate food security and nutrition for future generations are not compromised" and further recommended that states better align with five principles, which have since been adopted by the FAO,[3] in order to build sustainable food systems: (1) improve the efficiency of resource use; (2) protect and enhance the sustainability of natural resources; (3) protect and improve rural livelihoods, equity, women's empowerment, and social well-being; (4) enhance people's communities and ecosystem resilience; and (5) ensure responsible and effective governance. While these guiding principles are useful for thinking through the dimensions of sustainable food systems, there are opposing viewpoints on how to go about implementing them in practice. Hence, as the discussion in the previous section underscored, it is precisely the means by which to construct sustainable food systems – meaning the practices and underlying ideologies that shape these practices – that spurs debate. This section will examine two interrelated issues concerning food system sustainability – food security and climate change and the controversial topic of seeds – among agrifood actors to illustrate how different approaches to constructing sustainable agrifood systems ideologically collide, and in doing so, demonstrate the depth of political contention that characterizes these debates.

Climate change and food security: agroecology vs. climate-smart agriculture

Climate change is currently the most pressing environmental issue facing the global community and it has immense implications for food system sustainability. In a recent report, the FAO (2016, p. 1) observed that, "The effects of climate change on our ecosystems are already severe and widespread, and ensuring food security in the face of climate change is among the most daunting challenges facing humankind" (p. 1). The anticipated impacts of climate change on food security are extensive and will affect all four dimensions of food security, which include the availability of food, physical and economic access to food, the biological utilization of food determined by healthy and adequate food intake and preparation, and the stability of the first three dimensions over time.[4]

The FAO (2016) argues that climate change will have "cascading" effects on food security.[5] In sum, climate change will initially impact agricultural production systems, or agroecosystems, thereby altering existing patterns of global food production. Broadly speaking, high variability in crop yields owing to the uneven geographic effects of climate variations and the consequences of these variations on agroecosystems is expected. Two major and interrelated issues are the impact of pests and diseases on plant crops and animal production, which is expected to have a negative impact on production, and a loss of biodiversity that can disrupt delicate symbiotic relationships between flora and fauna, ultimately affecting the survival of the species most affected by disruptions (FAO 2016). Tropical regions, where most of the world's most vulnerable populations reside, are expected to be hit the hardest by yield changes resulting from climate change (Wheeler and von Braun 2013). Beyond yields, climate change, and particularly extreme weather events, are also predicted to have effects on crop quality and post-harvest processes, such as storage, transport, and retail of agricultural products, which may lead to both food safety issues and decrease the availability and access to food due to supply losses and increased prices (Vermeulen et al. 2012). There is a broad consensus that action must be taken to foster sustainable food systems that are resilient in the face of climate change.

Food systems have substantially contributed to generating greenhouse gases (GHGs). Vermeulen et al. (2012) calculated the carbon footprint of the food system for the year 2008 and determined that the food system was responsible for between 19–29% of all GHGs (p. 198). They further explained that, while most of the GHG emissions were attributable to agricultural production activities, including livestock production, rice production, the burning of fields, and deforestation to expand spaces for cultivation, preproduction activities (e.g., manufacture of synthetic fertilizers and animal feed) and post-production activities (e.g., food processing, packaging, transportation, refrigeration, and retail activities) also contributed. For years, advocates of the alternative agrifood paradigm drew attention to ecological impacts of modern agriculture encompassed by Green Revolution methods. In particular, critics of modern agriculture have highlighted the issue of biodiversity loss, caused by the use of agrochemicals and the continued use of monocultures, as contributing to ecological vulnerability, as well as the more recent threat posed by GMO crops, which not only pose a threat to other species through interbreeding but also often require agrochemicals and are grown in monocultures (Altieri et al. 2015). This is a particularly important point given the fact that one of the factors that can increase the resilience of agroecosystems and, thus the food system in general, is biodiversity (FAO 2016, p. 11).

Maintaining and enhancing biodiversity by preserving the genetic base of plants and using polycultures are central features of production systems according to the alternative agrifood paradigm (Beus and Dunlap 1990). Thus, for adherents to the alternative paradigm, responses to climate change already exist, namely through the framework of agroecology. In addition to recognizing the immeasurable value of biodiversity for agrifood systems and the environment, agroecology also puts traditional practices and knowledge at the center of its model. According to Swiderska et al. (2011), five types of traditional knowledge that are useful for maintaining and strengthening biodiversity and climate change adaptation are those concerning climatically resilient local crop species, plant breeding, wild crop relatives, resilient farming and resource management practices, and climate forecasting (pp. 2–3). According to proponents of agroecology, small-scale farms where traditional practices are implemented are more resource conserving, productive, and genetically diverse than those managed using modern agricultural practices, and this diversity enhances ecosystem function and overall resilience to vulnerability (Altieri et al. 2015). Thus, advocates of agroecology, including members of the food sovereignty movement and increasingly the environmental justice movement, support agroecology and its principles as a framework for mitigating climate change and building more resilient agrifood systems.

The other approach for adapting to climate change is climate-smart agriculture (CSA). Introduced in 2010 by the FAO, CSA has three main objectives: (1) sustainably increasing food security by increasing agricultural productivity and incomes; (2) building resilience and adapting to climate change; and (3) developing opportunities for reducing green-house gas emissions compared to expected trends (FAO 2013). At the heart of CSA is the concept of sustainable intensification, which "entails increasing food production from existing farmland in ways that have lower environmental impact and which do not undermine our capacity to continue producing food in the future" (Campbell et al. 2014, p. 39). Proponents of CSA argue that the approach can help to mitigate climate change by reducing the amount of land that is converted to agriculture and making more efficient use of "ecosystem services," or the activities and benefits from ecosystem functioning that support life (Lipper et al. 2014). CSA has become the mainstream approach to adapting agriculture to climate change and it has been adopted widely by international agriculture and development organizations. Spearheaded by the FAO, the Global Alliance for Climate Smart Agriculture (GACSA) was created in 2014 at the bequest of the UN Secretary General at the United Nations Climate Summit. The alliance currently has a membership of 180 organizations, including states, private companies, farmer organizations, and agriculture and research organizations and universities, and several civil society organizations with observer status.[6] The broad mission of the GACSA is "to improve people's food security and nutrition in the face of climate change" and, echoing the strategy presented by the FAO (2013), it seeks to accomplish this with a focus on increasing knowledge and investment and creating enabling environments at multiple scales (local to global) for the adoption of CSA practices and policies to support the approach (GACSA 2014).

While there does appear to be some convergence between CSA and agroecology, particularly in terms of the emphasis of CSA on fostering environmentally sustainable agricultural production that is specific to local conditions and takes into account the wider landscape in which local agroecosystems are embedded – hallmark principles of agroecology – CSA also accommodates practices that are not compatible with agroecology, including the use of agrochemicals, GMOs, patented technologies and seeds, factory farming, and large-scale monocultures and biofuel farms (Pimbert 2015, pp. 289–290). This is unsurprising given the representation of private sector agribusinesses, particularly agricultural input producers, and agriculture development firms in the GACSA and other CSA platforms. For example Monsanto, famous for its production of GMO seeds, is the co-chair of the Climate Smart Agriculture Working Group of the World Business Council for Sustainable Development (Monsanto 2017), which is a member of the GACSA. Thus, while CSA may appear to overlap with several core agroecological tenets, in reality, it is questionable how much CSA actually differs from industrial agriculture in practice, especially given the role of global agrifood corporations and the continued focus on productivity, trade, and markets for economic development (Pimbert 2015).[7]

Agroecology proponents have largely rejected the CSA approach. In response to the call for creating the GACSA, a group of over 100 national and international organizations and farmers movements signed an open letter opposing the GACSA for three main reasons: (1) lack of criteria to define what and what does not constitute CSA, thus leaving the door open to industrial agrifood approaches; (2) continued role for carbon offsetting policies to fund CSA projects, which in turn could threaten smallholder livelihoods; and (3) role for agribusinesses in CSA initiatives, particularly those that have contributed to social injustice and environmental degradation.[8] Citing the IAASTD report, the signatories of the letter argue for the necessity of policy change, stating:

> The International Assessment of Agricultural Knowledge, Science and Technology for Development concluded in 2008 that business-as-usual in agriculture *is not an option*; instead, a thorough and radical overhaul of present international and agricultural policies is essential to meet the challenges of the future.

There was a follow up to this initial condemnation of the GACSA by national and global civil society in 2015 when 59 international and 309 national civil society and farmer organizations released another statement prior to the COP21 conference to once again denounce CSA and the GACSA and implore decision makers to look to agroecology as the framework through which to address climate change.[9] This statement once again cited the potential for "greenwashing" by agribusinesses belonging to CSA initiatives and the lack of concrete attributes to define CSA and mechanisms to hold stakeholders accountable. Furthermore, it warned policymakers that "Climate Smart Agriculture must not be confused with agroecology." The inclusion of this caveat was not without reason: supporters of agroecology were becoming increasingly concerned that elements of agroecology, and the term itself, were being co-opted by advocates of CSA and other supporters of post-productivist solutions to climate change. This has generated a lofty critique from advocates of the alternative paradigm, particularly food sovereigntists for whom agroecology is a movement to resist the productivist and post-productivist industrial model, as this co-optation of terms can lead people to conflate agroecology with the post-productivist industrial model, thereby weakening the legitimacy of agroecology and the strength of the movement behind it (Holt-Giménez and Altieri 2016; Pimbert 2015).

Seeds: GMOs and the movement for seed sovereignty

Seeds are a vital part of sustainable food systems, as within them lies the base of genetic resources needed to ensure plant diversity, seen as essential to ensuring resilient agroecosystems and achieving food security, especially in light of climate change (FAO 2016). Traditional and indigenous agricultural systems are well known for being treasure troves of plant genetic diversity, and farmers have engaged in plant breeding and selection for thousands of years. However, this has changed significantly with the advent of modern agriculture. It is estimated that, between 1900 and 2000, 75% of genetic diversity in agricultural crops disappeared, and this was mostly attributable to the development and use of hybrid varieties during the Green Revolution that displaced traditional varieties in the developing world (FAO 1993), as well as the use of monocultures and agrochemicals, both of which served to erode local biodiversity. Today, 90% of global food intake is dependent on only 30 species of plants (FAO 2017b). The erosion of plant genetic diversity disproportionately affects the rural poor, who depend on biological resources for most of their needs (FAO 1993).

Present-day controversies over seeds are among the most contentious and are multidimensional. The roots of seed politics can be traced back to the immediate post-WWII period when seed breeding programs were initiated and then expanded in the 1950s and 1960s by the CGIAR. As Kloppenburg (2010a) pointed out, up to the 1930s, farmers had "seed sovereignty," meaning that they essentially had complete autonomy over decisions regarding their seeds – whether to save or plant their seeds or give them to someone else, and the sharing of seeds played an important role in maintaining and strengthening biodiversity and resilience in traditional agroecosystems. Slowly, this began to change with the advent of hybrid seeds, which could no longer by saved and shared by farmers and rather needed to be obtained from the producer of the seed and used in conjunction with fertilizers and pesticides to achieve the best results. This created opportunities for private companies to produce and market seeds, which was the first step towards reducing the seed sovereignty of farmers.

The advent of biotechnology in the 1980s and the introduction of the first genetically-modified seed varieties in the early 1990s ushered in a new era in which transnational "life sciences" companies, like Monsanto and Syngenta, invested heavily in R&D to produce genetically-modified seeds based on desirable traits – and sought patents to protect their technologies. The first kinds of seeds that were introduced to the market were herbicide tolerant and insect-resistant varieties, and by 2010, there was about 140 million hectares of land in 29 countries (mostly in the United States, Canada, Brazil, Argentina, and India) dedicated to the annual production of corn, soybean, cotton, and rapeseed using GM varieties (Barrows et al. 2014, p. 101). This has since increased to 189.1 million hectares across 19 developing countries and seven industrialized countries, with the same five countries mentioned above leading the world in the adoption of GM crops (ISAAA 2016). Adoption is likely to increase across developing countries with the introduction of GM rice and drought resistant varieties.

Proponents of GM crops argue that they have the potential to contribute to food security by increasing yields while providing a more environmentally sustainable option to that of the previous productivist model. In particular, some of the benefits outlined by supporters include less applications of pesticides, as pesticides are not needed for insect-resistant varieties and less harmful herbicides can be used with herbicide resistant varieties; less fuel consumption, as less chemicals are applied using farm machinery; and sustained, if not enhanced, biodiversity through the introduction of new varieties (Barrows et al. 2014). Land degradation can be mediated through the introduction of high-yield varieties (von Braun 2010). Furthermore, GM varieties can be engineered for climatic conditions, like drought, which presents an attractive solution to climate change and variation and could potentially conserve water normally required for irrigation.

Despite these claims, the environmental impact of GMOs is still unclear. Critics of GMOs, including the food sovereignty and agroecology advocates, cite a number of environmental concerns. First, despite the assertion that GMOs do not negatively affect biodiversity, critics state otherwise, citing two reasons: the possibility of genetic drift, as was found in Mexico where transgenic molecules were detected in traditional varieties of corn (Pineyro-Nelson et al. 2009) and the continued use of monocultures, which means increased vulnerablity to land erosion and pests and diseases. Another problem is that herbicide tolerant varieties can become tolerant to the herbicides designed to be used with them, thus necessitating stronger herbicides to reach the same effect. In fact, it has been argued that the risk of GM varieties becoming tolerant to agrochemicals is greater than it is for non-GM varieties (Barrows et al. 2014). But critics of GMO crops point out another issue and that is the privatization of genetic resources through the patenting of seeds. As the IAASTD (McIntyre et al. 2008, p. 8) noted, this has particular implications for developing countries (where the majority of agricultural smallholders live):

> . . . patents may drive up costs, restrict experimentation by the individual farmer or public researcher while potentially undermining local practices that enhance food security and economic sustainability. In this regard, there is particular concern about present IPR [intellectual property rights] instruments eventually inhibiting seed-saving, exchange, sale and access to proprietary materials necessary for the independent research community to conduct analyses and long term experimentation. Farmers face new liabilities: GM farmers may become liable for adventitious presence if it causes loss of market certification and income to neighboring organic farmers, and conventional farmers may become liable to GM seed producers if transgenic are detected in their crops.

In response to the risks associated with GMOs and the privatization of seeds by life science transnational corporations, advocates of seed sovereignty have formed numerous initiatives to create local seed banks and other mechanisms to counter the patenting of life and put genetic plant resources back into the hands of farmers, indigenous groups, and local communities. Initiatives include forming local seed banks and encouraging seed exchanges. Another broader initiative is called the Open Source Seed Initiative[10] that is premised on the open source software movement. As Kloppenburg (2010b, pp. 161–162) explains, the purpose of the approach is to encourage the free movement and use of plant genetic resources while at the same time preventing the patenting of plant life, preventing biopiracy and bioprospecting, and inhibiting the appropriation of peasant and farmer derived plant genetic resources in proprietary breeding programs, and impeding the spread of GMOs.

Figure 12.1 Native sorghum and bean seeds for sale at a farmer's market in Estelí, Nicaragua. Photo Credit: Arely V. Araica.

Looking to the future

As discussed in this chapter, food systems worldwide are currently in the midst of multiple crises with social, economic, political, and environmental dimensions, and there are different opinions as to how to address this complex situation. Post-productivists have adopted an "integrated approach" to achieving food system sustainability that seeks to optimize production while being environmentally sustainable. They generally advocate market-based approaches to food security and sustainability, thus seeing a clear role for private enterprise and international trade, and emphasize scientific knowledge and innovation. On the other hand, recent iterations of the alternative paradigm, particularly agroecology and food sovereignty, argue that ecologically-attuned modes of production embedded in local economies that value local and traditional knowledge are the path towards sustainability. While not being against trade, they advocate measures that limit the power of markets to infringe on the rights of the less powerful, thus exemplifying their deep concern with all forms of justice.

The likelihood of forging a consensus between these two competing frames is unlikely, at least in the short term. This is because facts are needed to demonstrate the viability of certain practices over others. For example, Green Revolution practices did not change until there was enough solid evidence to delegitimize these methods of production, and even so, practices such as using pesticides and growing in monocultures are still employed widely around the world. Forging change takes time – time that we very well may not have, given the depth of crisis that we are facing with the onset and intensification of climate change.

But there is another dimension to the issue of overcoming divisions between the post-productivists and alternative frames, which is that not all of the differences between them are issues that can be rationally solved by appealing to facts. At the crux of some of the key debates, as seen in the examples discussed above and echoing the work of Beus and Dunlap (1990), are competing values, especially about nature–society relations, knowledge, and governance. For example, the domination and commodification of nature, which is central to the industrial frame, is in stark contrast to the alternative paradigm that sees people as being part of nature and ecosystems. Likewise, when it comes to knowledge, the industrial model values science, technology, and innovation to manipulate nature, while the alternative paradigm has traditionally drawn on local knowledge and ecological systems to emulate nature. Finally, there is the question of governance and how this is shaped by the centralization and decentralization of power and resources. At the heart of food sovereignty and recent alternative food movements is the concept of food democracy as a means to creating more just food systems. The industrial model, with its accommodation of neoliberalism, faces important limitations in terms of creating conditions that can lead to more economic and political equity, as in practice, the model has led to the concentration of wealth and power. It is this set of factors that will more likely render the task of reaching consensus around building sustainable food systems a lofty goal at best and, more likely, an improbable one for the foreseeable future.

Notes

1 The High Level Task Force on Global Food and Nutritional Security (2015a) defined a food system as "the elements (environment, people, inputs, processes, infrastructure, institutions, markets and trade) and activities that relate to the production, processing, distribution and marketing,

preparation and consumption of food and the outputs of these activities, including socio-economic and environmental outcomes."

2 See AGRA website (http://agra.org) for more information.
3 See the FAO webpage on Sustainable Food and Agriculture: www.fao.org/sustainability/en/.
4 For a more detailed discussion of the four dimensions of food security, see www.fao.org/docrep/013/al936e/al936e00.pdf.
5 See FAO (2016, p. 4) for a helpful figure depicting how climate change's initial effects on agroecosystems carry over to impact agricultural production, followed by the livelihoods of agricultural producers and others, and finally affect overall food security and nutrition.
6 See GACSA website (www.fao.org/gacsa/) for full list and additional information.
7 For discussion of the role of international trade in CSA and the Green Economy, see Module 1 of the *Climate Smart Agriculture Source Book* (FAO 2013).
8 The rejection letter (dated September 2014) is available on the Climate Smart Agriculture Concerns website: www.climatesmartagconcerns.info/rejection-letter.html.
9 The 2015 statement (dated September 2015) is available on the Climate Smart Agriculture Concerns website: www.climatesmartagconcerns.info/cop21-statement.html.
10 See website for more information: http://osseeds.org.

Further reading

Clapp, J. (2016) *Food*. Cambridge, UK: Polity.
Conway, G. (2012) *One Billion Hungry: Can We Feed the World?* Ithaca, NY: Cornell University Press.
Gliessman, S. (2007) *Agroecology: The Ecology of Sustainable Food Systems*. Boca Raton, FL: Taylor & Francis.
Patel, R. (2010) *Stuffed and Starved: The Hidden Battle for the World Food System*. Brooklyn, NY: Melville House Publishing.

Recommended websites

International Panel of Experts on Sustainable Food Systems: www.ipes-food.org
International Planning Committee for Food Sovereignty: www.foodsovereignty.org/
CGIAR: www.cgiar.org
Global Alliance for Climate Smart Agriculture: www.fao.org/gacsa

References

Altieri, M. A. (1995) *Agroecology: The Science of Sustainable Agriculture*. Boulder, CO: Westview Press.
Altieri, M. A., Nicholls, C. I., Henao, A. & Lana, M. A. (2015) Agroecology and the Design of Climate Change-Resilient Farming Systems. *Agronomy for Sustainable Development*, 35(3), 869–890.
Barrows, G., Sexton, S. & Zilberman, D. (2014) Agricultural Biotechnology: The Promise and Prospects of Genetically Modified Crops. *Journal of Economic Perspectives*, 28(1), 99–120.
Beus, C. E. & Dunlap, R. E. (1990) Conventional versus Alternative Agriculture: The Paradigmatic Roots of the Debate. *Rural Sociology*, 55(4), 590–616.
Campbell, B. M., et al. (2014) Sustainable Intensification: What Is Its Role in Climate Smart Agriculture? *Current Opinion in Environmental Sustainability*, 8, 39–43.

Clapp, J. & Fuchs, D. (2009) *Corporate Power in Agrifood Governance*. Cambridge, MA: The MIT Press.

Clapp, J. & Helleiner, E. (2012) The Global Food Crisis and the Politics of Agricultural Derivatives Regulation. *Review of the International Political Economy*, 19(2), 181–207.

Climate Smart Agriculture Concerns (2014) Corporate Smart Greenwash: Why We Reject the Global Alliance on Climate-Smart Agriculture. [Online] Available at: www.climatesmartagconcerns.info/rejection-letter.html (last accessed 15/09/2017).

Conway, G. (1997) *The Doubly Green Revolution: Food for All in the Twenty-First Century*. Ithaca, NY: Cornell University Press.

Dahlberg, K. A. (1986) *New Directions for Agricultural Research: Neglected Dimensions of Emerging Alternatives*. Totowa, NJ: Rowman and Allanheld.(last accessed 13/09/2017).

FAO (1993) *Harvesting Nature's Diversity*. Rome: Food and Agriculture Organization of the United Nations.

FAO (1996) Rome Declaration on World Food Security and the World Food Summit Plan of Action. World Food Summit, Rome, Italy, 13–17 November. [Online] Available at: www.fao.org/docrep/003/w3613e/w3613e00.htm (last accessed 13/09/2017).

FAO (2006) *The State of Food Insecurity in the World 2006: Eradicating World Hunger—Taking Stock Ten Years after the World Food Summit*. Rome: Food and Agriculture Organization of the United Nations.

FAO (2009) *High Food Prices and the Food Crisis—Experiences and Lessons Learned*. Rome: Food and Agriculture Organization of the United Nations.

FAO (2010) *The State of Food Insecurity in the World: Addressing Food Insecurity in Protracted Crisis*. Rome: Food and Agriculture Organization of the United Nations.

FAO (2013) Climate Smart Agriculture Source Book. [Online] Available at: www.fao.org/docrep/018/i3325e/i3325e.pdf (last accessed 13/09/2017).

FAO (2015) *The State of Food Insecurity in the World*. Rome: Food and Agriculture Organizations of the United Nations.

FAO (2016) Climate Change and Food Security: Risks and Responses. [Online] Available at: www.fao.org/3/a-i5188e.pdf (last accessed 12/09/2017).

FAO (2017a) *The Future of Food and Agriculture: Trends and Challenges*. Rome: Food and Agriculture Organizations of the United Nations.

FAO (2017b) Plant Genetic Resources. [Online] Available at: www.fao.org/nr/cgrfa/cthemes/plants/en/ (last accessed 14/09/2017).

Feldman, S. & Biggs, S. (2012) The Politics of International Assessments: The IAASTD Process, Reception and Significance. *Journal of Agrarian Change*, 12(1), 144–169.

Friedmann, H. (2005) From Colonialism to Green Capitalism: Social Movements and Emergence of Food Regimes, in Buttel, F. H. & McMichael, P. (eds), *New Directions in the Sociology of Global Development*. Amsterdam: Elsevier, pp. 227–264.

Friedmann, H. & McMichael, P. (1989) Agriculture and the State System: The Rise and Decline of National Agricultures, 1870 to the Present. *Sociologia Ruralis*, 29(2), 93–117.

GACSA (2014) Global Alliance for Climate Smart Agriculture (GACSA) Framework Document. [Online] Available at: www.fao.org/3/a-au667e.pdf (last accessed 13/09/2017).

Geier, B. (2007) IFOAM and the History of the International Organic Movement, in Locheretz, W. (ed.), *Organic Farming: An International History*. Oxfordshire, UK: CABI, pp. 175–186.

Ghosh, J. (2010) The Unnatural Coupling: Food and Global Finance. *Journal of Agrarian Change*, 10(1), 72–86.

Heckman, J. (2006) A History of Organic Farming: Transitions from Sir Albert Howard's War in the Soil to USDA National Organic Program. *Renewable Agriculture and Food Systems*, 21(3), 143–150.

Heffernan, W. D. (1998) Agriculture and Monopoly Capital. *Monthly Review*, 50(3), 46–59.

Heffernan, W. D. & Constance, D. H. (1994) Transnational Corporations and the Globalization of the Food System, in Bonnano, A. et al. (eds), *From Columbus to ConAgra: The Globalization of Agriculture and Food*. Lawrence, KS: University Press of Kansas.

HLTF on Global Food and Nutrition Security (2015a) *Compendium—Final Report Global Hunger Challenge Working Groups: All Food Systems are Sustainable*. Rome: FAO.

HLTF on Global Food and Nutrition Security (2015b) Compendium—Final Report: Zero Hunger Challenge Working Groups. [Online] Available at: www.un.org/en/issues/food/taskforce/pdf/All%20food%20systems%20are%20sustainable.pdf (last accessed 13/09/2017).

Holt-Giménez, E. & Altieri, M. A. (2016) Agroecology, Food Sovereignty, and the Green Revolution, in Méndez, V. E., Bacon, C. M., Cohen, R. & Gliessman, S. R. (eds), *Agroecology: A Transdisciplinary, Participatory and Action-Oriented Approach*. Boca Raton, FL: CDC Press, pp. 113–120.

IFPRI (2002) *Green Revolution: Curse or Blessing?* Washington, DC: International Food Policy Research Institute.

ISAAA (2016) *Global Status of Commercialized Biotech/GM Crops: 2016. ISAAA Brief No. 52*. Ithaca, NY: International Service for the Acquisition of Agri-Biotech Applications.

Kloppenburg, J. (2010a) Impeding Dispossession, Enabling Repossession: Biological Open Source and the Recovery of Seed Sovereignty. *Journal of Agrarian Change*, 10(3), 367–388.

Kloppenburg, J. (2010b) Seed Sovereignty: The Promise of Open Source Biology, in Wittman, H., Desmarais, A. A. & Wiebe, N. (eds), *Food Sovereignty: Reconnected Food, Nature and Commodity*. Oakland, CA: Fernwood Publishing.

Lang, T. (2010) Crisis? What Crisis? The Normality of the Current Food Crisis. *Journal of Agrarian Change*, 10(1), 87–97.

Lang, T. & Heasman, M. (2004) *Food Wars: The Global Battle for Mouths, Minds and Markets*. Abingdon, UK: Earthscan.

Lipper, L. et al. (2014) Climate-Smart Agriculture for Food Security. *Nature Climate Change*, 4(12), 1068–1072.

Lynch, J. P. (2007) Roots of the Second Green Revolution. *Australian Journal of Botany*, 55(5), 493–512.

McCalla, A. F. (1993) Agricultural Trade Liberalization: The Ever-Elusive Grail. *American Journal of Agricultural Economics*, 75(December), 1102–1112.

McIntyre, B. D. et al. (2008) *International Assessment of Agricultural Knowledge, Science and Technology for Development (IAASTD): Synthesis Report with Executive Summary*. Washington, DC: Island Press.

McKeon, N. (2010) *The United Nations and Civil Society: Legitimizing Global Governance: Whose Voice?* London: Zed.

McMichael, P. (2005) Global Development and the Corporate Regime, in Buttel, F. H. & McMichael, P. (eds), *New Directions in the Sociology of Global Development: Research in Rural Sociology of Development, Volume II*. Amsterdam: Elsevier.

Monsanto (2017) Driving Innovation in Agriculture to Combat Climate Change. [Online] Available at: https://monsanto.com/company/sustainability/articles/climate-smart-agriculture-practices/ (last accessed 13/09/2017).

Murphy, S. (2008) Globalization and the Corporate Concentration in the Food and Agriculture Sector. *Development*, 51(4), 527–533.

NGO Forum to the World Food Summit (1996) Profit for Few or Food for All: Food Sovereignty and Security to Eliminate the Globalisation of Hunger. [Online] Available at: www.fao.org/wfs/begin/paral/cngo-E.htm (last accessed 27/08/2017).

Patel, R. (2012) The Long Green Revolution. *The Journal of Peasant Studies*, 40(1), 1–63.

Pearse, A. (1980) *Seeds of Plenty, Seeds of Want: Social and Economic Implications of the Green Revolution*. Geneva: UNRISD.

Pimbert, M. (2015) Agroecology as an Alternative Vision to Conventional Development and Climate-Smart Agriculture. *Development*, 58(2–3), 286–298.

Pineyro-Nelson, A. et al. (2009) Transgenes in Mexican Maize: Molecular Evidence and Methodological Considerations for GMO Detection in Landrace Populations. *Molecular Ecology*, 18(4), 750–761.

Reardon, T. et al. (2003) The Rise of Supermarkets in Africa, Asia, and Latin America. *American Journal of Agricultural Economics* 85(5): 1140–1146.

Sage, C. (2014) Food Security, Food Sovereignty and the Special Rapporteur: Shaping Food Policy Discourse through Realising the Right to Food. *Dialogues in Human Geography*, 4(2), 195–199.

Sustainable Development Network (2009) Framework Document for a Global Agriculture and Food Security Program (GAFSP). [Online] Available at: www.gafspfund.org/sites/gafspfund.org/files/Documents/GAFSP%20Framework%20Document%20FINAL%20(external).pdf (last accessed 12/09/2017).

Swiderska, K. et al. (2011) *The Role of Traditional Knowledge and Crop Varieties in Adaptation to Climate Change and Food Security in SW China, Bolivian Andes and Coastal Kenya*, London: IIED.

Vermeulen, S. J., Campbell, B. M. & Ingram, J. S. (2012) Climate Change and Food Systems. *Annual Review of Environment and Resources*, 37(1), 195–222.

Vogt, G. (2007) The Origins of Organic Farming, in Lockeretz, W. (ed), *Organic Farming: An International History*. Oxfordshire, UK: CABI, pp. 9–29.

von Braun, J. (2010) Food Insecurity, Hunger and Malnutrition: Necessary Policy and Technological Changes. *New Biotechnology*, 27(5), 449–452.

Wheeler, T. & von Braun, J. (2013) Climate Change Impacts on Global Food Security. *Science*, 341(6145), 508–513.

Williams, M. (2009) Feeding the World? Transnational Corporations and the Promotion of Genetically-Modified Food, in *Corporate Power in Agrifood Governance*. Cambridge, MA: The MIT Press.

Windfuhr, M. & Jonsén, J. (2005) *Food Sovereignty: Towards Democracy in Localized Food Systems*. Warwickshire, UK: ITDG Publishing.

Young, E. M. (2004) Globalization and Food Security: Novel Questions in a Novel Context. *Progress in Development Studies*, 4(1), 1–21.

Forest politics, neoliberalism and the limits of international environmental policy

13

David Humphreys

Introduction

The conservation and sustainable management of forests became a politically important environmental issue in the mid-1980s when international concern over deforestation led to the first tentative international initiatives to tackle the problem. This chapter begins by explaining deforestation as an international political issue using public goods theory. It then presents an analytical overview of international forest politics, beginning with the forest negotiations that took place at the 1992 United Nations Conference on Environment and Development in Rio, before tracking the aftermath of the Rio process, which has seen the establishment of a series of international forest bodies within the United Nations (UN) system. These bodies have agreed several non-legally binding outputs but, and despite several attempts, there is still no consensus that a global forests convention should be negotiated.

The absence of a forest convention explains, in part, why international forest policy is spread over several international organisations. It is argued that, in order to fully comprehend the international policy responses to deforestation, an understanding of neoliberal discourse is needed. Neoliberalism promotes certain types of environmental policy, in particular those that are voluntary, business-led and market-based. In this respect, neoliberalism establishes the parameters of international forest policy. The paper concludes by arguing that the World Trade Organization (WTO) has served as a powerful driver in the expansion of global neoliberalism, providing neoliberal principles with a political and legal force that environmental objectives lack in global governance. Using forests as a case study, therefore, the chapter draws out some points of broader relevance to global environmental politics.

Forests as public goods

Like other international environmental issues, deforestation is politically significant as it has a public goods dimension. Public goods are those that benefit a broader public; a *publicum*. Depending on the public good in question, the *publicum* may vary considerably, extending from the local to the global. In the case of global public goods, all humanity is the *publicum*. Forests play a major role in the regulation of the Earth's climate – a classic global public good, as everyone benefits from a stable atmosphere – by taking up carbon dioxide, a major greenhouse gas, from the atmosphere, breaking it down by photosynthesis and storing it in trees and plants. Public goods have two attributes in common. First, they are non-excludable. For example, no one can be excluded from the benefits of a stable climate. Second, they are non-rival in consumption; the consumption of a public good by one person will not affect what is left for others.

Forests serve as habitat for as much as 80% of the world's terrestrial species. They thus contribute to the global public good of biological diversity conservation, and the maintenance of the diverse global gene pool necessary for resilient and adaptable species and ecosystems (Perrings and Gadgil 2003). At a local level, forests may satisfy recreational or spiritual needs for a local *publicum*, such as a village of indigenous peoples, and provide local and regional soil conservation and watershed management functions. Forests thus provide a range of public goods for both proximate and distant users. In this sense, forests are shared – not in a spatial or ownership sense, but in the sense that they provide life support functions for all humanity.

Part of the problem of deforestation as an international political issue is that, while forests contribute to the maintenance of global public goods such as atmospheric regulation and biodiversity conservation, in international law, forests are a sovereign resource of the state. Some tropical country governments are particularly assertive on sovereignty. For example, successive Brazilian governments have made it clear that no other country has the right to interfere in how the Brazilian Amazon is used. Since the 1960s, Brazil has sought to develop the Amazon for economic development, exploiting Brazilian forests for the harvesting and mining of private goods. Private goods are those that can be bought and sold on markets. In contrast to public goods, private goods are rival in consumption (for example, the more timber that a business extracts from an area of forest, the less is available for others) and excludable (as those who own a private good can, legally at least, prevent others from using it). The private goods that forests provide include timber, nuts, berries, rattan and rubber.

In neoclassical economic theory, the provision of private goods is best realised through markets. But, because markets work best when goods are both rival and excludable, they undersupply, or do not supply at all, public goods. Furthermore, the overharvesting of private goods can lead to public good depletion. This is particularly the case with deforestation, which is often the result of forest clearance to harvest timber or to free land for alternative land uses, such as cattle ranching, crop agriculture or mineral mining. The degradation of public goods is an example of what economists call market failure, when the routine functioning of markets fails to bring about an allocation of resources that maximises the collective welfare of society. Forest politics is, in large part, an attempt to manage the tension between conserving the public good attributes of forests and exploiting the private goods that forests, and forest land, can realise. This tension runs in different guises throughout all forest policy and forest-related political conflicts, from the global level to the local. Conceptually at least, the tension has been overcome by the idea of sustainable forest management (SFM), which has served as a guiding concept in international cooperation on forests for nearly two decades. SFM may be defined as the maximisation of the yield of the private goods that forests can provide, but only to the extent that this does not deplete forest-related public goods.

There are divided views on how forest public goods can best be realised. Some argue that, like private goods, the provision of public goods should take place through the creation of a new generation of environmental markets (below). Others argue that the supply of public goods requires interventions in markets and tough regulatory action from publicly accountable authorities, such as states and intergovernmental organisations. In the negotiations that took place prior to the 1992 United Nations Convention on Environment and Development, the so-called 'Earth Summit' in Rio de Janeiro, it was suggested that forests should be governed by a global forests convention that would aim to prevent deforestation, conserve forests and achieve SFM. It is to these negotiations that we now turn.

An unconventional approach to international forest politics

The two most significant outputs from the 1992 United Nations Conference on Environment and Development (UNCED) were the Convention on Biological Diversity and the Framework Convention on Climate Change. Because forests are a major sink of carbon dioxide and an important habitat of biodiversity, it was suggested by developed country governments and the UN Food and Agriculture Organization that a third convention should be agreed – a global forests convention that would support the forest-related provisions of the biodiversity and climate change conventions. However, states failed even to commence negotiations for a convention, eventually agreeing only to a non-legally binding instrument commonly called the Forest Principles (United Nations 1992a).

The main reason for this is that the negotiations were characterised by a clear division between the developed countries of North America, Europe and Japan and the developing countries of Asia, Latin America and Africa. North–South differences are often overstated in international relations literature. However, at the UNCED, all the developed countries of the North argued for a forests convention, while all the developing countries of the South – speaking through their UN caucus: the Group of 77 Developing Countries (G77) – argued against. The European Union (EU), United States, Canada and Japan argued that the concept of sovereignty should be linked to two other principles: stewardship (the principle that countries with forests should manage them for the common good of humanity) and common responsibility (the notion that all countries share the responsibility to manage forests sustainably). Some delegates from the North suggested that forests themselves could be seen as a common heritage of mankind or a global common. This was a clumsy attempt to recognise the contribution that forests make to global public good provision, but it drew forth a retort from the Malaysian delegation that concepts such as global commons had a supranational character and were an attempt by the North to erode the sovereignty of developing countries over their forests (Humphreys 1996: 95). The G77 argued that sovereignty should not be delimited by linkage to other principles.

Timothy Ehresman and Dimitris Stevis argue that the governments of the South view international negotiations through the lens of justice (Chapter 6). This was the case during the UNCED forest deliberations, when many G77 position statements centred on issues of equity and responsibility. The G77 argued that the countries of North America and Europe bear a disproportionate responsibility for deforestation, as not only have they deforested significantly compared to their pre-Industrial Revolution forest cover, but they continue to drive deforestation through high levels of consumption of forest products. Hence, argued the G77, states should agree not to the principle of 'common responsibility' but instead to 'common but differentiated responsibilities', thus denoting that some states have more responsibility than others for causing deforestation and, therefore, more responsibility for financing future conservation measures.

The G77 also introduced the concept of 'compensation for opportunity cost foregone'. The concept of opportunity cost has its origins in neoclassical economic theory; if an economic resource is used in one way, the opportunity cost is the value of the next best alternative that the resource could have been used for. The opportunity cost of conserving forests is that they cannot be cut down. The G77 used the concept of opportunity cost foregone to signify that utility maximizing forest owners and the governments of forested states will rationally opt for forest conservation if they are compensated with a financial sum that exceeds what they would receive from deforestation and conversion to other land uses. The G77 also introduced the issue of external indebtedness, noting that payments from developing to developed countries for debt servicing and repayment exceed official development assistance transfers from developed to developing countries, resulting in net South-to-North financial transfers. The G77 argued that any agreement on forest conservation should be tied to debt relief, increased financial assistance and increased transfers of environmentally sound technology. The negotiating strategy of the G77 was summed up by the Malaysian prime minister, Mahathir bin Mohamad, shortly before the UNCED: 'If it is in the interests of the rich that we do not cut down our trees then they must compensate us for the loss of income' (Mahathir 1992). The UNCED forest negotiations did not, therefore, focus exclusively on forests and saw protracted deliberations on broader economic concerns of salience to developing countries.

Two theoretical explanations may be offered for the failure of the UNCED forest negotiations to lead to a forest convention. The first relates to cognitive theories of international cooperation. Cognitive theories focus on the role that shared ideas, beliefs, norms and values can play in fostering international agreement (Jönsson 1993; Hasenclever et al. 2000). International agreement is more likely when states can agree on a formula, principle or set of ideas that informs the negotiations and around which actors' expectations converge. However, there was no agreement on core concepts to guide the Rio forest negotiations: instead, different states invoked different concepts. But, these conceptual differences exposed deeper differences between North and South over past and future responsibilities and distributive justice, in particular what constitutes a fair and equitable distribution of the world's natural, financial and technological resources. The negotiations may also be viewed as a crude price negotiation in which the North pressed the South to implement strong forest conservation policies in the form of a global forests convention, while the G77 responded by introducing its economic concerns, arguing that all issues needed to be settled in a comprehensive package. So the G77 raised the price of forest conservation during the UNCED forest negotiations, a price that the North was unwilling to pay (Humphreys 1996).

This leads onto the second explanation, which centres on power. Powerful states possess the material capabilities to block the aspirations of other states. The neorealist view of international politics explained by John Vogler in Chapter 1 of this volume – according to which states will seek to preserve their relative advantages over other states and, where possible, to achieve relative gains – is relevant here. Both tropical and developed states have the power to grant or, alternatively, to thwart the aspirations of each other. Tropical states possess resources in the form of their rainforests, which produce private goods (such as tropical timber) and public goods (such as carbon sinks) valued by other actors. Meanwhile, the North has the power to satisfy the aspirations of the South for increased financial and technological transfers and debt relief. The enhanced value that the developed countries now attach to tropical forest conservation has provided the governments of tropical forested countries with enhanced bargaining leverage.

Realising this, the G77 attempted to translate the concerns of the developed countries over tropical deforestation into hard economic gains. But the developed countries of the North could not meet the G77's bargaining demands without eroding their relative advantages in international trade and finance. The costs that would be borne by tax payers and businesses in the North to meet the G77's demands on, say, financial and technological transfers would be extremely high. While Northern-based governments have been prepared to make modest increases of aid on a bilateral basis, they are unwilling to agree to large scale transfers on a multilateral basis that would enable developing countries to realise relative economic gains. In any case, donor countries are only likely to agree to significant North to South resource transfers if they can extract some binding commitments from the South on forest conservation targets; and this would touch upon developing country sensitivities on sovereignty. From this gridlock, the non-legally binding and heavily caveated statement of Forest Principles was agreed as a compromise between pro- and anti-convention states (United Nations 1992a).

The UNCED negotiations on forests were fractious and divisive. Two years later, in 1994, representatives from the governments of Canada, which had lobbied more strongly than any other state for a forests convention at Rio, and Malaysia, which led for the G77 against a convention, initiated a confidence-building dialogue to which selected other countries were invited. The result of this initiative was the creation of an Intergovernmental Panel on Forests with a two-year life span. This met four times from 1995 to 1997 and negotiated a series of non-legally binding proposals for action, namely policy recommendations for governments and other actors. With most developing countries remaining wary of international forest commitments, most of the proposals for action suggested actions that could be taken at the national level. Indeed, one of the main areas of agreement of the Intergovernmental Panel on Forests was the recommendation that all states should formulate and implement national forest programmes, which should be holistic, intersectoral and iterative programmes that recognise and respect the rights of local communities (Humphreys 2003).

By now, there had been some significant shifts in position on the convention question. First, the United States was opposed. The United States appears to have favoured a convention at Rio as an instrument that would focus principally on tropical forests. It did not envisage a convention as an instrument that would entail significant costs for the United States, for example, in the form of financial assistance to developing countries or raised standards for the American forest industry (Davenport 2006: 131). Second, Malaysia, the strongest voice against a convention at Rio, now argued in favour. As with the United States, the reason for this lies with domestic factors. The shift of position by Malaysia followed a change in the ministry with lead responsibility for forests, from the Ministry of Foreign Affairs, which viewed forests strategically as a sovereign resource, to the Ministry of Primary Resources, which saw a forest convention as an instrument that could promote the international trade in forest products to Malaysia's advantage (Kolk 1996: 162). Indonesia and most of the Central American states also changed position to support a convention. Meanwhile, Brazil and its Amazonian Pact allies remained resolutely opposed, while the EU remained broadly in favour.

With no consensus for a forests convention, but with increased confidence between countries on the forests issue, the decision was taken to replace the Intergovernmental Panel on Forests with the Intergovernmental Forum on Forests; to all intents and purposes, it was the Panel, with a different name and revised agenda. Created for three years, the Intergovernmental Forum on Forests met four times between October 1997 and February 2000. Its activities were very similar to those of its predecessor. It negotiated further proposals for action. Between them, the Panel and the Forum agreed approximately 270 proposals for action; the exact number is slightly unclear, as there are areas of duplication and overlap between different proposals.

During this period, another international forest initiative took place; namely, the formation of a World Commission on Forests and Sustainable Development. World commissions usually comprise an elitist 'eminent persons' membership of between 20 and 30, who set out to examine an international problem with a humanitarian or public goods dimension that is either being ignored in international politics or which requires some innovative thinking. The World Commission on Forests and Sustainable Development was the brainchild of a former prime minister of Sweden, Ola Ullsten. The organising committee for the Commission was convened shortly after the UNCED, but it was not until 1995 that the full Commission first met. Its final report was issued in 1999. The Commission made a serious effort to broaden the international discourse on forests and to emphasise the public interest, both global and local, in forest conservation. It argued that the custodial role that local communities play in maintaining and conserving forests is not always valued and made a commendable effort to rehabilitate the public goods values of forests in international politics (World Commission on Forests and Sustainable Development).

However, the impact of the Commission on mainstream international politics was negligible. There are three reasons for this. First, the organising committee started with the assumption that a forests convention was necessary. This led many developing countries to question the objectivity of the initiative, which was seen as starting with a pre-ordained political agenda. Second, and related to this, the Commission did not achieve formal endorsement from within the UN system. The approval of the UN secretary-general was sought, but not given. This is in comparison to the Brundtland Commission, which had been called for by the General Assembly. Finally, the initiative was eclipsed by the creation of the Intergovernmental Panel on Forests and the Intergovernmental Forum on Forests (Humphreys 2006: 48–65). Overall, the Commission failed to gather a critical mass of support from the world's governments, with only a few governments – Canada, Sweden and the Netherlands – expressing any support.

By now, states were poised to elevate the international forest policy dialogue within the UN system. In 2000, the decision was taken to create a new body – the United Nations Forum on Forests (UNFF) – to report directly to the UN Economic and Social Council (Figure 13.1). In addition to its elevated position within the UN system, there were two further differences between the UNFF and its predecessors. First, a multistakeholder dialogue segment was introduced during which stakeholders, such as forest businesses, indigenous peoples, farmers and scientific organisations, could engage both with each other and with government delegates. Second, some UNFF sessions included a ministerial segment. Throughout 2002 to 2004, the UNFF negotiated resolutions on a number of forest-related issues, such as forest health and productivity, maintaining forest cover, scientific knowledge and the economic aspects of forests. However, there was little evidence that the multistakeholder dialogues and ministerial segments had any real bearing on the negotiation of the resolutions. By now, UN forest institutions has entered a phase of diminishing marginal returns, and the UNFF resolutions added little, if anything, that was new.

In an effort to rejuvenate itself, UNFF set out in 2005 to agree a new international forests instrument. Once again, there was no agreement for a convention; states agreed to negotiate the unimaginatively-named 'Non-legally binding instrument on all types of forests', which

Figure 13.1 The United Nations building in New York: home to the United Nations Forum on Forests.

was concluded in 2007 (Eikermann 2015). During the negotiations, the EU, Canada, Costa Rica, Mexico, Norway, South Korea and Switzerland pressed hard for time bound and quantifiable targets; for example, that states would commit towards reducing their rate of deforestation by x%, or increasing their forest cover by y thousand hectares, by a stipulated date. However, the anti-convention states, principally the United States and Brazil, opposed any mention of time bound or quantifiable targets, or even of voluntary commitments to such targets. The instrument contained only four generalised 'global objectives' and that states agreed to make progress towards their achievement by 2015; namely (in abbreviated form):

- Reverse the loss of forest cover worldwide through SFM;
- Enhance forest-based economic, social and environmental benefits, including by improving the livelihoods of forest-dependent people;
- Increase, significantly, the area of protected forests worldwide and other areas of sustainably managed forests; and
- Reverse the decline in official development assistance for SFM and mobilize significantly increased, new and additional financial resources from all sources for SFM (United Nations 2007: para. IV).

With the exception of these objectives, there is no new commitment in the non-legally binding instrument that is not in the 1992 Forest Principles, the proposals for action agreed between 1995 and 2000 and the UNFF resolutions. Once again, developed states vetoed any suggestion they had a mandatory or legal responsibility to transfer finance and technology to the global South.

In 2015, states agreed to continue with the UNFF until 2030, with a mid-term review to take place in 2024 (Humphreys 2015). The non-legally binding instrument agreed in 2015 was renamed the UN Forest Instrument, and the timeline of the four global objectives on forests was extended until 2030 to align with the timeline of the 2030 Agenda for Sustainable Development (United Nations 2016).

In summary, a body of non-legally binding law (or soft law) on forests has been agreed at the UNCED and by various UN forest bodies. The United Nations Forum on Forests is arguably the best possible option in the absence of an international consensus for a convention. But international forest politics is not confined just to the UNFF. It is also scattered across a wide range of public and private international organisations, as the next section shows.

Neoliberalism and the fragmentation of international forest policy

Apart from the failure to agree a forests convention, there are two other reasons why the coordination of international forest policy has proved to be so difficult. The first relates to the nature of deforestation as a political issue; because forests provide such a wide range of public and private goods, international forest politics inevitably encroaches upon the jurisdictions of several international legal agreements with a forest-related mandate, in particular the Framework Convention on Climate Change, the Convention on Biological Diversity and the International Tropical Timber Agreement. International forest politics is characterised by a form of institutional 'turf war' in which the UNFF, which has no budget for forest policy implementation, both collaborates and competes with other international organisations.

The second reason concerns the broader international political and economic context. Forests became an international political agenda item in the 1980s, the same decade that neoliberal economic policies became ascendant. The theoretical origins of neoliberalism can been traced to Hayek (1944), who argued that a strong role for the state in the economy would destroy individual and economic freedoms, and to the monetarist Friedman (1962, 1963), who argued for deregulation, privatisation, government spending cuts and the control of the economy through the money supply. The prefix 'neo' (for 'new') indicates that neoliberalism is a contemporary variant of liberalism. Neoliberalism has adopted the liberal belief in free international trade that underpinned nineteenth century laissez faire economic policies, and it draws from neoclassical economics, in particular the notion that the common collective good is best realised when individuals compete in the market place. According to Harvey (2005), the first country to implement neoliberal policies was Chile in 1973–1974, although it was only when the United States under Reagan and the United Kingdom under Thatcher adopted neoliberal programmes of privatisation, government spending cuts, deregulation and marketisation that neoliberalism became ascendant internationally. The United States and United Kingdom, backed over time by other developed countries and international organisations such as the World Bank and International Monetary Fund, have successfully promoted neoliberal ideas such as trade and investment liberalisation in developing countries.

Neoliberalism has structured how policy makers think about and interpret the world (Castree 2008a, 2008b; Heynen et al. 2007; Larner 2000). Neoliberalism is a discourse in the sense that Foucault (1994) employed the term, as a more or less coherent set of understandings and ideas that shape the boundaries of thought, and thus of action. Proponents of neoliberalism favour certain environmental policy responses, such as market-based policies, voluntary commitments and business-based solutions. Neoliberalism has influenced international environmental policy in three important respects. The first is the emphasis on market-based solutions. Neoliberals argue that natural resources are most likely to be conserved when their functions are valued and priced through market mechanisms. A central difference between liberalism and neoliberalism is that, under the latter, the state uses its agency to leverage new spaces where market forces can operate. One example is the creation under the Kyoto Protocol of an international system of tradeable emission permits, under which some states are granted permits to emit an agreed level of carbon dioxide. These permits can be traded between countries; states that wish to exceed their emissions quota need to purchase permits from low polluting states with unused permits to sell.

Second, neoliberals advocate an enhanced role for the private sector. In this view, natural resources will be more effectively managed when placed under private, rather than state, ownership. Developed countries have argued, in the UNFF and other international organisations, that the forests of developing countries will be more effectively managed if privatised. However, developing countries, most of which view their forests as sovereign natural resources, have been reluctant to privatise their forests, as under current international trade and finance rules, any business would have the right to bid to purchase forests in other countries, and forest-rich developing countries could, over time, expect to lose control of their forests to powerful business corporations from the developed world. However, private businesses have a major role in developing countries through forest concessions. This is a mechanism under which a public authority hands over an area of state-owned forests to a private business for management or for logging for a prescribed time period.

Finally, neoliberals emphasise voluntary action rather than regulation. To neoliberal orthodoxy, public regulation creates market distortions and is thus burdensome and inefficient. Deregulation frees markets, enabling them to work more effectively. Instead of the public sector setting environmental targets and standards, any targets adopted should be those to which business itself agrees, for example, through corporate social responsibility and voluntary codes of conduct. Where regulation is necessary, it should be soft and optional if markets are to work most effectively. The emphasis in neoliberalism on deregulation helps explain the aversion of some states to time-bound and quantifiable targets for forest protection.

As a result of these two contextual factors – the large number of international institutions with a forest-related mandate and the neoliberal international policy environment – international forest policy is highly fragmented among a diversity of international organisations, as the following four examples illustrate.

Forest certification and labelling

In the late-1980s, with concern about tropical deforestation growing, an attempt was made to introduce an international timber labelling scheme through the International Tropical Timber Organisation (ITTO). Created in 1985, the ITTO is the first, and so far the only, international commodity organisation with a conservation mandate. In 1989, Friends of the Earth in London lobbied the UK delegation to the ITTO to table a proposal for a timber labelling scheme that would not have banned the international trade of unsustainably-managed timber, but would have provided for the labelling of timber from verified sustainably-managed forests. The proposal was rejected after opposition from the tropical timber producer caucus, in particular Malaysia, Indonesia and Brazil, which saw it as a veiled attempt to infringe upon national sovereignty and to interfere with the international market for tropical timber. However, even if the proposal had been agreed, it is unclear whether it would have been consistent with international trade rules, in particular the provision in the General Agreement on Tariffs and Trade (GATT) that prohibits discrimination between 'like products' on the basis of manufacture, a provision that could be interpreted to mean that discriminating between sustainably – and unsustainably – sourced timber is illegal under international trade law. There was also a concern that the ITTO scheme would have discriminated between tropical and non-tropical timber in international trade.

The ill-fated ITTO timber labelling proposal made it clear that any international timber labelling scheme would need to apply to all timber, not just tropical timber, and that any such scheme would need to be consistent with international trade law. In the early-1990s, the World Wide Fund for Nature, which had supported the Friends of the Earth proposal, worked with other environmental NGOs (nongovernmental organisations) and several environmentally concerned businesses to create, in 1993, the Forest Stewardship Council (FSC) (Cashore et al. 2004). The FSC is a voluntary, non-state, private scheme for the certification of forest products harvested from well-managed sources. It is governed by a novel institutional structure with three chambers – social, environmental and economic – each of which has one-third of voting rights with equal representation between developed and developing countries. As a voluntary, non-state, private organisation, the FSC does not admit governments as member organisations. The exclusion of governments as members is necessary for the FSC to avoid charges that it is a form of intergovernmental organisation, and thus bound by international trade law.

The FSC, and other international timber labelling schemes that have subsequently been created, such as the Programme for the Endorsement of Forest Certification (PEFC), has thus been deliberately constructed to be compatible with international trade law which has, in effect, set the parameters within which all certification and labelling schemes must operate. This is also the case with respect to the EU's efforts to address the international trade of illegally-logged timber.

International measures to curb illegal logging

Illegal logging and the international trade in illegally-logged timber pose an increasing threat to tropical forests. There is no multilateral agreement to ban the trade in illegally-logged timber. Agreeing such a ban is possible in principle, although there would likely be technical difficulties, as different countries have different definitions of illegal-logging. A multilateral ban would need to be agreed, either through an international environmental agreement or through the WTO. There are several precedents for multilateral trade bans on environmental grounds, including ozone-depleting substances (the 1987 Montreal Protocol to the 1985 Vienna Convention for the Protection of the Ozone Layer), hazardous wastes (the 1989 Basel Convention on the Control of Transboundary Movements of Hazardous Wastes and Their Disposal) and endangered species (the 1973 Convention of International Trade in Endangered Species of Wild Fauna and Flora, or CITES).

With no multilateral ban on the international trade in illegally-logged timber, no state can impose a unilateral ban without falling foul of the WTO. Somewhat ironically, therefore, a unilateral ban on the import of illegally-logged timber would itself be illegal under international trade law. Since 2003, the EU has taken an international lead in promoting policies to counter the international trade in illegally-logged timber, and has opted to take the only action that is available to it consistent with international trade law, namely voluntary action. Under its Forest, Law Enforcement, Governance and Trade (FLEGT) action plan (European Commission 2003), the EU is looking to conclude voluntary, but legally-binding, bilateral partnership agreements with timber producing countries which undertake to export to the EU only timber from verifiable legally-logged sources. Trade between such countries and the EU will be licensed and monitored. The obvious weakness in this scheme is that criminals can circumvent it by exporting illegally-logged timber to the EU via a third country that does not have a voluntary agreement with the EU. In 2008, the EU agreed its first voluntary partnership agreement with Ghana, since when a further five agreements have been concluded (with Cameroon, Central African Republic, Indonesia, Liberia and Republic of the Congo). In 2013, the EU Timber Regulation came into force under which it is illegal to introduce illegally-logged timber into the European Union. With no multilateral support for a comprehensive worldwide ban on the international trade of illegally-logged timber, the EU Timber Regulation and its voluntary partnership scheme are the strongest measures permissible under current international trade law.

A third long running dispute in international forest politics is whether knowledge of the properties of individual species should be patented. Here, too, the WTO plays a central role.

Knowledge patenting and benefit sharing

Over time, local communities and indigenous peoples have accumulated knowledge of the properties – for example, as foodstuffs and medicines – of the plant and tree species that form part of their environments (Berkes 1999). For example, indigenous forest peoples have developed knowledge on which plants can be used to treat burns and abrasions, which can be used to treat migraines and stomach ailments, and so on. This knowledge, usually called traditional knowledge, has been passed on from generation to generation, often orally, and comprises what is, in effect, a public good that is freely available to all. However, under intellectual property rights law, and especially under the WTO's Agreement on Trade-Related Intellectual Property Rights (TRIPS), business corporations have the right to patent knowledge on biological species (providing that no prior patent has been filed) and to charge royalties to other businesses that wish to use this knowledge for commercial ends. Dozens of such patents have been filed by agricultural, pharmaceutical and biotechnology corporations. One argument that the proponents of patents make is that, by assigning economic value to biological resources, patents make it more likely that these resources will be conserved and sustainably managed.

Under the TRIPS, all financial benefits from the commercial use of knowledge flow to patent holders. The TRIPS is opposed by two main groups of actors. First, the governments of biodiversity-rich countries, principally tropical forest states, argue that a share of the financial benefits from patenting should accrue to the government of the country where the species grows. Second, indigenous peoples and local communities have opposed the TRIPs. Two different views have been expressed from these actors. The first is that knowledge on biological species should be freely available and there should be no patenting of such knowledge. The second view accepts patenting as a practice but insists that, when a patent is based on traditional knowledge, a share of the royalties should flow to those communities and indigenous peoples that originally discovered or developed the knowledge.

Given that traditional knowledge has developed over many generations, over which it has been passed onto many different social groups, there are clear definitional problems with agreeing who the traditional knowledge holders are and, therefore, who should receive a share of the benefits. However, it can be argued that this does not invalidate the general principle. Indeed, the principle that the financial benefits from patenting should be shared has status in international law; the Convention on Biological Diversity provides for 'the equitable sharing of the benefits' that arise from the utilisation of knowledge with the original knowledge holders (United Nations 1992b: article 8(j)). In 2010, the Nagoya Protocol on access and benefit sharing was agreed, entering into legal force in 2014. However, while this upholds equitable benefit sharing as a principle, it does not indicate a formula by which benefits should be shared between the three main claimant groups: commercial patent holders, governments and local communities/indigenous peoples.

The politics of patent rights to biological resources is thus played out between different legal instruments: the WTO and TRIPS on the one hand, and the Convention on Biological Diversity and Nagoya Protocol on the other hand. Different political actors favour those instruments that best promote their interests. The TRIPS agreement reflects the interests of those actors that were instrumental in its negotiation, namely developed states and corporations seeking to promote the commodification of nature and the private ownership of knowledge on biological resources; these actors wish patent rights, like other 'trade-related' issues, to be kept firmly under the purview of the WTO. Meanwhile, the governments of biodiversity-rich countries and community and indigenous groups argue that this debate should be settled by parties to the Convention on Biological Diversity and its Nagoya Protocol. Pending a resolution of this issue, royalties from patent rights continue to accrue to commercial patent holders, although the governments of tropical forested countries assert that their sovereign right is to decide which corporations may access their biological resources and which may not.

Valuing the carbon sink function of forests

The role of markets occupies a central place in neoliberal thinking and has been central to international climate policy since the agreement of the 1997 Kyoto Protocol. In 2007, parties to the Framework Convention on Climate Change initiated a policy debate on how to reduce carbon emissions from deforestation and forest degradation, especially in developing countries (United Nations 2008). The debate was initiated by Papua New Guinea and Costa Rica, later attracting support from Bolivia, Central African Republic, Dominican Republic, Nicaragua and the Solomon Islands. The decision was premised on the idea that financial incentives should be put in place to encourage developing countries to reduce their deforestation rates.

The incentivizing of forest conservation through valuing the carbon that is stored in forests, in order to prevent deforestation that would otherwise occur, has become known as 'reducing emissions from deforestation and forest degradation' (REDD, also known as REDD+). The basic idea is that countries that reduce their deforestation above a certain baseline will create carbon credits that can be sold to countries who wish to exceed their agreed emission levels in a post-Kyoto market-based global carbon trading scheme. The baseline is the background (or 'business-as-usual') rate of deforestation. Such a scheme has the potential to restructure international forest and climate politics. When emissions from deforestation are included, then Indonesia and Brazil become the world's third and fourth largest emitters of carbon dioxide, after the United States and China (The Economist 2006).

In addition to the methodological and technical issues that will inform baseline measurement, there is a further problem: developing countries may bargain for generous deforestation baselines before agreeing to participate. The European Union's Emissions Trading Scheme (ETS) illustrates the problems that an international REDD+ scheme might face in this regard. In order to establish the ETS scheme, the EU allocated permits to some businesses with high levels of carbon dioxide emissions. The EU was accused of agreeing generous baselines by overestimating the past emissions levels of these businesses in order to secure their participation. Businesses that had taken measures to reduce their emissions prior to the implementation of the ETS scheme were not rewarded. Against this, it can be argued that more stringent emissions baselines would have attracted fewer businesses, thus compromising the long-term effectiveness of the ETS. How baselines are agreed thus has a bearing upon both participation and effectiveness. Similar considerations inform REDD+. A tropical forest country will have more incentive to participate in such a scheme when its baseline of estimated future deforestation is overestimated, as that country would then be able to claim a higher level of reduced deforestation than has actually been achieved. The country would gain financially, as it would generate additional carbon credits for sale to high emitting states (Humphreys 2008).

In environmental terms, this is clearly self-defeating. Not only would the developing country have less incentive to take proactive policies to reduce future deforestation, but lenient baselines would lead to an oversupply of REDD+ credits, which could depress the price of credits worldwide. High-emitting countries would thus be able to purchase credits at a lower price than if more accurate baselines had been used, and would consequently have less incentive to invest in clean technology to reduce their emissions at source. Generous baselines will thus reduce the incentives to reduce deforestation in developing countries and to reduce carbon emissions in high-polluting countries.

The REDD+ debate also brings to the fore the question of justice. It might be argued that, provided the baselines are accurate, a REDD+ scheme can promote the principle of intergenerational equity, which holds that environmental risks and harms should not be passed onto future generations. A counter-argument is that REDD+ focuses only on the carbon stock value of forests, which will promote a narrow emphasis on one forest-related public good – climate regulation – at the expense of others, such as biodiversity habitat, watershed services, sociocultural values and so on. Furthermore, it may be argued that REDD+ violates another dimension of justice, namely intragenerational equity. This is the principle of fairness between different groups and countries in the present generation, according to which all people within any one generation have a fair and equal claim to the world's ecological space, including the atmospheric commons. Under the principle of intragenerational equity, REDD+ can be viewed as a morally unjust mechanism that enables some states to continue polluting by purchasing carbon sequestration in other countries, in effect colonising the ecological space of other people. Indigenous forest peoples' groups such as the Forest Peoples' Programme are critical of REDD+, claiming it will lead to elite control over nature, with most of the financial benefits flowing to national treasuries rather than to communities (Griffiths 2007).

Table 13.1 International forest politics timeline: select dates

Dates	Event
1992	United Nations Conference on Environment and Development (UNCED): with no agreement for a forests convention, states agree a non-legally binding statement, the 'Forest Principles'.
1993	Forest Stewardship Council is created.
1995	World Commission on Forests and Sustainable Development is created. It meets several times before disbanding in 1999.
1995–1997	Intergovernmental Panel on Forests agrees a set of proposals for action.
1997–2000	Intergovernmental Forum on Forests agrees further proposals for action.
2000	United Nations Forum on Forests (UNFF) is created.
2003	EU agrees its Forest Law Enforcement, Governance and Trade (FLEGT) action plan.
2007	UNFF agrees a *Non-legally binding instrument on all types of forests*.
2008	The EU agrees its first FLEGT voluntary partnership agreement with Ghana. UN REDD programme is established.
2013	EU Timber Regulation enters into force.
2014	Nagoya Protocol 2010 on access and benefit-sharing enters into force.
2015	The UNFF is renewed until 2030. The *Non-legally binding instrument on all types of forests is renamed the United Nations Forest Instrument*. Paris Agreement on climate change.

In 2008, the UN established the UN-REDD programme to help developing countries develop national REDD+ strategies. Countries supportive of REDD+ pressed for a strong endorsement of national REDD+ programmes in the 2015 Paris Agreement on climate change. However, while the Paris Agreement mentions the importance of reducing emissions from deforestation and forest degradation (United Nations 2015: article 5.2), the idea of REDD+ as a strategy was not endorsed. Table 13.1 below provides a timeline of some important events in international forest politics since 1992.

Conclusion

It is often suggested that a forests convention would rationalise and harmonise global forests governance. According to VanderZwaag and MacKinlay (1996: 2), a convention would promote a more effective and holistic approach to global forests governance and address the increasing fragmentation in the activities of international forest-related organisations. Against this, it can be argued that there is no legal reason why a forest convention should have a higher standing than any other freestanding legal instrument. Indeed, a forests convention could, by adding another layer of international regulation, lead to further legal uncertainties and complications. As Skala-Kuhmann (1996) has argued, 'the notion of a "superconvention", designed to serve as a kind of umbrella over existing conventions and harmonize the areas they cover, is unprecedented in international law'. In any case, there is no international political consensus for a convention.

Like its predecessors in the UN system, the UNFF has been unable to provide a coherent coordinating focus for international forest management issues. Global forest policy has developed not according to any rational design, but incrementally across several international institutions. It has been argued in this chapter that international forest policy has been strongly guided by neoliberalism, which favours voluntary action and business-led, market-based initiatives, while eschewing regulation and a strong role for the state. Both forest certification and the idea of REDD+ are based upon the principle of voluntary action through international markets. States have no role in forest certification. In the case of international tradeable emission permits, the role of states has been confined solely to creating a new generation of property rights – the right to pollute – and establishing the conditions for the international trading of these rights, after which the state stands back and allows the market to set a price for carbon that will, hopefully, reduce carbon emissions and incentivise forest protection. Similarly, states have created the right to patent knowledge on biological resources as an intellectual property right. Voluntary action characterises the EU's policy to counter illegal-logging. However, EU member states would have taken stronger action to tackle illegal logging had they been able to do so. They have not done so because they were constrained by WTO rules. Overall, therefore, neoliberal principles have constrained and weakened international action to conserve forests.

This leads onto a broader point that is relevant not just to international forest politics, but more broadly to international environmental politics. International environmental law is considerably weaker than the international legal instruments that promote neoliberal principles. International legal instruments on trade, investment and intellectual property rights are now consolidated under the auspices of a single international organisation: the WTO (Larner 2008). Gill (1995, 2002) has argued that there is now a 'new constitutionalism' that codifies not the rights of people and publics, but the rights of business and investors. To Gill, the WTO promotes 'disciplinary neoliberalism', namely neoliberal principles that are backed by powerful developed states that exert influence and control over international organisations. International environmental law is scattered across several legal instruments and international organisations, whereas the WTO agreements are administered by one body. For business corporations and other proponents of neoliberalism, this has an advantage, as the WTO has stronger enforcement mechanisms than international environmental law. States are required to implement WTO law, including making any necessary changes to domestic law, on pain of sanctions. International forest policy has been constructed so as not to fall foul of the WTO. On other environmental issues, governments have become increasingly self-censorious, avoiding any trade restriction measures that might not survive a WTO challenge (Eckersley 2004). The WTO agreements have a stronger normative force than international environmental law, and in this respect, they have established the limits of international environmental policy.

References

Berkes, Fikret (1999) *Sacred Ecology: Traditional Ecology: Traditional Ecological Knowledge and Resource Management*. Philadelphia, PA: Taylor and Francis.

Cashore, Benjamin; Auld, Graeme; Newsom, Deanna (2004) *Governing Through Markets: Forest Certification and the Emergence of Non-State Authority*. New Haven: Yale University Press.

Castree, Noel (2008a) Neoliberalising Nature: The Logics of Deregulation and Regulation. *Environment and Planning A*, 40(1), 131–152.

Castree, Noel (2008b) Neoliberalising Nature: Processes, Effects, and Evaluations. *Environment and Planning A*, 40(1), 153–173.

Davenport, Deborah S. (2006) *Global Environmental Negotiations and US Interests*. New York: Palgrave Macmillan.

Eckersley, Robyn (2004) The Big Chill: The WTO and Multilateral Environmental Agreements. *Global Environmental Politics*, 4(2), 24–50.

Eikermann, Anja (2015) *Forests in International Law: Is there Really a Need for an International Forest Convention*. London: Springer.

European Commission (2003) COM (2003) 251 final, 'Communication from the Commission to the Council and the European Parliament: Forest Law Enforcement, Government and Trade (FLEGT), Proposal for an EU action plan', Brussels, 21 May.

Foucault, Michel (1994) *The Archaeology of Knowledge*. London: Routledge.

Friedman, Milton (1962) *Capitalism and Freedom*. Chicago: University of Chicago Press.

Friedman, Milton. (1963) *Inflation: Causes and Consequences*. New York: Asia Publishing.

Gill, Stephen. (1995) Globalisation, Market Civilisation and Disciplinary Neoliberalism. *Millennium: Journal of International Studies*, 24(3), 399–423.

Gill, Stephen. (2002) *Power and Resistance in the New World Order*. London: Palgrave Macmillan.

Griffiths, Tom. (2007) *Seeing 'RED'?: 'Avoided Deforestation' and the Rights of Indigenous Peoples and Local Communities*. Moreton-in-Marsh: Forest Peoples Programme.

Harvey, David (2005) *A Brief History of Neoliberalism*. Oxford: Oxford University Press.

Hasenclever, Andreas; Mayer, Peter; Rittberger, Volker (2000) Integrating Theories of International Regimes. *Review of International Studies*, 26(1), 3–33.

Hayek, Friedrich (1944) *The Road to Serfdom*. Chicago: University of Chicago Press.

Heynen, Nick; McCarthy, James; Prudham, Scott; Robbins, Paul (eds) (2007) *Neoliberal Environments: False Promises and Unnatural Consequences*. London: Routledge.

Humphreys, David (1996) *Forest Politics: The Evolution of International Cooperation*. London: Earthscan.

Humphreys, David (ed) (2003) *Forests for the Future: National Forest Programmes in Europe—Country and Regional Reports from COST Action E19*. Luxembourg: European Communities.

Humphreys, David (2006) *Logjam: Deforestation and the Crisis of Global Governance*. London: Earthscan.

Humphreys, David (2008) The Politics of "Avoided Deforestation": Historical Context and Contemporary Issues. *International Forestry Review*, 10(3), 433–442.

Humphreys, David (2015) Negotiating the Future Under the Shadow of the Past: The Eleventh Session of the United Nations Forum on Forests and the 2015 Renewal of the International Arrangement on Forests. *International Forestry Review*, 17(4), 385–399.

Jönsson, Christer (1993) Cognitive Factors in Explaining Regime Dynamics, in Rittberger, Volker (ed.) *Regime Theory and International Relations*. Oxford: Clarendon Press.

Kolk, Ans (1996) *Forests in International Environmental Politics: International Organizations, NGOs and the Brazilian Amazon*. Utrecht: International Books.

Larner, Wendy (2000) Neo-liberalism: Policy, Ideology, Governmentality. *Studies in Political Economy*, 63, 5–26.

Larner, Wendy (2008) Neoliberalism, Mike Moore and the WTO. *Environment and Planning A*, 41(7), 1576–1593.

Mahathir, bin Mohamad (1992) 'Speech by the Prime Minister of Malaysia, Dato' Seri Dr Mahathir bin Mohamad at the Official Opening of the Second Ministerial Conference of Developing Countries on Environment and Development, Kuala Lumpur, on Monday, 27 April 1992' (mimeo).

Perrings, Charles; Gadgil, Madhav (2003) Conserving Biodiversity: Reconciling Local and Global Benefits, in Kaul, Inge; Conceição, Pedro; Le Goulven, Katell; Mendoza, Ronald U. (eds), *Providing Global Goods: Managing Globalization*. Oxford: Oxford University Press/United Nations Development Programme.

Skala-Kuhmann, Astrid (1996) 'Legal Instruments to Enhance the Conservation and Sustainable Management of Forest Resources at the International Level', Paper Commissioned by the German Federal Ministry for Economic Cooperation and Development and GTZ, July.

The Economist (2006) So Hard to See the Wood for the Trees. 19 December. Available online at: www.economist.com/world/international/displaystory.cfm?story_id=10329203 (last accessed 02/03/2017).

United Nations (1992a) A/CONF.151/6/Rev.1. 'Non-legally binding authoritative statement of principles for a global consensus on the management, conservation and sustainable development of all types of forests', Rio de Janeiro.

United Nations (1992b) *Convention on Biological Diversity*. New York: United Nations.

United Nations (2007) A/C.2/62/L.5. *Non-Legally Binding Instrument on All Types of Forest*. New York: United Nations.

United Nations (2008) FCCC/CP/2007/6/Add.1 'Report of the Conference of the Parties on its thirteenth session, held in Bali from 3 to 15 December 2007', Decision 2/CP.13, Reducing emissions from deforestation in developing countries: approaches to stimulate action, 14 March. Available at: http://unfccc.int/resource/docs/2007/cop13/eng/06a01.pdf#page=3 (last accessed 02/03/2017).

United Nations (2015) Paris Agreement. Available at: http://unfccc.int/files/essential_background/convention/application/pdf/english_paris_agreement.pdf (last accessed 02/03/2017).

United Nations (2016) A/RES/70/1999 'United Nations forest instrument', 16 February. Available at: https://documents-dds-ny.un.org/doc/UNDOC/GEN/N15/450/10/PDF/N1545010.pdf?OpenElement (last accessed 02/03/2017).

VanderZwaag, David; MacKinlay, Douglas (1996) Towards a Global Forests Convention: Getting Out of the Woods and Barking up the Right Tree, in *Canadian Council on International Law* (ed), *Global Forests and International Law*. London: Kluwer Law International.

World Commission on Forests and Sustainable Development (1999) *Our Forests, Our Future: Report of the World Commission on Forests and Sustainable Development*. Cambridge: Cambridge University Press.

Conclusion

The future of global environmental politics

Gabriela Kütting

This book has attempted to explain what it means to study global environmental politics: the history of environmental politics, the theoretical or conceptual frameworks within which to situate debates, and the analytical lenses employed, as well as a variety of issue areas / case studies that form the biggest challenges today.

While the study of global environmental governance is important and continues to occupy a predominant position in global environmental politics, many chapters here have shown that it is important to see governance attempts as a particular juncture in the understanding of the global environment. Global governance becomes a wider field when we include the importance of non-state actors, as Lucy Ford showed in her chapter and as indeed many governance forms today incorporate. However, it is not only the actors but also the fields of action that have changed considerably in recent times. While until not so long ago attempts at regulating the causes of environmental problems focused on getting states to agree to certain targets, we now have the options of economic tools, such as cap and trade, of getting non-state actors involved in finding solutions to problems, and also of taking into account new perspectives of how to conceptualize problems. For example, the concept of sustainable consumption, as explained by Doris Fuchs and Frederike Boll, shows that including society and how individuals behave both as political and economic entities brings vital new dimensions to the field that become increasingly important, the significance of which was overlooked for a long time. The same goes for ideas of justice and equity. While justice had for a long time been looked at in terms of fair burden sharing between states signing an international environmental agreement on a particular problem, it has become clear that justice or equity is a lot more than that, and global solutions to global problems need to be more accountable – that is, respect the rights of all. Timothy

Ehresman and Dimitris Stevis discussed a variety of issues and concepts related to international and global justice and equity, the main message being that the rights of communities have to be respected at the local, regional, national, and global level for legitimate solutions to environmental problems, particularly in the field of climate change.

Above all, the conceptual chapters have demonstrated how connected the political and economic, the theoretical and the practical, the individual and the institutional, and the local and the global are. John Vogler's chapter on theories and concepts as much as Thomas Hickmann and Markus Lederer's chapter on global political economy and North–South issues connect in ways that are complemented by Lucy Ford's non-state actor emphasis. The focus on consumption and justice are explored in detail in chapters five and six, but play prominent roles in nearly all the chapters, be it in Lucy Ford, Hickmann & Lederer, or the case studies. Hannah Hughes' chapter focusing on environmental security shows how framing aspects also have a huge bearing on how states perceive environmental problems. Kyle Herman's chapter shows how many different countries are not coming up with their own clean technology solutions. Together, what all these chapters show is that it is exactly this plurality of approaches that helps us to conceive of global environmental politics as a whole, and such a plurality is needed for analyzing, interpreting, and finding solutions to global environmental problems.

These gains in the development of global environmental politics are naturally complemented by how we, as a global society, approach these challenges to our planet, our lives, the lives of our children and their children, and ultimately all of our livelihoods. Here, our case studies have given us important clues. The case studies are about some of the most pressing problems; some of these are specific issues, some are difficulties particular sectors are facing, and they all vary in scope and complexity. First of all, the case studies show that a one-size-fits-all approach to global environmental problems clearly does not work, as each and every problem and challenge is different and needs different solutions. Yet, it is also clear that all problems and challenges need solutions at the global level – solutions that have to be based on the current tools political scientists and policy makers have at their disposal.

In terms of who has the responsibility for meeting the environmental challenges of the 21st century, the resounding answer is all of us in all political, social, and economic spheres. Political action cannot be a top-down approach with governments telling their citizens what to do – it also has to be bottom-up with the citizens telling their representatives what they expect of them. Bottom-up movements must likewise be buttressed by sustainable business models and government institutional supports for these new synergies. The economy must not simply become more sustainable with producers adopting more environmentally friendly production methods; there also has to be a rethinking of how and what we, as people, consume – and how we want our economy to be organized. Do we want an economy based on a concept of infinite growth, or do we want more of a steady-state economy? Do we want environmental problems to become security threats and have them approached from this lens? Or do we see the roots of the problem in the organization of the neoliberal political economy? Can we achieve change through activism? And do we want to be active through non-state channels, or do we make the way we consume our political action? These are a lot of questions and they require a lot of thought.

However, we believe one of the biggest lessons of this book is that the environmental problems of the 21st century cannot be resolved through global environmental governance alone – their mechanisms, roots, and possible solutions are so complex that they require a wider angle and action on more than one front. It was the aim of the authors and contributors of this volume to provide you with the tools to understand this complex web.

Index